The Great North Road

The Great North Road

A JOURNEY IN HISTORY *by* *Frank Morley*

The Macmillan Company *New York* *1961*

© Frank Morley, 1960, 1961

First Printing

Printed in the United States of America

The Macmillan Company, New York
Brett-Macmillan Ltd., Galt, Ontario

Library of Congress catalog card number: 61-7433

To my old friend the enemy
A. W. Wheen

And to the memory of
2/Lieut. Patrick McLeod Innes, Royal Garrison Artillery
2/Lieut. Donald McLeod Innes, Royal Highlanders

Contents

I » Farewell

At the end of the last war I revisited London. There was many another who came from overseas to gloom among craters in a ruined City, and to poke around to find what remained. Each made his own investigation in his own way. As like as not it was a lonely way. My way started with St. Paul's. I had always believed that a first axiom of London was never to fail to look at St. Paul's from every possible angle. A miracle at the end of the war was that St. Paul's was there to be looked at.

The huge dark frame of St. Paul's was at that time islanded in devastation. A square mile of the City east, north, west, and southwest of St. Paul's had been burned and flattened; more than flattened—excavated. The scene was hard to admit. The mind preferred not to grasp it. The experiences of St. Paul's could scarcely be expected to relive themselves to anyone who had not been close at hand toward the end of 1940. To read about experiences afterward is hardly the same thing. The high-explosive bomb which early in the morning of 12 September fell near the southwest tower, and the

extraordinary feat of its removal; the incendiaries of 29 December
which caused the burning of the City—how may these things communicate? You would think that if you had intimate memories of
individual buildings, of Stationers' Hall [1] or the City Livery Club,
or if you had known Paternoster Row like the back of your hand,
you might form some idea of what went on in the City in that
December night of 1940: but no—the eye might recognize erasures,
yet even that was difficult. Where was . . . Had it been there . . .
or there? There was no doubt of the totality which had perished for
want of fire fighters or water or both. Is it true, as I have read,
that an exceptionally low tide in the Thames was partly the explanation of the extent of the burnings? That when other sources of water
failed, London River itself failed the demand? So it has been said:
The river water was so low as to be impossible to reach, and pumps
and hoses from that life stream brought up nothing but mud. [2]
There were so many fires because there was no means of extinguish-
ing them. How St. Paul's Watch managed that night to deal with
their own fires is not easily imagined. The Watch did so. At the
end of the war the cathedral stood there, hurt and dirtied, islanded,
but still upstanding. I used to start my postwar explorations from
St. Paul's.

I shall be brief about this personal tour, a short swing from St.
Paul's and back again. Distances, in the City, if not recollections,
are trivial. Eastward of St. Paul's there was not much point in
going far along Cheapside, for most of Cheapside had disappeared. Surprisingly, the Cheapside Tree was still alive at the
corner of Wood Street. The Cheapside Tree was the ordinary,
elderly, unbeautiful plane tree which, so long as I could remember,
had been defended against the encroachment of shops and offices;
it grew, or at least existed, in a small patch of hallowed ground,
which used to have a narrow border planted by somebody with
tulips, or, later in the season, with geraniums. The Cheapside Tree,
I say, had been defended. It had often been attacked for occupying
possible office space, but it had been defended by Act of Parliament: it had been granted the right of Ancient Lights. At the period
of my postwar expeditions it did not require much of that kind
of protection. The leaves and branches were not then threatened
by many buildings. It looked indeed a bit mournful, the buildings

having gone, leaving around its roots only a certain amount of grime and rubble, and though it might have been tulip time there were no tulips. Nor do I recall that the Cheapside Tree was cheered with any bird song, any twittering of sparrows. Nevertheless the tree was there, and I went into what used to be Wood Street. "What used to be"—for here I was at once in no man's city. Here was the square mile of exposed and blackened cellars of the past, acres of jagged holes half filled with rubble: bracken and willow-herb struggled to grow in crevices. Far and wide it was a sea of desolation, with a surprising number of white church spires, each like the mast of a wrecked ship standing above a burned-out hulk. A dead sea, a dead land, a desert. I might recognize this or that white church spire, but there were few other compass marks.

I remember the bewilderment at not being able to find my way. There was the damaged shoulder of Goldsmiths' Hall, but where was the Goldsmiths' Arms, the pub where the Pickwick Club started? I thought I could have found it in the dark. But this was a new darkness, in which it wasn't there. I carried on northward, across Gresham Street, to find where Little Love Lane used to turn off to the right. Huggin Lane used to be on the left. In other days when I might be pointing out sights to a visitor, I would explain that the name Huggin Lane had nothing to do with little love, but was a corruption of Huguenot. There was no longer much point to the explanation, for Huggin Lane and its shop fronts with Hugue-not names had vanished. I had to outflank the ruins of Little Love Lane and fetch around for some yards to the eastward to find what I was seeking. I was seeking for the remains of a church called St. Mary Aldermanbury. The reason for finding that particular church was that in prewar years there was in front of it a garden. It was a pocket handkerchief of ground, fenced off from the lane by iron railings, with room for a few garden benches around a statue in the center. It was one of numerous tiny City gardens, many of them in front of churches, restful little places in which a rambler might sink upon a bench to take the weight off his feet, or in which typists from surrounding office buildings might eat lunchtime sandwiches.

In the devastation I was searching for this garden, in which, as I said, there used to be a statue. It had never been much of a statue. It was not to be specially praised as a work of art. There had been a clumsy brown pediment which supported a conventional bronze bust of Shakespeare. You had to look twice to discover the peculiarity of the statue. The peculiarity was, this statue of Shakespeare was not dedicated to the man Shakespeare. It was dedicated to the memory of two other men—two other men, both of the parish of St. Mary Aldermanbury. These two men, John Heminge and Henry Condell, had published the first folio of Shakespeare's works. If Heminge and Condell had not collected and printed the plays, the world might not have had them. On the pediment of the statue was a phrase or two from the preface to the first folio: "We have but collected them and done an office to the dead . . . only to keep alive the memory of so worthy a friend and fellow as was our Shakespeare." The action of Heminge and Condell seems in its way as worthy a defense of a fabric as the action of St. Paul's Watch. At any rate, in the nineteenth century the gallantry of their action operated vigorously on a gentleman named Charles Clement Walker of Lilleshall Old Hall, Shropshire. Mr. Walker insisted there should be a statue to the memory of Heminge and Condell. So there the statue had been placed, in the garden in front of St. Mary Aldermanbury. The bust was the bust of Shakespeare, but the praise was praise to his publishers. At the time when I was a young book publisher, prowling around London with James Bone,[3] we named that particular statue the Publishers' Shrine, and that was why at the end of this war I poked about to find the site, to stand and stare at its destruction.

But the statue had not been destroyed. The statue survived. The church of St. Mary Aldermanbury had barely survived. The square tower stood upright. The body of the church was black and gutted. The garden was a misery. Such battered benches as remained were unusable, for the iron gateway to the ruined church and garden was now padlocked. Yet in the midst of the grief and grime the statue was just as it had been, and I confess it gave my heart a bounce of joy to see it.

That is not the end of that story, but it is the beginning of this book. If you go now to seek out St. Mary Aldermanbury, you will find brand-new large cubes of office buildings, gleaming for the moment like so many icebergs, overhanging many of the smaller City churches, which persist as pieces of dark wreckage underneath.

St. Mary Aldermanbury is, as I write, still such a piece of dark
wreckage, but the garden has been restored, the gate is open, the
benches are there to be sat on, and you are invited in by a notice
which requests you to keep the precincts FRESH AND TIDY. Long may
that notice beckon one in; but as for the beginning of this book I
wish to go back to the immediate postwar mood. It might at that
period have been winter, spring, or summer that I made expeditions to this part of the waste city. There must have been some
pulling power over and above the normal claims of business, for as
I look back on it, it is hard to explain the trips from New York at
a time when transatlantic travel was not convenient and certainly
not pleasurable. There must have been some element of pilgrimage.
I remember in particular a July day, calm, cool, bright as a July day
can sometimes be in London, when I again made precisely the same
round which I have been mentioning. It must have been some years
after the war, because the rubble had been cleared away from the
roots of the Cheapside Tree, and a brave new spirit had planted
geraniums in the narrow border of that hallowed ground; and an
indignant spirit it was too, for in the front row of the geranium bed
there was a gap, and a short stick bearing a cardboard placard
had been stuck into the gap; and on the placard was the statement:
ONE STOLEN. Ah, well! I went along Wood Street as before, and
here or there a bombed site had been turned into a car park, but
there were many holes that did not seem to be turnable into anything. There was the same problem of finding the way, when so
many landmarks had continued to have vanished. Where was my
favorite Brewers' Hall, in Addle Street? Notice boards had been
put up to show where such famous haunts had been. They were
white notice boards, each with the shield of the City of London,
with its red cross and red dagger, and each sign, where once there
had been a famous building, was like the placard for the geranium:
ONE STOLEN.

The Publishers' Shrine, on that July day, was still locked up, the
garden still grimy and desolate. The statue was still there. I wandered on with an errand to do before swinging back to St. Paul's.
The quiet breeze carried a flicker of drifting seeds. They were
seeds from the willowherb, this year growing more strongly in the
desolate cellars. What is the phrase from the *Jungle Book*—"the Cold

Lairs"? North of the Cheapside Tree nobody was planting anything. It was the letting in of the jungle: advance guard of bracken and willowherb. The seeds drifted in the July air like specks of memory I couldn't quite catch. The forlorn churchyard of St. Alphage's: hadn't that churchyard once been a garden? I thought I could remember it as such, with children roller-skating. Yes, there was still the stone tablet placed in the rough wall at the back of St. Alphage's churchyard to celebrate that in 1872 the churchyard had been made open to the public. There was nothing about the tablet or the wall to indicate anything more than that. The wall was a rough wall, six or eight feet high, a backstop for the garden. I did remember the garden as it had been. I remembered the children roller-skating, and the unholy noise they made. I did not seem to remember the wall. I don't suppose I had ever noticed it.

On this day it was my errand to look at the wall of St. Alphage's garden. I did not eye the south face of that wall with any favor. The garden itself was simply a strip of blackened desert. Nobody was there, no children, no roller skates, no noise, no sparrow. There was the white tablet commemorating the opening of the garden in 1872. There were some other tablets commemorating some people who had been expected to spend the rest of all time in St. Alphage's churchyard. So far as concerned the south face of St. Alphage's wall, that was that. But my errand was concerned with the north face of this same wall, so I went round St. Alphage's to the north side, into Fore Street, to have a look. Here in Fore Street was another of the City's white wooden signs. It was inscribed as follows:

> On this site at 12:15 a.m. on the
> 25th August 1940, fell the first
> bomb on the City of London in the
> Second World War

My errand was to note what use was being made of the destruction caused by this and later bombings.

For I had heard that when all the buildings hereabouts were razed to their cellars, there had been disclosed a long, continuous section of the northern face of the original Roman Wall of London. Concealed for the many centuries, the north front of the Wall was now disclosed in length and to its full height, as it was *ab urbe*

condita. As had many people, I had seen bits and pieces of the Wall
before. I knew the Bastion (Bastion XIX) which resides underground in the yard of the General Post Office, where its foundations are laved by the only trickle of the Fleet River which most
Londoners are likely to see nowadays. I have said I had just been
looking at the south side of the garden wall of St. Alphage's, and
had found it unimpressive. But from the south side of St. Alphage's
all that one had seen were the uppermost strata of the Wall, au-
thentic enough, yet by my time so patched and tableted and inter-
fered with as to be unrecognizable. Now, and from the northern
side, one had a continuity in all its courses, from the original Roman
stonework foundations to the medieval brickwork at the top. Along
the whole northern face of the Wall holes had been pecked into it
as the housings of a thousand years and more had attempted to
jostle each other and to nestle against it. If your mind's eye could
get down to the ground level—the ground level as it had been in
Boadicea's [4] time—you could see the Wall standing as a cliff, as a
rock cliff facing the north with fierce, angry hardness. Looking at
it even now, from the present level of Fore Street, you couldn't be
patronizing about it. The myriad holes pecked in the cliff—here for
a beam, there for a joist, there perhaps for a rafter—were as pin-
pricks the Wall had never noticed. The housings had now gone
away. You did not feel the Wall had noticed that fact either. The
Wall stood. There was nothing soft about it. It faced you with a
coarse and contemptuous dignity. It forced you to the contemplation of dirty and sordid drama.

I had gone on my self-imposed errand, for I imagined that some
day the Roman Wall would be covered and built over again. I had
heard there was a plan to keep a segment of its flank, if only fifty
yards or so, exposed for posterity to look at. I wished the plan well,
naturally; and yet as I looked, I felt that when a mere segment of
the Wall was tidied up for exhibition it would inevitably come to
seem only a museum piece. Something of the present impression
was bound to be lost. For it was not just a piece of the Wall that
the blitz had exposed: you could see the whole line of it. The line
of it, like the back of a prehistoric monster, humped through the
sea of rubble toward Cripplegate. It humped and reared that way,
almost as if this monster of the past had come alive. One might

hope that all except a token of the Wall would be covered again and never again exposed. But I felt that my errand had not been wasted. The naked length of Wall would never depart from the mind's eye. I wandered on beside the Wall toward Cripplegate.

There must have been something dreamlike about that July afternoon in the ruined City. I think it was a feeling shared by many, that it was strange to contemplate that we had survived, and there was necessity to contemplate what else had survived. What were the significant survivals to be thought about, as you stumbled westward along Fore Street? In Fore Street it was not easy to think. It was doubtful if you could call a street what was only an open potholed way, with nowhere on either side. You couldn't think, you had to watch where you were going. There was a remnant of fabric and spire ahead: St. Giles's Cripplegate.[5] How curious to find such two great symbols as the Roman Wall and St. Giles's standing beside each other, crippled, but standing! For if the Wall had made you think about Caesar and the Roman Empire and the Roman Church, St. Giles's made you think of Cromwell and of the British Empire and the English Bible—for at the moment formative for the creation of the Authorized Version, St. Giles's was the "living" of Lancelot Andrewes. Stumbling along this fifteen-minute journey, what had I found emergent from the rubble? St. Paul's, Shakespeare, the Wall and Caesar, St. Giles's and Cromwell and the English Bible—what sense did one make of it? What sense did one make, not so much of the survivals, but how did the things which survived come about in the first place? How did they come into being?

Fore Street, on that July afternoon, was not much of a place for consecutive thought on the mysteries about which no amount of consecutive thought is likely to provide a satisfactory rebuilding; but it certainly provided a scene to make one try to think. In the wilderness of rubble I kept an eye on the direction finder and swung around toward the "riding redoubtable dome of Paul." I had to pause before crossing Aldersgate Street. Aldersgate Street was not so much worth looking at as the things at which I had been looking. And yet a thought did come to vivid focus. Aldersgate Street was part of the Great North Road.

The Great North Road.

It was difficult at that moment to have pride in the Great North Road if you paused to look at Aldersgate Street. The destroyed and deserted Aldersgate Underground Station, if it said anything, said that travel nowadays, so far as it was concerned, had ceased. But Aldersgate Underground Station had never represented the kind of traffic I was trying to think about. Aldersgate Underground Station was only a local east-west punctuation mark. I could recall lots of things about Aldersgate Underground Station, but they were trivial. The thought of the Great North Road was not trivial. Look south, you saw it stretching all the way to Rome. It had been in its time the road to Rome. Look north, it was the road away from Rome. The Great North Road had carried—well, now, what hadn't it carried, and how far, and where not, around the world? What hadn't it caused to be carried? The ruin of Aldersgate Underground Station was as nothing. It had little to do with the muscular movement of the Great North Road, long-distance movement of body, word, and spirit, up and down. Old wars or recent war, war or no war, that traffic was continuing. On the tour that I've described, I found few habitable buildings hereabouts in Aldersgate Street, but the traffic lights were working on this, the major working road of Britain. The traffic was continuing. Before you could cross the Great North Road you had still to watch the traffic lights.

When I had crossed over Aldersgate Street I found I had crawled from a sea of devastation to some sort of foreshore. It was a foreshore, because there was a shore line of buildings. Behind the shore line there were shocking gaps. Old Charterhouse was in ruins except for the chapel. West Smithfield (strangely enough, considering its history) provided the return to civility. The cattle market, with its iron lacework and architectural filigree, was as it had been in Victorian times. St. Bartholomew the Great had had its bells removed for safety during the war, but the square flint-darkened tower and the timber and plaster gatehouse were now being renovated by Dove Brothers, Ltd. The south side of West Smithfield was still bounded by the long and beautiful façade of Bart's Hospital. As those who know the City have perceived, my tour had now brought me round to the entrance to Little Britain, an acre of considerable importance in the development of the Western world. But I can deal with that later, and resist for the moment the side-

wise temptation into Postmen's Garden. I resisted all temptations
on that July day, even that of inspecting the immense respectability
and efficiency of the London General Post Office. The bombing
had not seriously impaired the Post Office. After all, there are limits
to impertinence. The bombing had, though, opened up a new view
of the cathedral as I came to it by way of Little Britain.[6] And there
I was, back at St. Paul's.

I must now cast round for a different beginning.

This is a book about the Great North Road. What is the Great
North Road? Physically it is a strip of roadway in Britain connecting two capital cities, London and Edinburgh. The geometry is
inconsiderable: about four hundred miles.

There is no mystery about the Great North Road. There is not
much that is photogenic. What motive then suggests the undertak-
ing of so short and unadventurous a journey?

There would be nothing wrong in attempting to answer this
question in scientific terms. The problem is easily restated. After a
war a man returned to Britain to look at things which either in
themselves or regarded as symbols exhibited a power of survival.
In a few repeated half-hours of poking around in a part of the City
of London he spotted a few such things. Seeking for a common
causative element in the original formation of these things, it was
worth looking at something which might have been causative, or
at any rate contributive, or which at the least was concomitant with
the growth and form of the various survivals. The survivals might
be accepted as characteristic of the civilization of Britain. They
represented things which had not stopped in the nighttime. Part
of the question was, How did they start? One element, causative,
contributive, or concomitant, was open to inspection. It was not
showing off, nor was it in hiding. It was the Great North Road.

There is nothing new in the idea that specific roadways may be
studied as having affected the growth and form of specific civilizations. There is a respectable realm of science called hodology
(*hodos* being the Greek work for *road*). As a science it derives
from D'Arcy Thompson, as D'Arcy Thompson derived from Goethe
what Goethe derived from Aristotle. D'Arcy Thompson's best-
known contribution was a book called *Growth and Form*. It was a

study of the ways in which physical forces were to be observed as affecting the specific forms assumed in the process of growth of a great variety of things. A merit of the book was that Professor D'Arcy Thompson was preoccupied with things which were reasonably simple. He was preoccupied with many and delightful organic forms of life: with the manner of growth in flowers and shells, in fir cones and guillemots' eggs, in dolphins' teeth and the narwhal's horn, in deers' antlers and spiders' webs, in many types of concretions, spicules, agglutinated skeletons and the branching of blood vessels. *Growth and Form* was and remains a wonderfully alert and stimulating book, an eye opener to the science of "morphology": the study of the interrelations of growth and form, and the part which physical forces play in this complex interaction.

Jusserand's *English Wayfaring Life in the Middle Ages* was another contribution to the science of morphology. This was an account of the English roads of the fourteenth century and of conditions to be met with by the ordinary traveler and the casual passer-by. It described the lay wayfarers, herbalists, charlatans, minstrels, jugglers, tumblers; it described the messengers, itinerant merchants and peddlers; it described outlaws, wandering workmen, tinkers, and peasants escaping from bond. It also described the religious wayfarers, the wandering preachers and friars, the pardoners, and all who went on pilgrimage. Jusserand's book was almost wholly descriptive; he was too wise and wily to be drawn into discussing the causation of the everyday things which he so well described; but if in your boyhood you had read Jusserand with D'Arcy Thompson's book also in mind, you derived a lasting feeling that the preexistence and physical condition of the roadways of the fourteenth century had a great deal to do with causing and shaping the life of that period. You derived the feeling that roads had played an active part in the great formations, language, law, and order and so forth, which arise in an energetic society. You saw that the great roads of the world should be studied, not merely for the ways in which they exhibited various heydays of various civilizations, but for the ways in which heydays of civilizations came into being. You saw, in short, that in the great academic department of morphology there had to be a special room devoted to the study of roads.

Boyhood was the age for enjoying fragmentary sciences, and if I am dwelling on the science of hodology it is because I enjoyed it in boyhood and it has not lost a fascination for me to this day. What a wrestle it was, to attempt to extend D'Arcy Thompson's suggestions to the larger formations of civilized life! The idea that there were physical concomitants in the great concretions and agglutinations of social order—what more pleasurable exercise could there be than to attempt to isolate such coefficients! Dull indeed would have been the mind which couldn't be stirred into curiosity by thinking about roadways. From each great road, did you not obtain a feeling, and a proper different feeling, for each civilization? Was not the road to Athens made for conversation? Were not the roads of Italy precursors of the Renaissance?—not merely as pathways for wandering scholars, but in picture and painting. Consider Pico della Mirandola discussing the merits to be looked for in a road (*Si modo mare, modo montes . . .*) and there the road was, with the merits Pico mentions, always in the background of the Renaissance picture.[7] Roads suggested problems that were logistical and topographical: How do you open up a New World? Consider North America: rivers at first had the advantage. Roads beat the rivers for transportation soon after men made railroads of them and altered longitude to latitude, altered direction of ideas from north and south to east and west. How do you open up an Old World? The best part of Kipling's *Kim* is his description of the Grand Trunk Road of India. I am scampering over the surface of matters which the contemplation of roads could and did suggest to the innocent mind. The topographical elements were always interesting: the spiritual elements, the interaction of the causes and uses of roadways, were much more curious.

A study of the causeys, causeways, hard highroads of the world is, I have said, a respectable science. It is a science which is pleasurable to study, for it suggests all sorts of thoughts, and is not so pretentious as to suggest that whatever it teaches comprises a complete answer. As for the complete story of Mankind:

> The fretful foam
> Of vehement actions without scope or term,
> Called History.

As for its contribution to the whole picture, the science of hodology is properly modest. There are other fragmentary sciences of about the same size, each suggestive of special elements causative in the make-up of this or that civilization. Each of these little sciences is for a scope or term put on the stage and given a run. There is, for instance, a scientific study of the "play-element." It was to nobody's disadvantage that Professor Huizinga isolated the "play-element" as a mainspring in the causation of culture, and made "play" into a science of academic respectability. "Play," as we shall have occasion to agree, is no soft word; "play" is a hard word: "horseplay," "swordplay," "gunplay." It was a serious and sensible assertion which Professor Huizinga made, that "civilization arises and unfolds in and as play." He devoted his life to thinking about the assertion, and in his last book, *Homo Ludens*,[8] gave a considered judgment:

In myth and ritual the great instinctive forces of civilized life have their origin: law and order, commerce and profit, craft and art, poetry, wisdom and science. All are rooted in the primaeval soil of play.

This is no unsupported statement. Professor Huizinga brought to his thesis a full professional equipment of references and illustrations, and it is fascinating and beneficial to follow him trailing and tracing the arising and unfolding of civilization "in and as play." Others have taken up Huizinga's idea, and you may pursue his and their studies and decide for yourself the size you wish to accord to the science of "play." You may decide that in the department of morphology the "play-element" should have a large room or a small room, but you may have to agree it should have a room of its own. All that I am asserting is a similar academic respectability for the science of hodology. Chapter by chapter and paragraph by paragraph, if a student of sufficient maturity and leisure were to wish to set himself to the task, Professor Huizinga's exertion on behalf of the "play-element" in history might be paralleled on behalf of the "road element." The hodological approach equally has thoughts to suggest as to the growth of complicated formations in a civilization: formations of "law and order, commerce and profit, craft and art, poetry, wisdom and science."

But having declared and said that there might be a real and

proper scientific way of looking at the Great North Road, I have
to confess that that is not going to be my method.

Somebody asked George Mallory why he wished to climb Mount
Everest. "Because it is there," said Mallory.

I have attempted to travel the Road, and if I speak of hardships,
I speak whereof I know. The object of the exercise is not so im-
modest as to claim that I have anything to tell about the Great
North Road; the object is to let the Great North Road tell me. I,
at the age of sixty, with whatever equipment I have been able to
lug along, am not content to avoid this journey. The challenge of
the journey is "to learn." The verb "to learn" goes back to an original root which meant "to follow a track." The track is "there." I
must have written to no purpose about my postwar strolls in the
City, if I failed to convey the importance to me of the Great North
Road being "there." So that is why I have rejected a scientific attitude. I am not a dispassionate pilgrim. I care too much. When I
called the Great North Road the major working road of Britain, I
was using the word "working" in an old sense, as when you say
yeast is working. I was thinking of the ferments. Along this conduit
and at any time for a couple of thousand years you could examine
Britain's peristalsis. I rejected a scientific attitude because I don't
greet an old friend in that manner. I might go so far as to say,
"Your pulse, ma'am, your pulse is horrid"; but chiefly to remind
myself that her grandmother lived to the age of two thousand.

To study the Great North Road has not been for me an impersonal
affair. It has not been a journey to be tossed off in a few hours. The
Great North Road is not at all the straight four hundred miles you
thought. If you and I speak English, it is your history and mine; and
that is quite a subject. But let the Road answer, in its own way,
what it has to tell about its own ribbon development of history.

The ancients, when starting out on any ambitious journey, were
accustomed to indulging "a Voluntary before the March." It was
one of the polite "Beates and Points"[9] of marching manners, and
that is all that I have so far been attempting. I may have struck a
wrong note. Soon enough, I am very conscious of it, we shall be
in trouble. I am not doing much good by excusing myself, saying
this little tour is only a personal essay. "Farewell" was scarcely the

right word with which to start. "There," with its challenge, is the
Great North Road. Seldom has faring on that way been well or
easy. I accept a first correction:

> Not fare well,
> But fare forward, voyagers.

II »» *Fare Forward*

Where does the Great North Road begin? Plenty of Londoners will state with an easy assurance that their Great West Road begins at Hyde Park Corner, and that distances along it are measured from that point of origin. I don't know if that is a right answer, but it is a precise answer readily given and believed. If you ask the corresponding question about the point of origin of the Great North Road, although it is the premier of all the roads of Britain, the Route A1, the chances are that your informant will have no answer at all.[1]

The topographical answer is not hard to find out. Technically the Great North Road is the post road from G.P.O. London to G.P.O. Edinburgh. The beginning is at the Post Office, beside St. Paul's. But I had been asking myself a different question. I wasn't bothered so much about the technical geometrical point of origin of the Great North Road, but where is the beginning on the time scale? What was the original push? What caused this causeway which I was claiming to have been causative in the history of the

English-speaking world? What was it that the long, harsh north-ward-facing stretch of Roman Wall, as one saw it humping through the rubble of a square mile of the ruined City—what did that compel one to think about?

My theory is that on the time scale the beginning of the Great North Road resides in Julius Caesar's decision to make his second expedition to Britain; and that was a very peculiar decision. It is indeed worth repeating this initial simple question: After Caesar's first expedition to Britain, why did he make a second expedition in the following year?

The question does not seem to me remote or academic. It is remote in time. It involves a long swing. But as soon as the question grasps you, it becomes interesting. The dates of Caesar's two expeditions to Britain are given as 55 and 54 B.C. I suppose that so far as possible we should attempt to regard decisive moments of history—moments which subsequently appear to have been decisive—according to the circumstances of those moments, when there may have been factors which are difficult for us to assess. Into such guesswork I enter with humility and caution. At the same time, if you ask a direct question it does no good to wince about expressing your answer. Why, after his first reconnaissance of Britain, did Caesar return in force in the following summer? Britain was at that moment completely off the Roman map. As Dio was later to say, Britain was "out of this world." Caesar's first reconnaissance revealed very little of material or political advantage to suggest that the expedition should be repeated; and he promptly repeated it in the next year with an army of 40,000 troops—an army as large as that with which he had subdued all Gaul. Of Caesar's first expedition to Britain, Romans in Rome might well say: "Wherefore rejoice? What conquest brings he home?" Why did he make the second expedition?

Caesar, like Cromwell, until he was in his forties had no military experience of handling troops in the field. Then, in Caesar's Gallic campaigns, there is the familiar picture that everything that he set out to accomplish was secured. There is the familiar picture of Caesar exhibiting his wonderful combination of patience and velocity; the devotion he inspired in other men to serve him with fidelity and skill; and, as perhaps his most central characteristic, that "he meant to have his way in Rome." I am sure we may take it as an axiom that in Caesar's time Rome was the be-all and end-all of ambition, that Rome was the great theater for genius and exertion. If that be so, I return to my question, What was Caesar's motive in the repetition of visits to the faraway, unimportant island of Britain?

Regarding the welter of opinions about Caesar, whether his character should be regarded as that of hero or villain, one has to bring in another axiom, that behind the legendary figure there must have been a man. A question then is, Where or at what secret moments was the man converted, for good or ill, to his megalomania? When did Caesar cease to be tentative about his capacity to do whatever he chose to do? When was there alteration in his character from uncertainty of success to certainty of success, from hesitation to unhesitation about the taking of momentous action? I am here thinking of military action, the realm in which Caesar, until he was in his forties, was inexperienced. Can you isolate a climacteric in Caesar's military career, after which his pulse beat differently? It would be a very gross impertinence to think so; and yet the question of the second expedition to Britain remains nagging at the mind. No ordinary explanation for the second expedition seems to make sense. On any score it was a peculiar move. That much is fair comment. Of Caesar's character, of the ferments working in him, better men than I have spent lifetimes of study. I am drawing attention only to the oddness of one particular military move: Caesar's second expedition to Britain.

The remoteness of Britain from the actualities of Rome in Caesar's time provokes me to the paradox that it was because of Britain's remoteness that Caesar perceived an opportunity. Opportunity for what? Opportunity for unobserved military exercise. What were the actualities in Rome? Caesar's relations with Pompey, the great Pompeius Magnus, were not as yet openly hostile. What were the secret feelings? Pompey had achieved unrivaled glory as a soldier; he had a seasoned army at his command; he was having spectacular success, campaigning in and looting the wealthy East. Pompey was favorite of the Senate, and darling of the populace. The spoils that Pompey was sending back to Rome were so notable that piracy in the Mediterranean became a major business. To put down the piracy Pompey had to pay a good deal of attention to sea warfare.

By contrast with Pompey's achievements, what had Caesar to offer to Romans in Rome? In land warfare he had made the name of Caesar the first and earliest Latin word to enter the Teutonic dialects; he had made Caesar a name of fear and respect wherever he chose, almost anywhere in the inhospitable and unprofitable Northland. Into a wilderness Caesar carried extraordinary and unprecedented displays of Roman power. He commanded his engineers to build the famous bridge across the Rhine; he noted that the feat was accomplished in ten days. He recorded the building of that bridge as a spectacular achievement. What did it mean to Romans in Rome? For what purpose was the bridge built? What loot came back across it? Teutonic volunteers, perhaps, for Caesar's army; what else? In the same year in which Caesar built the bridge across the Rhine he made his first expedition to Britain, presumably in ships commandeered from Northmen. I don't know what evidence there may be about the ships; it is however to be regarded as Caesar's first serious sea venture to a hostile seacoast. And despite the striking power of the force Caesar had gathered, the first expedition to Britain was a failure.

On that first expedition of Caesar's to Britain, in 55 B.C., ships and men were lost by gale damage. Such reconnaissance of the island as was undertaken revealed no wealth. I have to respect such an authority as Cicero, who reported to a friend: "It is now known that there is not a pennyweight of silver in the whole island, and no hope of plunder except in the form of slaves." Caesar himself made mention of the political advantage of overawing British chieftains so that they would not give aid and comfort to Rome's enemies in Gaul; but it was difficult to maintain, after a first inspection of Britain, that the aid and comfort which British chieftains could give to Rome's enemies were a matter of major importance. Yet in the very next summer Caesar made the unprofitable expedition to Britain all over again. Could any move have been less popular with anybody?

If you rearrange the chess play as I am rearranging it, you get a picture of Caesar's second invasion of Britain which I have to admit is unorthodox. I have tried to be explicit about my main axiom: which is, that the chessboard was Rome. The play upon

the fringes of the world was as to what sort of power one was
going to bring back to the center. Pompey, famous soldier, was
bringing back loot. Caesar, hitherto famous playboy, was bringing
back military proficiency. That, and that alone, was what Caesar
could gain in the Northland. I have been suggesting that the fact
of life, the constant preoccupation, was Rome. It might be said
that by 54 B.C. Caesar's contest with Pompey was not as yet overt.
But personal ties had gone. Julia, daughter of Caesar and wife of
Pompey, had died. Crassus, who with Caesar and Pompey had
formed the Triumvirate, had died. As early as 54 B.C. it may have
been clear to Caesar that there was going to be nothing between
him and Pompey except a straight fight. This is a bold assertion
to be made two thousand years afterward by a journeyman who
has no claim to be a scholar. From scholars, the nearest information
I can find is the cautious remark that by 54 B.C. it might have been
doubtful if Pompey would feel himself either bound or inclined to
allow Caesar anything except, in Rome, a second place. Somehow,
somewhen, and put it where and when you will—I feel it was
somewhen in the Northland—Caesar had jumped over an inner
Rubicon, had secretly cast his die: *Aut Caesar aut nullus.*

I am indulging myself in fantastic guesswork; but if you travel
the Great North Road, you have to guess what caused it. Let me
restate. I wondered why Caesar made his second expedition to
Britain. In an inhospitable Northland, not without struggle and
not without the devoted service of such a deputy as Labienus,
Caesar had conquered the fiercest of barbarians, Franks, and
Teutons. Many of them he had enrolled and had taught them
legionary discipline. But Caesar's first sea venture to Britain had
been a failure. That, I suggest, was a factor in the immediate
repetition.

I must be fair to the orthodox view, which is that Caesar was
seriously intending to capture Britain but, and because of mis-
calculations, failed, after two goes, to do it. That might be the
right view, and who am I to squabble with teachers who (this
side idolatry) I do revere. I revere Collingwood and Myres.[2] They
present, none better, the orthodox view of Caesar's second expedition to Britain. That view is that on his second expedition Caesar

took so large an army as 40,000 in order to make quick conquest of the island; that he had expectations of wintering in Britain; but that he was prevented from prolonging his successful summer campaign because of uprisings in Gaul. That is, of course, Caesar's own story. As well as most other historians, Collingwood and Myres respect it. They speak about Caesar's "frustrated plan of conquest." They say that in the autumn of 54 B.C., before the equinoctial gales should come, Caesar "crowded all that was left of his army and prisoners in the few ships he had, and on a calm night made his last crossing in safety." Collingwood and Myres ascribe Caesar's failure to "the mistake which he made when he set out to conquer Britain before he had pacified Gaul."

I wonder about that "mistake" of Caesar's. When Caesar set sail in 54 B.C. for the summer in Britain, did he regard Gaul as "pacified"? He pretty much says so, but throughout you have to keep an eye not merely on what Caesar said but on what he did. In 54 B.C., when Caesar sailed for Britain, there was certain to be more fighting in Gaul. There was rebellion on the eve of his departure. Caesar's absence might even invite trouble. What, I would speculate, were the relations at that time between Caesar and his deputy, Labienus, to whom he left the management of Gaul? Within a few years Labienus was to quarrel as bitterly with Caesar as did Pompey. Did Labienus and Caesar trust each other in the year 54? I don't know. What I see is Caesar going off to Britain for a summer's military exercise, to repair a first failure, to make certain how to embark an army, land it on enemy coast, and return again. Return, to what destiny? Whether or not the destiny had been formulated, it was certainly not as yet to be proclaimed.

My view is that the reconnaissance of Britain in 55 B.C. had humiliated Caesar as to one military operation in which he was not yet expert: the landing of an army on an open coast, the establishment of a beachhead, and the protection of his ships. Caesar's second landing on the coast of Kent in 54 I find instructive. Caesar anchored his ships and landed his army. Then he engaged the VII Legion in storming Bigbury Fort above the valley of the Stour. About this action Collingwood and Myres are indignant:

He made a mistake for which he paid dearly. While he lay encamped in the Stour valley a gale got up from the east. His ships dragged their anchors, fell foul of one another, and were thrown by scores on the beach to be hammered by the full force of the rollers. The crews left on board could do nothing, and by morning very few of the vessels were undamaged . . . forty of his ships were a total loss, and the rest were not to be repaired without much labour. . . . But it was not enough to repair his fleet; he now at last realized that he must protect it from like damage in the future. The only way in which he could do this, in the absence of a safe harbour, was by beaching every ship above high-water mark and then entrenching them against enemy attack. This took ten days, which could ill be spared from the short campaigning season; but it had to be done, and Caesar did it.

The negligence with which he exposed himself to a repetition of the same disaster which he had suffered in 55 is difficult to understand. . . .

I would comment that it was not repetition of the same disaster. In 55 Caesar's ships had merely been beached below high-water mark, whereas in 54 they were left in what was reputed to be safe anchorage offshore. But it was certainly a disaster, and Caesar had at once to attend to it. What arouses heat in Collingwood and Myres is that Caesar did not attend to the disaster in what they consider the right way. Caesar failed to scout round for a safe harbor for his remaining ships; for, if the conjectural site of his landing is assumed to be correct, there was a harbor nearby at what is now called Richborough, two or three miles away:

Why should he not have moved them there after the storm instead of spending ten precious days in beaching them? Richborough was a perfectly good harbour in the time of Claudius; it cannot have been a bad one in the time of Caesar.

Collingwood and Myres take the view that Caesar was working against time to conquer Britain as speedily as possible; hence their very reasonable impatience with him for wasting those "ten precious days." If Caesar had really been thinking first and foremost about conquering Britain and wintering on the island, his delay in finding a harbor is not very understandable. But consider the converse. If Caesar was not thinking about a speedy conquest and a long-term occupation of Britain so much as of mastering a technique whereby he might land an army and protect his ships on any flat shore, anywhere in the world, regardless of harbors—then the picture is different. In that case to find a harbor would not be to work out the problem. It would have given him Britain, but not experience which he could apply elsewhere. Why should he want Britain? To be able to establish a safe beachhead independent of harborage, and to know how long it would take—therein lay knowledge. I am not at all sure that Caesar regarded those ten days as wasted.

Interpret the episode either way, Caesar chose to spend those ten days as he did. Throughout that summer of 54 I ponder not only Caesar's words but his actions. Many of the episodes of Caesar's second summer in Britain give an impression of summer maneuvers. The storming of Bigbury Fort, which took place just before the emergency with the ships, creates the feeling of an exercise contrived for the training of the VII Legion. The mastering of the British charioteers is undertaken as if it is merely the working out of an interesting tactical problem. In example after example, there is the feeling that a superb professional soldier is giving lessons, scarcely so much to the enemy as to his own men. It seems that Britain, as such, is of no particular importance to Caesar; though a good training ground. Cassivellaunus is the only British leader who is given credit for putting up a real struggle; but Cassivellaunus is dealt with. The other leaders are brushed off, or they capitulate. Caesar's main concern seems to be to wind up the visit, leaving to the Britons memorials of his invincibility, but also creating faith in his invincibility among his own troops. The question about Caesar's second expedition to Britain thus suggests as a possible answer that by making it he had satisfied himself that he had men to count on: that he had an army which, having followed him off the known map of the world, would follow him anywhere.

In what direction, for Caesar, was that "anywhere"? The awkward rebellions in Gaul brought Caesar back from Britain to the Continent; it is impressive how those allegedly awkward rebellions kept on providing reasons for Caesar to move southward. The campaigns of 53 and 52, culminating in the defeat of Vercingetorix, involved the terrible fights we read about in boyhood; but always the vivid troubles of pacifying Gaul seem to have nudged Caesar steadily back from the Northland, always back to the border of Italy. By 51 Caesar was at the Alps; by 50 he was on the southern side of the Alps, at Ravenna. Ravenna was within striking distance of Rome.

It was, for Caesar, a four years' travel from the river Thames to the brook Rubicon, and it is hardly for me to speculate in detail on all the political and personal disputes in Rome during those four years. I pick out as significant that in those years there was continuing and increasing acrimony in the Senate between the partisans of Caesar and those of Pompey. I pick out a dramatic change in the relationship between Caesar and his at-one-time most devoted deputy, Labienus. Caesar, at Ravenna in 50 B.C., within reach of Rome, had only one legion with him. Labienus, who had served with Caesar throughout all the Gallic campaigns, now chose to leave him. It must have been clear that Caesar was going to force the issue of the Roman Civil Wars. It must have been clear to Labienus that it was no longer possible to go along with Caesar's megalomania. Caesar at Ravenna with one legion —Labienus preferred to join cause with Pompey and the Senate. Caesar, with no fighting force behind him except his single legion, must indeed have seemed a madman. Caesar must have been stung by the desertion of Labienus, but not even that deterred him from challenging Rome. Caesar jumped the brook Rubicon, with the phrase, as reported by Suetonius, *Iacta alea est:* the die is cast.

In these meditations I seem to be getting a long way from the Great North Road; but I don't believe so. I think we have to find the point of origin of the Great North Road on the time scale, and that is what we are doing. Caesar was the first great Roman to have crossed the Thames. I think we have to follow him across the Rubicon before we can come back. Here the master on whom I rely is Professor Ronald Syme (*The Roman Revolution*). After the crossing of the Rubicon, says Professor Syme:

It had confidently been expected that the solid and respectable classes in the towns of Italy would rally in defence of the authority of the Senate and the liberties of the Roman People, that all the land would rise as one man against the invader. Nothing of the kind happened. Italy was apathetic to the war-cry of the Republic in danger, sceptical about its champions.

So (Professor Syme gives the full story) Caesar's action was not so reckless as it had seemed. It is true that he had only one legion at hand, but as well as the legion he had a legend. Suetonius gives us the spirit of that legion by giving us its marching song:

Ecce Caesar nunc triumphat qui subegit Gallias

The tread and the noise of that line are like thunder, and as Caesar swept forward, down the east coast of Italy, the song gathered for Caesar more troops as he went. Within two months of the crossing of the Rubicon, Italy was mastered.

This swift success of the adventurer was not to be regarded as fatal to the forces of the Republic. Pompey with several legions had crossed the Adriatic; there he had had forces from the East behind him, and in Spain Pompey could count on his experienced and loyal legions. Between these pincers, in Italy, Caesar was trapped. I get the impression from Syme that Pompey, Labienus, and other regular soldiers could almost laugh at Caesar's predicament.

What Caesar did was to lash out at Spain, and against all calculations he landed, outmaneuvered and outfought Pompey's legions there. He had conquered Spain by August; in that month returned to Rome and was named dictator; he at once set forth across the Adriatic to have the final round with Pompey.

Yet even so [says Syme] until the legions joined battle on the plain of Pharsalus, the odds lay heavily against Caesar.

In Caesar's own history of the civil wars he minimizes his reverses, but it stands out that he did not find it easy to get at Pompey. Caesar's attack at Dyrrachium (Durazzo) was repulsed with heavy loss. Caesar's forces were regarded as being in a bad way. Pompey, with reinforcements, confidently forced a decisive battle at Pharsalus. It was the most astonishing of Caesar's victories.

At Pompey's council of war before the Battle of Pharsalus, as Caesar describes in the third book of the *Civil Wars*, Labienus mocked at the dictator and his tattered forces. If anyone had been affected by the strength and power of the shout "Ecce Caesar" then Labienus was the man to puncture that boast. "Do not suppose, Pompeius," said Labienus, "that this is the army that subdued Gaul and Germany. At all those battles I was present: not much of that army survives." Labienus then swore that he would not return from the field except as Caesar's conqueror, and Pompey and the other generals all swore the same. Caesar is putting these words into the mouths of his opponents, perhaps to rub in the bitterness of the fight. There is no doubt of its bitterness, nor of the carnage, where Roman killed Roman, friend killed friend.

"They would have it thus," said Caesar as he gazed upon the Roman dead at Pharsalus, half in patriot grief for the havoc of civil war, half in impatience and resentment. They had cheated Caesar of the true glory of a Roman aristocrat—to contend with his peers for primacy, not to destroy them. His enemies had the laugh of him in death. Even Pharsalus was not the end. His former ally, the great Pompeius, glorious from victories in all quarters of the world, lay unburied on an Egyptian beach, slain by a renegade Roman, the hireling of a foreign king. Dead, too, and killed by Romans, were Caesar's rivals and enemies, many illustrious consulars, while Cato chose to fall by his own hand rather than witness the domination of Caesar and the destruction of the Free State.

That was the nemesis of ambition and glory, to be thwarted in the end. After such wreckage, the task of rebuilding confronted him, stern and thankless. Without the sincere and patriotic co-operation of the governing class, the attempt would be all in vain, the mere creation of arbitrary power, doomed to perish in violence.

Two more quotations from Professor Syme's great book wind up this part of the story. Of the intolerable situation in which Caesar found himself toward the end, and of Caesar's own personal despair, Professor Syme says:

That he was unpopular he well knew. "For all his genius, Caesar could not see a way out," as one of his friends was subsequently to remark. And there was no going back. To Caesar's clear mind and love of rapid decision, this brought a tragic sense of impotence and frustration—he had been all things and it was no good. He had surpassed the good fortune of Sulla Felix and the glory of Pompeius Magnus. In vain—reckless ambition had ruined the Roman State and baffled itself in the end. Of the melancholy that descended upon Caesar there stands the best of testimony—"my life has been long enough, whether reckoned in years or in renown." The words were remembered. The most eloquent of his contemporaries did not disdain to plagiarize them.

Each of the sentences in this passage is documented. The contemporary referred to in the last sentence is Cicero. Caesar himself "could not see a way out" is the statement to be pondered. The second quotation from Professor Syme is to the effect that Caesar foresaw that he was likely to be assassinated; but "his removal would be no remedy but a source of greater ills to the Commonwealth, the Dictator himself observed."

I have now made most of the long swing to the point of origin, on the time scale, of the Great North Road. As I have sketched the story, Britain happened to be the most northerly and most distant exercise ground from which Caesar returned, moving steadily southward and more and more imperiously toward the dictatorship of Rome, from which there proved, for him, to be no way out. The Roman State was ruined. I turn now to the succession of Caesar's dictatorship, to that most enigmatic of Roman characters —Caesar's great-nephew, Augustus—that "chameleon," as Julian the Apostate called him.

Of all the enigmatic behaviors of Augustus I am concerned only with his behavior toward Britain. Augustus was nineteen years of age at the time of Caesar's assassination. What were the personal relations between Caesar and the boy whom he had nominated to be his heir? Did Caesar talk to him about his own career? Did the boy notice Caesar's melancholy, irritability, unpopularity, and draw conclusions of his own? Were there mentors who advised Augustus? Who can tell? All we see is that after the assassination of Julius Caesar there were seventeen years of chaos in Roman affairs: seventeen years of confusion, disorder and civil warfare. Then, when a most extraordinary series of hazards and events brought Augustus to the throne at the age of thirty-six, this unmilitary ruler proceeded to rule the Roman Empire for the unexpected and unequaled period of forty years.

Julius Caesar, after Pharsalus, when he had dealt with a number of distant affairs, returned to Rome in July 45 B.C., and seven months later was assassinated. Augustus was emperor for forty years. The contrast calls for attention. Undoubtedly by the time of Augustus all Romans were weary of the fighting. The old governing class was shattered; there was general will for peace, even if the price was despotism. *Pax et Princeps* was the generally accepted formula. But Syme points out the caution with which Augustus applied the formula. Caesar, dead, had become a god and a myth. The godhead was useful to Augustus, and he accepted the deification. The memory of Caesar the Dictator remained a red light of danger. "Augustus was careful sharply to discriminate between *Dictator* and *Princeps.* Under his rule Caesar the Dictator was either suppressed outright or called up from time to time to enhance the contrast between the unscrupulous adventurer who destroyed the Free State in his ambition and the modest magistrate who restored the Republic. In its treatment of Caesar the inspired literature of the Augustan Principate is consistent and instructive. Though in different words, Virgil, Horace, and Livy tell the same tale and point the same moral."

All that I am concerned to consider is the possibility of some kind of identification in the mind of Augustus of the idea of military dictatorship with the idea of the Northland. There was as yet no physical Great North Road. The one northward adventure by Caesar had wrecked everything. Julius Caesar had put Britain on the Roman map, but for Augustus it was a fixed idea to take it off again. Or, I must say, so it seems. If Augustus could prevent it, there was never to be a Great North Road. The inspired geographies of the Augustan reign bear out what Syme says about the inspired literature. In so far as Britain appears, it is coupled with the idea of low-grade, unscrupulous adventure. In the Augustan period I can find no reference to Britain which does not go out of its way to be derogatory. Many elements may come into this. The derogatory remarks may, for instance, have been based on observation of the island and may have been true. But they seem mostly to stem from observation of Augustus. Augustus, as a soldier, was never in a class with his great-uncle Caesar; and never wished to be so classed; and whenever he was pressured, as he was from time to time, to annex Britain to the Roman Empire he gave it out (as is remarked by Collingwood and Myres) "that Britain was too poor, too distant, or too friendly to make annexation expedient or necessary." This is the official line followed by Strabo in his *Geography.* Strabo makes some delightful embroideries. The inhabitants of Britain, Strabo says, are coarse in their eating habits, and have no aptitude for gardening. He has not been in that part of the world, but he has it on hearsay that the inhabitants of Ireland are even more disgusting than the Britons. The Irish are cannibals: when an old Irishman dies the menfolk of his clan sit up all night eating him. No wise Princeps would touch any part of Britain. So apparently said Augustus to the end of his long life. Before Augustus died in A.D. 14 he passed on to his successor, Tiberius, the advice (I am again quoting Collingwood and Myres) "that the frontiers of the Empire were best left unaltered, and in particular gave him a hint, which Tiberius treated (according to a phrase of Tacitus) as a command, against reopening the question of a British war."

So long as Tiberius lived (he ruled for twenty-three years and did not die until A.D. 37) he obeyed the instruction of Augustus, not to meddle with Britain. His abstention is more curious than that of Augustus, in that Tiberius was a more competent soldier and was under more pressure to make use of his surplus troops. Tiberius had finally settled the long troubles in Spain, and Spain was overgarrisoned. The frontiers of the Rhine and Danube were solidly held. The Near East, though it might be providing rumors of religious restlessness, was not presenting a military problem. Britain could be taken into the empire at any time, and by this time there were many in Rome who regarded it as worth the taking. The proposal to invade Britain moved up on the Roman agenda. Tiberius refused to pay attention to it.

What was the reason for this persistent taboo on Britain? It is an odd problem. Throughout the long reign of Augustus and the long reign of Tiberius the taboo persisted. If in some way the idea of adventuring in Britain had been identified by Augustus, and passed on to Tiberius, as having association with the tragedy of the first Caesar, that might for a time have explained the avoidance of the island. The thought is fanciful, and it would be a queer thing for such a superstition to persist for the better part of a century; yet it is also a queer thing that instantly after the death of Tiberius, and when the harm done by Julius Caesar was by many forgotten and only his glory remained, the first thought of new contenders for divine glory was the conquest of Britain, and the project was identified with Caesar, and presented as fulfillment of Caesar's cherished design. Caesar was no longer played down, but exploited. Had it not been Caesar's expressed intention to conquer Britain? Had Caesar not made a prophetic offering to the shrine of Venus Genetrix of a breastplate of British pearls?

I don't know where this story of the breastplate of British pearls comes from. It circulates in the reign of Tiberius, and what could be more symbolic? What better proof, indeed, that instead of being poor, Britain was rich in natural resources? Had Augustus not been timid and Tiberius aloof—so aloof was Tiberius to the citizens of Rome that toward the end of his life he refused to live among them—had these emperors been younger and more enterprising, Romans would for a long time have been profiting from Britain's raw materials, a wealth of metals, wheat, and cattle, as well as slaves. Earlier reports of Britain were now reversed. The metals of Britain were not only iron, lead, and tin, but silver and gold. The people, far from being ignorant savages, understood the arts of agriculture and of breeding livestock. The upper-class Britons understood the good things of life: they wore well-cut clothes of wool and linen; they wore jewelry; they had good table manners—to other delights of the table they had added oysters, not soft as were the Mediterranean oysters, not green as were the oysters of Gaul, but large and white and plump and succulent. Oysters full of pearls: Caesar had said so. This was the new propaganda which was going about in Rome at the time of the death of Tiberius. As soon as the ancient taboo was removed and the back-room boys in Rome decided to take Britain, the island came out of its long eclipse, and came out shining like the breastplate Caesar had offered to Venus Genetrix.

The first activity for the young and energetic Gaius, when he succeeded Tiberius, was to be the capture of Britain. Such a conquest would at once invest the new emperor with the god-like stature of the original Caesar. To make a pageant of that fact, Gaius was to put in a personal appearance in Britain on an appropriate field of action, where the manifestation of his presence would save the day.

In this idea of *deus ex machina* I find the origin of the physical Great North Road. This was the idea which governed the first big push from Rome to London. "Then the perilous path was planted."

There was no difficulty about the machinery. There were doubts

about the blustery northern ocean; yet the first Caesar had conquered it, and since his time there had been the advancements of
nearly a century in matters of shipping and of maritime equipment.
There could now be built a remarkable new lighthouse at Boulogne,
as beacon and gathering point for the Roman expeditionary force.
The lighthouse was designed and built, and under this northward-
looking eye of Rome the force against Britain was assembled, in A.D.
40. The catapult was poised—and then everything had to be called
off.

The machinery was all right. The trouble about using Britain
as a backdrop for this particular *deus ex machina,* was that this
deus was crazy. Gaius had turned out to be a maniac. Without
laboring the details, we note the result. Gaius was adjudged to
be impossible and was summarily assassinated. The light in the
lighthouse at Boulogne was put out. The invasion force was disbanded.

There must have been graybeards in Rome who thought about
the ancient curse on Britain. The episode of Gaius was a reminder
that emperors who shunned the Northland lived long lives, and
an illustration that those who didn't, didn't. There must have been
other Romans in Rome, to whom the episode of Gaius proved
only that Rome's pride was the more committed to the conquest of
Britain. It seems a repetition of the earlier question, Why did
Julius Caesar make his second invasion? Once again there was pride
involved, and the morale of troops. If, after the failure of Gaius,
the haughty chieftains of Ultima Thule had hoped to escape punishment, they were wrong. The light in the lighthouse at Boulogne
went on again. The Roman eye glared northward.

Claudius, who succeeded Gaius, was adjudged to be a safe *deus
ex machina.* Nobody, including Claudius himself, expected him
to display military genius. Roman military genius was ready to
hand: there was the field general Aulus Plautius, who had made
an excellent name in Pannonia, and there was choice among an ex-
cess of troops. The troops finally chosen for the invasion of Britain
by Claudius in A.D. 43 were Aulus Plautius's own legion, IX His-
pana, and three legions from the Rhine: II Augusta from Strass-
burg, XIV Gemina (with its capricorn emblem)[3] from Mainz,
and XX Valeria Victrix from Cologne. With auxiliaries, foot and

horse, it was a force of about 40,000; an army the same size as that of Julius Caesar, organized somewhat differently according to Caesar's recorded notes and advice.

A trouble with writing anything is that there is a tendency to be rude to one's betters, and I feel that in discussing Caesar's second invasion of Britain I may have been guilty of bad manners to Collingwood and Myres. There is no intentional insult in disputing a point. But as to the Roman Conquest of Britain in A.D. 43 I follow Collingwood and Myres most worshipfully: nobody, it seems to me, could possibly better the zest and skill with which they tell the tale—and what a tale it is! There was the same Roman scheme for Claudius as there had been for Gaius. The military force could be counted on to be thoroughly professional and effective; therefore the play was for Aulus Plautius to get himself into just the right amount of apparent difficulty with the British warriors, and then for Claudius to turn up in the nick of time with a force of elephants and a token portion of the Praetorian Guard. Claudius and the elephants were to save the day and accept the credit.

Claudius and the elephants: none of this is my invention. *Hypotheses non fingo.* There was nothing inherently fantastic in the idea that Claudius should bring elephants with him to Britain. Is it not one of the longest-lived of military traditions for invaders to bring with them weapons strange to the enemy? Without accepting all of the embroideries which got into the story of Hannibal's elephants, since the time of Hannibal there were elephants in Roman military myth and in Roman armory. Against well-trained troops they might be useless, but they were always good for pageantry, and wasn't the chief point of the personal appearance of the emperor to provide an impressive pageantry? Where in Britain was this pageantry to take place? If I read Collingwood and Myres correctly, the British were expected to make a desperate stand at London. But that was the expectation of the Romans. Were the Britons going to play up? As in any scene that needs two actors, one alone cannot carry it. Already, when thinking about the preinvasion publicity which was being put about in Rome, one had begun to wonder how the island of Britain was going to be competent, in actuality, to live up to the excessive expectations. Where was the expected wealth to spring from—the quantities of gold and pearls? How was a primitive marshy trading settlement at London to furbish itself up as an adequate setting for the arrival of Claudius, the Guards, and elephants? One had the uneasy feeling that something might go wrong with this world premiere. The premonition was correct. Something did go wrong.

Aulus Plautius made his landing in Kent and marched for London. The Britons did not wait to fight him at London; they interposed themselves at the river Medway. This Battle of the Medway [4] was unexpected by the Romans. What was bad for both parties, it was not a mere brush but became a real battle. It was a battle lasting two days, which was unusual in ancient times. The account is that throughout the first day the Romans were hard put to it, and that not till dusk of the second day did Aulus Plautius win the field. It is, I think, a point of importance that Aulus Plautius was startled, and as I interpret the matter, impressed by the ferocity of this encounter at the Medway. As for the Britons, in the end they were shattered. When the Britons finally ran, they kept on running until they were far beyond London. By the time Aulus Plautius could collect himself and reach London, the remnant of Britons were as far away as Colchester. And so for Claudius, toiling after the fighting forces with his elephants, the show was spoiled.

Although the audience had run out on him, Claudius appears to have caught up with Aulus Plautius in London, and Aulus Plautius then hurried the emperor on from London to Colchester, where he received the submission of many of the tribes, hastily patched up a political system for the government of his new province, instructed Aulus Plautius to look after all details and conquer the rest of the island—and as quickly as possible Claudius was then returned to Rome to celebrate his triumph. It was quick work. First to last, if we can believe the records, Claudius spent sixteen days in Britain.

What happened to the elephants?

I said *hypotheses non fingo,* sheltering beneath the great wing of Sir Isaac Newton; and yet I have noticed that upon occasion Newton was not above touching a hypothesis. The statue of Newton, on the Great North Road at Grantham, is some way ahead of us: I hope we may reach it in due course. I crave indulgence for the slowness of my journey; but I said my purpose was to find beginnings; and beginnings do demand hypotheses. That breastplate of British pearls brought back to Rome by the first Caesar (assuming there was such a breastplate) seems to be in at the beginning of a lot of trouble. Was the breastplate really decorated with real pearls, seed pearls, or what? Was there in Caesar's time a pearl fishery in Britain? Why did it die out? I fail to find such an industry now. Have British oysters changed their habits? That is a possibility. Oysters are particularly susceptible to unseasonable cold, and it is mentioned in the records that the year A.D. 684 was, all over Europe, cold beyond belief. Some such year may have killed off an old pearl-bearing stock of British oysters. Or there may never have been a pearl-bearing stock of British oysters. Caesar's breastplate may have been decorated, not with real pearls, but with pearl buttons made from mother-of-pearl. It may have been a garment made up more or less like the garments of the pearly kings and queens, as still worn by London costermongers. Caesar may have had the breastplate made to order, or it may have been a gift offered to Caesar: shell-fish and shells in those days had significance other than gustatory. The costermongers on Hampstead Heath on August Bank Holiday may be preserving thoughts which are more august than they or we know.

What I am trying to say is that you don't really know where you are with invasions, when they land on the coasts of illusion. Something happens, and that is what I am attempting to trace in this story of a road. As to what causes the happenings, it is extremely difficult to discriminate between facts and fancies. What are the facts of the matter? I also ask, What are the fancies? It is extremely difficult to decide which of those two *f*'s is which, and which in the long run proves more causative. Different planes of attention slip and slide. As far as you can, you lock a point in the one plane to a point in the other in a one-to-one correspondence; but the process is uncertain. There may be a connection between Caesar's breastplate and the pearly kings, but one can never know. If you ask yourself, What did happen to Claudius's elephants (assuming there were elephants), you step at once into the plane of fancy. You find that you have raised the question that while Julius Caesar in Britain in the year 54 B.C. was exercising his fighting men, how did he exercise his engineers? Did he put them to building a first London Bridge?

The question has sometimes been asked, but never answered. Caesar was at the time bridge-minded. He wrote in great detail about his bridge over the Rhine. If he did build a London Bridge why didn't he say so? That is an argument against the speculation.

An argument for the speculation (though as an argument I confess it is only the shade of a shade) derives from the story of Claudius and the elephants. The argument runs this way. If on the accession of Claudius it was in Rome decided that the new emperor was to put in a personal appearance in Britain, with his Guards and the elephants, it must have been thought that there was an adequate showplace. It is hard to imagine that the elephants should have been walked from Rome, or from wherever it was they had to be walked, and ferried then across the Channel, without somebody having some idea of an eventual destination. The speculation is that the destination was London. If so, London in the Roman imagination at the time of Claudius must have been (we don't know what travelers' tales the imagination was fed on) somewhat more important than is conveyed by the phrase I used: a marshy trading settlement. London must have been something approaching the status of a town. What then caused London to continue or improve its status between the times of Julius Caesar and Claudius? There was always London River; but bear in mind London River was not in those days or for another thousand years a river well charted for sea traffic. But supposing there had been a London Bridge? With river and bridge, a town would grow. A town had grown. *Ergo,* Caesar had built a London Bridge. *Ergo,* London Bridge would be the right place for an imperial pageant. That is how the elephant argument comes into history. I don't present it as fact. I present it as fancy. Sherlock Holmes, if he were viewing it, might have said it was time and high time to roll such conjectures into a gigantic ball and toss them onto the rack of the railway carriage.[5] Time and high time to stop theorizing about matters in which there is not a shred or vestige, not a jot or tittle, of hard fact.

But if you wish to find hard facts in ancient history, where do

you go? Facts, in a desert, are as much subject to sandstorms as
are fancies; and fancies may be durable, sometimes more durable
than facts. If the first Caesar had built a London Bridge in 54 B.C.
it was hardly likely in A.D. 43 to have been in fit condition for
elephant traffic; and yet it is conceivable that once a bridge had
been started there would have been effort to keep it up. At any
rate it is my fancy·that in the time of Claudius there was a London
Bridge, and north of it a smith field and on the south bank a play
field. North of the river weapons were made and mended; south
of the river was the place for shows. Proof is impossible and proof
would be irrelevant, for I am not speaking here in the plane of
proof. I am deliberately in the realm of fancy when I say the
south bank was the place for Londoners to expect to see strange
spectacles. That is where it pleases me to "place" Claudius's elephants. It is on the south bank of the Thames that I visualize
London's first zoo. I doubt if those elephants ever escaped from
it. We have seen that the Claudius pageant was mistimed. The
play had failed. When Claudius scuttled for Rome, I imagine the
elephants were expendable. No such good fortune came their way
as came to the horses which the Spaniards reintroduced to the
American continents. The horse experiment of the Spaniards was
to prove a biological experiment of immense fecundity. Some
learned men assert it was the most exciting contribution Spaniards
made to the New World. But with Claudius's elephants in Britain
there was no such physical success. They did not reproduce themselves. Perhaps they were not given time enough, or the right food,
or peace of mind. Perhaps they were the wrong kind of elephants
for the experiment: not tough cold-weather elephants but softies
from a southern clime.

Were there ever any elephants at all with Claudius? Isn't the
whole story a myth? It became a myth, and that is why I attend
to it. A myth starts somehow, and sometimes a myth abides by a
locality. I made it clear that we are not here on a plane of conviction, but where you may feel as you will and as you like. I feel
that Claudius did bring elephants, and I admit they did die out,
but in the world of myth they did not die but went on breeding.
The world of myth is not of the physical world, but is engaged
with the physical world. There is an Elephant south of London

River today. The name, no doubt, from the name of the tavern, the Elephant and Castle, most famous of the hostelries in the area for Elizabethan stage shows. There are fifty different explanations for the inn sign Elephant and Castle. They are all ingenious explanations, and although each contradicts each other, each is convincing. What is common to the contradictory explanations for the inn sign is, it is averred, a peculiar stubborn genius of the low-class Briton for translating high-born phrases into facetious double talk. Do what one will with the Londoner, his common speech is afflicted by his talent for corruption. Precisely so; the common fellow likes to translate his inn sign into a term which he regards as humorous, homely, and familiar. But why does there reside in this particular part of London a focus of corruption whereby any other term should be translated into "Elephant"? Why on the south bank of the Thames is so exotic a phenomenon as "Elephant" to be preserved as a familiar, homely, and accepted symbol?

Why Elephant? Why on the south bank does the term seem so natural? Whenever I hear *Twelfth Night:*

> In the south suburbs, at the Elephant,
> Is best to lodge,

astonishment renews itself. In comes the Elephant, as if of natural right. Try any other name in that place, and I doubt if it would have such a special chord of association. Call it Twelfth Night, or call it What You Will, there is suggestion that Shakespeare is toying with tribal memory. This is Illyria, lady, says Shakespeare, suggesting a coast of illusion, a place out of this world where plays go wrong and end up rightly; and in the middle of Illyria:

> In the south suburbs, at the Elephant,
> Is best to lodge.

What wonderful nonsense! Illyria, and likewise Elephant, in the south suburbs of London, the play place at the southern end of London Bridge! You can't pin anything on Shakespeare, but there is this much to pin; that the play business is a practical game, and some touches are more practical than others. Anything you

may wish to use is here or now or just around the corner, or somewhere in the memory.

> To the Elephant.
> I do remember.

We have finished with Claudius. Not immediately after his return to Rome, but not many years after, he was assassinated. Some
blamed his wife Agrippina, saying she had fed him a poisonous
mushroom. Some blamed a rather sinister personal physician.
Some said Agrippina and the physician were both framed. But
we have finished with Claudius and with Romans in Rome. The
task is now to cross over the Thames and to see what Aulus Plautius
was to make of the Great North Road within Britain.

III »» The Road

Dimidium facti qui coepit habet: He who has begun his task has half done it. Claudius at Colchester may have taken comfort in that Roman thought. In A.D. 43 the immediate first activities at Colchester were the laying out of an imposing new city on the hilltop to the southeast of the older, lower town which had contented Cunobelinus. "In all probability," say Collingwood and Myres, the hill-top at Colchester was to be "the official residence of the propraetor and the seat of Roman government; and here in the centre of the city, surrounded by the porticoes of a forum, was to stand a temple, a vast and massive building where Claudius was to be worshipped as a God."

I derive the impression that Aulus Plautius, to whom as resident propraetor the task had been given of subduing the whole island of Britain, did not regard that task as half completed just because there had been a beginning. What we now call Sussex and Kent and East Anglia were at any rate for the moment under strong Roman control, but there was the unknown area to be conquered

39

which spread fanwise from the Thames estuary westward and northward. The method of conquest was to be by separate military columns, each working in one direction, but by what Collingwood and Myres call "a general radial movement," dividing and ruling the new territory. Each column as it worked forward was to commence the construction of a permanent military road.

Although Colchester [say Collingwood and Myres] was the capital of the new province, the centre from which these radiating lines diverged was at London. The building of roads was an essential instrument of conquest, and most of the main Roman roads in Britain must have been laid down at a very early date. When we find London the centre from which one road, Watling Street, runs north-westward to Wroxeter, another northwards to Lincoln, and a third westward to Silchester, we can hardly doubt that these were the roads built for this triple advance, and that London served as the supply-depot and base for the three columns.

Why was there this quick shift of the Roman center from Colchester to London? It begins to look as if, despite the extreme tenuity of the elephant argument, there may have been a London Bridge at this early date. For a thoroughgoing triple advance into Britain there had to be a supply depot north of the Thames. Why couldn't it have been at Colchester, the first seat of Roman government, with the intended official residency, forum, temple and so forth? There were potential ports near Colchester; for instance, Harwich or Brightlingsea. What was so sacrosanct to the Romans about their early ports of Dubris (Dover), Rutupiae (Richborough), or Regulbium (Reculver)? True, the sea journey from Boulogne to any of these ports of Kent was shorter than the sea journey to Harwich, and the crossing of the unchartered waters outside the Thames Estuary would have been troublesome. But consider the extra handling: if you landed your gear at Harwich, there it was without much further trouble at Colchester. If you offloaded it at the Kentish ports there was quite a long haul to London, and then the problem of transfer from a marshy south bank to the north bank of the Thames. Yet Rutupiae seems from the beginning of the Roman Conquest to have been the favorite "safe and quiet" harbor, and it became so famous as Britain's principal port that the adjective "Rutupine" was used by the Romans almost as an equivalent for

"British"; and despite the transport problems the north bank at London became the Roman supply depot for the military columns —London, not Colchester, became the point of origin for the three greatest military roads. Did Aulus Plautius select London because there was already available the convenience of a London Bridge? If not, so soon as Aulus Plautius had chosen London as the point of origin for his radial roads, there must have been pressure on him to build a bridge.

Bridge or no bridge, there was another factor in the selection of London, instead of Colchester, as point of origin for the Roman road system. I emphasized the view that Aulus Plautius, as his first experience of British tribes, had found the Battle of the Medway an unexpectedly near thing; and if so, then thereafter and in no circumstances should any great concentration of rebellious Britons be permitted. The maxim for Aulus Plautius, after the Battle of the Medway, had to be: Divide and rule. It was, as I see it, of instant importance to him to divide Britain into compartments. For such purpose of dividing the island London was a better point from which to start carving than Colchester. A short portage from Harwich to Colchester might have been convenient for the handling of gear; but the roads from Dover and Richborough, joining at Canterbury and thence straight as a die through Rochester to London, formed not only a means of transport but a rampart dividing the Southland from anyone attempting to cross the Thames Estuary. Of greater military urgency, since they were to penetrate regions as yet unpacified, were the three chief roads splitting the island north and west of London: our own North Road, the road toward Wales, and the road toward Cornwall. If the purpose of the main roads was not merely one of transport, but, and even more purposefully, the purpose of partitioning the island, then London as common point of origin for the radial roads, was a center far better than Colchester.

The radial roads from London did not begin as haphazard tracks through forest or wilderness. From the start they were pushed out as straight as possible, as level as possible, as solid as possible; and they were hammered forward, regardless of the time it took. Consider the manner of construction of a Roman road, as quoted by Jusserand:

1. Pavimentum, or foundation, fine earth, hard beaten in.
2. Statumen, or bed of the road, composed of large stones, sometimes mixed with mortar.
3. Ruderatio, or small stones well mixed with mortar.
4. Nucleus, formed by mixing lime, chalk, pounded brick or tile; or gravel, sand, and lime mixed with clay.
5. Upon this was laid the surface of the paved road, technically called the *summum dorsum.*

Jusserand is careful to add that not every Roman road in Britain was built with so much care or in such enduring fashion; yet it was normal construction for an ordinary second-class main road, width twenty or twenty-four feet, metaled for summer or winter use, and provided with stone bridges or paved fords. But Jusserand possibly understates the impressiveness of the really first-class Roman military roads in Britain. Figures given more recently by Ivan Margery are startling. Of Roman roads in Britain, a first-class road of maximum width meant an actual roadway of ten yards wide. That was the width of the road surface, constructed on a raised causeway, the *agger.* On either side of the *agger* was a deep scoop ditch, then a cleared space almost equal to the road width, and then a narrow, shallow ditch delimiting the road zone. The whole road zone for such a first-class road comprised a strip twenty-eight yards in width, which is six yards wider than the length of a cricket pitch, or two yards wider than the length of a lawn-tennis court. Allowing for the probability that sections of such roads may have been narrowed whenever the terrain was particularly difficult to negotiate, it must nevertheless have been an impressive phenomenon for natives of Britain to observe road works on this scale dividing their countryside. A secondary class of Roman military roads in Britain had a road-zone measurement of twenty yards two feet across. If we can trust these measurements, they suggest that the purpose of the Roman military roads was much the same as the purpose of building a wall; they suggest a method of separating the territory on one side of the road from the territory on the other. They translate the maxim of divide and rule into harsh practicality; a breakup of the country into pieces; a containment of the peoples in concentration camps.

Nowadays we are so accustomed to thinking of a road as a means of transport from one place to another that it is something of an effort to regard a road also as a wall or boundary. But there would scarcely have been such investment in construction of the main Roman radial roads merely for purposes of transport. Consider the Great North Road. Take an outline map of Britain; draw a heavy straight line from London to Newcastle-upon-Tyne. That represents a first section of the Great North Road. It takes thirty seconds to draw the line upon an outline map. It took the Romans thirty-two years (some authorities say thirty-five) to build the road that far. But they built not only one road, but another one parallel to it. The route from London to Lincoln was doubled, and it was doubled from Lincoln to the Tyne. No doubt these were most important lines of communication and supply between London and the North, alternative routes to be used as such. Merely for purposes of transport, though, the investment seems excessive. It looks as if the doubled roads were intended as a double barrier between East and West. It looks as if the primary design was to confine the natives of what we now call East Anglia to East Anglia; to separate them from the natives of what we now call the Midlands; the other roads designed to separate the Midlands from the West Country, and so on. The purpose of such extraordinarily massive and durable investment in Roman military roads is hard to explain otherwise: hard to explain except as, at any rate in part, a design for fragmentation of the islanders. The first of the generations of Britons who watched the slow, inexorable construction of the Roman *viae*, or who as slaves were forced to work upon them, were intended to see the *viae*, as David Jones says, as "at once the sign of something and the chief agent of what they signified, namely: the desert of an imposed peace." [1]

It is completely guesswork to trace back the incentive for the Roman road system in Britain to the unexpected violent check which Aulus Plautius received at the Battle of the Medway; but if an idea stemmed from that battle of thereafter preventing the island tribes from getting together, in a short-term military sense it was a wise idea. British rebellions could be handled if localized. The story of Caractacus proved that. The story of Boadicea is of even more significance. Here the IX Legion was exterminated at Lincoln, and London itself was momently overwhelmed, burned, sacked, and hu-

miliated. Had the mutiny become general, the Romans might have
been expelled; but even that rebellion was contained by the road
system. The immediate result of British rebellions was more and
more attention to Roman roadwork. I should be surprised if there
was any other Roman province, comparable with Britain in small-
ness, with so many Roman roads. For a description of the network
I turn again to Collingwood and Myres:

The 5,000 miles of Roman roads which are known to us in Britain
form a system intelligible enough in its main lines, but obviously planned
to serve the needs of conquest and government rather than those of civil
traffic. The whole system radiated from London, and gives the impression
of having been designed so as to provide the most direct communication
from point to point of a network whose nodal points are the *coloniae*,
the legionary fortresses, and the tribal capitals. If London was the seat
of the provincial government, nothing could have been better arranged
to suit the needs of a legate who wished to keep in touch with the score
or so centres of administration. But, useful as it was for such official traffic,
and consequently also for through traffic of a private kind, whether in
passengers or in goods, the system was of little service to local traffic.
Instead of running along belts of relatively dense population like the
North and South Downs or the Cotswolds, its main lines cut them cross-
wise, in order to penetrate as quickly as possible the belts of sparsely
inhabited forest that lay between them.

The Roman roads were going to be the bony structure of a living
Britain; the life was bound to be affected by the skeletal structure;
and that thought brings in a large and vexing question.

Why are we not speaking Latin?

The Romans ruled in Britain and worked and talked in the island
for four hundred years. One would think four hundred years to
have been a reasonably long time for a language so universal as
Latin, and so well established in other Roman provinces, to have
settled upon the peoples of Britain. Yet the awkward fact has to
be faced that the flexible living language that we speak today is not
a Roman language and does not derive from Latin.

Roman London, within the London Wall, which after Boadicea's
insurrection was rebuilt, strengthened, and heightened, was about
the size of present-day Hyde Park, or about half the area of Central Park in New York. One feels it to have been, say by the second

or third centuries, a Romanized, crowded, Italianate town. I don't
suppose there were actually many Italians, but I do suppose that a
polyglot population was thoroughly Romanized. Within Roman
London there is little need to question that the prevailing language
was Latin. It was the official language, and throughout the four
hundred years of Roman occupation such records and inscriptions
as remain are all in Latin; naturally so. But there is evidence that
Latin was not merely an official language in London, and that the
writing or reading of Latin was not confined to clerks. At the Guildhall Museum in present-day London (housed at the moment in the
Royal Exchange) is the Austalis tile. This is a large square red tile
which was dug up in Warwick Lane. It is on view to anybody. On
that tile, in a legible and cursive hand of whatever date you wish to
attribute—somewhen plus or minus A.D. 300—there is a pleasing inscription. *Austalis dibus xiii vagatur sib cotidim,* which has been
translated: "Austalis for the last fortnight has been wandering off by
himself every day." Whatever your interpretation of the message, it
is evidence of a homely living Latin in the streets of Roman London. The presumption is that the "humor" of Latin was not merely
a specific of the officer class; the presumption is that merchants
from the Levant bearing rugs and also carrying garnets, and Franks
bringing their containers of Rhenish wine, and miscellaneous peddlers who hawked brooches and gewgaws, and London butchers
and bakers and purveyors of lamp oil, all had a smattering and
palavering of Latin. In what other common language did they pa-
laver? What else can you assume except that the common language
of the streets of Roman London was, and for a long time, Latin?

Why then are we not speaking Latin today?

We must believe that the Latin language radiated from London
along the radial roads. The roads carried reading matter of a lighter
kind than official edicts and orders. Martial, writing in the first century, records with a mixture of pride and sense of injury, that his
epigrams are read upon the roads of Britain. Pride, in that his so-
phisticated, scabrous, and witty verses could percolate to so out-
landish a province; sense of injury, in that from such far-flung
circulation his purse derives nothing. Authors may be prone to
exaggerate the circulation of their books, but there is no particular
reason to doubt that Martial's epigrams were read and repeated in

Britain, or that other Roman writers were occasionally read also. Such reading was not confined to Romans. For those of the Britons who welcomed the main roads, for those who wished to get aboard the Roman bandwagon, there is no doubt that Latin was the ticket. Tacitus says of Britain under Agricola that "in place of distaste for the Latin language came a passion to command it." Tacitus is speaking of "the sons of the chiefs" whose preferments resided in the patronage of Rome. "In the same way," says Tacitus, "our national dress came into favour and the toga was everywhere to be seen. And so the Britons were gradually led to the amenities which make vice agreeable—arcades, baths and sumptuous banquets. They spoke of such novelties as 'civilization,' when really they were only a feature of enslavement." Upper-class thoughts which went Romeward were naturally thought of in Latin. Yet apart from use by Roman officials and Romano-British collaborators, and in complete contradiction of the fact that in Roman London and along the main roads Latin must have been the living and lively language, as a language it took no root in Britain.

Every time one reviews it, the statement remains surprising. Most other European provinces which were under continuous Roman rule exhibited, and in modern dress continue to exhibit, a "romance" language, the structure of which is derived from Latin. In all such European provinces the Latin language struck roots. In Britain, despite four hundred years of Roman occupation, despite what I have tried to say about the vitality of the Latin speech and writing in London and along the roads, as soon as the Romans retired from their network of roads the Latin language, within Britain, vanished. It was as something which had never been.

That remark is so preposterous it must be looked at. In ordinary English speech today, and wherever English is spoken, there is an immense number of Latin words and words derived from Latin. But the structure of the two languages is different, and if you look closely into the adoption of Latin words (as for instance Owen Barfield looks closely in his *History in English Words*) [2] you find at least four distinct layers of adoption. I am at the moment talking about the earliest layer: such Latin words as were generally adopted by Britons within the four hundred years of Roman rule, and which remained when the Roman rule departed. Such words are few. Apart from place names in Britain such as *York* (Eboracum) which retain in a more or less corrupted form the particular titles given to them by their Roman founders, Mr. Barfield finds only two Latin words which can be proved to have been generally accepted by Britons within the period of the Roman rule, and afterward retained. The two words are *port* (in the sense of seaport) and *castra* (in the sense of a fortification) surviving today in *Chester* and in the ending of other town names.

Four hundred years of Roman occupation, and within that time span all the necessities of communication, and all those roads—and at the end of it, when the Romans pulled out, no remnant of language structure, and only two Latin words generally and grudgingly accepted by the Britons! What an inhospitality! To dwell upon the point with some astonishment is not to be disrespectful to the manner in which other layers of Latin words were subsequently built into the English language. There were the Latin words which seeped in because they had been learned on the Continent of Europe by the tribes which, when they came to invade Britain, brought the words with them; of such words imported by Teutonic invaders, but only after the Romans had gone, Mr. Barfield gives examples: *camp, mile* and *street*. There is then another layer of Latin words such as *altar, candle, nun,* which came into Britain with the Christian missionaries, a considerable time after the Roman occupation. There is then the much later and thicker deposit of Norman-French words derivative from Latin, and the even yet later and enormous amount of scholarly and literary borrowing from Latin sources. But here I am not thinking of the later ages when a newly created and thriving English language was stretching out for words and pulling them in with as many arms as an octopus. I am thinking here of the four hundred years of Roman occupation of Britain, when among British tribes there was no common vernacular, and when in spite of the thoroughness of the Roman Conquest, the Latin language failed to take. Perhaps others than Mr. Barfield may prove that there were a few more Latin words accepted generally throughout Britain than the two words *port* and *castra*. But if Mr. Barfield has trouble in finding two examples, other examples are unlikely to be numerous.

It is a mystery why the Latin language, vulgar in Roman Lon-

don, lively along the roads, should have vanished in Britain when
the legions and officials moved away. It is a mystery more strange
in that within the four hundred years of Roman occupation, Romans and Romano-British proprietors lived on the land and spent
at least part of their daily lives not in town centers but in villas and
holdings all over the settled parts of Britain. They lived that way,
father and son. Latin-speaking country gentlemen must have had
intimate conversation with those who did the farming for them;
their domestic slaves must have been able to tell children's stories
in the language of the masters. Here or there, one thinks of the
equivalent of an Uncle Remus. It stands to reason that within four
hundred years the Latin language must have been firmly entrenched
throughout the Romanized part of the island. Yet apparently it
wasn't.

I can only suppose that off the main roads and away from town
centers the native Briton exhibited a good deal of local stubbornness about his local language. A Roman gentleman on the east
coast, whose name might have been Aeneas, might wish to send
a consignment of oysters to his friend Montanus in Rome. I mention
such a transaction because Juvenal mentions that Montanus, an
epicure at the court of Domitian, was familiar with such consign-
ments. Assuming oysters were sent by his hypothetical friend
Aeneas, Aeneas in some language must have discussed the matter
with the oyster dredgers of Mersea Island, the fatters at Whitstable,
and the shippers at Richborough. Aeneas's original command
might be in Latin, but somewhere along the line he or his deputy
would have to talk local; would have to know such terms as *cultch*
and *spat*, and *shram* and *tingles;* would have to know the east-coast
meaning of a *didal.* Oystermongers would not be likely to adapt
their terms to the terms of the master language. One imagines
then, all over Britain, a good deal of pidgin talk: but essentially
local pidgin talk. If Aeneas, after corresponding (in Latin) with his
friend Balbus in the Cotswolds went to visit the Cotswold villa,
he perhaps talked Latin with his host; but if Balbus was having a
wall built round his garden to keep away the deer or badgers
(there were as yet no rabbits) it would not have been a vallum
but a dry-stone dike—the point is there would have been local
terms, whatever they were, used by Balbus's gardener for the

way he preferred to plant the lettuce and the cabbage, or the peri-
winkle in the flower garden, and local terms for the operations of
wall building or the construction of the Roman bath—and the
point is, the vernacular of the Cotswold mason and the vernacular
of the oyster dredger of Mersea Island were different because of
the original determination of Aulus Plautius to keep the tribes
apart. The picture then is of a common master language, not mixing easily with local dialects, and local vernaculars not mixing with
each other. It would have been the same picture had our itinerant
Aeneas gone on to Wales or Cornwall. When Aeneas visited a
Roman they might converse in Latin, but owing to the fragmentation of the island there was no common native vernacular, and such
adaptations as were forced upon the Latin language were, as I visualize it, forced upon it differently in different districts. This, I feel,
contributed to the weakening of the master language.

My assertion is that a factor in holding the British tribes apart
was the construction of the monster radial roads, by intention ramparts. This prevented the growth of any common British vernacular
with the unintended eventual result that Latin itself failed, within
Britain, to remain a common language. Somehow the disappearance
of Latin must be explained, and this is as near as I can come to it.
It seems to me the Roman road system unintentionally fragmented
the Romano-British country dwellers, and tended to make them
locals. It was the drift from the towns to country places, possibly
tax evasion, which was eventually to sap the Roman discipline. The
toga was a town wear; you can't ride horseback in a toga; in the
country you resumed your toga in the spirit of dressing for dinner;
as when Balbus was visited by Aeneas they resumed their proper
Latin; and this Roman civility could and did go on for a long time;
but it was vulnerable.

It is a thesis to be treated with moderation, that a Roman road
system originally intended to be divisive for Britons but connec-
tive for Romans turned out to be, disastrously, divisive for the
Romans themselves. It is, however, noticeable that the prime purpose of the road building which throughout the Roman occupation
continued to go on, was to increase the grip of the provincial government so as to respond to increasing demands from Rome for
dividends. The roads were being built by soldiers for the tax-

gatherer. Shall we look at one of the road builders? David Jones
gives a picture:

At mass, supposing it is a mass of the modern Roman rite, we may
hear words of the prayer: *Domine non sum dignus ut intres sub tectum
meum . . .*. and we may be moved to recall that these are the words of
a warrant officer of the Roman army. True they were no part of the rite
until a thousand years after the last Roman soldier was dead, but
that does not prevent us from recalling this most typic man who, you
will remember, went on to say: "For I also am a man set under authority,
having under me soldiers, and I say to this one: Go, and he goeth . . ."

At all events in considering what were the agencies whereby these *viae*
of Britain came to be I found myself thinking of this Roman soldier whose
words the Roman rite now employs. So let us second to a unit stationed
in Upper Britain this centurion of auxiliaries serving in the Tetrarchate
of Galilee.

"I would invite you," says David Jones, "to envisage this figure. . . . I would like you to try and see him disposing some work-
ing-parties on a partly levelled road-site on rather high, open
ground somewhere on the chalk of what is now southern England."

The blackthorn is out and the thrush sings but though she is in April
there are no English there. Beneath the starry, white-budded black bough
of the windy tree he sits on a pile of white rubble eyeing a work in
progress. His rain-proof cloak is of fine-wove British goat-hair fabric in
Silchester-dyed cockle-red . . . it keeps you dry—which is more than
can be said for the issue woollens they run off the subsidized looms at
Venta. And it keeps you warm, and, what's more, the more it is in the
wind and the rain and the more times it has been rinsed in the launder,
the more—especially in a certain rake of light—especially under the pluvial
light of Britain, will it seem to look as near the Purple as dammit.

So we'll see him as he would fancy himself most; and which in a
vicarious and legatine fashion, is no whimsy, but the truth. So we'll see
him in the sacred *murex* . . . in Caesar's cloak. And as he directs the
making of this particular section of road, we can hear him say to this one,
Vade, and to another, *Veni,* and to a third, *Fac hoc.* We are in no doubt
about the going, the coming and the doing—a doing which is, in this
case, a making: a *praxis* which is also a *poesis.* For the Rectilineal Plan
has its poesy. But for the kind of things made by that sort of making you
had to have the men in the purple cloaks, the Directors of Toil.

It would seem that road building in Britain went on even after there began to be doubts in Rome whether the investment in Britain, because of troubles in Italy and elsewhere, could be held on to. Toward the end of the fourth century I would think the tax returns from Britain were of value to Rome, but a consideration was whether the manpower for policing and guarding the distant island could any longer be spared. Unknown perhaps to the Romano-British, the Aeneas and Balbus of whom I was speaking, the centurion as described by David Jones—unknown to them, at the center of things, Rome, Britain was slipping down on the agenda. For the time being, work and play went on as usual, and I would think a few more Latin words did get into British vernaculars, and remain in all parts of the country. Among slaves who were ordered around by the Directors of Toil, I can imagine that some of the terms of command were back-twisted in an ugly and retaliatory way. The command *Fac hoc* might have been resentfully muttered and repeated and understood anywhere, though not recorded in our dictionaries. I see a word or two which may have come in through play. Although among British tribesmen there must have been hostility to the way in which the Roman ramparts broke up the forest land, for some of the British youngsters the first suggestion of a flat paved road may have been a good place to play games. Games of the type of *Red Rover, Red Rover, Come Over, Come Over* suggest themselves, and there are further suggestions, some say evidence, that games of hopscotch and curling were played on the roads; and it is hard to refrain from thinking that there may have been whipping tops, marbles, and primitive ball games. It is difficult not to suppose that Britons learned to play games on the streets and because the streets were there to play on. It is difficult to suppose that urchins everywhere did not attempt to trail the legionaries and beg for scraps of their rations; we must later reflect on the acceptance into the English language of the word "cheese." Here, my point is that road building in Britain went on even after the Romans in Rome were getting doubtful about their investment in Britain. The purpose of the road building, as Collingwood and Myres emphasized, was not to assist local traffic. The soldiery went on road making for the effectiveness of government and taxgatherer. And as I see it, if children played games on the roads, those from whom tax could be gathered did their best to stay away from them.

Aulus Plautius had begun his work too well. The main roads split up British tribesmen, but in the end also split up the local Romano-British proprietors. And in the end, the roads which had been efficient for the imposition of government were equally efficient for a rapid and complete withdrawal.

David Jones makes a cautionary remark:

In Britain the "end of the world" came slowly and as perhaps befits the elusiveness, severalty and contradiction seemingly implicit in the things of this island, that "end" was a patchy and complex affair. What happened here, didn't there and something different again, perhaps not so far off.

Those of us who have lived through the whole, or even part, of the first half of the twentieth century understand, or should understand, that the end of a world brings radical but by no means uniform change.

But, accepting the caution, as soon as decision was reached in Rome that Britain was to be written off, the roads were the means for an evacuation whereby the departing Romans took with them everything they could, including their language. I got into this long excursus by wondering why we are not speaking Latin; I get out of it only by supposing that Latin, once effective on the military roads, never really got off the military roads. It was part of the impedimenta which could be taken away. Symbolic once of conquest, Latin had become symbolic of retreat.

The end of Roman Britain, as David Jones rightly cautions, must have been a patchy and complex affair; but when Rome needed troops elsewhere the evacuation along the roads was swift and swiftly noticed. It is interesting to observe that the northward-facing walls in the north of Britain had never been so effective in dividing up the island as the original radial roads had been. Scotland had never been hammered (perhaps the Romans thought not worth the hammering) as the rich Southland had been thoroughly hammered, and a thinning of patrols along Watling Street was less dangerous than a thinning of troops along Hadrian's Wall. Even before the complete withdrawal of the legions from Hadrian's Wall there are stories of the Picts, in force, swarming over it. There are stories of the Pictish invasion of about the year 368 which mentions the storming of York, the sacking of Lincoln, the burning of Caistor-by-Norwich "and the rest." Britons, accustomed to the Roman protection for which they believed their taxes to have been paid, made urgent appeals to Rome. There are stories how one such appeal was met, not by reinforcement of Roman legionaries, but by the forcible transportation into Britain of a captured Alamannic tribe called Buccinobantes, as a bulwark against the Picts. This may or may not have been the beginning of the Teutonic settlements in Britain. As the Romans thinned out, we must pay more and more attention to the Teutonic settlements. Anglo-Saxons had on their own account been cautiously nibbling at undefended sections of "the Saxon Shore." The horror of "Saxon Robbers," added to the horror of the Picts, was represented to the Emperor Honorius. The answer of Honorius, in 410, was to the effect that it was all too bad, but the Romano-British were not to count on further help from Rome. They would have to look after themselves.

This must have been a terrible jolt to the friends we were speaking of, Aeneas and Balbus, for if the roads were not Roman-patrolled they were not safe, and if they did not dare to use the roads, they were separated; their friendly customs and their master language would die out. It was impossible to think Rome had deserted them. Thirty years after the warning of Honorius the Romano-British were continuing to appeal to Rome, as recorded in the famous passage in Bede's *History,* where he says the "wretched remnants of the Britons" sent the letter which began: "To Aetius, thrice consul, the groans of the Britons." This party of Romano-Britons thus unfolded their calamities: "The barbarians drive us to the sea, the sea drives us back to the barbarians; between them spring two sorts of death: we are either slaughtered or drowned." No help from Aetius; powerful though he was, he was at the time engaged in "most serious" wars with Attila, who had "ravaged almost all Europe." It was the final word. The remnants of Britons had to look after themselves.

In respect to the wretched Britons it must be said that for four hundred years Rome had been the center of everything. At Rome itself it must be recalled that the island had been taken as a long-term investment; much effort had been made to make it pay; if it did not pay, rulers, officials, soldiery could be withdrawn at Rome's disposal. A difference to be noted about the Anglo-Saxon invasions of Britain, is that, unlike the original Roman invaders, they had no capital behind them. To the Germanic peoples of the North Sea margins, pushed from behind and wondering where to go, what Britain offered was a new world: not an investment which might be discarded, but a place in which to live and stay. Anglo-Saxons who came to Britain came in a spirit which was other than Roman. They came for good and all. They were not annexing anything to anything. They came because they had to go somewhere for keeps. Unlike some of the Romans, they had no Rome to retract to. The Anglo-Saxons who came to Britain had burned their boats.

Some scholars blame the Picts, some blame the British king Vortigern, some blame Aetius the Roman, and some blame Attila the Hun for the migrations of Teutonic peoples into Britain. It is agreed by one and all that it is a complicated story. When Rome itself was under increasing pressure from the Huns along the Rhine and Danube boundaries, the stiffening of the Roman barrier and the pressure of the Huns squeezed all the Teutonic peoples on the northern fringes of the Continent. It is pictured that the squeeze accelerated the Anglo-Saxon invasions of Britain. It is also held that apart from such Roman actions as importing a captured tribe of Buccinobantes, the British leader Vortigern invited other Germanic peoples to defend him from the Picts. We know of Vortigern that he was a king in Wales; that when some of the "wretched remnants" of Britons despaired of their groanings to Rome, they named Vortigern, somewhen about 440 or 450, as their dictator. This was in the area of Celto-Roman civilization, the lowland South Country of Britain, "where Celtic elements," say Collingwood and Myres, "were more and more prevailing over Roman. Latin must have been less and less used. Rome was becoming a memory."

For this period of the end of a world I rely on C. F. G. Hawkes: [3]

All the Germanic peoples of the North Sea margins in the fifth century, the Franks of the lowermost Rhine no less than those northeast of them, knew Britain well. In 443 a body of those farther peoples, Angles and Saxons and probably Frisians already too, had been invited to eastern Britain by Vortigern to defend him from the Picts; more and more of them went over; the land was good, and in leaving their over-crowded homes they were leaving also the menace of Danes pressing west from southern Scandinavia, and of Attila and the Huns in central Europe. . . .

Professor Hawkes is discussing how one of the Germanic peoples, the Jutes, came to occupy Kent:

In 453 opportunity in Britain widened. Vortigern wanted still more Germans: this time to hold the old "Saxon Shore" of south-eastern Britain, from a central base in Thanet, against a possible invasion by Aetius. . . .

A possible invasion by Aetius! How so? Because Attila, the dreaded leader of the Huns, was dead. Aetius as Roman Commander of the West was free at last to respond to the "groans of the Britons," to reestablish Roman control in Britain, devoutly wished for by most of the Romano-British. This would mean Vortigern's extinction. Without united support behind him, Vortigern's only hope of resisting Aetius was to invite more Germans:

The Jutish German Hengist was ready to lead an armed settlement to meet Vortigern's need in Kent. . . .

The irony was that as soon as Hengist was firmly settled in Kent, Aetius was murdered in Rome. Any expectation of the restoration of Roman power in Britain died with Aetius, and Hengist was under no external threat. He sized up Vortigern, and within a year of the death of Aetius, Hengist tore up his treaty:

The whole bulk of the Germanic federates in Britain burst out against Vortigern, and Hengist in particular defeated him in Kent and soon drove the resisting Britons out, "in great fear," to London.

When "the Saxon Robbers" took London, nobody knew the shape of things to come, but all knew that an old shape of things had gone. The Celtic flare-up under Vortigern had flickered out. Nor had the Romans left behind them anything but remnants of Roman strength and Roman will power. The Roman spirit withdrew from the roads by which it had entered. A bitter twist is lent to that brave statement: *Dimidium facti qui coepit habet*—for the task the Romans began in Britain was never more than half done. So soon as Roman civilization seemed to be flowering in Britain, it died on the vine. It was wholly dependent on the distant authority, and had no life of its own when the root in Rome was cut. The loss of heart in which the Roman occupation of Britain ended, the paralysis which in the fifth century afflicted the island, is looked at in a clinical way by Collingwood and Myres. Their diagnosis is that in the bad times many of the major towns of Roman Britain, most of the smaller towns, a great many of the villages, and practically all of the individual villas came to an end "not by fire and sword, but by decay and evacuation. They were abandoned and left to fall down."

A kind of building which might be abandoned but which of its nature could not fall down was the Roman road. Now we contemplate the part played by the roads in the transformation of a paralyzed, marcescent Britain into the Anglo-Saxon invention of Merry England.

IV »» Merry England

Nobody can blame me for being a slow traveler on this personal journey. My last chapter reviewed four hundred years of the Road, and so shall this one. No sensible traveler can travel faster than that.

I had reached the question, How did a marcescent [1] Britain turn into Merry England? The adjective *marcescent* is not commonly used; it has apparently been dropped from some of the concise dictionaries; but it is a precise and descriptive term for flowers such as the morning glory or the evening primrose, brave in their beauty yet symbolic of the brevity of life.

> Fair daffodils, we weep to see
> You haste away so soon.

The ultimate root of the word *marcescent* means brevity or short-ness, and carries the connotation of sadness for all that is transitory, all that lasts for only a short while. From the same word root

comes the word *merry,* with connotations which are exactly oppo-
posite. *Merry* connotes all the qualities which in a happy sense make
time pass quickly. From the marcescent Romano-British civilization, the groans of the Britons, the unsuccess of Vortigern and
the Celtic twilight, we turn to consider the newcomers who came
into Britain in "one of those mass-migrations" to which Vortigern
had "unwittingly opened the flood-gates."

Angles, Saxons, Jutes, Frisians—there is little need for us to
sort out what tribal differences there may have been among these
peoples while they were glued to their North Sea margins of
Europe. Bede tries to sort them out, but generally speaking to the
then indigenous inhabitants of Britain, whether Britons or Romano-
British, the newcomers were all indiscriminately "Saxon robbers."
In a way equally derogative, they might be called *Angelcynn,*
a term to some extent adopted among themselves for people of
Angle race. A point is that as newcomers to a new land the various
Anglo-Saxons were aware of a unity among themselves. Whilst
Britons and remnants of Romans were repeating the refrain "dispersed are we," the Anglo-Saxons, of whatever tribal origin, stuck
together. Little evidence can be adduced until there were written
records; but so soon as there are any records, Dr. Dorothy Whitelock, who has examined all available material, emphasizes that any
original tribal differences among the Anglo-Saxon invaders had
ceased to have much significance:

Men were far more conscious of their common Germanic origin.
Bede refers to this again when speaking of Egbert's desire to convert
heathen races in Germany, and Boniface's appeal to all the English to
further the conversion of the continental Saxons, since they were of
"one blood and one bone" with them, called forth a letter from Torhth-
elm, bishop of Leicester, in which he refers to the pagan Saxons as
"our people." The Anglo-Saxon poem called *Widsith,* with its list of
rulers and heroes of ancient German tribes, and the allusions to such
persons and their exploits in *Beowulf* and *Deor,* reveal the close interest
taken by the Anglo-Saxons of Christian times in the stories of other
Germanic peoples, although only fragments survive of narrative poems
on these heroic legends. No doubt the consciousness of common origin
was kept alive among the Germanic tribes settled in Britain by their
nearness to Celtic peoples speaking a different language. . . .[2]

The problem of language is bound to obsess anyone who begins to think about it. The assumption is that the Germanic invaders had sufficient common language to understand each other, and that before the period of which Dr. Whitelock is speaking, their common language was helping them to keep together; whereas Britons and Romans in their division and confusion had no one universal tongue. We have a picture, then, of a mass intrusion of Germanic immigrants, united by language, bonded by being new-comers-all to a land richer than the lands to which they had been accustomed, with mighty evidences of stone constructions impressive to peoples who had been living in wooden shacks on a foreshore which had been sinking under them into the North Sea. The astonishment was, many of the stone constructions were theirs for the taking. There is an echo of the astonishment of what the newcomers found in Britain in a gnomic poem prefixed to one of the manuscripts of the Anglo-Saxon Chronicles:

Cities are visible from afar, the cunning work of giants, the wondrous fortifications in stone which are on this earth.

There is evidence of superstitious awe in the way in which the early Germanic invaders avoided settling inside, and usually set-tled outside fortifications deserted by the Romans: witness Durovernum. But I don't think there was any superstition which prevented the invaders from using the Roman roads. The roads were there as initial conditions, and a highly convenient feature, of the new-found land.

I suppose the course of a mass migration of humans may be much the same as the migration of plant life. In the middle of the nineteenth century the Canadian pondweed, *Udora Canadensis,* was accidentally introduced into the English canal system, and, in this new and favorable environment, ramped in such a famous way as to give H. G. Wells the idea for his story *The Food of the Gods.* The pondweed seriously impeded canal traffic, and was a factor in the rapid growth of railways. Then the "alien" weed settled down, became a "colonist," and came to terms with the indigenous inhabitants. The parable perhaps applies to the Anglo-Saxons, when they were introduced to the ready-made road system of Britain. "Those sea-wolves," as they were bitterly described, "who live on the pillage of the world," were spared a great deal of time in their conquest not merely by the weakness of the opposition but by having the roads; but what one goes on to wonder about is the effect upon the Saxons of the evidences spread before them of an older civilization which, if in decay, had nevertheless been in its time "the cunning work of giants." The speed with which the Saxons altered from "aliens" into "colonists," however you explain it, was remarkable: the way they settled down to tackle the problems of self-government, the way they began their own system of law and order which—Anglo-Saxon, not Roman— remains the foundation of the common law of Britain and America. I don't know how to phrase it except to say that the Saxons came into Britain not with contempt for what they found but with respect: that the desire to create their own institutions and their own form of life was rendered no less creative by recognition of the monuments of another heritage. Aided and tempered by the environment, the Saxon Conquest of Britain rapidly developed as an experiment in self-government.

The experiment could take its own course because Rome, in a military sense, was now out of the picture. To the islanders, Rome was now as distant from Britain as Britain had once been distant from Rome. The Latin language had vanished from the roads, and so had the religion of the legionaries.

The conversion of the Saxons to Christianity cannot be mentioned without wonderment why, in the four hundred years of Roman occupation of Britain, the religion of Mithra had not more firmly taken hold. The Rev. S. G. F. Brandon, Professor of Comparative Religion in the University of Manchester, was moved, on a recent visit to Rome, to put the question:

The Church of San Clemente in Rome is one of the oldest and one of the most interesting of the many ancient churches of that venerable city. As it is now constituted, it comprises a basilica of the eleventh century, beneath which are the remains of another Christian basilica dating from the fourth century, and below this in turn is a Mithraic sanctuary of still earlier date. Thus, when visited today, the church affords concrete evidence of a most dramatic kind of the victory of the religion of Christ over that of Mithra; for while the saviour-god, who came from Judaea, is still worshipped there in a noble liturgy, the Iranian saviour is only remembered by the broken fragments of the statues which once adorned his shrine.

The ordinary visitor to this Roman church of St. Clement is probably impressed by the seeming rightness of this demonstration of the defeat of Mithra by Christ, because, being educated in the Christian tradition, he will instinctively see Mithraism as a false religion which was rightly supplanted by Christianity. Unless he is of a particularly reflective frame of mind, it is unlikely that such a visitor would go on to consider what once had made Mithraism into a living faith of men, even though it was ultimately defeated as a world-religion by Christianity. Yet here is a subject worthy of deep consideration by all who wish to understand a period of history which was crucial in the formation of that culture and civilization which underlies the so-called Western way of life.[3]

More dramatic even than the contrast provided by the church of San Clemente in Rome is the contrast in the City of London. Here, hard by the huge fabric of St. Paul's, the rebuilding after the last war revealed a shrine of Mithra. It is to be kept as a museum piece, and the broken fragments of statuary, and relevant photographs of the excavation, are in the Guildhall Collection housed in the Royal Exchange. There was in London of our day and age a demonstration of unusual curiosity, in the length of the queues of people who waited to watch the excavation of this ancient and defeated shrine of Mithra: the representation of what in Roman London had been once a living, if now a ruined, faith. But I was not so much puzzled about contemporary curiosity in the shrine of Mithra below the dome of Paul's, as by Professor Brandon's question, Why in the early ages of Britain was Mithraism superseded?

If you think of Mithraism as a mystery cult which was of Persian origin and which was specially favored in the Roman army, you tend to beg the question. To people in Britain, when they first began to hear of Christianity, the new faith centering round the Saviour Christ may have seemed no more than another mystery cult of Eastern origin presenting, intellectually, much the same pattern as Mithraism; for Mithraism was based upon a very realistic evaluation of life, and its doctrine commands intellectual respect. In Professor Brandon's words, the central mystery in Mithraic thought was that "the salvation of Man was in some way connected with an act of sacrifice, performed with apparent reluctance by Mithra, which had the effect of passing the individual from the dominion of Finite Time, which connoted decay and death, to the dominion of Infinite Time, which correspondingly would signify immortality." How Mithra by his active slaying of the bull was thought to have achieved his saving act of mediation between these two forms of Time is not easily apprehended; especially difficult to those of us to whom the symbolism has become emotionally repulsive. But the sculptured representation of the crucial moment of sacrifice constituted, as Professor Brandon says, the focal point of every *mithraeum*, and to initiates the mystery was holy. In all the representations it is not difficult even for the uninitiated to see that if the blood of the bull is being spilled, the seed from his genitals is being carefully preserved: the blood is spilled; the race remains. In the bull-slaying scene there are symbols which the uninitiated may find it difficult to comprehend: the animals which collect the semen of the fated bull into an urn are usually a lion, a snake, and a scorpion. Curious and perhaps repulsive as Mithraic ritual may seem to us, there is no doubt of the power it had over the minds of men upon the Roman roads. In many of the Mithraic temples you will find the credo *Hominibus vagis vitam.* This has been interpreted as meaning, to bring "life to wandering men." In that interpretation the word "wandering" strikes me as somewhat weakening the credo. Mithraism was a faith not only for vagabonds: it represented the humility and mystery universally required by purposeful strong men: life to men who were going places.

In Britain, Mithra was worshiped in Roman London, and along the main Roman roads. Why was it that this religion failed, as also the Latin language failed, to get off the roads? It is possible, and without irreverence, to consider some of the adventitious aids which may have helped Christianity in the contest with Mithraism. Mithraism was a soldiers' religion; it was identified with the legionaries; it was identified with the roads. That brings me to a small and trivial thought, which I present as being no better than it is. We had a glimpse of a Roman centurion in charge of a working party slicing one of the Roman roads across Britain, compelling British slaves to make a scar across the native wilderness. I reflect a moment on the engineering. I have made no special study of

Vitruvius, but I would wager that in his time a customary method of Roman road engineers for sighting ahead and obtaining the levels of the road to be built was the use of what have subsequently in our language been called boning rods. Boning rods are commonly used in the construction of new roads today; it would require a lot of contradiction to persuade me they were not used in the time of Vitruvius. A boning rod is a vertical upright with a horizontal crosspiece—a miniature Christian Cross. My thought is that in a mere engineering way the Roman roads in Britain were preceded by the planting ahead of the miniature crosses: that what the remorseless effort of the Roman road builders was effecting was the posting of a symbol before it was a symbol. I am sure the boning rods which preceded the roads would have been signals for resentment and hostility such as a modern landholder may now feel when served with notice that pylons are about to be marched across his property by authority which he is powerless to resist. According to my speculation, the signal of the cross may have been made familiar and hateful to the Britons by the very same Roman soldiery who were advancing their own civilization and their own religion of supremacy. Looking at the cross as a British slave might see it, as symbol only at first of the contemptuous humiliation of a powerless people—so soon as it was put about that it was on the cross that Christ had been crucified, it would help to make Him one of us.

I would not wish to press this speculation about a symbol preceding the symbol, the Cross preceding the roads, and yet it is reverent to consider adventitious matters which may have helped Christianity to oust Mithraism. It is reverent to ask why should the pale Galilean have power of conquest over Mithra, the bull-slaying mediator, among the incoming Germanic tribes? One fact perhaps, that many Mithraic temples were deserted, and represented unsuccess. But why were the temples deserted? They should have represented a last stand. I think of only one answer: Mithraism was a man's religion, a soldiers' religion, and the soldiers went. What about women, in the four hundred years of Roman Britain? I don't find much answer to this question in the books. I do find some evidence to support the invention of imaginary Romano-British characters, Aeneas and Balbus; I can see something

of their customs and actions; but who were their wives? Were
there, in Roman Britain, many Roman matrons or Roman brides?
Who was the wife of Balbus in his Cotswold villa, or of Aeneas
in the town now called Ipswich? The women of Roman Britain
don't emerge; you don't know who they were, and—always subject
to correction—you suspect that Roman Britain was a man's world.
With the Anglo-Saxon migrations there is a vital change. The
Anglo-Saxons brought their womenfolk with them, and the Germanic women who came with their men came with equal status.
No authority can be quoted for that remark until we reach the
era of documentary evidence; but as soon as there is documentary
evidence, there is no discrimination in the legal status of the sexes.
The inference is that Anglo-Saxon women and men, by initial
assumption, had equal rights. After that, women in Britain were
not down-graded until the Norman Conquest. The equality between
the sexes in the Germanic tribes I regard as an adventitious aid
to the acceptance of Christianity; for if St. Paul and many Fathers
of the Church tilted the Christian ritual in man's favor, one nevertheless feels that the Christian rites had much more to offer than
Mithraism to that half of the world which is women.

My guess is that Anglo-Saxon women played a part in the
conversion of Britain to Christianity. It is no less interesting to
brood upon the part women played in the formation of that
astonishing invention, the English language. I had come to the
point of accepting, as fact, that even after four hundred years of
Roman occupation, Latin had not got off the Roman roads. It
was, I felt, too much a ruling tongue, and it departed with the
rulers. In my conception I tied the Latin language in Britain to
the road system, and therefore I was wide open to the question
that when the Roman power wilted, and a road system in Britain
was free and available to incoming Germanic peoples, would that
of itself be sufficient to explain such a miracle as the creation of a
new language?

The creation of the English language was a miracle, and miracles
are not to be explained, but one may go on commenting on adventitious aids. In my first thoughts I had hoped to find that as soon as
a rigid Roman rule departed from Britain and the roads were open
to anybody, a common language would emerge. A little more

reflection made the problem seem less simple than that. The freeing of the Roman roads of Britain comes in as a necessary condition for the formation of a new language, but considered just by itself, a freedom of the roads is scarcely a sufficient condition. Let me illustrate by skipping a good many more than a thousand years and reflecting on the situation in which Mr. Peggotty found himself when he went away from Yarmouth for his long journey through France:

"Alone, and on foot?" said I.

"Mostly a-foot," he rejoined; "sometimes in carts along with people going to market; sometimes in empty coaches. Many a mile a day a-foot, and often with some poor soldier or another, travelling to see his friends. I couldn't talk to him," said Mr. Peggotty, "nor he to me; but we was company for one another, too, along the dusty roads."

I should have known that by his friendly tone.

I am sure we did well to stress a sense of unity among the Germanic invaders, and do well to stress a desire for fraternizing with indigenous Britons—for though we may believe there was plenty of fighting, we can't believe that everyone was fighting every minute—but all the same, a wish for a new common language does not automatically produce it. For a characteristic of the English language, though it grew out of Saxon stock, is that it flowered as something entirely new.

When I first read Jusserand it seemed satisfactory to ascribe the creation of a new common language to the wandering life of peddlers and traders and cozeners in general. I am not disregarding the certainty that wayfarers have always brought words with them. Before the Germanic peoples crossed the sea to live in Britain, they had learned and brought with them such words as *kitchen, dish,* and *kettle;* such other domestic words as *chest* and *pillow.* The Saxons brought across the sea the word termination *-monger,* used as in *costermonger, ironmonger, fishmonger,* and supposedly a corruption of *mango,* a Roman name for a trader. A word which the Saxons brought into Britain as *ceapian,* meaning "to buy," and which we preserve in such forms as *chap, chapman, cheap,* is traced back to *caupones,* a Roman word for wine dealers. So, and before the Saxons crossed the sea, we have the picture of peoples accustomed to the visits of itinerant vendors, awaiting the visits with expectancy, and thereby gaining new vocabulary. As Logan Pearsall Smith said, we have "a dim picture of Roman traders, travelling with their mules and asses along the paved roads of the German provinces, their chests and boxes and wine-sacks, and their profitable bargains with our primitive ancestors."

If we don't scrutinize the dim picture too closely, it seems apt and ready enough to present itself as adequate to explain the invention of a new language. Look more closely at the conditions of itinerant chaffering, despite the fact that chaffering seems fully as necessary to the creation of common talk as was Mr. Peggotty's desire to get along with the French—although wayfaring provides a congenial explanation for the creation of language—and a doubt comes in, whether wayfaring was sufficient. Transfer Logan Pearsall Smith's picture to the frame of Britain in Saxon times. It is easy and perhaps too easy to imagine at a road junction in Britain the existence of a "local," a *mansio* or *taberna*, with a bush pushed out on a long pole for a stop sign to indicate that a new brew of ale was available. It is easy and perhaps too easy to imagine such "pubs" as being hospitable to "commercials" and as being useful in a civilized way both for trading and talk. But those who have made the most careful scrutiny of Britain in Saxon times are not encouraging about so congenial a picture. Neither Sir Frank Stenton nor Dr. Dorothy Whitelock mentions any noticeable spiritual uplift along the roads of Britain in Saxon times just because the roads were relatively free. The experts are not encouraging as to the amount of casual trade to be done by itinerant traders in country parts of Britain, or as to local "pubs" being readily available either for conviviality or commerce. A realistic problem was shortage of coinage. Pearsall Smith's phrase about the itinerant trader's "profitable bargains with our primitive ancestors" is up against a touchstone: Who was going to pay for what, and to pay for what with? Roadways begin to fade from the trading picture. The likely places which might repay a commercial traveler for a visit were a market town on market day or fair day, or the offices and kitchen quarters of a monastic institution, or the corresponding quarters of a manor house.

I had hoped to be able to think that uninhibited road traffic, in

Saxon times, would of itself have explained the creation of the English language. Road traffic as such does not prove to be an adequate creative cause. Furthermore, road traffic in Saxon times can scarcely be thought of as uninhibited. As soon as there are documents to look at, they indicate that Saxon society in Britain had become exceedingly rigid. "The division of society," says Dr. Whitelock, "into three classes, nobles, ordinary freemen and slaves, seemed to a writer of the latter part of our period so ancient, inevitable and in accordance to the divine scheme that he derives them from the three sons of Noah." Not only was the slave (in Saxon areas the words Briton and slave were equated) tied to his master's estate with death penalty for leaving it, but the *gebur* of low station "could not go where he would," and many a so-called freeman had to seek permission or invent an excuse to visit a market town. Nor were the market towns of Britain, in Saxon times, such as we would regard as bursting with excitement. They were not great centers of trade. "In the early period," says Dr. Whitelock, "trade was not of such volume as to bring large con-courses of persons together near harbours or where travel routes met, and, though several crafts were carried on, such as those of the goldsmith, the weaponsmith and the blacksmith, the carpenter and the leather-worker, such persons were often in the employ of some lord and did not tend to congregate in towns to any great extent. London, however, was of some significance already in Bede's day; the kings of Kent had a hall in it, and we hear in-cidentally of a Frisian merchant there."

So much for the London pride of that moment: the kings of Kent had a hall in it, and we hear incidentally of a Frisian merchant there. What has happened, then, to my promise of Merry England, and my hope of discovering the causation of the English language, which most certainly did somehow emerge and spread over Eng-land even before, politically, a unified England existed? Slaves could not of themselves invent a universal language, nor, appar-ently, could the free trader. What aids do we look for—the influence of Christian missionaries, the efforts of King Alfred, or the exist-ence in Saxon times of country houses? All of these coefficients are worth examining, and all of them, in contrast with the previous marcescence, are influences comparatively merry.

On a Saxon country estate a dominant thought was to make the time pass quickly. I am speaking here not of the slave or the *gebur* but of the top class of society. Unlike the underlings, the top class of Saxon society seems to have been accustomed to perpetual motion. It was a regular thing for the top class of nobles to move around. Part of the impulse one supposes to have been simple and practical. In primitive tribes all over the world one observes periodical impulses to feasting, and to make one's own feast more lavish than the neighbor's. As societies integrate, procedures may change, but original impulses persist. I said that in considering the Saxon conquest of Britain we did not have to discriminate between Angles, Saxons, Jutes, Frisians; I stressed the solidarity of the different tribes; but concomitant with their integration, as wealth developed we may suppose a development of competitive hospitality and social rivalry. One imagines top people being invited to travel from estate to estate to consume the perishable products as they were accumulated at each spot; and to exchange and return such visits. It was difficult to transport local specialities and there was no refrigeration: therefore the invitation to the cloudy locusts to move themselves and their appetites from one house party to the next. The exchange of visits from manor house to manor house is attested, as well as anything can be in the Saxon period. My case is that in the mutual hospitality of the top people of the country, factors are to be found for the creation of new language.

The problem of a Saxon hostess at a manor house was how to make the long twilights pass quickly: what show to make with food and drink and entertainment. About the foods and drinks in Saxon times we know very little—we know less of the details than we know about in Roman times. But we know, or suspect we know, something about Saxon hospitality. As top people moved from one house party to another, there was an appetite to be cared for other than the appetites for food and drink. There was sex. In primitive Germanic tribes (there is no reason to exempt them from a general primitive practice) it was probably as natural to offer sexual comfort to a distinguished visitor as any other form of respect or amusement. The genius of the Saxons in Britain seems to me displayed by a desire to codify the rules. I don't know of any other people who actually spelled out the rules of play; but there it is, among the earliest of the Anglo-Saxon laws of Britain—a Catering Wages Act written out in the reign of King Æthelbert. It specifies the scale of charges to be observed for sexual entertainment. The code is strictly stated: "If a man lies with a maiden belonging to the king, he shall pay 50 shillings. . . . If she is a grinding slave he shall pay 25 shillings; if she is of the third class, 12 shillings. . . . If a man lies with a nobleman's serving-maid, he shall pay 12 shillings. . . . If a man lies with the serving-maid of a ceorl, he shall pay 6 shillings; if with a slave of the second class, 50 sceattas; of the third class, 30 sceattas."

What is curious to us about this document is that there is not the slightest suggestion of immorality, except to get the prices understood and agreed. I quote the tariff from Lady Stenton's book *The English Woman in History*. She provides the references, and the gloss that a *ceorl* is a free farmer, and that the *sceatta* is roughly equivalent to the later silver penny, though how to equate that to present currency remains a matter of conjecture. But the suggestion of the law is that the purpose of the tariff was not one of fines against a sin of ravishment, but a regularization of recognized house charges where everyone concerned was a consenting party. The suggestion is it did not preclude individual bargaining above the basic scale, but it was a basic scale of payment to be observed at any proper manor house.

I take the existence of such a law to be an indication that by the time of Æthelbert there had been a long heritage of acknowledged sexual entertainment, extramarital yet not indiscriminate, in Saxon society. The offer of such entertainment to visitors was a form of hospitality common to many tribes other than Anglo-Saxon; but the open lawmaking about it, the posting as it were of the house charges, was something to make people talk. I mean that seriously, that insofar as Æthelbert's law was effective it was an aid to the creation of the English language. For Æthelbert's published tariff is expensive. One must imagine that there was as yet no other severe inhibition against sexual entertainment. There is no evidence of fear of venereal disease until much later times, no evidence such as one might expect if disease had been prevalent; nor in Saxon times was there as yet any firmly established condemnation of sexual performance by the Church on the score of immorality. No doubt that in Saxon times there were jealousies between mistresses and the housemaids who were required to be in the house for dual purpose. The Church was by degrees on the side of the mistress, and Æthelbert's tariff does seem very severe on house guests. One cannot imagine that shillings or even sceattas were easy to come by in quantity, or that the quantity would last very long for a succession of house parties. So in the formation of Merry England I single out a necessity imposed upon a successful hostess of providing alternative twilight pastime for the guest who was short of cash. By the great Saxon ladies some kind of floor show had to be offered after dinner to guests of quality who might be too poor to slink off.

We have Lady Stenton's portrait of the Saxon hostesses. "In their natural setting of the great hall, which was the centre of early social life, these ladies appear as figures of grace and dignity, overseeing the entertainment of the guests, or rewarding a poet who had recited acceptable verses before the company. . . ." I cannot but feel that this is the decorous side of a Saxon evening; that to some of the company of hard-riding sportsmen, prevented from escaping from the hall to other pleasure, it may have been a sorry exchange to have poetry recited at them. There must have been other after-dinner floor shows which were more generally acceptable. I would think the great hall, in the sense of music hall, in the sense of "variety" and "vaudeville," in the sense of "turns," was of immense aid in the development of new language, and in due course of literature. It was the music-hall atmosphere of the great hall, with emphasis on song and dance and gift of the gab, which I would think was of inestimable importance in the development of vernacular speech, understandable both above and below the salt. The entertainers, one imagines, came as a rule from below the salt; and they had to be good if, even with Æthelbert's help, they were to hold their own against the oldest profession of all. Here, with a sigh of relief, I do begin to see the roadways starting to play an important part in the development of the English language. For if, on this estate or that, there were some acceptable ham actors, in the competition between Saxon hostesses there would I think have been needed the importation of itinerant professional entertainers; the "stars." If the quality moved round the country, so did their star entertainers; and if we were disappointed about expecting creativity of speech among the likes of Mr. Peggotty, or if we discounted the business to be done along the roads by peddlers, we find more incentive for the creation of language among the itinerant entertainers who would find on the roads a certain amount of their material and a certain amount of their practice.

If the roads of Britain when free of the Romans were not free to slaves or even to free men, they were free to nobility and free to those who were commanded, or who could pretend they were commanded, to follow on as entertainers. In one figure in particular, that of the Jester or Court Fool, we see someone who had considerable privilege of freedom. The Court Fool, adroit in double talk, was in his own way a mediator between matters of time infinite and time temporal; we see in him the suggestion of a memory of Mithraism. For him we see protection on the roadway, not only by his office but by his wit and his appeal, in whatever society, to antic instincts. It is possible he had a right of entry anywhere: that when he so wished, and whether he had a sceatta or not, he would have been welcomed in *mansio* or *taberna*. But if, as I have been maintaining, an expansion and universalization of vernacular speech derived in great part from a desire for entertainment, there was another kind of Fool, who whether or no he had title to do so, walked the roads of Saxon Britain proclaiming another kind of Mediator between the temporal and the eternal, and offering an attitude which was not that of merry cynicism or cynical merriment. I see the Christian missionary as fully as important as the entertainer in breaking the adhesions of vernaculars and forming speech understandable to all. There is a school of thought which maintains that the Church of England was founded "not by peripatetic preachers overwhelming an indignant heathen population by their enthusiasm, but by diplomats, lawyers and architects, who worked Christianity into the framework of the State." That is the phrase of a modern Romanist, and it is not to be disregarded as to the formation of the fabric of the Church, the work started by Augustine (who died in 604) in Canterbury.[4] Yet I am discussing the formation of language, and here the problem for missionaries was not how to impose a framework in the Latin language, defunct in Britain and vanished from the roads, but how to express their message in words that were alive. A German preacher, Botolph, preaching at Botolphstone (Boston) understood that he was among peoples to whom he had to speak in their own terms. A most remarkable woman, Hilda of Whitby, recognized that if other Saxon hostesses had to provide entertainment which could replace or compete with sexual hospitality, the Christianity to which she was dedicated had to provide its attraction in language which would be superior in contest with the flippant entertainment of the worldly world.

As, in the Old Testament, Ezra is accorded greatness partly for his effort to transform the oral Torah into the written Talmud ("We shall write down the Word and put a ring of fire round it") so, in the history of the English-speaking world, Hilda of Whitby seems to me a great figure. The Saxon hostesses mentioned by Lady Stenton were on occasion competent to discern and to work into their entertainment programs talent which emerged in their own kitchen quarters. Hilda, Abbess of Whitby, was able to discern and to transform into an instrument of competition with lesser kinds of entertainment, a talent which emerged in the cow byre of her abbey. "The Venerable Bede, in a charmingly told and commonly known story, has related how a certain Cædmon, who towards the end of the seventh century was a servant of the monastery of Whitby, under the great Abbess, Hilda, having had to leave festive meetings owing to his inability to use and accompany with song the harp which was handed round, was miraculously inspired to write sacred poetry." I have borrowed that sentence from George Saintsbury, who treated the preliminaries of English literature with infectious gusto.[5] What was the poetry which Cædmon composed? Here is a recording, simplified from a manuscript written two or three years after Bede's death:

> Nu scylun hergan hefænricæs uard,
> metudæs maecti end his modgidanc,
> uerc uuldurfader, sue he uundra gihuæs,
> eci dryctin, or astelidæ;
> he ærist scop aelda barnum
> heben til hrofe, haleg scepen.

Tha middungeard moncynnæs uard,
eci dryctin, æfter tiadæ
firum foldu, frea allmectig.

Here is Dr. Dorothy Whitelock's translation of the passage into our contemporary English: "Now we must praise the guardian of the heavenly kingdom, the powers of the Creator and his thoughts, the works of the Father of Glory, as he, the eternal Lord, appointed the beginning of every wondrous thing; he, the holy Lord, the Guardian of mankind, first created for the children of men the heaven as a roof. Then the eternal Lord, Ruler Almighty, afterwards adorned the world, the earth, for men."

Hilda's extraordinary contribution to our world was that not only did she take pleasure from the piety of Cædmon in the cow byre, but that she also caused his words to be written down. Is it strange that the above transcription looks uncouth? It was a baffling problem, and not one to be solved in a moment, for scribes well versed in Latin to devise a notation for this fluid, low-class alien language. How could they do other than to make it look barbarous? But we must believe the Anglo-Saxon speech, though visually it looks to us so frightening, was easy to the ear, else why should it have been effective for ordinary entertainment or for preaching or, in that passage from Cædmon, have had the effect of poetry? The message of Cædmon's passage, in the paraphrase, is simple enough, but the voicing of it must have been music, or why should Hilda have so much insisted on the devising of a notation? It is not a matter of surprise that early efforts of abstract notation look uncouth to later ages. In communication, the visual arts have an advantage over the arts and sciences which cannot be transferred from peoples to peoples without being written down; and the devising of symbols, of notation, is of immense importance. Once you have a notation, no matter how strange it looks at first, it becomes of its own right suggestive, and asserts a power of creativity. Notation in effect takes charge. To Hilda of Whitby we ascribe the first writing down of Anglo-Saxon spoken poetry. First steps are difficult; to her the honor of insisting on this first step: *Dux femina facti.*

If in Saxon society in Britain women were equal with men, men were equal with women. Bede, though it is not recorded that he wrote in language other than Latin, was as quick as Hilda to perceive the importance of her idea of providing notation for the vernacular tongue, and lent his authority to the experiment. Authority must have been needed to induce clerks, whose vested interest was in the Latin language, to attempt a new form of transcription. As early as the middle of the eighth century, from Hilda's foundation at Whitby and Bede's foundation at Jarrow a strange and scrappy cargo was being carried southward along the Great North Road from Northumbria: bits and pieces of experimental writing in a vernacular which was Northumbrian, yet which, with sufficient curiosity, an intelligence in Wessex might also appreciate. If wandering scholars whose delight (if we remember the *Attic Nights* of Aulus Gellius) resided in discussing the niceties and fine distinctions and pedantries of Latin grammar should have been intrigued to compete in the relatively disreputable game of recording a vernacular language, that, in so far as it happened, would be further tribute to something lyric and compulsive in the sound of Anglo-Saxon: something fresh and interesting about the new game, some feeling that the old game was played out. I don't think it was only the authority of Hilda and Bede which sent the scraps and bits of writing up and down the Road. The inoculation of the new writing took and spread of its own accord.

Within the four hundred years of the Saxon occupation of Britain there are many evidences of a new and lively busy-ness. To speak of Merry England is forcing the pace of our journey, for there was as yet no single polity which could be called "England." There were kings and kinglets; and by and large one pictures a plantation life, with slavery at the bottom of society and political bickering and feuding at the top. Among the nobles one pictures a love of sport, and you cannot look at the jewelry found at Sutton Hoo without crediting wealth and appreciation of beauty and craftsmanship to the Saxon possessors. There was overseas trade, but little outside interference in the affairs of Saxon Britain. There was a link with distant Rome through the Church, but in the correspondence of the early Christian Fathers, so far as the correspondence relates to Britain, one feels the Saxon Church was controlled with a loose rein. One feels it was almost a handicap to Augustine that he came to Canterbury under instructions in

Latin. There was a Roman tradition of organization in the Saxon Church, and a rapid spread of churches, shrines, and monastic foundations, but the control was mild. It is possible that women such as Hilda could not only preach but administer the Sacraments. In the fragment quoted from Cædmon, which gave Hilda pleasure, there is exhibited no theology except that of a mild deism. The correspondence of the early Fathers (such correspondence as comes down from Gregory, Basil, and others) [6] is much concerned with the art of growing vegetables, and we may credit the Saxon Church with introducing into Britain new varieties of cabbages and lettuces. What seems to have delighted Saxon ingenuity was civil law rather than canon law. There is a mock trial reported by Werfrith (see Professor Earle, *Anglo-Saxon Literature,* page 197) of the devil, when he was accused of possessing a nun. The defense of the devil was a counteraccusation:

Ic saet me on anum laehtrice, tha com heo and bat me.

Or, as Professor Saintsbury edited with relish:

I sat me on a lettuce, then came she and bit me.

One notes the mock trial is conducted in "English," not in Latin.

It is mentioned by Asser, the biographer of Alfred the Great, that Alfred could not read till he was twelve; what is significant, and perhaps intentionally symbolic, is the suggestion that he learned to read English before he learned to read Latin. In the long run, the English language was the weapon, and Alfred saw it as such, with which to beat the Danes.

For, after four hundred years of easygoing isolation, Saxons in Britain had to face an old enemy. In came the Danes.

V » » *The North Road*

There is another long stretch of four or five centuries before there is conscious unification in England, and any sense of nationality with such feeling of elation as is expressed by Robert of Gloucester:

Enge | land is a | right good | land, I | ween of all | lands the | best

That [1] is a thirteenth century feeling; but in the ninth century, in Alfred's time, apart from such unity as was felt within the Saxon heritage, there was no such entity as England. There was the invasion of Danes. Apart from border raids, the descendants of the Germanic tribes had been able to hold their territory against the peoples of Wales and Scotland, but the Danes were Scandinavian robbers who when they came "in great host" occupied the whole center of Britain and completely divided the island. Our question is, in these new circumstances, What part did the Great North Road play?

The Germanic immigrants into Britain had been granted about

four centuries of isolation in which to come to terms with their new land and to create their new civilization, a civilization which seemed to me in some ways stiffly integrated, in other ways loose and easygoing. But it was a civilization which seems to have been intensely alive, so there was one immediate difference between the Saxon and Danish invasions of Britain. The Saxons had found relatively little physical opposition; the Danes, when they invaded, found Saxons in possession.

When the Danes (or call them Vikings, Northmen, whichever you prefer) unexpectedly attacked and despoiled the Holy Isle of Lindisfarne off the coast of Northumberland (you may catch a glimpse of the Holy Isle today as you drive up the Great North Road), they established an unforgettable memory. The documentary records of the period are those which were preserved in monasteries, and what they preserve are the institutional reactions. The shudder of the churchmen at the first Viking raid was instantaneous, and was communicated throughout Christendom. I quote from Dr. Dorothy Whitelock:

Alcuin's letters show the consternation and horror aroused by this event; never before had such a terror appeared in Britain, nor had such an inroad been thought possible. Such an attack on this holiest of sanctuaries could surely not occur without a divine warning, and men interpreted in retrospect certain portents seen earlier in the year, flying dragons and bloody rain, as foreshadowing the wrath of God and the imminence of his vengeance.

I pause over the two portents mentioned, the "flying dragons and bloody rain." "Dragon" is a symbol so ubiquitous, so representative in a general way of that which has its cold and evil eye upon you, so representative in all mythologies of the ever-watching enemy, that we may need to recall that at the time of the first Danish raid the term had, as well as its general interpretation, a specific interpretation for Churchmen. Gibbon in *The Decline and Fall* points out that Leo the Iconoclast used the term "Dragon" as the official title for the Imperial Inspector who was charged with the special duty of dissolving religious communities. The "Dragon" was provided with soldiery for the specific purpose of destroying the Church. Gibbon says that Leo's successors continued to use the term, and this suggests that throughout Christian communities "Dragon" conveyed a particular physical thrill of fear. Never before had this persecution by the "Dragon" extended to Britain. One doubts whether when the Danes built their ships with dragon prows they were deliberately adopting Leo's symbol. One doubts if the motive of the Danish dragon prows was other than to strike general terror and to frighten Danegeld from whomsoever might be met. But what may be intended by the attacker as a general insult may also be interpreted by the victim as an individual, specific threat. Church documents would indicate that after the first shocking Danish raid the monks and chroniclers regarded the dragon prows as being directed wholly and especially at them. The churchmen's only way to meet the menace was to put God's House in order by repentance and reform. The popes, when applied to, recommended to the Saxon Church a stricter observance of the marriage laws and less cohabitation with nuns.

The year of the Viking attack on Lindisfarne is given as 793. In the following year Bede's monastery at Jarrow and Hilda's abbey at Whitby were sacked and looted. I have a reason for speculating on the time of year: there is a possible hint in the second portent mentioned, the "bloody rain." "Bloody rain" is a not uncommon medieval phrase for what we call Northern Lights. A reference comes to mind in Guy Gibson's *Enemy Coast Ahead*. Gibson is describing night-flying bomber operations in the last war, and makes the remark:

> In the north is that bomber-boys' bad dream—the glow. Some scientists call it the Aurora Borealis, but you ought to hear what we call it when there are fighters about! [2]

I am told by the experts that general weather conditions in the North Sea area are unlikely to have changed in the past thousand years; in other words, that the present edition of the *North Sea Pilot* probably represents the weather problems as faced by the early Danish navigators. A phenomenon of "bloody rain" is apt to be most noticeable in the North Sea area in early spring or late autumn when the sky is otherwise dark. In early spring the prevailing winds are north or northeast or east. At other times the prevailing winds are southwest, with possibility of fog. It was in the

months about Eastertide that wind direction was favorable for
the Danes to sail for Britain. In months about Eastertide the boys
in the Bomber Command in the last war complained of "the glow."
The suggestion is that it was in those months that Alcuin, back in
the eighth century, linked up the portents of dragons and bloody
rain. The suggestion is that the original raiding of Britain by Danes
may have been an Eastertide activity.

If the raids coincided with the period of the Easter festival, that
might have added to the horror within the Saxon Church. How
far or in what way all this might conceivably tie in with the subsequent myth of St. George and the Dragon must be pushed to
the back of the mind. Here I must turn to the probability that the
sport-loving Saxon warriors who were ruling in Britain would
not have been unduly flurried by the earliest Danish raids. The
Church was horrified, and recorded the fact. There is no corresponding record of the attitude of Saxon warriors. They may have
been busy with their own feuds. It is possible that some were not
so devoted to the monasteries as to be greatly agitated at the news
that there were cats among the pigeons. By the first hit-and-run
methods of the Northmen, Saxon fighters, I imagine, would have
been rather provoked than dismayed. This is probable, in that the
more ambitious of the warrior class of Northmen did not attempt
at that time any serious inroads upon the island. After a first
inspection of the coasts of Britain they sailed on southward for
richer pickings elsewhere. What, after all, was gained by pillaging
Lindisfarne, Jarrow, and Whitby? The proudest of the northern
adventurers went on to vie with each other in ransacking the
Continent of Europe. Some of these Northmen raided south to the
Mediterranean; some attacked Sicily, others attacked Constanti-
nople; and when pushed back, they nevertheless remained in
France and developed a heartland and a courtier game in Normandy. This courtier game in Normandy one feels to be far
removed in spirit from the spirit of the rabble of Danish settlers
who more than a generation later than the initial raids—forty
years later is what is indicated by the chroniclers—began to seep
into the eastern side of Britain "in great host."

It may be unfair to speak of the later wave of Danish invaders
as "rabble," but it seems correct to stress that the invasion of the

great host of Danes was no invasion with banners. It was an invasion of immigrants with axes, settlers who were intent upon cutting down forests and building farmhouses. First had been the Viking raiders, but the later and more serious invasion was the infiltration into Britain of men with no higher ambition than to be farmers or backwoodsmen or tradesmen. They came in small boatloads to the east-coast estuaries, but they came in numbers and, as Saxons had done earlier, they brought their women with them. Throughout the ninth century their migration continued, and by the end of that century they had muscled in to the whole of a monstrous cantle of the island, from London to Chester and from Carlisle to the mouth of the Tees. This was the Danelaw.

A traditional view of the Viking civilization is conveniently given in Douglas Jerrold's *History of England;* he quotes from Hodgkin and others a description of the court of Harold Fairhair in Norway—the Harold who united all Norway for the first time toward the end of the ninth century. This is the picture of Harold's court:

> Everything is gay with the bright colours and the gilt of the Viking age. The fighting men are not allowed to marry, but their generous lord has organized prostitution as he has organized amusements. . . . "Very magnificent," says a contemporary poet, "is the life enjoyed by the glorious champions who play chess at Harold's court. They are enriched with money and with splendid swords, with gold and with girls from the East. . . ."

At the same time the king's poets "encouraged the king's warriors to despise the allurements of peace, the indolence and luxury of life indoors. The man who was indeed a man sought adventure on the sea even in the storms of winter. . . ." Strip it all down a little, and there is a recognizable gangster quality about this picture of a Danish king and his hangers-on which matches the quality of his opposite numbers in Normandy and perhaps his opposite numbers in Anglo-Saxon Britain. But it does not seem to have been the likes of Harold Fairhair who came to settle in the Danelaw. It seems to have been a less ambitious order of Northmen, artisans and fishermen, who for the most part came to be

the settlers. Nobody mentions any notable leaders. The bulk of
the Danish immigrants seem to come in as escapists, and if I have
called them a rabble it is what I suspect Harold Fairhair would
have called them.

One must distinguish between the settler and the pirate. Some
historians regard the history of Viking piracy as more important
than the story of the settlers. Much is made of the superiority of
Viking warships as they were built about the year 900: "They were
the decisive military invention of the ninth century and solved in
terms of the warfare of those days the eternal military problem of
giving mobility to mass." The sentence is so well phrased that one
tends to forget that so far as concerns Britain the Viking warships
produced no military result which could be called decisive. I admit
Mr. Jerrold is persuasive: "The appearance of these brightly-painted
ships, with their striped red-and-white sails, the great dragon
heads at their prows, the coloured pennants streaming from their
mast-heads and the brilliant shields of the raiders hanging over the
gunwales, must have been an inspiration to the Vikings themselves and a source of awe to their victims." Sometimes, no doubt,
the unexpected appearance of a Viking warship had the desired
effect of extracting Danegeld, and we believe that into Alfred's
time the pirates were exerting nuisance value. But the military
importance of the Danish raids upon the south coast can be exag-
gerated. According to Mr. Jerrold, the whole of the south of
Britain was wide open to the Danes: "The once brutal and ferocious
Anglo-Saxon had lost alike his fury and his skill. The sea which
had been his servant had become in the course of time a stranger
to him." Test the statement by considering the submarine morphology of the Thames estuary; there are other tricky estuaries, but
for our purpose the Thames will serve. To the navigator, no matter
how seaworthy your ship, when you have made a landfall you
have to know the bottom and the tides; prosaic matters such as
sandbanks and mudflats can shake a lot of color out of would-be
raiders. It is doubtful if their own sea was a stranger to the ninth
century Saxons; I gather that in the troublesome Thames estuary
they knew the then equivalents of what we nowadays call the
Barrow, Sunk, and Long Sand; I gather they knew the transverse
swatchways—the word itself is Saxon, from *swaeth*, a track. Monas-

tic chroniclers tend to write as if dragon prows were to be expected up any estuary at any moment. To believe that is unrealistic. There is a chronicler's account that a "great army" of Danes wintered in London in 871, the year Alfred came to the throne. My conjecture is that if an army of Danes did remain in London for a year or two after 871, its main lines of communication and of subsequent retreat were not up and down the Thames but overland. A further reason for the lack of any lasting military success by the Danes in Britain south of the Thames was that in any sort of pitched battle the "once brutal and ferocious Anglo-Saxon" had not lost his fury.

Mr. Jerrold makes handsome amends, if not to the Saxon seamen, at least to Saxon warriors. Initially, I suggested Saxon lords may have been less stirred by Danish raids than the churchmen. It was the churchmen who had special cause for horror, and we may believe that atrocity stories were fostered in the monasteries. As Danish settlers, rather than pirates, kept on seeping into the Danelaw in numbers and with intent to stay, the Saxon warriors began to have cause for their own special indignation. Mr. Jerrold puts his finger, I think, upon this annoyance. The trouble was, the Danish immigrants who came into the Danelaw showed no disposition to play the game as recognized by warriors and gentlemen. If a Harold Fairhair had arrived in Britain to contest for sovereignty, there could have been notable and worthy sword play. The Danish immigrants who were intruding, the artisans, farmers, tradesmen, displayed no interest in the political sovereignty of Britain. Two centuries later, when Harald Hardrada landed at York, the Saxon Harold could fight him honorably as an equal, and beat him. But in Alfred's time the immigrants into the Danelaw were, according to the code of Saxon warriors, not equal, and presented nothing to be beaten. The Danish pirate was special enemy to the churchmen; the Danish settler was a most awkward enemy to the sport-loving Saxon lord. The raiders, in Alfred's time, were chased away. The settlers remained, and there was no sportsmanship about them. This was a very special cause of fury, for in any game not even a cheater is so unpopular as a spoilsport.

My picture, then, is that Saxon warriors, not at first much fluttered by the raiders, came to be much provoked by the Danes who infiltrated as settlers. In Alfred's time there seemed to be nothing final for the Saxon warriors to do about the Danish settlers. Give or take a battle here or there, it made no difference. You could chase the Danes out of the South Country and contain them behind the great rampart of Watling Street, the central of the three greatest Roman roads by which Aulus Plautius had divided the island. You could chase them out of London, but you could not go far along the North Road, because that was in their guerrilla territory. You could not decisively beat the Danes because they were not interested in setting up kings who could be conquered or institutions which could be destroyed. There was no decisive way of hurting them. Had Northern lords, such as the predecessors of Edwin and Morcar, been friendly with Saxon lords of Wessex, had they agreed to combine against the Danes, perhaps the Danes could have been exterminated. But there was no solid Saxon agreement, and short of extermination no way of getting rid of Danish settlers; and one does not get the impression that the Danish settlers would have been easily exterminated. One gets the impression they were ingenious, energetic, hard-working, practical tough peoples. They were in good country; their wives were with them; they intended to make a go of it in their self-contained Danelaw; and beyond that intention they cared for nobody, no, not they.

How was it that these unwanted, uninvited, independent intruders who had grabbed the center part of Britain forsook their own language and began to talk English?

Questions, such as I never thought of till I began to travel the Great North Road, are piling up. I asked, What part was the road going to play when it was wholly enclosed within the Danelaw? I am now being asked another inconvenient question: Why did not the Danelaw remain an enclave within Britain, an enclave faithful to its own language, like the French enclave in Canada? Why did the Danish settlers in the Danelaw forsake and forget their own language? Why did the Danes forsake their own speech and speak English?

I remember the colored map of Britain circa 900 as it was presented to the eye of a schoolboy. That map was visually rememberable. It was pretty. Britain was a bedquilt of hard and fast shapes and colors. Each colored piece of the map was sure of itself, and distinctive. The Danelaw was a hard yellow trapezium across the

whole middle of Britain. There was no doubt about the Danelaw
dividing the island, blocking off the pink of the Anglo-Saxons
south of the Thames and the purple piece of Mercia from a rather
more tentative Northumbria—I say Northumbria was rather more
tentative to the mapmaker, because it was not solidly colored but
only outlined in brown. There was nothing tentative about the map
presentation of the Danelaw. There it was as a yellow chunk, a
block across the map, bounded on the southwest by the rampart
of Watling Street. What then had happened to the double rampart
of Roman roads north from London? The Great North Road had,
apparently, no longer any base. The Saxons had reoccupied London. The Great North Road was rootless, and wholly enclosed
within the Danelaw, and the mapmaker (who was concerned with
political boundaries) had not bothered to draw it. So far as that
map was concerned, the Great North Road did not exist, circa 900.

Other arguments were put about in schooldays to argue that
the Great North Road was out of existence by Alfred's time. One
argument was that for military purposes the Northmen always
preferred shipwork to foot slogging. That was a dubious argument.
It overlooked the distinction between the Danes who were pirates
and the Danes who were settlers. One would think that ships were
preferred by raiders, but the great host of the Danes were settlers
who possibly resented piracy on the east coast as much as Saxons
resented it in the South. Another argument was that all Roman
roads in Britain must have deteriorated in Saxon times because
Saxons had lost the peculiar skill of the Romans in the mixing of
mortar and the maintenance of stonework. On this theory, when a
Roman bridge fell down, it could not be repaired. Wherever that
happened, nothing was left but a stone ford; hence the corresponding place name, Stamford; and since there were a number of places
called Stamford or Stamford Bridge, the inference was that by the
time of the Danelaw road traffic was handicapped by bad condition of the roads. This, in boyhood, seemed an ingenious argument, but I am now less certain than I was in boyhood that Saxons
or Danes were incapable of repairing such roads as they wished to
keep in repair.

The easterly branch of the Roman road from London to Lincoln—
Ermine Street—went in part through low ground which was subject

to flooding. Men of the fenland were at times amphibious; there is the ballad about King Canute:

> Merrily sang they, the monks at Ely,
> When Canut the King he rowed thereby;
> Row to the shore, men, said the King,
> And let us hear these monks to sing.

Hereward the Wake "rowed away for Crowland." As late as the early years of the nineteenth century, when George Borrow's mother brought him as a child from Peterborough to Norman Cross, it was commonplace for them and other travelers to cross that part of country by boat. Yet in Danish times, when floods subsided there is no reason to suppose that Ermine Street was unusable; and there was always the westerly branch of the Roman North Road, which follows the edge of hard ground. The two causeys go through the heart of the Danelaw like a high-tide mark and a low-tide mark; and though by the time of the Danelaw the roads may have lost political importance as a doubled Roman rampart separating East Anglia from the Midlands, I don't think they lost, but gained, importance for domestic traffic. For unless those roads were carrying traffic north and south, from and to London, precisely at the period when the mapmaking of our school-days expunged them from the colored map of Britain, I can't explain how the Danes were seduced to give up their own language, how and why they were seduced to speak English. That seems to be a cardinal matter to brood about. When descendants of peoples of the Danelaw set out, much later, to pioneer in New England, few of them bothered to learn the language of the Delawares or Choctaw; but the original Danish pioneers of the Danelaw discarded their own heritage of language, and learned English. The Danes had a common heritage of language: Swedish, Norwegian, and Danish are languages not very far apart today. But among settlers of the Danelaw, this common heritage was given up. The Danes learned English.

It will be remembered that when Danish pirates first attacked the Saxon monasteries and churchmen applied to the popes for advice, the advice was to put God's House in order and to cease cohabitation with nuns. God's House may have been put in order, but that did not stop the infiltration of Danish settlers. When King Alfred was applied to by the churchmen, he reproved them for "neglect of learning." When Alfred's warriors complained to him about the desirability and difficulty of eliminating the peoples of the Danelaw, he chided them, it seems, with the same reproach: "neglect of learning." To churchmen, to warriors of the time that recorded remark of Alfred's must have seemed—and seems to us of later time—obscure. What did Alfred mean by it, as the approach of a Saxon king to the practical problem of coping with the intrusion of the Danes? What did Alfred mean by "neglect of learning?"

To the churchmen Alfred was tireless in uttering two words of advice: "Write English." What sort of English? Here is a piece from the preface of Alfred's version of St. Augustine's *Soliloquies:*

> Then I gathered for myself staves and props and bars, and handles for all the tools I knew how to use, and crossbars and beams for all the structures which I knew how to build, the fairest pieces of timber, as many as I could carry. I neither came home with a single load, nor did it suit me to bring home all the wood, even if I could have carried it. In each tree I saw something that I required at home.[3]

The fact that the spelling has been modernized, and that if we read the passage aloud our pronunciation may differ from Alfred's, does not alter the impression that Alfred's notion of "learning" was no small narrow notion. The language he was advising churchmen to learn was not only church English but also field English. Here was a King defining learning as the learning of English; and this "English" of his was an arrow directed at a country mark. Neglect of learning was neglect of hitting the mark. Over and again you notice that when a document which Alfred is translating is, in the original Latin, remote or abstract, what he adds to it is the direct simile, and a simile equally understandable throughout the most of Britain, to Saxon and Dane alike. Could any style be better adapted to the incoming ancestors of "Robinson Crusoe" or John Bunyan than such an example of Alfred's as I have just quoted? The churchmen could not disregard Alfred's piety nor the extent of his "Latin learning"; therefore by his example "English learning" could not be regarded as unrespectable. If to the churchmen Alfred said "learn to write English," what he said to his warriors was consistent. Here again, as a fighter his conduct was not to be despised. He had been active in the field, had reoccupied and refortified London, had beaten the Danes in a notable fight near Hertford, and had built ships of Saxon design "full twice as long" as those of the Danes. Alfred's ships were able to chase the raiders from the south coast. Yet, if I understand him rightly, I think he saw that there was nothing to be done permanently or dramatically, in a military way, about the Danish settlers who had seeped and were seeping into the Danelaw. Alfred's testament to his fighters before his death (in 900 or 901) was in effect: "These Danes are here to stay. The sword will not get rid of them. They must be taught to understand." That is what I think Alfred included in his term "learning."

Whatever weight you give to the coefficients which brought it about, the most notable victory of Saxons over Danes was the victory of language, whereby throughout the Danelaw settlers came to adopt English. In so far as Alfred was responsible for this victory, he had quietly won one of the decisive battles of the world. What made it a lasting victory was that the Danes forsook their own speech as if of their own accord, as if they had as much right to take over the language of the Saxons as they had to take over the land of the Danelaw. It is a curious phenomenon. I can think of no exact parallel. I think that everyday traffic along the Great North Road must have played some part. There was now a common language on the Road which had also managed to get off the Road, and when there was a common tongue (with whatever local variations) from the south of Britain to Northumbria there was by no means an end to internal squabbling, but there was the possibility of an eventual single polity, an England which Alfred may have hoped for, though he could not live to see. I dwell on this business of language with the more interest, when I think about the temper of the Danish settlers in Britain. I said Harold Fairhair might have regarded them as a rabble, and so might the forebears of William of Normandy, or many of the Saxon nobles; but the passage of time was to prove that the Danish element in Britain was to be, in spirit, notably independent, unruly, nonconformist, and anarchic. The British peoples on the western fringe of the British heartland were no more rebellious. They refused to take to the English language. The Gaels in the far North refused it. The Danes from the beginning took to the English language and then proceeded to defend it with as much spirit as if it had always been their own—with more spirit than they had defended their own. The corollary to that is, without the defense of the English language which was put up by the Danelaw, we might now be talking Norman-French. In the warfare of languages that is the final large contest we have to consider—the contest between English and Norman-French. It was a contest in which, in the end, English decisively won.

Before I struggle with the impact of the Norman Conquest, and with what in Norman times Professor Saintsbury calls the "shaking together" of Latin and French elements into the English language, I try to review for myself the characteristics of the main invaders of Britain, an island much invaded, much overrun. I said the Great North Road was not photogenic; yet these are the snapshots which the Road demands. The Romans—I thought about the military invasion, the road making, the towns with temples, arcades, club gossip; the country villas with central heating, baths, and the amenities of dining. Remains at Verulamium or Bath or Wall in Staffordshire (once called Letocetum) impress one with the persistence with which, in the provinces, the Roman gentleman attempted to keep up a Roman way of life. Any Roman with any official pretensions dressed for dinner, was interested in manners of dining and in niceties of food. The ox, the goat, the sheep, the deer—none of which animals were indigenous to Britain—had probably been brought to the island long before Roman times; but who but the Romans would have imported the edible dormouse? This fat little fellow, with a tail like a squirrel, still known by the name of *Glis glis,*[4] traveled to Britain with the Roman epicure. *Glis glis* was reared in a grove of oak or beech trees, he was fed upon currants and chestnuts; for final fattening he was put into a special earthenware vessel called a *glirarium.* A good dormouse grew so fat it was necessary to break the pot to remove him; after that ceremonial he was then cooked and served with a honey sauce. In the British climate the edible dormouse hibernated seven months of the year, sleeping with his tail wrapped over his head; but when he waked to be stuffed with food, he was available for the table during the months when it was traditional to avoid the oyster. The edible dormouse was so much esteemed that scales were brought to the banquet to record his weight before he was eaten. Possibly some of the original stock of edible dormice may have managed to escape; it is interesting that *Glis glis* exists in England today in an area which is particularly rich in Roman remains, extending from the Great North Road westward through Amersham in Buckinghamshire. He exists forever also in *Alice in Wonderland,* although in Tenniel's illustration for the Mad Tea-Party his *glirarium* appears as a silver teapot, into which the March Hare and the Mad Hatter attempt to insert him upside down.

Innumerable little details bring to life the lives of Romans in Britain. There is the Austalis tile in the Guildhall Museum; in the same museum is a pair of leather drawers worn by some Roman slave girl; somewhere there is the counterfeit Roman coin which was dug up near Gerrard's Cross—a coin held to be counterfeited not in later times, but counterfeited in the Roman times, which tells some sort of story. Coins, tools, and ornaments all help to picture the domestic life; and, for the Roman period, there is the advantage of being able to check one's impressions from the wealth of information about Roman life in Rome itself. I am thinking of such works as Becker's *Gallus;* with appropriate caution it ought to be possible to apply to the life of Roman provinces some of the customs which were initiated at the center of things. For instance, Becker suggests that the rule of the road on the Appian Way was to drive on the left.[5] If it was natural for the Roman patrician in his two-wheeled *lectica* to drive on the left of the paved road, it would seem a natural assumption that legions, when passing each other in formation would keep to the left, and that the custom would extend to all the paved roads of the empire, wherever the Roman writ ran. Many a thought about Roman life in Britain, perhaps not provable by evidence within the island, may be legitimately projected from what is known—or said to be known—about Roman life in Rome. The importance of road customs to the Romans is, in this present book, to me a matter of primary interest. How did that particular dimension of four feet eight and a half inches come to be the gauge for English railways, and subsequently for railroads in many other parts of the world? If, as I trust, I can hump along in my journey as far as Northumberland, I can discuss how George Stephenson came to choose the dimension which was laid down by the Romans in military manuals as the double marching step for the legions, and, understandably, as the dimension of the "yoke" under which tribesmen passed in token of submission. Road customs in Roman Britain are attested by the direct evidence, such as that of the burial of cinerary urns parallel to the roads and as near to the roads as possible. Outside a town (for instance Letocetum) a Roman cemetery extended for long distances on both sides of a main road, rather than extending to areas inland. It is as if there was belief the dead could continue their interest in and find company with the living who were passing to and fro; and possibly too, that the living would remember the dead. Indirect evidence that tombs by the roadside were the regular thing is derived from contemplating the Appian Way. There was a custom which the Romans derived from the Greeks, of offering at a shrine which had special meaning, a token garnishment of parsley. There is no direct evidence, but the indirect evidence suggests that parsley may have come into Britain to sustain a Roman custom of respect for the dead.

So, and wherever you turn, there is a wealth of suggestion about the character of Roman Britain, and the heritage from Rome. The Romans did not directly bequeath us some of the big things (law and language and self-government) but many little things. The Saxons bequeathed us the big things, but, although I have speculated (perhaps wildly) about their domestic affairs, I feel at a disadvantage in forming for myself any thumbnail sketch of Saxon character. There is very little indirect evidence of what Anglo-Saxon lives had been like in their homelands, which we believe they were glad enough to leave; and for direct evidences of their daily life in Britain we are reduced to digging up their graves. Apart from the macabre interest, there is sometimes an element of humor revealed by the raking of Saxon graves. There have been found (notably at Sutton Hoo) most beautiful and worthy death gifts to someone of the nobility, but often enough, as the Roman counterfeit coin was evidence of a desire to cheat a living fellow man, there is a Saxon example of readiness, if possible, to cheat the dead. Mr. T. C. Lethbridge, in *Dark-Age Britain* (Methuen, 1956), page 114, writes about Saxon burial customs:

The Anglo-Saxon did not for preference bury the best and latest available objects with the dead. The dead person had to be provided with ornaments or weapons for the next world, but they were dead things like himself. The more valuable objects went to the next of kin. A perfect example of this was found in Grave XI at Holywell Row. Here a girl, perhaps ten years old, was buried with brooches, girdle-hangers and other things, which were worn or patched at the time of burial. She was provided with festoons of beads much too big for her. She was not buried with her own jewels, but with old and worn-out objects, which probably had not even belonged to her mother. They had been picked out of some old remnants chest. The cracked brooch with its missing garnets, the girdle-hangers roughly patched for the occasion—these may have belonged once to her grandmother or great-aunt . . . I could go much farther than this. I could point to spears whose edges were so ground away with sharpening that they were no longer fit for battle; or to patched bronzed kettles picked from some nail in an outhouse.

It is possible, then, that objects found in Saxon graves may have been out of date at the time of burial, and that the objects found are not always representative of the best craftsmanship, but sometimes represent deliberate discards. Mr. D. B. Harden, in discussing glass vessels of the Saxon period, exclaims that "it is not true, as has so often been stated, that dark-age glasses will never stand upright." He points out that the imperfect and unstable examples of glassware come from finds in the graves.

If the picture I have of Saxon life is sketchy, and if it includes poignant contrasts of pride and penury, what do I select as characteristic of the life of the Danelaw? I wonder if it is odd to single out a love of color. I was the more inclined to give some credence to the account of the highly-colored court of Harold Fairhair because I thought of the variety of color still to be seen in East Anglian farm buildings and in old cottages. I may be wrong, for I am giving only personal impressions; but contrast the color of the cottages in an old Suffolk village with the grayness of a corresponding village in Wales. There remains in East Anglia the same instinct as is exhibited in the red barns of Sweden. I suggest that among the Saxons bright colors were used to deck lords and ladies, and that among Danish farmers bright colors were used to deck farm tools. It saved time in looking for the tools if they were garish. The bright colors of the modern farm implements manufactured today by the International Harvester Company may derive from a tradition which came into the Danelaw with the Danes. The color I most associate with the Danes is red. I might check this with the history of clothmaking in one of the most important towns of the Danelaw, Lincoln. The story of Lincoln is well documented, and scholars may correct me if I go wrong.[6]

Lincoln, Lindum, was a notable town from the start. Londinium to Lindum, was Ermine Street. A glance at the Ordnance Survey Map of Roman Britain will indicate the importance of Lindum in the Roman scheme. Lindum was the junction of Ermine Street and the Fosse Way which came across the island from the far south-west, from Isca, nowadays Exeter. Lincoln in Roman times was a garrison town, one of the four *coloniae* for the settlement of time-expired soldiers; the other three were York, Colchester, and Gloucester. Physically, Lincoln did not start by being a large town, according to Roman standards. It was a hill town (it may still startle the tourist to find how steep the hill is), and the rectangular layout of the original Roman town fitted exactly the top of the hill. Within the stone walls with their gates at the four points of the compass the Roman streets were laid out in chessboard pattern, with the town hall (*basilica*) at one end of the market place (*forum*), and with the customary Mithraic Temple. But the area within the early walls of Lincoln was only forty-one acres, contrasting with the 330 acres of London, 240 of Cirencester, 200 of Verulamium. What was, however, unusual about Lincoln, was that it was one of the very few towns which in Roman times was materially enlarged. The town at the top of the hill was two hundred feet or more above the river Witham; as the town proved itself an important road junction, so also there was perceived the possibility of a twofold river connection. The Romans (it is believed) cut the canal called the Fossedyke, which connected Lincoln with the river Trent at Torksey, a distance of eleven miles. To Lincoln traders this opened up the extensive waterways of the Trent, the Yorkshire Ouse, and the Humber. What is provable is that in Roman times (probably third century) the town of Lincoln was extended southward down from the hilltop to the river, and this extension, more than doubling the whole area, was likewise walled. One takes the extension to have been due to the river connection, and caused by extension of trade.

Trade with whom, and with what commodities? That, in Roman times, is guesswork. Access to the Trent was access to the North Sea. It is certain that by Danish times Lincoln, like York, was busy with exports. In the Domesday Survey the number of Lincoln's burgesses was exceeded only by London and York, and like York its fee farm was £100, only London paying more. It is conjectured that from Roman times a source of wealth at Lincoln and York was the export of woolen cloth. There is plenty of testimony that the Romans understood the essentials of wool manufacturing, and that they carried their knowledge of weaving into all the provinces in which they settled. In no province was an impervious warm cloth more essential than in Britain. In the passage about the Roman road building we quoted David Jones's impression of the centurion's concern for his woolen cloak—the "British warm." As sheep provided the ewe's milk for the staple ration of the legionaries—cheese—so wool was available for weaving, and weaving seems to have been a natural occupation in the various *coloniae*. But if, in Roman times, there was desire for woolen cloth within Britain, it is probable there was demand for the warm cloth in the non-Roman territories across the North Sea. One imagines the British export of woolens to the Northmen began in Roman times. The wool trade may indeed have been one of the inducements for the Saxon and Danish settlers to seep into Britain.

It might be an exaggeration to say that the Danish settlers, when they came to the Danelaw, came for the wool rush; but they displayed an aptitude for cloth manufacture which transcended the work of the Romans and Saxons. It is another instance of the failure of the Latin language within Britain, that the term that got into British speech was not *lana* but *wool*. Words in the English language associated with "wool" seem to be of Teutonic or Danish introduction—the word *wool* itself, and *weave, sheep, shearing*—none of them are of Latin origin. These were words well settled in the language long before the Norman Conquest, and for the French word *laine* there was no entry into the English wool trade.

But I am not yet ready to discuss the contest between the English and French languages. I am endeavoring to maintain a thesis that Danes within the Danelaw showed aptitude for wool manufacture, and showed desire to stain their woolen cloth in hard and fast bright colors. I think they had exceptional desire for bright colors. At Lincoln in particular there was in Danish times special attention to the dyeing of cloth; and therefore special desirability for cloth of Lincoln "grain."

"Grain" and "green" are two words which are so inextricably mixed up that I have no hope of disentangling them. Grain was the small stuff which, whatever it was, when dried and pounded, produced a lasting dye. Grain might be seeds, might be berries, might be worms, might be spiders, such as cochineal. A grain most likely to be used at Lincoln was the *chermes* or *kermes,* a widespread little aphid, in Sanskrit called *krimi,* in Arabic *girmiz.* This little aphid I understand to favor forest conifers, the spruce to lay its eggs in and the larch on which to grow. The female of this species, when dead and dried, produces kermescic acid, which can lastingly dye cloth red. Cochineal came into European use much later, from Mexico; but it is from the evergreens of Scandinavia that we posit an early importation of chermes to Lincoln. The insect by some was thought to be a berry, and the "grain tree," as bearer of this berry, appears in the crest of the Dyers' Company. Possibly the dyers of Lincoln had a secret of mixing berries with the chermes to achieve a brighter color, for kermescic acid by itself produces a dark red, and the cloth for which Lincoln became famous was bright scarlet. In Danish times and in the eleventh and twelfth centuries, Lincoln was producing a scarlet cloth with a hard and fast color which was thoroughly engrained. I have found many people to be annoyed with me at the suggestion that the best Lincoln "green" may have been scarlet. But I am not alone in the hypothesis. Professor Owen writes (with proper caution) in *The Times Trade and Engineering Supplement* (February, 1936) that "the scarlet dye was derived from the 'grain' (greyne) or 'al-kermes,' an insect resembling cochineal. . . . It seems thus possible that one, perhaps the earlier, of the Lincoln greens is this grain or scarlet." In J. W. F. Hill's *Medieval Lincoln* (Cambridge University Press, page 325) I find a telling reference. In 1181–1182

"the sheriff of Lincoln bought, presumably in Lincoln . . . 90 ells
of scarlet . . . 12 ells of green . . . 9 ells of grey." The references,
which give the costs, are in the Pipe Rolls, P.R. 26 Henry II, page
48 and P.R. 28 Henry II, pages xxvi, 50. The Lincoln scarlet cloth
was the most costly: it cost half a mark for an ell. The standard
length for an ell (usually assumed to have been forty-five inches)
is for my purpose irrelevant. It is the proportionate costs of the
three colors of which I have need. How much half a mark in the
twelfth century would amount to in our money is also irrelevant;
all that I need is the proportionate costs. These we can get. Assume
that the half-mark for the scarlet Lincoln grain was anything you
like, say six shillings eight pence. On that scale the green Lincoln
grain cost three shillings and the gray Lincoln grain cost one shilling eight pence. The coefficients don't matter, but the proportion
does. Scarlet Lincoln grain was esteemed best in the Danelaw.

What I have attempted is a short reminder of three characteris-
tically different peoples who used the Great North Road, before
the Normans conquered Britain. Of the three peoples, I sketched
the Romans as having something of a gift for provincial life, the
Saxons as having a wonderful gift for creating the institutions
for a lively, self-governing society, the Danes, as practical, ingenious backwoodsmen, artisans, and tradesmen. Such general-
izations are forced upon me by a rapid journey, and are agreed
to be subject to every correction. If on the Road you can do better,
hypocrite lecteur, I'll draw over to the hard shoulder and let you
pass me. I resented not being able to get much of a picture of the
Saxons; I resent that I don't seem to get any sufficient picture of
the Danes. Yet in some ways the Danish intrusion into Britain
had more than anything else to do, when it gathered steam, with
the future of the island. In their beginning in the Danelaw, so
long as they had no political ambitions, they were in a military
way unbeatable. As soon as they were infected with a disease for
sovereignty, Saxons could beat them. Danes made an organized
push in 1002, and were beaten. Canute achieved his uneasy reign,
but with the death of Hardicnut in 1042, the idea of a Danish
dynasty was ended. From the distance of nearly a thousand years
it would seem that the importance of the Saxon-Danish contest
for total sovereignty over the whole of the English-speaking

polity was that both sides became vulnerable to the fourth important conquest from abroad.

Up to the time of the Norman Conquest of Britain the story remains provincial. After the Norman Conquest the story of the Great North Road becomes dynamic.

VI »» *The Questing Beast*

Though both branches of the Great North Road (high-tide and low-tide marks) are straight as can be from London to Durham and Newcastle, there are occasional sharp bends, which makes the run along it "tortive and errant from his course of growth." I am now at a sharp bend. I leave behind the views so far half seen, and see ahead another landscape. It is a landscape of legend.

The status of the Great North Road was completely altered by the Norman Conquest. In Saxon times, and more especially in Danish times, I pictured the Great North Road within Britain as a mere fragment of what the road had been in Roman times. I pictured it as a section, self-contained within the island. Cut off from the Continent, the section had become parochial. I maintained this did not mean it had become atrophied; rather, indeed, that when the segment was parochial it was playing an active part in the process whereby Danes forsook their own tongue and talked English. The Norman invasion suddenly made this piece of road once more a main military road, and linked it with the

97

Continent. What I have now to struggle with are the consequences of this linkage.

I was satisfied, at any rate momentarily, with the explanations I could find for the Saxon and Danish immigrations into Britain. I found suggestions, though admittedly sketchy, as to the activities and characteristics of these intruders. What sort of sketch can I make for myself of the Normans?

Insofar as one can generalize, I find that the Northmen who originally penetrated the Continent, who fought in Italy and France and settled and married there, had become in the course of two or three centuries a very complicated people. I mean that the character of the Normans in Normandy seems to me to have become complex, even in some psychical ways self-tortured. Like the lower-class Northmen who had remained in Britain, they forsook their language. But the language they took to was wholly different. They were aware of Italian; they spoke French. They were converts to the Roman Church, and like many converts, fierce in their new convictions and self-repressions. The effect on the Northmen who had penetrated into the Mediterranean area was vastly more complicated than the lowlier contest being worked out in Britain between Danes and Saxons.

It is easy to describe the conquest of Britain by William of Normandy in terms of ordinary economic pressures, coupled with William's prowess as a military opportunist. On this view, William is pictured as being squeezed in Normandy, as being surrounded by a strong force of needy adventurers, and as seizing upon Britain as a plum fine and ripe for the picking. I am not disregarding that view. The Norman Conquest can be looked at as a glorified version of the earliest type of Viking piracy. By 1066 Britain had become well-to-do: worth taking. It is natural to suppose that Danegeld was in the minds of many of William's adventurers. For earlier Northmen, Danegeld had been the sporadic and local shakedown of an accessible town or monastery. But within Britain the conception of Danegeld had been altering. Æthelred organized Danegeld as a levy to be raised in anticipation of raids from outside; as a levy against possible future contingencies, a general war chest. If there were no raids from outside, so much the better for the king's treasury. Canute found the

Danegeld to be a useful general tax; his levy of Danegeld in 1014 brought him £83,000. It was a temptation to William that Britain was accustomed to anteing up Danegeld on that scale, and convenient for him to come in and scoop the kitty. William levied Danegeld, after the Conquest, at least three times in the early years of his reign. Then, to make the levy more complete, there was the energetic compilation of the Domesday Survey, which provided not only a proportionately fair method for a general shakedown, but a list of title deeds available for distribution to resident or nonresident Norman nobility.

All this seems reasonable enough: William's impact shaking together the peoples of Britain under one military aristocracy, a single polity. "England," brought into being as if by a Norman-French equivalent of the phrase *Ein Reich, ein Volk, ein Führer.* But it doesn't explain the cathedrals.

Visually you can't escape the Norman Cathedrals in England. You can't look at a cathedral and just take it for granted. The beauty and the grandeur of it may be breathtaking; and then you wonder, Why is it there?

This opens a train of thought which makes me groan, because I am incompetent to follow it. When I reread the letters which St. Augustine wrote from Carthage—not the lesser Augustine of Canterbury, but him whom I regard as the greater Augustine—I sometimes think I can see the origin of the impulse for the building of cathedrals.[1] What the Church was to do about the physical fabric of the house of God is a subject of much concern to Augustine. Plagued by a population of Carthage which was rowdy and excitable, Augustine is worried as to how the Church may arrange for orderly and seemly Christian services. Pagan associations with pagan places of worship have associated them often with licentious outings, at times with sexual orgies. How can low instincts be transformed and low parodies of the highest forms of devotion be controlled? The tombs of saints and martyrs, the holy shrines, are outside the towns. The very places which should be sacred are by their isolation available for desecration. A deliberate positive pleasure in doing what is wrong achieves an added kick if it is done at a sacred site. To simple-minded people, licentiousness and absolution are somehow conjoined if the setting is holy. It is not only the orgies of the ignorant, but the deliberately wicked parodies of Christian ritual by the knowledgeable blasphemer which cause the most unbearable grief to St. Augustine—the treatment of the Last Supper as a banquet, treatment of the Communion of wine as a drinking bout, and other practices of witchcraft and Black Mass. What can be done about customs of Parentalia and Feralia, what can be done about preserving sacred tombs from desecration, unless, St. Augustine ponders, churches and shrines might be consolidated at the centers of towns, where a general social pressure ought to reduce misconduct.

It took about five centuries for Augustine's precept to be observed; only in the tenth century did the church begin to reach the town center. Long after that, country churchyards throughout the Continent and in Britain continued to be regarded, on occasion, as places of right in which to have night pastimes, revelries, and drinking bouts. Giraldus Cambrensis describes a witch dance in a churchyard in Wales in 1188 (*Itinerarium Cambriae* i. 2). Frequent and repeated prohibitions by Church councils failed to repress such customs. The building of churches at the centers of towns did exert, as Augustine predicted, a measure of seemliness. Came then a competition in the size and magnificence of church buildings; came then the age of great cathedrals.

What I find myself incompetent to deal with is the complicated and bitter religious warfare which developed coincidentally with the beginning of the building of great cathedrals. By and large, all I can make of the complex of religious feelings in Italy and France is that the Cathar cults and a movement such as that of the Albigenses were animated by a variety of passionate intentions for reformation and "purification" within the Church; that there was a cluster of beliefs and practices which seemed to the popes so sinister that it was branded as "the Heresy"; and that the fighting about "the Heresy" was implacable and cruel, even beyond the cruelty of most religious wars. Broadly, the idea of "the Heresy" was the formation of a church within the Church, a secret self-elected "pure" within the generality, with chivalry as the outward élite. As a short and brilliant essay on the whole theme, I greatly commend *The Arrow and the Sword* by Hugh

Ross Williamson.[2] Canon Demant has pointed out that a chief
value of Mr. Ross Williamson's book "is that it strings on one
thread a number of tendencies often of diverse historic roots but
of a cognate religious temper which is clearly identifiable." Canon
Demant's comment continues:

At the period in which he is most interested the representatives
of this movement can be conveniently called the "Cathari." One phase
of the movement, that of the Albigenses, is perhaps the best known to
historians. But the importance of the sketch given in this work springs
from its showing the "Cathar" cults as representative of a very deep-
rooted and recurring religious force. To mention only its roots in Mithraism, its links with the Gnostics, its theological dualism, its asceticism, the
rituals of life and death as cosmic mysteries, the appeal of the troubadours, Arthurian legends and the cult of the Holy Grail, the passions
aroused for and against witchcraft, the intimate connection between sex
and religion—all these things are sufficient testimony to the deep-rooted
vitality of a stream of religious consciousness which cannot be superficially dismissed. . . .

I feel "the Heresy" cannot be superficially dismissed, but neither
can it be superficially summed up. That's why I thankfully refer
to Mr. Ross Williamson. For my purpose it is sufficient to emphasize
that the Normans on the Continent had run into a very heady
mixture of religious ferment; that many of them became strongly
of the church within the Church; and that when William invaded
Britain he brought with him "the Heresy."

If William was pushed from behind by ordinary economic pressures, he was equally pushed by religious pressures. If there were
with him adventurers looking for Danegeld and property, there
were also with him priests and religious warriors with no baggage
other than passionate convictions. If some of William's companions
were greedy for worldly goods, others were intensely ascetic.
The development of chivalry in southern France had been accompanied by a championing of platonic or uranian love, the
soldierly love of man for man, expressed as in David's lament for
Jonathan—"your friendship for me was beyond all love of woman"
—and it was homosexual love which was most extolled by the
troubadours. Whether or no there was less immunization, less
history of skepticism, among Northmen in France than among

Mediterranean peoples about identifying virtue with "purification," about identifying worth with "chivalry"—whether or no this contributes to the explanation—I would accept the thought expressed by others before me, that among the Normans who came to conquer Britain there was an élite more extreme in its views of "purity" than those of the élite who remained in France. On the Continent there was the ruthless repression of the Albigenses; after the Norman Conquest there was room in Britain for militant extremists.

I have said that in my run along the Great North Road I have reached a sharp bend which causes me to look at a landscape of legend.

I regard the story of Harold, Saxon King in England; Harald Hardrada, King in Norway; and William the Conqueror—as legend. I regard it as legend with, so to speak, a high factual content.

Let me as swiftly as I can recall the story of the autumn of 1066. It is succinctly given in General John F. C. Fuller's *The Decisive Battles of the Western World*. General Fuller recounts Harold's activities in September, 1066, when he was presumably in London, attentive to the threat of William's invasion from Normandy. At this moment Harold received the startling news that Harald Hardrada, accompanied by Harold's own half-brother, Tostig, had invaded the North of England. I now quote General Fuller:

Hardrada sailed from the Sogne Fiord, near Bergen, with 300 ships to the Shetlands and the Orkneys, and next, turning south, he picked up Tostig and his followers off the Tyne. He plundered and burnt Scarborough, rounded Spurn Head, entered the Humber, and thence rowed up the Ouse to Riccall, ten miles south of York. There he disembarked his army, set out for York, and at Gate Fulford, two miles from the city, met the Yorkshire fyrd, under Edwin and Morcar. On 20 September a fierce battle was fought, which is poetically described in the saga. Its outcome was the rout of the two northern earls. The Chronicle mentions "heavy casualties and many of the English host were killed and drowned," and the saga informs us that so many English were slain that "they paved a way across the fen for the brave Norsemen."

This is excellent persuasive writing. Everything is put in a way that is so factual and precise that it carries conviction. The exaggeration of the saga is agreed to as poetic licence. Hardrada,

whom Sir Frank Stenton described as "the greatest northern
warrior of the age," had won a notable victory at York. I continue with General Fuller's narrative, which goes on immediately
from the preceding paragraph:

When he learnt of Harald Hardrada's invasion, Harold took his house-
carles and such men of the fyrd who had not yet been disbanded—almost
certainly a mounted force—and "went northwards day and night." On
the 24th he rode into Tadcaster, and on the following day, when
Hardrada was negotiating over hostages with the two earls, he surprised the invaders, forced a passage over the Derwent, and after a
prolonged and desperate struggle at Stamford Bridge all but annihilated
them. Not only did Hardrada and Tostig perish in the fray, but when
the battle was over, we are told that no more than twenty shiploads of
the enemy were left. These Harold allowed Olaf, Hardrada's son, to
take back with him to Norway. That Harold's losses were heavy is recorded in the Chronicle, and Ordericus Vitalis, writing between 1123
and 1141, informs us that in his day great heaps of bones still lay on the
battlefield, "memorials to the prodigious number which fell on both
sides."

The importance of these two actions cannot be overestimated, coming
as they did less than a month before the Battle of Hastings, for they
seriously reduced the strength of Harold's army. . . .

Here I begin to wonder about the dates and places which are so
precisely mentioned. One can so nearly accept the facts that there
is a feeling of shame at raising any doubts. The moment belief is
suspended, awkward doubts about the facts of the story do make
their shamefaced entry; and the moment doubts come in, whether
pertinent or impertinent, they are distracting. If Hardrada's defeat of Edwin and Morcar was as complete as is represented,
why did he not occupy York? His ships are said to be in the Ouse.
If Hardrada had reason to draw off from York to negotiate hostages,
why should he draw off to Stamford Bridge on the Derwent, eight
miles east and slightly north of York—away from his ships? I
would not be easily convinced that because eighteenth century
mapmakers gave the name Stamford Bridge to this particular
stone ford on the Derwent, that in 1066 it was the only stone
ford in the neighborhood of York; a site southwest of York toward
Tadcaster or south toward Selby would have kept the Norsemen

closer to their ships, and would have made subsequent actions less difficult to understand. It is not mere captiousness to question the traditional siting of the battle at Stamford Bridge on the Derwent. The difficulty is to reconcile that site with Harold's actions as narrated.

What were Harold's actions? "When he learnt of Harald Hardrada's invasion"—What was it Harold learned and when did he learn it? If what came to him was early information that Hardrada had plundered Scarborough and was sailing up the Humber, would he at that moment have summoned his house-carles and rushed northwards "day and night"? William's threat from Normandy was imminent. Harold is pictured as having to remain poised to face south or north. In the North, although in Fuller's phrase "Harold was no *persona grata*" to Edwin and Morcar, would he have started from London before knowing the result of their action against Hardrada? Had he done so, wouldn't he have arrived at York, from the point of view of the story, too early? But if as the story suggests it was the news of the calamity at Gate Fulford which spurred Harold, regardless for the moment of William, to face Hardrada's instant threat, one is in another difficulty. When did Harold receive the news about Gate Fulford? It is a full two hundred miles from York to London, by way of Tadcaster to Lincoln and thence by the Ermine Way—"which probably had not been repaired for 600 years," says General Fuller. I have been venturing some thoughts to the effect that the condition of the roads may have been better than usually believed; but even if so, how was the news of the disaster at Gate Fulford on the 20th to reach Harold in London in time for him to ride into Tadcaster on the 24th and on to Stamford Bridge on the Derwent on the 25th?

There is no suggestion that the news of Gate Fulford came to Harold other than by messenger; there is no suggestion that Harold and his house carles happened to be somewhere north of London. The suggestion is that after the Battle of Gate Fulford on the 20th, the message reached Harold in London (on the 22nd?) and that Harold and his armed men reached Tadcaster on the 24th, and were able to organize horseflesh to proceed on the 25th to Stamford Bridge on the Derwent for the surprise of

Hardrada and the prolonged and desperate and successful battle. The ride on the 25th from Tadcaster to Stamford Bridge presents some minor puzzles. The direct road runs through York—ten miles from Tadcaster—but with affairs as described, was York itself wide open? Could Harold count on riding straight through York on a green light? If not, one has to visualize Harold as somewhere crossing the Ouse, circling York, forcing the Derwent, to fall upon the unsuspecting Hardrada. It was because of prosaic topographical puzzles that I began to wonder if one might not solve them by locating some other stone ford more likely for Hardrada to have selected, and more convenient for Harold to have reached, if one holds to the dates as given.

The story goes on that Harold was at York, resting his men and celebrating his victory over Hardrada, at the moment that William of Normandy sailed into Pevensey Bay on the south coast. Some historians follow a source unknown to me and state the moment of William's landing as 9:00 A.M. September 28th. Harold is supposed to have had this news in York on October 1st. "Presumably," says General Fuller, "he set out on 2 October to cover the 200 miles to London, and pushing on at top speed he reached the capital on 5 or 6 October. There he remained until the 11th, collecting such forces as came in." On October 11th Harold set out from London to cover the further sixty miles to Hastings; on the night of the 13th–14th arrived at the site of the present village of Battle, and at 9:00 A.M. on the 14th the Battle of Hastings began.

I have chosen General Fuller's narrative of the Hardrada-Harold-William story because it does the very best that can be done to make the story appear to twentieth century readers as literal, factual history. I think everything *almost* fits on a factual level, though the totality of facts as stated persistently refuses to add up. This is a crucial moment at which to ask, What is one's view of "history"? This Hardrada-Harold-William story relates a vital, central episode in English history. Are we to write it off as a delusion because it is troublesome to get the facts to add up in a twentieth century adding machine? There is plenty of excuse for believing that if we delved deep enough the facts could be made to add up precisely. There is scope to pick and choose

between the "facts," and to award them different valencies. The
chief narrative source of English history for the time of the
Norman Conquest is what is sometimes called "the Anglo-Saxon
Chronicle." But as scholars have often complained, nothing is more
tantalizing than to find "the Chronicle" quoted as if it were a
single authority. There are three different versions which relate
to the period of the Hardrada-Harold-William story. These three
versions of the Chronicle are nowadays called versions C, D, E.[3]
Version C is a mid-eleventh-century manuscript which seems to
have been compiled at Abingdon, in Berkshire. It gives one view
of affairs immediately preceding the Norman Conquest, and ends
with the events of 1066. Version D is a compilation made in the
twelfth century, possibly at Worcester, possibly at Evesham,
possibly much of it compiled in the North of England, perhaps at
York. Version E was probably written out at Peterborough in the
twelfth century, but the copyist may have had before him a
version compiled earlier at Canterbury, and it may possibly supply
a Canterbury view of events. None of these compilations is especially concerned with topographical matters, but each has
details which one may emphasize or play down. It is not wholly
inconceivable that versions other than C, D, E might yet be discovered. There is plenty of room for pondering and arranging
the "facts" of this story, dramatic and central as it is in English
history.

Apart from the topographical details of the Hardrada-Harold-
William story, there are the details of timing. If the timing was
not stated so precisely, there would be less worry about the
topographical details. And here, as to medieval chronology, we
are in a realm of delectable confusion and uncertainty. Somebody
says William landed at Pevensey at 9:00 A.M. September 28th. Who
said so? No amount of repetition of a statement adds "factual"
validity to the original statement. Precise dates in medieval times
are sometimes accepted because they are presumed to be geared
to a Church calendar. Which calendar? If we go back to the
eleventh and twelfth centuries we have to make an effort of adjust-
ment to notions of timing which are wholly different from a twentieth century notion of timing. What is the date of Easter? Even
in the standardized twentieth century there remains a difference of

computation between Western and Eastern Churches. In the Middle Ages, within the Western Church alone, there were so many differences of calculation as to cause us immense confusion. It caused confusion to medieval men. In the eighth century Charlemagne had called Alcuin from York partly to help on an agreed computation for the date of Easter. Upon determination of that date depended other feast days. The result of Charlemagne's effort was an edict that every monastery of the Western Church should have at least one monk capable of computing the date of Easter. The edict indicates there was a problem, but does not indicate there was a universal answer. There was no universal answer for many centuries after Charlemagne. In the history of Church calendars there was no universal answer about the date of Easter and other feast days until after the invention of the printing press, with the circulation then of ecclesiastical timetables, as computed by Regiomontanus and agreed by others. Until the circulation of an agreed timetable, there was no agreement about the dates of feast days. No agreed timetable was in circulation in Britain much before 1500. In the twelfth century no agreement was even expected. Easter at Abingdon, Worcester, Evesham, York, Peterborough, and Canterbury was celebrated on days which may have been several weeks apart. There are stories of Easter being celebrated in a same place on different days, in the hope that one or other of the days might be the right one. So when one chronicler adjusts dates of the events which he is chronicling according to the feast days of his own monastery, and when another does so from another, there is no knowing where you are.

I have been recapitulating the details of topography and timing in the Hardrada-Harold-William story because it would seem to be possible, with ingenuity, to doctor it up to satisfy a literal, factual interpretation. It possibly could be made ready to pass through a twentieth century adding machine, with the sum of its details found to be correct. There might be a sigh of relief if this were done; but is it necessary? If the details could be tidied, would it improve the story's authenticity?—or if the details refused to be tidied, would that be cause to disregard it? It is a matter which deserves thought, because what the story represents is a central, crucial episode. Personally, I think it is a misconception to attempt to present it as a story to be made suitable to modern dress. That, to my mind, would be to miss the point that it was a story told effectively, and with important influence, in the eleventh and twelfth centuries. Regarding it as such, as legend, is not to reduce its "historical" importance; it is rather to invite attention to what the story says, and what it implies about the character of the people to whom it was addressed and who believed it; the people who evoke what they believe. This leads me to the thought that in his conquest of Britain, William was ready to exercise different policies in different parts of the island. I begin to see a general Norman policy all to the same end, but applied or evoked differently in the hitherto Saxon territory of the South, the old Romano-British territory of the West, and the territory of the Danelaw.

These different treatments of Britain I find reflected in three great legends. The first, in the South of Britain, is the almost factual story over which I have been lingering. What is interesting is that the Hardrada-Harold-William story should have been presented, or evoked, as so "almost factual." In the eleventh and twelfth centuries one might have expected a much higher content of the miraculous, of the supernatural, to be exhibited in a legend. It is as if this legend is deliberately tempered to, or tempered by, a factual-minded people. What does the legend say? It reports, on an heroic scale—but not wildly heroic—a drama of "conkers." Hardrada is a heroic warrior, easily beating Edwin and Morcar. Harold, with the support of his house carles, is an even better warrior, beating Hardrada. William is the best of warriors, beating the impetuous Harold. That is the essence of the legend. Scribes supply ramifications: in addition to the versions of the Chronicle, there are annals ascribed to "Florence of Worcester," narratives by William of Jumièges and William of Poitiers, and there is the picture-text of the Bayeux Tapestry. But the direct message of the legend is that in William of Normandy, England has found an all-conquering king; that Saxon fighters had nothing to be ashamed of—that they were let down only by their leadership. In the South of England there was to be new leadership, but otherwise "no change."

In the relevant volume of *English Historical Documents,* com-

piled and edited by Professor David Douglas, there is a good deal
to support the opinion that in the Saxon territory William at once
put it about that except for the change of leadership, there was to
be no change. It was a view not so much devised by William, as
devised by a matter-of-fact people who intended to view it that
way. Most of the Saxon nobility had to flee as fast as they could.
Some fled to Scotland, some to Flanders, and some as far as
Byzantium. At the time of the Domesday Survey in 1086 it is
rare to find a Saxon name among the greater landowners. Saxon
lands were preempted, but Professor Douglas emphasized that
William's discipline was rigid toward his fellow adventurers:
change of ownership, but otherwise, no change. William insisted
that an incoming Norman nobility should recognize, as to landholdings, the former Saxon customs. Disputes—and there were
many—among the new landlords were to be settled by legal
process, and in the great pleas which were characteristic of William's reign, appeal was regularly made to Anglo-Saxon precedent.
"It was thus under the cloak of an astute conservatism," says Professor Douglas, "that the territory of England was redistributed."

William's new polity, England, "was from its inception an
aristocracy, organized for war, and thus did it endure." England,
for the first time since the Romans, was a polity organized under
a single rule. "Of all the land of England surveyed in Domesday
Book, about a fifth was held directly by the king, about a quarter
by the Church, and nearly half by the greater followers of the
king," who were small in number and formed a close-knit group.
Under "the cloak of an astute conservatism" there was a suit of
armor. The Church had gained in landholdings; there was "the
church within the Church," preferment to the "pure," and an
increase of power to be exerted by monastic overlords. In the law
that related to landholdings, the appeal that could be made to
Anglo-Saxon precedent had to be put into the language of the
courts, which was a specialized French and Latin. The Domesday
Book was compiled in Latin. A noticeable social alteration was the
degradation in the legal status of women. The overt changes made
by the Normans seem all to stem from a conception that theirs
was a man's world, "organized for war." To the men who were to

fight for him, William went out of his way to talk in terms which
would appeal to their own pride. "It was by the service specifically
of *knights*," says Professor Douglas, "that the Norman aristocracy
held their lands, and the knight in England was himself a product
of the Norman Conquest." The word *archer* might replace the
English word *bowman*, but the all-important man on horseback
was not introduced to England as *chevalier*, but as *knight*. It paid
William handsomely to make his military service attractive to
English fighting men. There were already English soldiers in his
army when he marched against Exeter in 1068. Englishmen were
soon serving under William in his continental wars. "In 1073,"
says Professor Douglas, "many of them followed him to Maine,
and it was to an Englishman that he owed his life at the siege of
Gerberoi in 1079."

I was suggesting that the message of the Hardrada-Harold-
William legend was that it was altogether in order for a Saxon
fighter to transfer his allegiance to the king of greatest military
prowess. Among the fighters of the far West of Britain there was
a spirit not so much to be cajoled as to be revived. Here, waiting
to be reborn, were the tribal memories of Arthur, the legendary
quondam Rex que futurus, the once and future king. From under the
hill or from over the sea, Arthur would come again.

Concentrating on the affairs of Saxons and Danes, I have been
neglecting the remnants of Romano-British communities on the
other side of Britain; but if the peoples of the West had been
powerless by themselves to make head against the Saxons, that
does not mean that they had lost their memories. I would imagine
there were more memories of ancient Rome in the West country
and in Wales than in the east of Britain. A delightful example is
given to me by my mentor in such matters, Mr. D. M. Low. If in
the course of this and that you happened to wonder about the
pronunciation of Latin as the Romans might have pronounced it,
there would be small help in attending to pronunciations used
within the main bodies of the medieval church. Within Church-
dom, Mr. Low told me, there was never a standard pronunciation
of Latin. There were as many divergencies as there were in computing dates. Erasmus remarks (round about 1528) that by his
time vernacular pronunciations of Latin had gone so far astray

that speakers of different nationalities had difficulty in understanding each other's grotesque variations. Which pronunciation
was nearest to the antique Roman? Mr. Low confirmed the thought
that within this island the Britons of the West were the most
likely to have retained in use a pronunciation of Latin descending
directly from the days of the Roman occupation, and possibly
nearer to the old-fashioned usages of ancient Rome than the usages
which in Rome itself had become newer-fangled. Mr. Low reminded
me of the preface which the Saxon schoolmaster Ælfric wrote
for his school Latin grammar about the year 1000. It was courteous
of Mr. Low to remind me (for Ælfric's preface is not the sort of
drivers' license one habitually carries) and even more courteous
of him to translate for me a remark of Ælfric's which is most pleasing for its own sake:

I find it very extraordinary [said Ælfric] that many people shorten
syllables in prose which are short in verse, because prose is free from
any metrical rule. For example, they say păter in the British fashion and
mălus and so on with other syllables which are short in verse. I think
however that it is better to pray to God the Father in a dignified manner
with a long syllable rather than to shorten it as the Britons do, because
God is not to be made subservient to grammatical rules.

If Britons in the West of Britain preserved the old Roman short
syllables, it is the more probable to suppose they were retentive
of old Roman memories. The glories of the past were still to be
recited—the recollection of the *Comes Britanniae,* the *Dux Bello-
rum,* the *Imperator,* or, as the sound of the word is represented
in one of its Welsh forms, *Ameraudur.* The two carbon points
between which the arc light of legend might flare up brightly
were the readiness of the Welsh to reinterpret their ancient memories, and the readiness of the Normans to promote the reinterpre-
tation. So, to change the metaphor, the threads which pleased both
parties were picked out and woven into the great tapestry of
Arthurian legend: a re-creation of West Country pride, and an
identification of the form in which their king had come again.

A feeling about the "once and future King" is one which never
dies out among Gaelic peoples. John Rhys [4] recorded that in 1906
the time had scarcely gone

when the shepherds of North Wales used to entertain one another with stories describing one of their number finding his way to the presence of Arthur and his Men, all asleep in a Snowdonian cave resplendent with untold wealth of gold and other treasure: the armed sleepers were believed to be merely awaiting the signal for their return to take an active part in the affairs of this world. In South Wales an elaborate but popular story lodges Arthur and his Knights in a cave at Craig y Ddinas, in Glamorgan.

Stories of that kind had been traded between Britons and Bretons before Ælfric was writing his preface, and while the pious Ælfric (whose simple deism reminds us of Caedmon) was attempting to convert the Britons to a more sonorous pronunciation of the phrase for God the Father, the Normans were in a position to assist the setting off of a violent explosive power in the Briton-Breton myths. A century before their expedition into Britain, the Normans had taken over the eastern half of Brittany. Before the time of William there was talk on the Continent of "the Matter of Britain," and by degrees the stories of Arthur "under the hill" were elaborated by Norman minstrels. Arthur became a hero on the Continent, a protagonist of the "Northern" chivalry, as "real" to the imagination of the Northmen as were the other Norman heroes, Roland and Oliver. The most likely way in which the Arthurian stories reached Italy is that they were taken there by the transiently Norman conquerors. There is no doubt that the stories did reach Italy. In a primitive mosaic on the pavement of Otranto, Arthur rides again. In the Treasury of the Cathedral of Genoa there was claim to the possession of the Holy Grail. Under the crater of Mount Etna, or Mongibello, Re Artù (King Arthur) was rumored to lie buried and to await the summons to renew his championship of the Faith. What is significant is not the acceptance here or there of good stories, but the acceptance in different places of the same stories, articulated into one pattern of a chivalry of a kind at which orthodoxy in Rome might well look askance. The anger with which Rome fought "the Heresy" was partly responsible for pushing the Normans back northward and, in William's time, to Britain; and in Britain the code of chivalry which they brought with them was as acceptable to the Celtic peoples as it had been felt to be noxious in Italy, and the south of France, and Spain.

The poetical content of the Arthurian legend had special appeal in the West of Britain. It was just as much a renewal of pride for Celtic peoples in the North of Britain. There is an old volcanic vent at Edinburgh which to this day is called Arthur's Seat.[5] It is impossible that Scots would have retained the name unless some of them had wished to. No conceivable alternative derivation for the name of Arthur's Seat can alter the fact that the rock has become willingly identified with the legend. So elsewhere in Scotland. Southwest of Edinburgh, in the Border Country near Melrose, are the lovely Eildon Hills. Under those hills also sleeps Arthur, as retold for example by Leyden, who speaks of the enchanted sleep to be broken at length by someone:

> That bids the charmèd sleep of ages fly,
> Rolls the long sound through Eildon's caverns vast,
> While each dark warrior rouses at the blast,
> His horn, his falchion, grasps with mighty hand,
> And peals proud Arthur's march from Fairyland.[6]

As eventually elaborated, the Arthurian legend is identified almost as much with the North of Britain as with the West. In Malory's version it was from Orkney that King Lot's wife came richly bisene, with her four sons Gawaine, Gaheris, Agravine, and Gareth, to espy the court of King Arthur. "She was a passing fair lady, therefore the king cast great love unto her, and desired to lie by her; so they were agreed, and he begat upon her Mordred." This was the beginning of the doleful end of the whole legend, for King Lot's wife was Arthur's sister on his mother's side, and Arthur and his misbegotten son Mordred were fated to slay each other. Launcelot, the most notable of all the Arthurian heroes, is identified with the North of Britain. When Sir Launcelot's great heart was broken, and he died, his body was put in the "same horse bier that Queen Guenever was laid in tofore that she was buried" so that, according to his prayer, his corpse might be borne to his castle of Joyeuse Gard. "Some men," says Malory, "say it was Alnwick, and some men say it was Bamborough." So "they all together" went with the body of Sir Launcelot daily, "and ever they had an hundred torches burning about him. And so within fifteen days they came to Joyeuse Gard." After which, Launcelot's brother, Sir Ector, who over and again throughout the legend is pictured as seeking for Launcelot—when Ector in his seeking came to Joyeuse Gard and "heard such noise and light in the quire" he found, as he had feared, his brother dead. Ector's lament can never be forgotten:

Ah Launcelot, he said, thou were head of all Christian knights, and now I dare say, said Sir Ector, thou Sir Launcelot, there thou liest, that thou were never matched of earthly knight's hand. And thou were the courteoust knight that ever bare shield. And thou were the truest friend to thy lover that ever bestrad horse. And thou were the truest lover of a sinful man that ever loved woman. And thou were the kindest man that ever struck with sword. And thou were the goodliest person that ever came among press of knights. And thou was the meekest man and the gentlest that ever ate in hall among ladies. And thou were the sternest knight to thy mortal foe that ever put spear in the rest.

"Then there was weeping," said Malory, "and dolour out of measure."

The superb poetry and majestic sweep of Malory's version of the *Morte d'Arthur* need not prevent us from observing that the legend puts forward and extols ideas much more harsh and austere than the ideas which had obtained in Saxon society. It is the whole of Britain which is now to be comprehended in a military way. If Wales is given its place in the sun, so is Scotland. Eight of Arthur's twelve battles are represented as taking place in Scotland or Northumbria. The legend is fantasy, but the fantasy is a gloss upon an intention that the whole of the island was to be brought under the hegemony of Norman chivalry. The Roman roads spring back to a military importance which they had not had since Roman times. The roads north from Newcastle, the coast road past Alnwick, Bamborough, the Holy Isle and on from Berwick to Edinburgh, and the more direct Roman road from Corbridge and Hexham at the midpoint of the Wall across the Cheviots to Jedburgh and on to Edinburgh past Melrose and the Eildon Hills—these are pathways for the Norman legend. The physical end point of the Great North Road is now Arthur's Seat at Edinburgh. Even the farther North is brought into touch with the Great North Road. I mentioned that Orkney is brought into prominence with the fantasy of King Lot's wife and her four sons and the "many other knights and ladies" who rode southward. The riding, if we are to be practical about it, directs attention to the Great North Road. So does the fifteen-day procession which accompanied the horse bier bearing Launcelot's body, with the hundred torches, toward the "noise and light in the quire" at Joyeuse Gard.

Launcelot's body traveled the Great North Road. I find in that thought a striking contrast to the matter-of-fact part the Road played in the Hardrada-Harold-William story. The Saxon legend was, I said, a game of "conkers," reported as it were for the sports' page. Presently we shall have to deal with reactions in the South country, when it was discovered what Normans meant by "astute conservatism." But though there is contrast between the matter-of-fact Saxon legend and the wildly romantic Arthurian legend, each legend was to a large extent shaped by the peoples who accepted the Conquest either as a normal fact to be faced or as an unexpected and abnormal opportunity. The third of the great legends to be discussed—and it is perhaps the most lasting and effective of the legends of English history—was stimulated by the Norman Conquest, but contributed to not at all by the conquerors themselves. It was the legend which grew in direct hostility to the Arthurian legend. It was the legend of the Danelaw. It was the legend of resistance to authority imposed from outside. It was the legend of Robin Hood.

Launcelot's body traveled the Great North Road. I may be taken to task by those who say that the text of Sir Thomas Malory is not to be studied too literally. By the time (about 1469) that Malory had completed his compilation of the *Morte d'Arthur* from a number of French romances, the legend was no more than a storybook about a code of manners which had already passed away. But there had been a very hard core to Norman chivalry, laugh as we may at the coverings. It is not easy to describe the hard core of chivalry, because the description always involved a good deal of double talk. There are ambiguities in Ector's lament for Launcelot, as just quoted. There are ambiguities in the behavior of the Black Prince after the Battle of Poitiers:

The same day of the battle at night the prince made a supper in his lodging to the French king and to the most part of the great lords that were prisoners. The prince made the king and his son, the lord James of Bourbon, the lord John d'Artois, the earl of Tancarville, the earl of Estampes, the earl Dammartin, the earl of Joinville and the lord of Partenay to sit all at one board, and other lords, knights and squires at other tables; and always the prince served before the king as humbly as he could, and would not sit at the king's board for any desire that the king could make, but he said he was not sufficient to sit at the table with so great a prince as the king was. But then he said to the king: "Sir, for God's sake make none evil nor heavy cheer, though God this day did not consent to follow your will; for, sir, surely the king my father shall bear you as much honour and amity as he may do, and shall accord with you so reasonably that ye shall ever be friends together after. And, sir, methinks ye ought to rejoice, though the journey be not as ye would have had it, for this day ye have won the high renown of prowess and have passed this day in valiantness all other of your party. Sir, I say not this to mock you, for all that be on our party, that saw every man's deeds, are plainly accorded by true sentence to give you the prize and chaplet."

This is the account from Froissart, v. 64, 288. I note in a French edition of selections from Froissart, this is one of the passages left out. It is a passage favored by English historians as exemplifying the spirit of chivalry at its best. It is a passage not favored by the French, perhaps because within the protocol the Black Prince may be exhibiting the very mockery which he disowns. Within the élite double talk is habitual and elaborate and not easy for the simple to evaluate.

Outside the élite manners need not be explained, as later Don Quixote so exquisitely explained them to Sancho Panza. In the early days of Norman chivalry manners to the base-born need not be explained, only enforced. In the time of William the Conqueror the Norman's knightly manual was pretty much as in the twelfth century codification, written by Chrétien de Troyes and expounded from the ecclesiastical standpoint by Andrew the Chaplain. The code, as it applied to warfare, was that any base-born soldier who killed an enemy noble knight in battle was summarily to be hanged. This code is not represented in Malory as being out of date. Malory records as a matter of course that when the living Launcelot met an uncooperative carter, he struck him a "reremain," a blow on the back of the neck with his mailed fist, which stretched the carter dead. That was right conduct for a "kindest" knight, for the manners of courtesy demanded giving every "kind" of man his due. You, as the élite, determined what was due. In the spirit of chivalry as Malory records it, it would be totally wrong for the Lady Lionesse to accord to a kitchen knave anything but insults, or for Launcelot to deal with a carter except with a "reremain." Application of the code to base-born people of the Danelaw was going to lead to trouble. Launcelot's dead body, surrounded by a hundred torches, might be sent up the Great North Road; the people of the East of England preferred to invent their own symbol, the symbol of Robin Hood.

I recounted as a dearest wish of St. Augustine that a church at a town center would lead to orderly and seemly Christian behavior; yet when the house of God did begin to move to the town center, there came to be a rivalry of cathedral building which—and explain the coincidence how you may—was coincidental with the outbreak of fightings within the Church and with militant rivalries exhibited also in the Crusades. I said, you can't look at a Norman cathedral in England without wondering how it came to be there. Particularly I wonder as I stare at the great cathedrals along the Great North Road. Is it my fancy, or are they more and more like fortresses as you go northward?—St. Albans, Lincoln, York, Durham. The noble buildings are patently excessive to the needs or pride of local parishioners. The history of monastic institutions within the Danelaw suggests that for this territory St. Augustine's idea had gone wrong: a church imposed at a town center might exacerbate strife. It was where the Norman Conquest was least welcomed, and where a town life had been growing up with an independent civic consciousness, that the preemption of the town center by the Norman Church aroused the fiercest of Town and Gown feelings. Coventry, Reading, Bury St. Edmunds, or St. Albans, all within the Danelaw, might each be cited as an example of an extreme unruliness partially repressed by extreme Norman brutality. I choose St. Albans, partly because Sir William Savage, in *The Making of Our Towns*, provides the details.

From the quarter of the land of all England allotted by William to the Church came the revenues for the enormous new Church buildings. At St. Albans there was a good deal of building material ready to hand in the remains of the ruined buildings of the Roman town of Verulamium. The site of the abbey, in the present town, is across the valley from Verulamium; but the tower can be seen to have been built mainly from Roman bricks. At the beginning of the Norman régime it is likely that the building of the abbey was welcomed; there was a measure of safety in having a spiritual fortress against the possible exactions of king or barons. There were practical advantages to be expected—revenue from an influx of pilgrims, repairs to walls, roads, and bridges, and a promise of charitable aid. But if townsfolk expected too much pastoral care, it seems they were due for disappointment. Sir William Savage recounts that the direction of what was "due" seemed presently to be always due from the townsfolk to the Church:

Monastic overlords were particularly tenacious of their rights and by far the hardest from whom to obtain concessions. They represented a corporation which never died, and one bound by its constitution to oppose any relaxation of ownership or of rights. When a wise abbot realized the need for concessions he was apt to be reviled by the brethren, as when Abbot Sampson of Bury St. Edmund's Abbey commuted the servile harvest work which was in the bond for an annual reap-silver payment. The monasteries derived not only income but part of their food supply from the dues and services of the subservient towns. So long as the monastic idea represented a living spiritual force, and so long as the prestige and protection of the monastery was beneficial to the little growing town, the obligations from the town were not resented, but when the spiritual ideals of the people, and of many of the brethren, were blunted, the townspeople naturally compared their arduous lives with those of the idle well-fed monks who, to their ideas, battened upon their labours. The benefits received dwindled, the obligations remained unaltered, and they resented, sometimes with an exceeding bitterness, their prolonged servitude.

Of "impositions" by the Norman Church, Sir William Savage collects a formidable list: the most irritating, I notice, are from the Danelaw. I single out one obligation, the enforcement of which was irritating to everybody. It was the obligation to grind all corn at the abbot's mill. This, says Sir William, was objected to almost everywhere. "It was troublesome in journeys, costs charged were often high, while there were many complaints that the meal returned did not represent the grain handed over. A common evasion was for the townspeople to provide their own hand mills and occasionally, with more daring, wind or horse mills. The abbot's bailiff was constantly going round seizing and destroying hand mills and taking action in court against offenders. . . ."

It may be that apart from moneys concerned, many people actually preferred their hand mills, and found the job they could do with their hand mills was more to their liking. But they were up against a vested interest:

The townfolk of St. Albans by 1274 had gradually been using their own hand mills. . . . The bailiff of the Abbot searching houses for hand mills met with resistance. The Abbot retaliated by distraining on one of the richest townsmen for not using the Abbey mill and the burgess lost his suit in the Court and the hand mills had to be given up.

The hand mills took on symbolic importance:

In 1327 strife was much more serious. Twelve senior townsmen in the name of the inhabitants demanded from the Abbot a charter of liberties with rights of court, hand mills and the like. The Abbot took no notice so the townspeople attacked and besieged the Abbey and cut off all supplies. This went on for forty days when Edward III intervened and ordered the sheriff to restore order. He set up an Arbitration Court and this gave the burgesses most of what they wanted, but not the right to their hand mills.

Sir William Savage's narrative continues:

Only five years later the Abbot with the aid of great stores of provisions and wines for feasting the Justices, obtained a reversion so complete that the town community actually surrendered its deeds, charters, common seal, and community chest to the Abbot. After that the Abbot invited the humbled leading townsmen to dinners and an uneasy peace reigned for about fifty years. The confiscated hand mills were used to make a pavement in the Abbey cloisters. The charitable view is that they were convenient stones for a needed path but it is impossible to reject the possibility that texts about the Lord having placed his enemies under his feet may not have inspired the idea, or that pacing solemnly over them the hearts of the monks were warmed and uplifted.

All was not yet over at St. Albans:

The humbled townspeople saw their chance in 1381 when the Peasants' Risings broke out. A contingent went to St. Albans Abbey and demanded the restoration of the privileges they had lost fifty years earlier. They camped before the great gate, broke open the Abbot's prison and released the inmates. Later they burst into the cloisters and tore up the offensive pavement of millstones. The Abbot parleyed but had to give in and surrender the deeds relating to the lost liberties and these were burnt with great rejoicings near the Market Cross.

But that again was not the end of it:

The death of Wat Tyler soon after and the dispersion of the rebels quite changed matters and the King's officers came to the town, arrested the leaders and hanged some of them in the town (including John Ball) and the Abbey control was again established although shaken.

The final sentence of Sir William Savage's narrative about St. Albans is a short one:

When the Abbey fell at the Reformation no tears were shed in the town.

St. Albans, twenty miles north of London, is today an active, busy, shopping-conscious town. A long-distance motorist finds it not easy to stop. There is pressure of traffic behind. If you can stop, it is worth stopping at St. Albans. There is a reminder of the contest in which the hand mills became symbolic. In the market place of St. Albans there is a bell tower, not for church bells but for town bells. The ancient warfares have been to some extent composed, or altered. Most parishes in England are now I believe content to accept an impartial "siren" or "maroon" as a summons to people for what in the old phrase was called "fire or fray." There is no remnant of hostility between a civic summons and a summons by church bells. But here or there in the Danelaw (or what used to be the Danelaw) you find reminders of village bells which were in opposition to the Church: at Aldworth in Berkshire, for example, not far from Reading. Here at St. Albans, in the market square, remains the belfry set up by the town in opposition to the abbey. The earlier of its two bells dates from the fourteenth century.

As, today, you go east or north throughout the Danelaw Country, there are frequently traces of the especially bitter resistance with which the people of the Danelaw opposed the Norman Conquest in both of its aspects, the aspect of military command and the aspect of the Church militant. The evidence of Norman castles, keeps, and military strongpoints indicates the firmness with which the land had to be held; and one cannot look at the great hilltop cathedrals, Lincoln, York, Durham, without feeling that they are fortress-like. Against such obvious evidences of Norman strength one feels it is weak and puny to assert the Robin Hood legend. Yet it is interesting how the Robin Hood legend remains. Robin Hood is to this day identified with many specific localities: with Huntingdon, Sherwood Forest, Robin Hood's Hill near Sutton Bank in Yorkshire, Robin Hood's Bay five miles south of Whitby. The characters of Robin Hood's band of outlaws are each, in his way, in spontaneous opposition to characters of the Arthurian legend. This legend of the resistance was not written up by scribes, it was not brought together by a Malory; it was communicated mainly in ballads. The balladry was later on known by, for instance, Shakespeare and Ben Jonson, but there was never in it a book to reach Court or Society with such acceptance as was given to Malory's *Morte d'Arthur.* Yet the balladry was vital enough to invite the kind of treatment which a society often accords to a criticism which is too subversive to be accepted, but too general to be ignored; I mean the turning off of a criticism which is serious, by adopting it as a story suitable only for children.

This procedure whereby a hostile legend is adopted and accepted as being softer than it is, is familiar. *The Pilgrim's Progress* or *Gulliver's Travels* become books for children. The big legends are "editorialized" before being accepted. Antipathetic elements were removed from the *Morte d'Arthur* before (in Andrew Lang's version) it ever reached my youthful eye, and supposedly sympathetic additions were made to the Robin Hood story before (in Howard Pyle's version) it came to my nursery. Who, I wonder, was the first editor who felt the Robin Hood story would be the more acceptable by making him out to be the son of an Earl of

Huntingdon? And who, I wonder, took the color away from
Robin Hood, and clothed him, and Will Scarlet, in green? Green
was the color of a king's verderer; green was the color of a game-
keeper: it was a low trick, I think, to accept the legend of Robin
Hood by making him change his color.

It was all right, indeed it was necessary to the plot of the *Morte
d'Arthur*, to make Launcelot travel at times incognito. Was Malory,
I wonder, aware of the Robin Hood legend? If Launcelot was by
design associated with the country of the Danelaw, his character,
among the knights of the Round Table, was the least unsuited to the
part. In Malory's stories of Launcelot there are more than occasional
touches of ballad humor. One episode in particular makes me think
of Sherwood Forest. The episode as Malory tells it took place in the
forest of Windsor, where Launcelot was resting with a good hermit
(his name was Sir Brasias) before the joust which was to take place
"beside Westminster upon Candlemas Day":

And when he was come to the hermitage, wit ye well he had good
cheer. And so daily Sir Launcelot would go to a well fast by the hermitage, and there he would lie down, and see the well spring and bubble,
and sometime he slept there. So at that time there was a lady dwelt
in that forest, and she was a great huntress, and daily she used to hunt,
and ever she bare her bow with her. . . . So it happed this lady the
huntress had baited her dog for the bow at a barren hind, and so this
barren hind took the flight over hedges and woods . . . and so it
happed, the hind came to the well whereas Sir Launcelot was sleeping
and slumbering. . . . Right so came that lady the huntress . . . and
she put a broad arrow in her bow, and shot at the hind, and
overshot the hind; and so by misfortune the arrow smote Sir Launcelot
in the thick of the buttock, over the barbs. When Sir Launcelot felt
himself so hurt, he hurled up woodly, and saw the lady that had smitten
him. And when he saw she was a woman, he said thus: Lady or damosel,
what that thou be, in an evil time bear ye a bow; the devil made you
a shooter.[7]

There is in Malory a lot of detail about that wound, which was
"six inches deep, and in like long," and it "was passing sore, and
unhappily smitten, for it was in such a place that he might sit in
no saddle." But clearly it was Launcelot's own fault for sleeping
and slumbering in such a camouflaged way. In the hunting season

in the United States or Canada nobody but a nitwit would go into the woods except in the brightest of jackets, and in Sherwood Forest, what time Robin Hood and his trigger-happy bowmen were looking for deer, their sensible attire was not green but scarlet. There were, as we discussed, the three Lincoln "grains." I have no doubt Robin Hood rang the changes; but when he and his men wished to be conspicuous, I am sure they wore the best stuff, scarlet. The essence of the Robin Hood legend is, he and his men were not a beaten lot. They could do just as well for themselves as they chose. When it pleased them, I am confident that they wore red coats. That was their happiest recognizable uniform. I would rest the case upon the names—Robin Hood, Will Scarlet.

VII »» *The Road North and the Road South*

I was hoping to gain an impression of the Norman invaders
of Britain by contemplating their behavior in the hostile territory
of the Danelaw. It was obvious that the Conquest at once altered
the character of the Great North Road and made it into a military
highway based on the Tower of London. I believed this to have
been resented within the Danelaw with especial bitterness, and
believed the resistance to have been harshly put down. Historians
agree about William's harshness in Yorkshire. York was a point
of concentration for the resistance. William captured the town
in 1068 and planted a castle—some say more than one—with a garrison of, I suppose, partially Saxon soldiery. As soon as William
turned his back, the garrison was attacked and overwhelmed. William returned and burned the whole town of York. There is a scar
across the history of York in the late eleventh century. After William's revenge on York, he spent the next months ravaging the

manors and farms between the Ouse and Tyne, and occupants who resisted, according to the Chronicles, were simply slaughtered. "The desolation in Yorkshire," says Mr. Jerrold, "was enormous." This may not have killed "the sullen, self-willed, local Yorkshire nature" [1]—that was a phrase used seven centuries later at the time of the repression of mill riots in the 1850's—but the Norman terror would scarcely have encouraged much love for the great fortress-like cathedrals which, after the invasion, so demonstrably asserted the dominance, on the hilltops, of a seemingly cruel religion. Lincoln, York, Durham: you can't forget their militancy as you motor today along the Great North Road. Today they may all, if you wish, be by-passed: they could not be by-passed then.

Yet the moment you turn off the Great North Road you have, in Yorkshire, a more humane feeling about the Norman Conquest. I mentioned the hatreds, as at St. Albans or Bury St. Edmund's, where an abbey had been planted at the center of an existing town: sad comment indeed on Augustine's original pious hope. There is no such feeling where an order planted a monastic institution in a relatively vacant place and, afterward, a town accreted willingly around it: Peterborough, for instance. And I don't detect any emanation of hostility from Robin Hood when I contemplate the ruins of the Cistercian monasteries set away off the main road, in lonely places, not on the hilltops, but each of them low down, beside a bend of a small river. Among the many I would pick out Rievaulx. It seems to me a strange thing that Rievaulx was later on plundered and knocked down, and that the cathedrals at Lincoln, York, Durham remain. But that was, as it worked out, king's business. There is no record of hostility by Robin Hood to such a tempting low-set foundation as Rievaulx upon which at any moment, had he wished, his men could have dropped down from the hills. We have to explain to ourselves why unprotected Rievaulx was not molested by the Yorkshire countryman. The Yorkshire countryman might hate the Norman hawks with ineradicable hatred; but the hawks were too strong. The Yorkshire countryman might have plucked the sitting pigeons, the isolated monasteries, but he didn't. Why?

I am at one of those roundabouts in the road and have to make a choice of speculations. I am going to speculate about cheese.

When discussing the small group of words imposed by the Romans in Britain and accepted by Britons before the Roman legions withdrew, I wondered if the word *cheese* might not have been included. *Caseus* was the common term in Latin before the fifth century, adopted as the Italian *cacio*, Spanish *queso*, and Teutonic *kase*. (The Italian *formaggio* and the French *fromage* seem to come from the later Latin word *formaticus*.) Throughout the Roman occupation of Britain the staple issue in the army rations of those who built the roads was *caseus*, and I don't think linguists boggle at identifying *caseus* and *cheese*. So, having thought about road making in Britain, I began to think about cheese making. There is a treatise by Palladius on agriculture which describes Romano-British farming practice about the year 300, and the then cheese making methods, but that is too far to go back. Here what I wish to consider is a continuity of cheese making as developed by Romans in Britain, as then taken over by Saxons, as then taken over in the Norman times, and as obtaining, generally speaking, into the fourteenth century or later. I don't see how we can avoid thinking about the production of a most important staple food which could be stored against the winter.

Convinced that the story of cheese must be looked into, I sought out Miss Val Cheke's book on *Cheese-Making in Britain*.[2]

In Saxon times [says Miss Cheke] the shepherd milked his flocks of ewes twice daily and also made the butter and the cheese. His special concessions were the receipt of one lamb for the year, one bell-wether's fleece, and the milk from the flock over the seven nights after the equinox. He was additionally allowed to fold the flock on his own land for 12 mid-winter nights, so that his pasturage strips could have the benefit of the manure. During the summer he received a bowl of whey, or buttermilk, every night, but during the winter he seems to have had a hard time. His extras, in the form of the dried meat from one lamb, and rancid butter and lard, skim milk cheese from his seven days' allowance of milk, were little enough with which to improve his diet of cereals. If he were fortunate, he might also possess a few stock animals of his own.

The dairymaid also

. . . had a hard life, and in early days was bound to provide the lord's buttery with a hundred cheeses every year, and to make butter for his table from the "wring" whey. Such butter, later known as "whey butter," was churned from the waste fat obtained by skimming the whey. She was allowed to keep the buttermilk from the churnings, except for the allowance to the shepherd, and also the skimmed whey during the summer. Like other female serfs, she received additionally 8 pounds of corn, a sheep for winter food, and beans to use during Lent.

I remarked that an immediate effect of the impact of Norman chivalry was to downgrade the legal status of females. I learn from Miss Cheke's book it was not only ladies whose status was reduced, but also dairymaids. After the Norman Conquest, tasks which had hitherto been shared by men and women were regarded as women's work. The shepherd continued to milk his sheep, but was no longer responsible for making the milk into butter and cheese. He simply delivered the milk to the dairymaid, who had to take on all the rest of the work. She got no benefit from the extra labor involved. She was merely bidden "to keep herself clean and know her business."

After the Norman Conquest one begins to be more aware of the idea of division of labor. The manors and farms in Yorkshire which survived William's devastation were naturally, as before, concentrating on production and storage of winter food for both man and animals. A question is, Was there much surplus? The implanting of large new monasteries in country places makes one wonder about their own food supply. It is recorded[3] that Rievaulx Abbey under the third abbot, Ailred (1147–1166) was populated by 140 monks and 600 lay brothers, "so that the church swarmed with them, like a hive with bees." I never know whether to believe in statistics, but the stones of Rievaulx assure me that there was a large establishment to be fed throughout the year. One credits Miss Cheke's comment that such a monastery made an important contribution to the husbandry of its neighborhood; indeed, one credits that when such a monastery was planted in a wilderness it had to create a new husbandry. Thus one believes a monastery attracted employment and created a neighborhood. In Yorkshire the devastation attributed to William may have been to a considerable extent repaired by the planting of the monasteries. "The accounts of Bolton Abbey," says Miss Cheke, "show that 147 stones of ewes' milk cheese were consumed there during the year

1310." The lay brethren did not do all the work. "At Malhamdale the ewes were milked by women who were in the Prior's employ, and they made cheese." The prior made it a condition that "only old and ill-favoured females should be employed." Never mind the condition: it was a creation of employment. The employment had lasting effect. "For example, the monks of Jervaulx Abbey in Yorkshire possessed a method of making cheese from ewes' milk from which was eventually evolved the famous cheeses made in the Yorkshire dales."

One sees then the development in Yorkshire, as an adjunct to the monasteries, of cheese factories. This brings in a further thought about the number of ewes required. It is an arithmetical question: If Rievaulx Abbey in the twelfth century had 740 mouths to be fed the year round, how many ewes were needed for the cheese factory? And weren't there other mouths to be fed outside the boundaries of the monastery?

I think of Helmsley Castle, the ruins of which you see today not far from Rievaulx, and I think of the other Norman castles built in the Yorkshire dales. There are many of them. Stand and stare in the ruins: What did their masters eat? Even in so notable a castle as at Richmond I have not been able to conjure up a feeling that the castle represented a gracious way of living, or a way which represented any idea of being self-contained and homelike. Richmond, Bolton, Helmsley—I feel that when their rulers were for the moment at home they were, when possible, meat eaters. I am not surprised to find that the words *beef* and *mutton* were brought into our language by the Normans; and the word *butcher*. I have the fancy that the food which was most esteemed in the castles was that which was foraged. The word *venison* came in with the Normans, and in their usage meant the flesh of any game killed in the chase and used as food. Venison might be *fish, flesh* or *fowl;* the flesh might be that of *deer, boar, hare* or even *rabbit.* All of these italicized words, except *rabbit,* are found in the English language before the Normans came, but the Normans organized the hunting and hawking and dignified the product as game or venison. *Rabbit,* and the alternative word *cony* or *coney,* are both of Norman introduction, and as the animal has no native name in Celtic or Teutonic languages and as there is no mention of it in

Britain before the Norman period, the rabbit itself has been regarded as a late arrival in Britain and northern Europe. In the
earliest quotations it is the fur of the rabbit which is mentioned
and which was perhaps imported before the animal. When rabbits
escaped into the countryside, they soon became poor-man's venison
and poor-man's fur. The word *cony* occurs in the English Bible.
Smart, in his instructions to clergymen in 1836, remarks that cony
"is familiarly pronounced *cunny,* but cōny is proper for solemn
reading."

The esteem with which "venison" or "game" is still regarded in
Britain carries a feeling of its being regarded as an extra to the
routine, a special "treat." The word "treat," in this sense, is puzzling:
it comes into English from the French, and it carries an overtone
of condescension, but whether the word came in with the Normans is hard to say. I would be sure though that the steward
of a Yorkshire castle (the word *steward* seems to be Norman)
could not always count on a sufficiency of venison, especially
when coping with unexpected guests or late arrivals. The idea of
a "treat" carries with it the idea that diet was normally routine;
and thinking of Helmsley Castle I am wondering what the steward
did about such a routine item as cheese, or about preserving beef
or mutton for future eating. Vineyards had been planted by the
Romans in Britain, and it has been suggested that their vineyards
were not so much for the production of a wine for drinking as for
the making of vinegar as a preservative. After the Roman times,
vinegar as a word seems to fade; other words in English suggestive
of food preservation, such as *smoke, dry, salt, pickle, brine,* all
come in from Teutonic sources before the Norman period; and
then the word *vinegar* revives. I think it revives with the monasteries; they revived viniculture. Where did the steward of Helmsley
go for his vinegar? Where did he go for a sudden demand for
poultry or fish? Words connected with domestic fowl, such as
chicken, hen, goose, egg, are all well established in the English
language before the Norman period. I assume that monasteries had
their country suppliers; I assume that for the routine husbandry of
cheese, poultry, greens—and that puzzling problem, fish—monasteries were better equipped than castles. In other words, I see
Rievaulx Abbey as a food factory, large for its own needs, but also

enlarged for the needs of others: I see that for Helmsley Castle the monastery at Vievaulx was the "neighborhood store."

Lewis Mumford, almost thirty years ago, brilliantly expounded the thesis in *Technics and Civilization*,[4] that the Industrial Revolution might be regarded as an extremely rapid speeding up of a factory system which was already preexistent, and he associated the beginnings of the factory system with the sound of the monastery bell. I cannot explain the transformation of the Danelaw except by the thesis propounded by Mumford. And the transformation of the Danelaw is so striking that an explanation is cried out for.

The transformation of which I am speaking is forced on me by the contrast of two maps of Britain which are side by side upon my study wall. One of the maps is the Ordnance Survey Map of Roman Britain.[5] It is a colored map, and the colors are lightish colors, light greens and yellows and browns. The roads show up on the map, and the towns and ports of the East and South show nobly. Western ports scarcely exist: Bristol makes but a small mark, and Liverpool makes no mark at all. Apart from the roads, the dramatic features of the map of Roman Britain are the red necklace around the neck of Scotland, representing the forts imposed by Agricola, and the red breastworks, representing Hadrian's Wall, tightly stretched across the bust of England. Except for the removal of these red features a map of Britain at the time of the Norman monasteries would show little alteration. The map at the time of the Normans is still to be limned in light colors. But if I turn to the other map, a road map of Britain today, the alteration is, of course, fantastic. Where in the Roman map there had been the thin red necklace of Agricola's forts, there is on the present-day map the heavy black collar of factories from Edinburgh to Glasgow. Where on the old map Lincoln, York, Durham stand out boldly, on the new map, if I look at it across the room, they are difficult to descry. The inescapable dramatic feature of the present map is the wide black belt across the center of the island. Across the room I can see the black splodges which represent Leeds, Wakefield, Sheffield; Bradford, Halifax, Huddersfield; Blackburn, Bolton, Manchester; Preston, Liverpool. That is the Danelaw. Let your eye trace the ancient area southward through Birmingham to the great wen of London, it is the blackness which defines it on the map. Light-colored when the monasteries first arrived in the Danelaw, the area now displays itself on the map as black. How does such a change come about?

In Yorkshire there was an intermediate stage in the transformation; the decimation of the villages, the "enclosures." This was perhaps a general change all over the Danelaw: it is for Yorkshire alone that I happen to find the figures. I consider the figures before I consider the argument. On the time scale I am moving forward from the period of the Norman Conquest, when the Great North Road began to bring the great cathedrals and the monasteries and the castles into Yorkshire, to the middle of the fourteenth century, when it might be thought the new dispensation could have settled. It is at that point that the first great change in the map of Yorkshire is noticeable: the change from arable land to pasture—the increasing number of deserted villages, the detachment of peasants from "their" land. In the Lay Subsidy for 1344 there are 544 villages listed in the West Riding of Yorkshire. Of those villages, 30 have completely disappeared. In the North Riding, of 453 villages existing in 1344, 39 have disappeared; in the East Riding, of 366 villages in the mid-fourteenth century, 49 have disappeared. It is not strictly accurate to speak of decimation, for of the total of 1,363 Yorkshire villages tabulated in 1344 it is only 118 which have completely vanished; not strictly 10 per cent. The percentage is near enough to make the exaggeration pardonable; and though I don't know where I am with statistics, I admit a curiosity to have the figures explained. I take the figures from *The Lost Villages of England* by Maurice Beresford.[6] Mr. Beresford maintains that despite the initial harshness of the Norman Conquest the Yorkshire villages had scratched back into subsistence, that they had survived the Black Death, that they were no more than irritated by occasional inroads of Scottish raiders; but that what the villagers were powerless to resist was an ever-increasing demand for more and more sheep land.

The theme of "the man-eating sheep" was a preoccupation of Parliament and legislators and of moralists before and after Thomas More coined the phrase. Shakespeare regarded it as good theater to comment on the avarice engendered by the wool trade; Mr.

Beresford reminds us of the scene in the second Act of *Pericles,
Prince of Tyre,* wherein the shipwrecked prince is overhearing
a conversation between fishermen, who talk in allegory about
politics. Among the themes is the destruction of the villages of
England. The first Fisherman puts it this way:

> I can compare our rich misers to nothing so fitly as a whale. A' plays
> and tumbles, driving the poor fry before him, and at last devours them
> all at a mouthful: such whales have I heard on i' the land, who never
> leave gaping till they've swallowed the whole parish, church, steeple,
> bells and all.

Pericles, in an aside, remarks, "A pretty moral." That the driving
away of "the poor fry" from their habitat remained a perennial
theme is sufficiently recalled by Goldsmith's *The Deserted Village:*

> Ill fares the land, to hastening ills a prey,
> Where wealth accumulates, and men decay.

By Goldsmith's time wealth was accumulating from many sources
other than from the wool trade and cloth making, and the green
pastures of Yorkshire which for the sake of the man-eating sheep
had eliminated so many villages, were themselves in process of
elimination. Raw materials such as cotton were coming in from
overseas. The green lands were beginning to turn black with
"dark Satanic mills." The second stage setting of the map of Yorkshire had begun, but it had been suggested by the first stage setting.

And so, to swing back to the Great North Road at the time of
the Norman Conquest, the argument has been this: that when the
Normans revived it as a main military road and pushed their
institutions northward—cathedrals, castles, monasteries on a scale
much larger than had ever been known in the North Country
before—food factories became of increasing importance. As one
of the staple foods, I thought about cheese, and of cheese making
on a large scale as inviting a factory system. I couldn't do my
arithmetical sum, how many ewes required to supply cheese for
monasteries and castles all the year round, but I could imagine that
the cheese factory also produced a quantity of by-products:

mutton, parchment, wool. I could imagine the potential of those by-products, especially wool. I could think of Robin Hood looking down upon Rievaulx Abbey with a friendly eye because it was providing employment and food and clothing for those of his people who had an instinct for factory work. But there was almost too much of that instinct. Looking backward, if I had found a temptation to agree that the upper-class Norman had brought from France what we called "the Heresy," I felt an equal temptation to think that the Danes of the Danelaw had a particular bent for a heresy of their own. Even in those early days I felt there were incipient Puritans. It was perhaps a dangerous thing to introduce into green valleys the sound of the monastery bell, among people who could regard it mainly as a work bell. The by-product of wool emerged as having unexpected potentialities for a trade which could transcend monastic control. I may be forgiven for not attempting to pursue the economic consequences of the wool trade; my concern at this roundabout was to meditate that the Normans, pushing north through the Danelaw, provided impetus for the incalculable results of industrialization; and one of the harmless-looking little bombs which started things off, might, I thought, be cheese.

Despite the attention which the Normans paid to the development of that part of the Great North Road which stretched northward from the Tower of London, despite the firmness and the intended permanence of their hold on the Danelaw, I don't feel that William and his military élite ever forgot that their main interest was southward. Britain was to be captured, dominated, maintained forever as the "keep"; but the capture and maintenance of Britain was not the sole object. The Conquest exhibits a temper which is strikingly different from that of the previous Saxon and Danish immigrations. Saxons and Danes had each come to stay in the island, and however they bickered, were concerned only with domestic warfare. Saxons and Danes were both predominantly isolationist; it was within the island that each developed a way of life. But when I confessed that standing in the ruins of one or other of the Norman castles in the North Country I couldn't feel that their inhabitants had much feeling for a gracious way of living, it was, I thought, because their hearts were not really there—not even "there" to the extent of the Roman governor who planted periwinkles in his flower garden. Norman nobility was not inclined to stay home. The Great North Road was for the Norman nobility a road of capture northward, but so soon as Britain was captured, there was to be capture in the opposite direction, capture on the Continent. The rejoined Great North Road was to stretch south from the Tower of London, south as far as it had ever stretched, south as far as Rome or farther.

I am impressed not so much by William's instant militancy (as soon as matters in Britain were organized he was off to his foreign wars) as by the scale of the long-term intentions of William's successors. Here London Bridge comes again into the narrative, and this time there is no question mark about it. Before the Tower of London was completed, the new stone bridge was projected, to go across London River.[7] This was the famous London Bridge of which Jusserand speaks as "the great national wonder." Jusserand mentions that a previous wooden contraption had already been repaired by Peter Colechurch, "priest and chaplain"—and possibly it had been repaired many times before him—when in 1176 Colechurch was commanded to commence the new stone structure. The Frenchman Isembert, "master of the Saintes schools," was brought in to complete the work, and completed it was in 1209. In their first centuries in England the amount of building achieved by the Normans is almost incredible: consider this bridge. It had twenty arches, based upon wide stone piers. The thirteenth arch from the City side formed a drawbridge so that ships might pass. The bridge was wide enough to have houses on it on both sides, with a street in the center. It had its own chapel; it had defensive towers; since tolls were levied, it must have had tollgates or their equivalent. Jusserand says the houses on the bridge were suggested by a certain John Lackland, who vaunted that they would provide revenue to maintain the bridge for ever. The house idea caught on; there is the evidence of sixteenth century drawings that by that time the houses on the bridge had been built up to heights of four and five stories; they had cellars in the thickness of the piers; when the inhabitants needed water they lowered buckets by ropes out of the windows and filled them in the Thames. From the beginning London Bridge possibly did more to establish

Cockney pride than did the cathedrals, and it was certainly a phenomenon to astonish visitors. Lyly, in *Euphues and his England*, remarks:

Among all the strange and beautiful showes, mee thinketh there is none so notable as the Bridge which crosseth the Theames, which is in manner of a continuall streete, well replenyshed with large and stately houses on both sides, and situate upon twentie arches, whereof each one is made of excellent free stone squared, everye one of them being three-score foote in height, and full twentie in distance one from another.

This very remarkable structure was to remain London's only bridge for more than five hundred years, until the middle of the eighteenth century.

One could easily become preoccupied with the story of London Bridge. Sometimes there is a boisterousness about the story, and sometimes the story is not pretty. The houses do not seem to have attracted the best of London's inhabitants, nor was the house property at all times so profitable as John Lackland had predicted. It happened occasionally, Jusserand lightly remarks, that the houses, badly repaired, hung forward and fell in one block into the river. "A catastrophe of this kind took place in 1481." There must have been a lot of horseplay about the buckets let down into the river and about things flung down from upper stories upon passengers in the central street. There was on the bridge a horrible form of poll tax. On the City side of the drawbridge was the tower on the summit of which the executioner had the privilege of exhibiting, on pikes, the heads he had cut off. The better known the head, the better the ransom. The head of Sir Thomas More was exposed on London Bridge until the price of redemption was paid by his daughter, Margaret Roper. Such horrors were for a long time tolerated. There were eventually efforts to clean up the bridge. In 1576 a new, gay building called None-Such House, five stories high, made of wood, carved and gilt in the best Elizabethan "paperworke" style, replaced the previous executioner's tower. After that heads were no longer exhibited north of the drawbridge, but only on the next tower on the Southwark side.

Despite John Lackland's boast, revenue from the houses on

London Bridge was never regarded as the only revenue the bridge
could offer. There were tolls to be paid by passengers, animals
and vehicles of every quality and description. Jusserand quotes
from the list of tariffs of the year 1306, covering both the commodities which might cross the bridge, or which in ships might
pass through the drawbridge. Jusserand comments that the list
in full takes up no less than four pages of printed matter: stating
the tariffs on coals, timber, wines, beer, horses, sheep, butter and
cheese, fish, millstones, silk and other cloths; and sometimes "the
place they come from is given: Flanders, Normandy, etc." The
tariffs on bridge traffic may have been a stimulus to boatmen on
the Thames; I suppose the bridge revenue was mainly from horse
and wagon traffic. For river traffic up and down the stream the
bridge was never anything but a notable impediment. Coming
downstream, except at slack water and especially at nighttime it
was an adventure to "shoot" the bridge: an adventure from which
the Duke of Norfolk was luckily rescued from drowning in 1428;
some of his companions were drowned. For traffic coming up-
stream the drawbridge was from the beginning boycotted by
shipmasters. They preferred to berth below the Bridge, and so,
by degrees, was formed the Pool of London. To a shipmaster
London Bridge was a splendid inducement to sail anywhere else
the world over, except through the drawbridge. On occasion
I suppose the drawbridge was raised, but the only occasion I find
recorded—and recorded as an event which was unusual—was at
Wyatt's rebellion in 1554.

The fascinating story of London Bridge must not distract me
from what I regard as the original Norman intention, which was
to make it the beginning of the road for conquest southward.
The houses on the Bridge, the somewhat comical blockage that
it proved to be to river traffic, should not obscure what seems to
me the harsh austerity of the design. The dominant thoughts in
the Tower of London seem all to have been directed southward.
Southward, what was that solid bridge across the Thames to
carry? Soldiers. That was a first purpose. The bridge pointed to
any of the Channel ports, where the Road south took to the sea.
This meant a change of vehicle, no change of impulse. The many
who crossed the bridge could capture the channel:

Cheryse marchandyse, kepe thamyralte
That we be maysteres of the narowe see.

New edicts were issuing from the Tower of London: the narrow seas were to become the English Channel. The islanders were to be masters and to keep the admiralty. Nor was it only the narrow seas: the Bay of Biscay was to become an English lake. Nor was it only the Bay of Biscay: it was the Mediterranean.

The first occasion when there was need for a fleet of larger size was for transport for the crusade of Richard I in 1189. This fleet, which numbered upwards of a hundred vessels, purchased and hired from all the ports of England, Normandy, and Poitou, sailed as a unit. . . . All masters of ships were to show obedience . . . and at night a lantern was hung from the mast of the king's ship to keep the fleet together "as a hen gathers her chickens."

This is a quotation from Miss K. M. E. Murray's contribution to Austin Lane Poole's symposium on *Medieval England*. The phrase "need for a fleet of larger size" is explained, that it was under the Normans that English ships began to be offensive. Previously there had been English "war-ships" for defense of the island; there had been no fleets organized for the attack of foreign territory. Up to Norman times there had been an increase of English trading ships. By the time of the Conquest "the bulk of the ships engaged in the wine trade with Gascony were English, and the capacity of all ships was estimated in the number of casks of Bordeaux wine that they could carry, a ton in two casks occupying sixty cubic feet of space."

The size of ships is still gauged in tonnage, a measure of volume. The mention that in early days of the Bordeaux wine trade the ton was reckoned as sixty cubic feet is an interesting reminder of the ancient and persistent importance of the number "sixty," a number used in Babylon, and by the Phoenicians, and then by all Mediterranean peoples in the measurement of time and angles. "Sixty" goes on ticking away at us every minute, and it has played a formative part in the development of Western navigation. At the time the term "tonnage" was being co-opted into English shipbuilding, the navigators of Venice, Genoa, and Pisa were

using "sixties" as direction finders on long-range charts, dividing
the compass into 360 degrees, and constructing instruments which
were forerunners of the sextant. The Normans from Britain displayed small interest in such "art" of navigation, as it was in
their time developing among the Mediterranean peoples; they
displayed relatively little mercantile interest in "tonnage" as a
measurement for carriage of wine or trade goods; they displayed
enormous interest in the conversion of the trading ships, the
"round cogs," into fighting ships adapted for offensive action. It
was apparently the Normans who developed deckhouses (the
phrase is reminiscent of London Bridge) and even "castles" (of
which "fo'c'sle" is a relic) aboard ship. Awkward and clumsy and
indeed unseaworthy as their castellated cogs may have been, a
very great advance is indicated over the ships depicted in the
Bayeaux tapestry; but the advance, it seems to me, was dedicated
to the one purpose of military transport. It was the Great North
Road going south. So soon as the Normans had planted castles
all the way northward along the Great North Road, they shot the
road southward from the Tower of London, planting houses on
London Bridge and planting castles on their ships. They were not
out for exploration or primarily for trade; they were out to plant
their castles in France, in Spain, and in the Holy Land.

There may have been heady thoughts in the Tower of London.
There may have been ideas of a Holy Norman Empire, or thoughts
of capturing the papacy and transferring it to Canterbury. We
don't know what the Normans thought, but we can see what they
did; and of their deeds, what causes me astonishment is the
psychological fixation that the Normans, Northmen, had for the
South. It is as if they read the primitive compass needle, rubbed
with a lodestone and floating in water, the wrong way round.
Italian voyagers were beginning to probe westward, bringing
back canary birds to join their beccaficos, bringing back such
wondrous little things as fireflies, bringing back the beginnings
of dreams about the far side of the world—for those dreams were
starting in the Mediterranean while Northmen were dreaming
no other dream than the ancient dream of armed robbery in the
established South. While Mediterranean peoples were beginning
to think of discoveries, Norman types from Britain were still

obsessed with recovery of the Holy Grail, and with the general idea of plundering the southerners. The whole of the Southland was to be their hawks' meat, their venison. Incidentally their ships had to be sturdy, and Englishmen and English seamen had to learn to fight, for they were brought into brushes with Saracens, with the pirates of Tripoli, with Balearic slingers, with Spaniards who showed no softness to the Northern idea of planting castles in Spain.

The persistence of the Norman idea of driving their Road southward is demonstrated by their actions, and equally demonstrated by the myth which was built up that their Continental actions were successful; which, patently, they were not. The facts are simple. Despite notable battles and glorious victories told of and retold (Crécy and Agincourt) the Norman-English could not hold their winnings. For three hundred years or more they could cherish the belief that the crown of France was hardly more than a mark for English bowmen; yet all the while their persistent efforts were pushed back. The warships with the castles on them were of small use, and one by one the garrisons on land were given up. Gone were the far-flung dreams of the Holy Land, of Norman Empire on the Continent; the Norman leadership could not even hold France. From Gascony and Guienne, and later on from Bordeaux and eventually from Calais—Calais, no more than swimming distance from the south coast of Britain—the Northmen were evicted. The Great North Road was once more cut and was never again to be a highway for lasting territorial conquest on the Continent.

During that three hundred years of effort to push the Road southward from London Bridge, remnants of the expeditionary forces came back across the Bridge in mood less cheerful than the mood in which they had set forth. Hard-bitten leaders, unable to expend their militancy on the Continent, were the more ripe to quarrel among themselves. When the Great North Road was for the first time severed, that had led, I was maintaining, to the birth of the English language. When, after the Norman Conquest a southward push was stopped and the road was for a second time severed, the immediate result was the Wars of the Roses. The statement needs to be examined. It is accepted that when Norman adventurers found themselves penned up in the cockpit of England, they should fight among themselves and kill each other off; but what have the roads to do with it? They have this to do: that the same military roads which were initiated by Aulus Plautius to radiate from London were available as the main military roads to radiate toward London. When there were no real castles in Spain to be assailed, there yet remained one castle of enormous significance: the Tower of London. Not from that center, but toward that center, the military roads now led.

I pause to consider how frequently a noisy and dramatic action diverts attention from the real, if more quiet, business of the day. During the Wars of the Roses there were many remarkable headline flutters. There was the coincidence that when Lancastrian forces were marching toward the Tower of London along Watling Street (now on the road map called Route A5), the Yorkists with the same intent were simultaneously marching south along the Great North Road (our Route A1). The junction of those two great roads always has been, and is, at Barnet. By accident of timing the rival forces met at the road junction. Could they have made a common purpose they might, one feels, have captured London; but as each party was out for priority at the road junction, they paused to make such mutual havoc that neither party was able to get anywhere nearer the Tower of London. The Battle of Barnet was in effect no more than an unusually nasty street accident. What seems to me of more lasting moment is that at the time of the Battle of Barnet the Tower of London had already been quietly captured by a third party, and, however difficult to do so, it is of paramount importance in the story of the Great North Road to keep an eye on this anonymous party, the "City" of London. At the Battle of Barnet (in 1471) was killed Warwick the "Kingmaker," but the title was already an anachronism. The growing forces coming into being were Parliament and the City.

When the Great North Road was blocked to the southward, when that stone bridge over the Thames must have seemed, as to its original purpose, overambitious, when grandiose military adventurings kept on being talked about but kept on being clipped, what was it that shaped the institutions I have mentioned, Parliament and the City? Did each institution in its way exhibit a shared distaste for the wanton behavior of warriors who might have seemed fine men so long as they were overseas, but who were desperadoes when they hung around at home? Of what use within England was a chivalry as practiced in the daily life of Sir Thomas Malory? I quote from a study of Malory by Miss M. C. Bradbrook:

Sir Thomas Malory came from Shakespeare's county of Warwickshire, and his family estate was at Newbold Revell. As a young man, in 1436 he served in the train of the great Richard Beauchamp, Earl of Warwick. Later he entered Parliament. But such records as survive of Malory's middle years show the depressing picture of an old fighter turned gangster. He stole cattle and does; broke into an abbey; robbed under threats of violence; and even planned to ambush and murder the Duke of Buckingham. His one recorded amorous exploit is the felonious ravishing of Joan, wife of Henry Smyth, of Monks' Kirby, near Newbold Revell. All these events took place within some eighteen months of each other in 1450–1. Twice he broke jail, once by swimming the castle moat at Coleshill and once by fighting his way out at Colchester. So began his career of imprisonment, punctuated by spells of freedom, in which he later developed a taste for horse-stealing. He was imprisoned again, released again, and even returned to Parliament in 1456. Imprisoned yet again, and yet again set free; seen now with the Yorkists, but afterwards following Richard Neville, Earl of Warwick, it would seem, in his desertion to the Lancastrians. Malory was in 1468 twice excluded from general pardons granted by Edward IV. His death in 1471 must have come when he was about sixty, and some two years after he had finished the *Morte d'Arthur*. . . . He was buried in London, in the church of the Grey Friars near to Newgate, having tasted in his time most of the London prisons, including the Tower.[8]

A simple cause of many of Malory's imprisonments was debt. A carelessness about money, if other people supplied it, was an element in chivalry not much liked in the City of London or in Parliament, whether the spender was a mere knight like Malory, or a great baron like Warwick, or a king himself. I am brought to the conclusion that a main issue had arisen for Britain when the Great North Road was cut for the second time: when it was no longer a route for military conquests on the Continent. Contemplation of the Road has focused attention on the growth of two incompatible intentions. One, that the pushing of the Road north by stimulating the beginnings of factory work enormously stimulated a rise to money power of the factor, the merchant, and the City; the other, that the gradual stoppage of the push southward thwarted for the time being the piratical instincts which had been notably aroused. Neither of these intentions was going to die, and both were getting out of control. I said the monastery bell had got among a people who regarded it as a work bell; the monastery itself could be forgotten; the bell itself could go on to become the ship's bell of a trading ship. And, as the higher command withdrew from military enterprise upon the Continent, that meant an absence of control over seamen of the south coast, who could turn their equipment and skill toward sea piracy. If there was less and less military control over ne'er-do-wells who had been stirred up for southern conquest, there was certainly no ecclesiastical control. Those upon whom sea pirates might prey were Catholics; so the pirates were Protestants, as simply as that.

What the Road tells me is that the Normans brought into a self-contained Britain a number of ideas which among Saxons or Danes were going to be: some of them resisted, some of them absorbed, and some of them transformed. When the Road was cut for the second time, Britain was bound to be an explosive island. Among all the other crisscross of ideas one line of thought which the Road has here simplified for me is the line of thought about the northward and southward intentions, which I said were incompatible. So they proved to be. By the time of the Wars of the Roses the king's treasury was largely supplied by dues on the export of woollen cloth. To the City of London it did not matter so much who happened to be king, as it did matter that the wool trade could supply his expenses. Any Crown could be supported if there was foreign trade in wool. Toward this the misrule of English seamen in the Narrow Seas threatened to be disastrous. We must look ahead on the time scale to see how real the threat was. The final closure of the original Norman push southward was the loss of Calais in 1558. Calais was then sealed against English wool merchants. Piracy from the south coast of England had already achieved as bad a name as that of the corsairs of Tripoli. In 1563 it has been estimated that there were four hundred privateers at work in the Channel, mainly English, though some claiming to be Huguenot or Dutch. The result was Antwerp was closed to English traders in 1567 and Hamburg ten years later. The chief product of the North of the Great North Road was grievously impeded by the actions at the south end of the road. Henceforth how was the Treasury of England to be replenished or supplied? Who could say? ⁹

VIII »» *Little Britain*

The Great North Road had been cut for the second time. The
first time it was cut, Romano-British civilization had died on the
vine. Subsequent developments in the island were mainly domestic.
I pictured the Norman push as having released unpredictable
forces. I took the stone bridge over the Thames as a symbol
of ambitious design to extend the Road southward, to link
the new Tower of London with Norman demesnes on the Continent, as far perhaps as Rome itself. I brooded on the failure of
that design; and with the gradual but in the end complete blockage
of ambitions southward, I have now to watch what happened on
and to the truncated Road. One thing is certain: it showed no like-
lihood of withering. At the point I have now reached in my journey
I take as a symbol that acre of London between Smithfield and St.
Paul's which came to be called Little Britain.

I don't in the least know how that acre of London came to be
called Little Britain. It is easier to conjecture how Smithfield
obtained its name. There are two schools of thought about that,

as is natural, for in England there are two or more schools of thought about anything. But whatever the origin of the name Smithfield it is clear what made the name stick. From its site at the base of the Great North Road, Smithfield must have been a field of smithies—a field of blacksmiths, armorers, traffickers in horseflesh and in every kind of last-minute travel gear. Smithfield must have been the equivalent of a present-day filling station, though tradition indicates it was a filling station not so much for the wealthy and great as for travelers of poorer sort. Every literary reference to Smithfield from Ben Jonson and Shakespeare and Defoe to Thackeray and Dickens makes it a traditional synonym for all that was coarse and unsavory. Consider the use that Dickens makes of Smithfield in *Oliver Twist*. Dickens is drawing on a long-established conception of disgust for Smithfield when he makes it the region which Oliver is compelled to cross with Bill Sikes and Nancy after they had captured him and were taking him back to Fagin. The symbolic use which Thackeray makes of Smithfield is similar. The tradition of regarding Smithfield as a place of repulsiveness arose not from regarding Smithfield as a point of escape from London, but as the scene of arrival for the unhappy beast or man who was going to be slaughtered there. Thus far, to the gate of London, an animal from the North could be walked on its own feet; then killed.

So soon as the Great North Road was reestablished by the Normans as a military road extending to the farthest North of Britain, Smithfield was a foreordained scene of martyrdom. Granted that Smithfield may at times have had moments of rough gaiety, granted that we read of medieval hurly-burly there, of jousts and tournaments, of Bartholomew's Fair—the dominant theme of Smithfield was to be that of abattoir and brutal mockery. The message of Smithfield was that a transport southward along the Great North Road might be a Dance of Death. Speaking of the *Morte d'Arthur*, I felt that it was under the Normans that for the first time there was an intention of enlisting Scottish knights into the service of the Imperium. Only those knights, perhaps, who would accept the Order of the Round Table. Those who stood too much for an independence of their own people were to be shown the underside of chivalry. At Smithfield on St. Bartholomew's Day in

1305 William Wallace of Scotland was executed, together with his companion Fraser and two other Scottish knights. In 1307 a brother of Wallace and two brothers of Bruce were executed at Smithfield. One sees a pattern. Those dubbed as enemies are dragged the length of the Great North Road, are shown the hard face of the Roman Wall, and are butchered, not at the Tower of London, but at Smithfield, the place of indignity, the slaughter ground for common cattle.

Smithfield was the scene of death for Wat Tyler. In 1381 the dispossessed peasants, led by Wat Tyler, Jack Straw, and John Ball, made their march of protest against unemployment. From north and east they joined to come into London along the Great North Road. They halted at the northern side of Smithfield, the cattle-market side. It was, the books say, a day in June. The king, Richard II, was present. The king's forces were prepared against the marchers, drawn up in formation on the south and east side of Smithfield, in front of St. Bartholomew's—in front of the church and hospital which you may see today. Wat Tyler, as the story goes, advanced by himself across the field to parley with the king; Wat Tyler had begun to speak when Sir William Walworth, Lord Mayor of London, sprang from the king's side and killed the upstart Tyler with a dagger.

That episode is reputed to be the origin of the red dagger in the shield of the City of London—the shield which in my preamble I was so often noticing at bombed sites at the end of World War II. Sometimes Sir William Walworth's action has been regarded as if it were like Sir Launcelot's backhander which slew the carter: namely, a proper knightly way of dealing with any churl who should dare to speak with a king "out of order." There is another interpretation, that Sir William Walworth took violent action because he felt the king might listen, might even be too lenient to the complaint—that not only the people but the king should be taught that the City would strike for itself. Seen in that way, the dagger in the shield of the City of London is an assertion to all comers of the independence of the City toward feudal control.

The uprise of the City of London as a corporate entity which would take affairs into its own hands was something new in an age in which a king might regard a city as Edward III had regarded

Calais. A City myth which arose in parallel to the country myth
of Robin Hood is the myth of Dick Whittington. In the earlier
day of Robin Hood there was nothing to be done against Norman
rule except to escape from it. In the myth of Dick Whittington
it is recounted that an early impulse to escape was checked (the
myth says the impulse was checked upon the Great North Road,
at Highgate Hill) by the sound of the bells of the City, saying
Turn again Whittington. The cat is a curious element in the Whittington myth. Some have conjectured that Whittington did not
start as a poor apprentice but as a smart young operator in the
Company of Mercers, whose most successful trading vessel was
called the *Cat*. Without being sidetracked by odd conjectures, the
point of the Whittington myth is that a wool merchant of London
could become independent of Norman rule. Dick Whittington
was in his way as much of an outlaw as Robin Hood; that is to
say, the myth exhibits that merchants of London could resist
Norman command and throw out Norman law.

I mentioned earlier that William the Conqueror had insisted,
in a spirit of astute conservatism, that appeals in law were to take
account of Anglo-Saxon precedents; yet under the Norman rule
it was devised that the actual procedures of lawsuits were to be
carried out in the mixture of French and Latin. This meant that
any tradesman of London who wished to engage in legal action
had to employ a "conteur," later known as a "serjeant conteur,"
later still as "sergeant," to draw the count or pleading in the
language of the king's court. It seems that the first "conteurs" were
imported from the Norman courts, and that no others were allowed
to be heard. Hence, at the base and origin of the Great North
Road, there was the establishment of foreign-speaking lawyers
at the "parvis" of St. Paul's Cathedral. Chaucer mentions the
"parvis," where each specialist "conteur" or "serjeant" had his
allotted pillar, and where one or other had to be approached
directly by anyone who sought for litigation. Such legal rigmarole,
such business of being pushed from pillar to post, was intolerable
to merchants of London, as it was to landowners who came down
the Road [1] to seek legal redress for wrongs real or imagined. The
insistence of hearing their own lawsuits being ground out in their
own tongue was as stubborn as that of the townsfolk of St. Albans

of grinding their own corn in their own hand mills. The abolition of the compulsory use of Norman-French in law courts was recorded by Act of Parliament in 1362. Sixteen years later English became the official speech of Parliament. Three years after that was the Wat Tyler episode. All this is evidence that before the end of the fourteenth century the English language had proved itself far too strong to be ousted by the language of the conquerors. The Battle of Language seems to me of greater significance than the Battle of Barnet. In every institution, including Court and Church, English had become the language for expression of an emergent "national" feeling. It was as if the many failures to push the Great North Road southward had been in some way translated into a kind of triumph for the islanders, into an assertion that the Continent had not been able to conquer them. Let anybody try: he would meet with such rebellion that in the end his only use for legal Latin would be to say *captor, captus.*

Chaucer did not "choose" the language in which to recite and write his tales. By his time English was the language so mature and flexible and speedily understood at Court that even for a courtly audience there was no other choice. At Corpus Christi College, Cambridge, there is an illuminated manuscript of *Troilus and Criseyde,* probably written and illuminated in the late fourteenth century. The frontispiece shows Chaucer reciting the poem to a company of richly dressed nobles. The recitation may have been at the court of Richard the Second, or perhaps at the court of Richard's mother, Joan of Kent. But the point is, Chaucer is reciting to the nobles not as a novelty, but naturally, in English. That particular illustration represents a recitation on a summer's evening. One recalls Chaucer's own complaints of also having to entertain the Royal Court with recitations in winter. Then, he complains, the courtiers all gathered round the fireplace and monopolized it, and he had to perform at the other end of the room where it was cold. But again the point is that the language was English as the language quickly and naturally to be understood for subtleties as well as for broad jokes. I don't doubt that we who have been brought up in twentieth century town life miss a good many of Chaucer's country allusions, picked up readily enough by medieval courtiers who were closer to country than we are. It was customary for a medieval artist to put into his sketch-book studies of birds and beasts with the closest attention to char-acteristic actions which, if recognized by the viewer, is what gives pleasure. Chaucer's glance could fall like sunlight on such seen characteristics.

> This carter thakketh his hors upon the croupe
> And they bigonne drawen and to-stoupe.

Those two plowhorses in *The Canterbury Tales*—Brok and Scot—may have been ancestors of the Suffolk Punch, bred for his pulling power—the Suffolk Punch who will stoop to his knees before he gives up pulling.[2] It is not beyond possibility that Chaucer as a boy had watched a drawing match of plowhorses in the Suffolk part of the world. Chaucer's grandfather, if I remember rightly, was an Ipswich man. But yet once more my point is that the Eng-lish language had been already "readied" for such pleasurable brush strokes, laid on with directness and simplicity for people who could remember with their eyes and see with their ears. Chaucer was using, and improving, the language already accepted by cour-tiers, and in which they were quick in the uptake.

While Chaucer was using the English language for profit and fun, Wyclif was simultaneously using it for faith. It was in 1380 that Wyclif began to translate the Bible into English. Some of the clergy were as much shocked at the idea the Bible might speak direct to the people as Sir William Walworth was shocked at the idea the people might speak direct to the king.

He translated into English [says Knighton] that Gospel that Christ transmitted to the clergy that they might administer it gently to laymen and infirm persons. By him it is becoming more open to laymen than it used to be to clerks with a fair amount of learning. Thus the gospel pearl is trodden by swine.

The term "Lollard," meaning *mumbler* or *mutterer*, for one who spoke of Christian mysteries in the vulgar tongue, is older than Wyclif, yet it is after Wyclif that his followers became notorious as Lollards and persecuted by the Church as heretics: not merely for the speaking in English, but for an outrageous amount of uncontrollable "freethinking" which not only horrified the Church but disturbed both Parliament and City. In 1401 it was established in Parliament that "heresy" was to be punished by burning, and throughout the succeeding century every few years there is recorded the burning of some Lollard heretic.

The tradition of burnings at Smithfield had begun. When the conflict between Protestantism and the Roman Church came to its full violence and was exacerbated by the alternation of sovereigns and the reprisals by one side or the other, the tortures exhibited at Smithfield were such as to send a thrill of horror throughout the land. Executions at the Tower of London were a relatively private matter. When Henry the Eighth had Anne Boleyn's head struck off at Tower Hill, that was an affair within the family. When a lesson was to be driven home to the people of England, Smithfield was the scene of exhibition. It was at Smithfield that Henry the Eighth used John Forest as an example. Forest was prior of the Observant Convent at Greenwich. He denied the supremacy of the king's rule to the ruling of the pope. In 1538 the king had John Forest suspended in an iron cage at Smithfield over a slow fire until he was roasted to death. The reprisals in the three years' reign of Queen Mary were almost unbelievably numerous.

It is calculated [says Cunningham] that during the reign of Mary 277 persons were burned to death in England for heresy, and of these the great majority suffered at Smithfield. The usual place of burning was immediately opposite the entrance of the Church of St. Bartholomew the Great, the prior of which was generally present on the occasion. The victim faced the east and the great gate of the church.

I am recounting this chapter of horrors at Smithfield not for the sake of dwelling on the horrors but for the extraordinary way in which, as I believe, the world was altered by the simple topographical fact that Smithfield and the adjacent acre of Little Britain were at the London end of the Great North Road. I have been stressing that by the time of the worst horrors of Smithfield the island of Britain was self-contained: not much external outlet for internal warring forces. The over-all picture is that there was steam in the boiler and no safety valve. The detail in the picture with which I am concerned is the collocation of Smithfield, the acre of Little Britain, and the Road. If my view is right, there was here an interaction which altered the picture-at-large. There is here a conjunction of time and place which has to be attended to in social history, political history, and the history of literature and science. The first item on which to focus would seem to me to be the printing press, as brought into activity by what went on at Smithfield.

Fortunately, the story of the printing press does not require much elaboration. Among the early uses of the hand press on the Continent I believe I mentioned its convenience for reproduction of standardized ecclesiastical timetables and tables for navigators; and first usages in England may have included all-and-sundry purposes of handbills, pronouncements, pamphlets, ballads, with the consequent and tremendous importance of extending the habit of reading. The work of Caxton's press must be considered. Before his death in 1491 Caxton had printed for sale a hundred or more books. It should give anyone a thrill to look over Caxton's titles: *The Canterbury Tales, Morte d'Arthur, Aesop's Fables, Reynard the Fox, The Golden Legend*—what a wonderful publisher's list! A thought occurs: each is a reprint of a work which had already achieved recognition as a manuscript book. None of Caxton's titles are works printed for an author who was alive in the flesh. There was no risk of heresy, no danger of any form of censure. A hundred years later that fierce old Yorkshireman, Roger Ascham, might denounce the *Morte d'Arthur:*

The whole pleasure of this book standeth in two speciall poyntes, in open manslaughter and bold bawdrye; in this booke may be counted the noblest, knightes that do kill most men without any quarrell and commit fowlest adoulteries by subtlest shiftes; as Sir Launcelote, with the wife of king Arthure his master; Sir Tristram, with the wife of king Marke his uncle; Sir Lamerocke, with the wife of king Lote, that was his own aunte. . . .

But Ascham was reproving the Court of the sixteenth century. "Yet I know," he continues in his *Scholemaster*, "when God's Bible was banished the Court, La Morte d'Arthure was received into the princes' chamber." There might be this later reproval but there was no risk of unpopularity, no element of chanciness, in Caxton's time for any of his publications. Caxton's friends were among the nobility and gentry, from whom he solicited subscriptions in advance. *The Golden Legend* was issued at the suggestion of the Earl of Arundel, who promised to buy several copies and also to allow Caxton an annuity of a buck in summer and a doe in winter.

Caxton's house was in Westminster, beside the Abbey Precinct, in an area which was conservative and gentlemanly. The Norman lawyers withdrew to Westminster when they were driven away from the parvis of St. Paul's. I am not decrying the importance of Caxton's efforts to make the printed book respectable. Every form of his initiative was to the benefit of literature. He won an uphill fight to gain respect for the printed book. A glance at medieval manuscript books, and the manuscript books of Caxton's time, shows how they surpassed in beauty the uncouth appearance of the early printed page. Manuscript possessed an advantage over print by being, of its nature, something special. Caxton is hardly to be blamed for not putting his press at the disposal of contemporary writers, for to any writer of quality in Caxton's time the printing press was regarded as something very low. The manuscript-book retained the superior intimacy of communication which many people still feel for a handwritten letter over the letter which is typed. As late as Spenser, Spenser would not dream of presenting a copy of *The Faerie Queene* to the Queen's eye, unless it had all been fair copied by hand. To have a communication that you really cared about vulgarized by a printer was beneath the code of a gentleman. The impetus of Caxton and of his imitators in initiating a West End trade in printed books and of encouraging book collecting was of instant importance in creating a wider number of readers, even if it was only and for some time of minor importance as a direct encouragement to living writers.

There was one kind of writer to whom the invention of the printing press might have seemed a positive menace: the dramatist. Who got anything out of having a book printed? Financially, nobody but the printer, and he only if he could sell his product before somebody else pirated it. A fact to be carried in the mind is that there was no such thing as author's copyright until that right was invented in London in 1709, but not established as a property thoroughly protected against infringement until much later than that. So when it is observed, as it often is, that Shakespeare never cared to have his plays printed, there is an answer: Why should he give away an exclusive property, on the possession of which his livelihood depended? Why should Shakespeare have been so angry when texts of his, including *Hamlet,* were pirated? Would not printing, if it should make a text of his available to other actor-managers, damage his stock in trade? Shakespeare, at the height of his popularity, might have had his plays printed in the West End, had he so wished; but it was to his interest to resist publication. Before and after Shakespeare's time there was, however, many another writer who was itching to get into print, and this is where we return to Smithfield to observe how the facilities for East End printing began.

It was natural to wonder, when describing the killing of Wat Tyler, why the Peasants' Revolt should have collapsed so quickly. I suppose centralized power can always act more quickly than an undisciplined mob; following Walworth's act in London we saw how quick was the abbey at St. Albans to hang John Ball and other leaders of the peasants; whereas communication among a dispersed people was slow. But Smithfield was to become a center of communications from which passionate messages could travel in increasing numbers and with increasing urgency. Throughout the fifteenth century every burning of a Lollard at Smithfield sent a new impulse of anger along the line of communication, the Great North Road. Harold Goad has written:

Even as newsmen, the Lollards took the place of the Friars, when the latter for their begging and hearing confessions were each licensed only for certain rounds, whereas the former were free and usually on the run from place to place, naturally repeating all the scandals against the Church, including the reports of returning pilgrims upon the crimes, vices, and luxuries of Renaissance Rome. By the growth of a single language, England had become a sounding-board for anticlerical scandal. In 1524, Cuthbert Tunstall, Bishop of London, wrote to Erasmus: "It is no question of pernicious novelty; it is only that new arms are being added to the great crowd of Wycliffite heretics." [3]

"Every other man in England is a Lollard," exclaimed Tunstall; and Goad comments:

Undoubtedly the greatest "arm" of all was the English tongue, now unified by this new and largely anticlerical literature and, above all, by the printing presses.

These were the hand presses set up in Little Britain, because Little Britain was adjacent to Smithfield, and Smithfield was source of "news" which could be rushed to print, and the printed product launched at once upon the Great North Road. I have small doubt the printing trade of Little Britain started with the religious warfare and that the market served by Little Britain was a market for horrors and flammatory diatribes. This was in extreme contrast to the book trade which Caxton had started in Westminster. Caxton had established a carriage trade in reprints of great works of the past, of the literature which might communicate lasting pleasure without any of it being socially disturbing. We know the name of Caxton. We don't know the names of the earliest printers of Little Britain. We can surmise that they did their best to hide themselves, and Little Britain was a warren of narrow alleys in which they could hide. It was an acre even less savory, if possible, than Smithfield. The principal thoroughfare was the narrow passage, a hundred yards or so in length, leading from the corner of Bart's Hospital and St. Bartholomew's Church—leading, that is, from the site of the burnings—to St. Paul's. The name of this principal thoroughfare was Blow-Bladder Lane. There was a network of sidewise passages from Blow-Bladder Lane to Aldersgate. As "news" from Smithfield multiplied, we may believe the number of hand presses in Little Britain multiplied, and in Mary's time it would have been as hard for authority to find them and to control their products as at that same time it was hard to control the privateers upon the English Channel.

The point on which I should concentrate is that the spirit of the printers in Little Britain was to deal with up-to-the-minute, heretical, violent, surreptitious, fugitive writings as speedily as possible. The point is not whether all the news they printed in the form of broadsides, pamphlets, protests, was true or justified; the point is not whether more common English people learned to spell out their letters in order to read horror stories than in any other way; the point is that before the age of Elizabeth there had been developed in Little Britain a capacity for quick printing and quick distribution. The point is, Little Britain had become an instrument for communication. The motive for using the instrument was, I suppose, a mixture of passion and commerce. One does not have to believe that the printers were imbued with a spirit more exalted than the spirit which their printed protests condemned. The "pardoners" of the Church sold pardons; the "protestants" sold horrors. The horrors were ready-made at Smithfield. Then, with the death of Mary and the advent of Elizabeth, there was a marked decline in the supply of horrors.

It would be convenient if one could correlate the upsurge of Elizabethan literature with the dearth of other "news" with which to feed the presses. It would be too simple a theorem to propound, that the existence of a mechanical facility for book production was the sole inducement for the creation of imperishable books. Nevertheless, the capacity of the hand presses of Little Britain to cope with anything that was handed to them is part of the story. Somehow, in an unsavory acre of City land, there had come into being a "printing plant" which grew apace. To a printer of the present day the small hand presses of the Elizabethan period seem hardly more than primitive, clumsy toys; yet by 1611 with these toys a number of little jobbing printers could combine to produce the King James Bible. As soon as Shakespeare's death in 1616 released his texts for the public domain, and when Heminge and Condell had "but collected them," the hand presses could tackle the job of the First Folio. The wonder is not that there were some misprints: the wonder is the job could be tackled. We don't know much about the economics of the seventeenth century book trade. The printing must have been paid for, somehow. Indignation, from the beginning, was one sort of spur in Little Britain. Milton was in trouble with the Stationers' Company for publishing pamphlets without license; his reply, published without license, was *Areopagitica*.

Lords and Commons of England, consider what nation it is whereof ye are, and whereof ye are the governors; a nation not slow and dull, but of a quick, ingenious, and piercing spirit; acute to invent, subtile and sinewy to discourse, not beneath the reach of any point the highest that human capacity can soar to.

I can understand the willingness of a jobbing printer to run a risk in issuing *Areopagitica,* if only to express a proper pride; but the publication of *Paradise Lost* was a more formidable investment. To set up *Paradise Lost* on a hand press was risking a great deal of laborious effort. The job was undertaken. More difficult jobs than that could be undertaken in Little Britain. Four years after the publication of *Paradise Lost* a young man of twenty-nine had been elected to the Royal Society (then meeting at Gresham College, across the Road from Little Britain) and was hounded by the Secretary (he was really only Clerk, or Assistant Secretary) to get a book into shape to justify his election. The Clerk was Halley, whose name is still attached to the comet; the young Fellow he harried was Newton; the book was the *Principia.* That it could be printed was taken for granted. It was written in Latin, but any printer could print Latin. It had a good many diagrams and symbols: that presented more of a difficulty. Paper—I wonder where the paper came from: Holland? A considerable quantity of paper was required for such efforts as the various English Bibles, the First Folio, *Paradise Lost* and Newton's *Principia.* I have read histories of literature and science which blandly ignore the Mary-Martha problem; which just assume there was somebody to look after the housekeeping. But it interests me very much that Little Britain had somehow "growed" into an organization which could handle Newton's *Principia.* That was a job which Halley insisted should be completed in a hurry. Money was not the primary problem with the *Principia*—Halley was prepared to pay the printing bill out of his own pocket. But the interesting thing is, the services were available. Joseph Streater, the principal printer concerned, farmed out portions of the *Principia* to half a dozen other printers. The surprise is that half a dozen printers could be found close-handy to combine on such a job.

To go back to the Dissolution of the monasteries, it is not difficult to visualize that with the redistribution of Church properties there was a considerable shifting around of families and individuals. One example is going to be of the greatest importance to my story in the next chapter, and I may as well foreshadow it here. Thomas Cromwell, "the iron-handed servant of Henry VIII, the famous sledgehammer of the monks," had a nephew, Richard, "a Welshman

from Glamorganshire." After the Dissolution Henry VIII gave Richard a knighthood and, among other spoils of the Church, gave him
the revenues and manors which had belonged to the priory of
Hinchingbrook and the properties of the abbey of Ramsey in
Huntingdon. This meant that in a third generation, but as a direct
result of the Dissolution, there was going to grow up on property
immediately adjacent to the Great North Road a man who was
going to make extraordinary use of the Road: Oliver Cromwell. The
story which grows out of the transition of the Cromwell family is
something we must attempt to rise to in the next chapter; here,
in Little Britain, I contemplate the transfer, after the Dissolution,
of other individuals whose aptitudes and skills, before the Dissolution, might have found employment in this or that monastery. The
Dissolution meant a release or dispersal of the clerks and the book-
minded. After the Dissolution, where were such people to go?

London. Little Britain. It was a stinking quarter of the City,
but it supplied companions who knew what you were talking
about. Oxford and Cambridge might absorb some of the scholarly
type, but Thames was a wider stream than Isis or Granta, and across
London Bridge were the open-air beer gardens, the playground of
London, and what could contend with the South Bank for the exhibition and rivalry of dramatic talent? There is an old rhyme:

> Turkeys, heresy, hops and beer
> Came into England all in one year.

We need not be too precise about the year—some put it round-
about 1527. We can try to be precise, if we like, about the turkeys
—they were in the beginning what we now call guinea fowl, which
were introduced from the Levant and legitimately called "turkeys,"
a name then later misapplied to the larger birds from Mexico, and
later still misapplied to the "turkeys" of the Atlantic seaboard of
North America. Hops came from the Netherlands, where they were
first used to flavor ale, which in England had previously been
brewed from barley only and which, without hops, must have been
insipid. Ale could be drunk in enormous quantities. Anne Boleyn
as a Maid of Honor had an allowance of two gallons of ale a day—
perhaps to be shared with others?—but to make such ale interesting
it was served in possets and caudles, the warmed sweet liquor

mixed with honey, spices, roasted "crabs" or anything else which took the fancy. Then the strongly hopped "bitter" beers brought in a change of taste. The weaker ales were relatively "baby food." Elizabeth, when queen, issued repeated regulations in defense of weak ale and against strong beer; yet for herself, although she was abstemious, when she wished for a nip drank beer "so strong as there was no man durst touch it." This I suspect to have been an advertising story put about to increase the sale of the beers brewed south of London Bridge: the Elizabethan mighty "double-double" and "Elephant ale."

I was connecting the development of the hand presses of Little Britain with the demand for the horror stories from Smithfield, and the continuing circulation of heresy from Little Britain up the Great North Road is to be borne in mind. What the demand for horrors had created were presses and printers able to cope with rapid, surreptitious, up-to-the-minute work. Then, with the accession of Elizabeth, there was the dearth of Smithfield horrors. What should some of the little presses be put to but ballads, bawdry, crime, and even lyric poetry? I see Elizabethan lyric poetry coming into Little Britain as at first a mere substitute and by the back door; but that was Little Britain's contribution to literature— it was accustomed to the knock at the back door. The fact that a young man was being chased by the Star Chamber was no slur in Little Britain, and even if the young man had nothing more sensational to offer than a short poem, *Come live with me and be my love,* a small hand press was versatile enough to handle a thing like that. Indeed, a book of such verses, to be entitled *The Passionate Pilgrim*, might even be encouraged. There were by this time some patrons about with sufficient loose money to pay for such printings and, perhaps surprisingly, there were readers prepared to read such stuff instead of "news" of horrors. For *The Passionate Pilgrim* other items could be borrowed from Marlowe's companion, Shakespeare, whose first long poem, *Venus and Adonis,* was already being reprinted. *Venus and Adonis* was indeed reprinted nine times in Shakespeare's lifetime. The printing of poetry may have come into Little Britain by the back door, but proved itself not a bad thing to do. So it came about that if it was a short piece like *Drink to me only with thine eyes* or if it was a long piece, as long as

Chapman's *Homer*, there was a receptivity among printers of Little Britain to see what could be done about it.

It was that receptivity, by-product of heresy, which made Little Britain a more attractive common room for writing men, for scholars and for clerkly types, after the Dissolution, than anything that could be offered by the universities. To answer my question, How could you find half a dozen jobbing printers capable of producing, quickly, the *Principia?* I say that for a century before the *Principia* Little Britain had become receptive to the extramural scholar who in scholarship as in spirit surpassed many of those who holed up in easy livings. The receptivity of the printers of Little Britain toward doing anything, had drawn there men capable of producing anything. And so, in turn, printers who worked with George Chapman and Ben Jonson are not to be regarded as ignorant journeymen. I was wrong then to suggest it was a "jobbing printer" who printed Milton's *Areopagitica*. It was somebody of "quick, ingenious, and piercing spirit." Where did Milton spend his last years? He spent them at the house of his printer, Millington, in Little Britain. Proud blind Milton was probably no easy guest. You might have met Milton on Millington's arm in Blow-Bladder Lane; but if so you would have met two men, both "acute to invent, subtile and sinewy to discourse." In all departments of scholarship the printers of Little Britain came up in the scale as scholars came to live and work with them, and by the time of the Restoration, when the Royal Society was formed at Gresham College, I am the less surprised to find that there were half a dozen printers capable of coping with Newton's fluxions.

If it was heresy which in the first instance promoted the hand presses of Little Britain, it was the hops and beer that promoted the growth of theaters across the river; and once writers of Elizabeth's time had begun to be attracted to the north end of London Bridge to see their poems through the press, it was natural there should be rivalry in the more lucrative contest of supplying plays to be produced across the river. This is where John Heminge comes before us a little more clearly than merely as a friend and fellow of Shakespeare. I am indebted to Robert Giroux [4] of New York for information (which I hope he will publish) about Heminge, who was, in brief, almost exactly Shakespeare's contemporary, a member of the Grocers' Company, and came to own the beer and ale concession at the Globe Theater. Until Mr. Giroux gets around to establishing this in print I cannot quote him, but it may certainly be said that he has a *prima facie* case for an interesting point of Elizabethan scholarship. Heminge owned a tenement adjoining the Globe, he was a grocer, and we know that people drank beer in the theater. There is a famous and amusing letter, quoted by Chambers, on the occasion of the fire which started in the thatched roofing over the stage, when the cannon was shot off for *Henry VIII;* this spectator, Sir Henry Wotton, tells how someone's "britches" caught fire and the man behind him doused it with his beer. The Globe burned to the ground. It was rebuilt, grander than ever, in 1613, three years before Shakespeare's death. So "old Heminge," as Ben Jonson liked to refer to him, had business interests which went hand in hand with Shakespeare's over London Bridge.

Impartially, the hand presses of Little Britain clacked on and on. They had started with horrors and continued with horrors. Foxe's *Book of Martyrs* was issued in Latin in the year of Elizabeth's accession. The first of innumerable editions in English appeared in 1563, and the book was food for itinerant preachers who championed the tradition, up and down the Road, of cherishing their supremacy of "the inner light" against all restrictions of external rule. As to the association of print and preachings we must not forget that what the "Pilgrim Fathers" considered as a most important item of equipment for their voyage in the *Mayflower* was a printing press. That particular hand press (bought, I have no proof but I have no doubt, in Little Britain) had an interesting future. I mention it here only to emphasize the obvious, that the temporary amnesty of religious war at the accession of Elizabeth was not going to last, that the excitement of using the presses for poetry, and when you could, for plays, was bound to be affected by the coming religious upheavals. The climate of Elizabeth's last decade, favorable for the beer gardens, favorable for literature, was bound to change.

While the happy weather lasted, what a rout of talent gathered in this portion of the City, and crossed and recrossed London Bridge! William Heminge, son of "old Heminge" the City merchant,

grew up amid the rout and left a good picture of it. The curious
may find among the Ashmolean manuscripts a lively item:

Mr. Thomas Randall the Poett, his finger being cut of [*sic*] by a Riot-
ous Gentleman, his frinde Mr. William Hemminges made this Eligie on
the same.

This pleasing piece of mockery is remembered chiefly for the
catalogue of poets whom young Heminge pretends to assemble
to do honor to the coffin enclosing Randall's finger.

> Ytt had byn drawne and wee In state aproche
> but websters brother would nott lend a Coach:
> hee swore they all weare hired to Conuey
> the Malfy dutches sadly on her way . . .

Among the poets who must "quayntly vse thayr feett," young
Heminge lists:

> The fluente Flettcher, Beaumonte riche In sence
> for Complement and Courtshypes quintesence,
> Ingenious Shakespeare, Messenger that knowes
> the strength to wright or plott In verse or prose,
> Whose easye pegasus Can Ambell ore
> some threscore Myles of fancye In an hower,
> Clowd grapling Chapman whose Aeriall mynde
> Soares att philosophie and strickes ytt blynd,
> Dauborne I had forgott, and lett ytt bee,
> hee dyed Amphybion by thy Ministrye,
> Siluester Bartas whose translatinge pate
> Twynd or was Elder to our Lawreatt,
> Deuyn composing Quarles, whose Lynes asspire
> to heauen, and rauysh the Celestiall quire,
> The Aprile of all poesy, Tom May
> that makes our Englishe speake Pharsalia,
> Sandes Metamorphised Into a nother,
> wee knowe nott Sandes, nor Ouid from each other,
> Hee that soe well on Scoppius playd the Man
> the Famous Digges, or Leonard Claudian,
> the pithy Danyell whose salt lynes afford
> A wayghty sentence In each little word,
> Heroicke Drayton, Withers smarte In Ryme,
> the verye Poett beadle of the tyme,

Pans Pastorall Browne whose Infante Muse did squeake
At eighteen yeare better than others speake,
Shirlye the Morninge Childe the Muses Breed
and sent hyme vs wth Bayes borne on his head,
Deep In a dumpe Iacke forde alone was gott
Wth folded Armes and Melancholye hatt. . . .

And so on. The "squoblinge Middleton and Heywood sage" and many more "worthyes Like to thes I could impart," but enough has been quoted to remind us of the supply of talent. If the hand presses of Little Britain were disposed to take on poetry, there was no lack of fodder. Even when the heyday of the "play-boys" was over—how long was that brief heyday, two, three decades? —what remained was not alone the works of literature but a tradition and capacity among printers to handle anything that came along in the future, according to the climate. Literature, politics, religion, or science: a means of communication was there.

IX »» The York Road

London of the sixteenth century—what was it like? I take a glimpse from Miss Hilda Prescott's book on *Mary Tudor:*

A crowded, noisy, bustling town it was, yet childishly small to us, the only thing in it like to our London, those glimpses of the river, seen down every narrow southward-running street from St. Paul's to Charing Cross. But in London of the sixteenth century, besides those constant glimpses of the river and the ships, you could not go far without seeing the tree-tops in the gardens. Nor indeed was any part of London far from country sights and sounds. A great deal—a shocking great deal—of building was noted by that observant man, Master John Stow, during his lifetime; but in the earlier part of the century fields and farms were close to the doors of Londoners. Stow could remember how, when he was a boy he would be sent to a farm of the St. Clare sisters just outside Aldgate, to bring back milk "hot from the kine." He remembered too the country-like pastimes in the streets of a holiday evening; when the "prentices used to fight with 'wasters and bucklers' outside their master's door," and "the maidens, one of them playing on a timbrel, in sight of their Masters and Dames, to dance for garlands hung thwart

163

the streets." On Midsummer Eve, and St. Peter and Paul's Eve "Every man's door being shadowed with green birch, long fennel, St. John's wort, orpine, white lilies," and trimmed with garlands, "had also lamps of glass with oil burning in them all night." Londoners were in fact in those days only countrymen living in town, and, like the villagers, had their own Maypole, set up yearly, until the "evil May Day" of 1517, at the top of Cornhill, and laid by again under a penthouse roof along the wall of a row of houses near the church of St. Andrew, named for its sake "St. Andrew Undershaft." Along the banks of the town ditch, that ran close to where now the trains rumble into Holborn Viaduct Station, anglers sat on summer evenings, and caught good fish there too; "as many men yet living," Stow declared, "who have taken and tasted them, can well witness." [1]

A pretty picture it is:

> For those were the days when the Thames ran clear
> Palace and shadowy lawn between,
> Window-bays glittered with stately cheer,
> And light feet danced upon Charing Green.

We have been contemplating the dark side of the medal; surely we have a right to look at the bright side. Whatever may have been the hereditary sources, there was to Londoners an undeniable appeal in pageantry, play acting and show business. Mary Tudor, not by nature especially inclined to pomp and ceremony, when in the summer of 1553 she was proclaimed Queen of England, had to satisfy the desire that her entry to London should be duly ceremonial. Mary came to London from Framlingham in Suffolk. She rested at Wanstead, and on 3 August rode on toward the City with over seven hundred gentlemen in velvet suits going before her, and her ladies after. Her younger sister Elizabeth rode to Wanstead to meet her, with a thousand horse, with spears, bows and guns, and all her gentlemen in green "gauded with white velvet satin taffety." I borrow these details from Miss Prescott, who continues:

It was 7 o'clock in the evening of August 3rd when Mary rode into the city. She had on "a gown of purple velvet, French fashion . . . her kirtle all thick set with goldsmith's work and great pearl . . . with a rich baldrick of gold pearly and stones about her neck, and a rich billement of stones and great pearl on her head," and she rode on a palfrey whose gold-embroidered trappings came down to the ground, her train being borne up by Sir Anthony Browne, who carried it over his shoulder. At Aldgate Bar the Lord Mayor greeted her, kissing the sceptre "in token of loyalty and homage," before he gave it into her hands. She thanked him, graciously remembering the city to have been always good to her. The people, excited and overwrought, wept for joy at the gentleness of her words, voice and smile. The Queen passed on, Elizabeth following her, then the Duchess of Norfolk and the Marchioness of Exeter, through streets fresh gravelled, and hung with cloths and tapestries, the city companies standing armed, trumpets blowing and guns firing "like great thunder." The children of Christ's Hospital stood ready with an oration, "100 poor little children . . . all dressed in blue with red caps."

Mary was personifying the Old Religion; when Elizabeth, regarded as personifying the Protestant cause, came to the throne in 1559 the pageantry was not less but more elaborate. Elizabeth, for her inaugural show, had a winter's day. It was on Saturday, 14 January, that the whole of Elizabeth's Court gathered at the Tower, and although it snowed a little, "their sparkling jewels and gold collars seemed to clear the air." Here I am quoting Sir John Neale's description:

In the afternoon the procession, which numbered a thousand people on horseback, set out on its slow progress through the streets to Westminster. Dressed in a royal robe of rich cloth of gold and wearing the crown of a princess, as yet without the emblems of sovereignty, the Queen was carried in an open litter, trimmed to the ground with gold brocade, and borne by two fine mules, covered with the same material. On either side of her walked the gentlemen pensioners in crimson damask, bearing their gilt battle-axes, while all round was a multitude of footmen in crimson velvet jerkins studded with massive gilt silver and ornamented back and front with a white and red rose and the letters E.R. As a contemporary remarked, "In pompous ceremonies a secret of government doth much consist." [2]

The numerous pageants prepared by the City authorities to punctuate Elizabeth's progress from the Tower to Westminster, each pageant equipped with its "noises of loud instruments," are described in detail by Professor Neale.

I hover over that phrase, "In pompous ceremonies a secret of government doth much consist." There were those who enjoyed the display, and there were those who regarded it as unnecessary and vainglorious expense. The presses of Little Britain began to send along the Great North Road comments which were almost as sour about the new dispensation of Elizabeth as they had been about the old dispensation of Mary. Elizabeth's Parliament, and the City, could not disregard an extreme uneasiness about idleness —which was their term for what we call the "unemployment problem"—and about money. Elizabeth listened to her advisers on these matters, Burghley and Gresham. As to monetary matters Henry VIII had been uncontrollable. Church properties had been looted and redistributed, but that was a destructive operation which could not be repeated. So far as Henry was concerned, the proceeds were soon squandered. His treatment of his creditors was simple: he minted silver coins which were more than half alloy. Such debasement of English coinage continued after Henry's death; in Mary's time a shilling was worth not fourpennyworth of honest metal. For mercantile dealings with the Continent this was all the more of a handicap in that the amount of gold and silver there was rapidly increasing. The raids on Mexico and Peru trebled the amount of silver and gold in Europe between the years 1500 and 1600. Gresham's phrase to Elizabeth, "Bad money drives out good," was accurate enough as an observation; foreign merchants were not going to accept shillings worth in weight fourpence: the old good shillings were going out of the land, and the invalid coinage remained. The drastic reform forced upon Elizabeth was to call in all coins issued since 1543 and to mint new issues which were "good." This to some extent restored England's credit, and Elizabeth could get foreign loans at half the rate of interest which had been asked of Mary. The inconvenience remained of the acute shortage of bullion in England. For the populace "good" money was hard to come by, and "idleness" increased.

The Dissolution had amounted to a major social revolution. Along the Great North Road the common wayfarer was worse off after than before. A burden of responsibility for such a mundane matter as road repair, which had been carried, well or badly, by the abbeys was to be shifted—to whom? What hospices were

there, what help for the hungry, the needy, and the dispossessed?
What remnant was left of that ancient Mithraic trace element,
Hominibus vagis vitam, the promise of life to wandering men? The
power of the Church to give assistance had in many places been
waning before the Dissolution. At the suppression of Rievaulx
in 1539 there were only 22 monks; the income of the abbey had
declined to £351; the place was already falling down; no longer
much employment to be expected there; after the Dissolution,
none. If you were an evicted farmhand and took to the Road,
I am sure you could meet with itinerant preachers, more perhaps
after the Dissolution than before, but where was there employment? Elizabeth's laws against vagrancy were as drastic as her
reformation of England's coinage; but the monetary reform actually intensified the problem of shortage of bullion, and the whipping
of "rogues and vagabonds" up and down the Great North Road, from
parish to parish, did not solve the problem of idleness. The workless
could echo the groans of the old Romano-Britons—their choice was
death or the sea. The sea was the answer.

Thus the Great North Road of Elizabeth's time took on a new
function, the function of being a spillway for vagrants who might
find some recourse by peeling away from it toward the sea. More
has got into the history books about the southern end of the spillway than about the northern end, but I think both ends are important. I think farmers and backwoodsmen of Danish heritage
were apt to retain the backwoods-farming instinct; that for a good
many of that breed, dispossessed of farms on land, there was
instinct to farm the sea. Fishing was sea farming, and arctic waters
were the backwoods. The difficulties of the Elizabethan wool
traders, the loss of business across the Narrow Seas, the boycott
in the Continental ports, forced more attention to the northern
waters and the produce those waters contained. If Elizabeth's
laws against vagrancy on the roads seem to us very harsh, part
of the intent was to siphon vagrants off into the fishing fleets,
which Elizabeth did her best to subsidize. Elizabeth ordained that
no one in England was to eat meat on Wednesdays, Fridays, or
Saturdays, or in Lent or on Ember days. The punishment for eating
meat on a forbidden day was to have a spell in the stocks. The
fishermen to be encouraged were not only coasters, but men who

worked the Banks of Newfoundland, the seas off Greenland, Iceland, and Spitzbergen. The arctic workings of the Elizabethan fishermen have received little attention because theirs were not dramatic voyages for exploration of new territory; they were less concerned with finding land than with keeping away from it. There were by-products which are relevant to my story of the Great North Road. These traders and backwoodsmen who were siphoned off the northern end of the Road learned from the distant fishing grounds how to build ships for the worst seas, how to handle them—and they learned about whales.

The history of whaling is never a digression to a man who spent part of his boyhood in Nantucket. I am approaching the time when the pulsations of the Great North Road are to spread East and West, when the spirit of the Danelaw is going to relive, with whatever sea change, within the spirit of New England. Habits of hand, and skills, and habits of trade are as important to my story as are the appetites of politics or theology; and I would not expect to get very close to an understanding of the port of Mystic, Connecticut, without some acquaintance, if only the briefest, with the story of whaling.

In the anecdote about the crusade of Richard Coeur de Lion, the lantern which hung from the mast of the king's ship to keep the rest of his ships together as a hen gathers her chickens was supplied with whale oil from Biarritz. Skipping intervening centuries, in sixteenth century London the "lamps of glass with oil burning in them all night" which Stow mentioned as a feature of Midsummer Eve were supplied with whale oil. The Midsummer Eve ceremonial correlates with the bonfires traditional to that date in Mediterranean countries, but on winter nights there was continuous demand for lighting in London, indoors and out. With tallow candles there was much trouble with the wicks. Almost any wick would burn in whale oil. So soon as fishermen from the East Coast of Britain found whales on their doorstep—so soon, that is, as the fishermen regarded the Arctic as their doorstep—there was development of skill and daring and tradition in whale hunting, some time before the Muscovy Company attempted to obtain a monopoly. There are no records of the "newfoundlands" at which Elizabethan whalers put in for wood with which to render down their whale oil, partly, no doubt, because each of these privateers would prefer not to publish his secrets. There is an amusing report dated 1611 of the Muscovy Company that after they had announced their sole patent for making "oyle" in Greenland (meaning Spitzbergen) their consignment was scooped by an "interloper" from Hull. Ships from Hull knew about Northern hideouts years before the Muscovy Company. The ports which established and maintained a brisk trade in whale oil were London, York, Hull and Whitby. Leith, Dunbar, Dundee came in to do a smaller trade. Bristol and Liverpool made starts now and then but never kept up in the whale race.

The northern whaling industry was helping to replace some of the unemployment among wool traders, when one of those southern privateers who had done so much to spoil "marchandyse" across the Narrow Sea, sailed west, and altered the whole picture. The first years of Elizabeth's reign, we have been saying, were plagued with poverty, unemployment, insecurity. Some of the unemployed manpower spilled off the northern parts of the Great North Road to the fishing grounds, near and distant; some spilled off the southern end of the Road. A "sturdy rogue" who had been whipped as far as the Whipmawwhopmaw Gate of York was possibly happy enough, for the moment, to find himself in a whaleship. His fellow number, if whipped across the Thames, in 1573 might have found himself in a ship commanded by the son of a naval chaplain at Chatham dockyard, Francis Drake. Nobody supposes that Drake knew precisely what he was going to achieve by his voyages. His first astonishing achievement affected the whole English economy. Keynes says in his *Treatise on Money:* "The boom period in England definitely began with the return of Drake's first important expedition in 1573, and was confirmed by the immense gains of his second expedition which returned in 1580." The dividend paid on Drake's 1580 expedition was 4,700 per cent. Elizabeth had a share in the investment; her profit, in the currency of the time, has been computed as £500,000. Her foreign debts at the moment amounted to something like £20,000. Drake was allowed to keep £10,000 of the treasure he brought home, and received his knighthood. Elizabeth paid off her foreign debts and had the large margin remaining for further investments. Others of the Court and City who had put up money for the adventure cashed in handsomely. "Indeed," says Keynes, "the booty brought back by Drake in the *Golden Hind* may fairly be considered the fountain and origin of British Foreign Investment."

After this extraordinary transition from rags to riches there was bound to be a spending spree. What is impressive is that some people kept their heads. To start with, Drake. He was not presuming to rely on repetition of his piracy. At a right moment he had fallen in with unprepared and unsuspecting Spanish treasure ships; but sooner or later that meant war with Spain. Drake and Hawkins, who was in charge of the English dockyards, worked steadily and patiently toward a new form of naval architecture. The object was to achieve the best combination of firepower with maneuverability. The idea of being able to fire a "broadside" had occurred under Henry the Eighth; a carvel construction made it possible to cut gun ports in a ship's hull without weakening it; and the development of the gun deck meant that top hamper could be cleared. Naval tactics for centuries had been based on the direct frontal attack, but the new object was to attack with a broadside. Thus the ships Hawkins built for Elizabeth were not of the type of cog or galleon, but were long, "lying low and snug in the water." The art of sailing them was to get closer to the wind than the enemy. The superiority of the English seamanship and of the firepower of the English ships was demonstrated by Drake at Cadiz and by the defeat of the Armada. This superiority was the result less of a sudden burst of bravery than of patient thought and training.

In the City, now there was money for foreign investment, various merchants seem to have been shrewd in laying it out. Piracy under Drake had demonstrated its phenomenal success, but permanent profits were to be looked for not in loot but in trade. There were some sour grapes in this philosophy. Discoveries of gold would have been welcome enough; but a second endeavor was to probe for trade in every likely direction. Which direction was most likely, nobody could tell; hence the search for a Northwest passage to India and the formation of the various companies of Merchant Adventurers—the Muscovy Company, the Virginia Companies, and the Levant Company. The Levant Company, originally

entitled "The Society of Merchants of London Trading into the
Levant Seas," more commonly called simply "the Turkey Merchants," was one of the earliest and one of the most interesting
of these endeavors. Elizabeth's patent to the Levant Company was
issued in 1581, and into the venture she put £10,000 of the money
she had received from Drake. This was no endeavor to raid the old
world of Arabia, but in a prosaic way to open a market there for
English woolen cloth. Such a trading station as Aleppo was to
replace the market which had been lost at Calais. In course of time
the return of raw material, notably cotton, was to prove of immense
impetus to English manufacturing. The East India Company was
eventually an outgrowth of the Levant Company. The philosophy
of the Merchant Adventurers was in total opposition to the idea
of piracy. When Sir Kenelm Digby set out in 1627 on a privateering expedition to the Mediterranean, perhaps with some memory
of Drake in mind, the Turkey Merchants buzzed with anger at the
interruption to their trade and the defamation of the reputation of
the English for fair dealing. They took immense pains and paid out
£20,000 to restore the credit impaired by Digby. Two items about
the Turkey Merchants may be tucked in; one, that the ship *Mayflower* worked for the Levant Company until she was deemed to
be too old for further service, and so could be hired cheaply by
the Pilgrims from Scrooby; the other, that a certain Henry Teonge,
Chaplain to H.M.S. *Assistance,* mentions that when that ship put
into Aleppo in 1676 there was, as if it were at that date a customary
procedure, a game of "krickett."

After Drake had struck it rich, if there were some who made
sober use of the dividends, there were others who did not. If there
were times when Elizabeth encouraged thrift there were also
times when she encouraged spending. Professor Neale has many
an amusing story to tell of what happened when Gloriana suddenly
felt that London was stale (and possibly plague-ridden) and announced that she intended a royal progress:

Officials did not share the enthusiasm. Progresses involved tremendous preparations. Along with the personnel of the Household went
hundreds of carts bearing the baggage, including furnishings for the
bare houses which often had to be got ready; and it was the reverse of
pleasure, in bad weather and on bad roads, to follow an advance guard

of this nature. Ten or twelve miles was as much as the stately procession traveled in a day. Moreover, it was often impossible to find reasonable accommodation for all the Queen's followers, and to add to their trials, Elizabeth had an increasing proclivity to change her mind and upset plans at the last minute . . .

Any town through which the Queen was to pass had a wonderful free pageant:

> No sooner was pronounced the name,
>   but babes in street gan leap;
> The youth, the age, the rich, the poor,
>   came running all on heap,
> And, clapping hands, cried mainly out,
>   "O blessed be the hour!
> Our Queen is coming to the Town,
>   with princely train and power."

But:

Elizabeth's descent on private houses was both coveted and feared; coveted for the honour, feared lest there might be some hitch, or the entertainment fall short of expectations. Apparently, there was no need to do more than surrender the house to the Queen's use: the cost of food, even the furnishings, would be provided by the Royal Household. But to do no more than this might be regarded as churlish behaviour, and in one instance certainly was so regarded, at least by the courtiers. There are many little incidents to suggest that Elizabeth herself was reluctant that smaller folk should outreach themselves on her behalf, but the extravagant preparations made by wealthier hosts, or by courtiers trying to outdo one another, tended to set a standard that made royal visits an expensive honour. In 1577 a four-days' visit cost Sir Nicholas Bacon £ 577; a ten-days' visit to Burghley in 1591 cost rather over £ 1000; a three-days' visit to Lord Keeper Egerton in 1602 cost as much as £ 2000.

In 1591, when Elizabeth was received by the Earl of Hertford at Elvetham:

Though only a three-days' stay, three hundred men were set to work beforehand to enlarge the house, erect a host of outbuildings for the royal train, and dig a pond, half-moon shape, with three islands representing a ship, a fort, and a snail. At her arrival she was saluted in

Latin verse by a poet clad in green to signify his joyful thoughts, with a laurel garland on his head and olive branch in his hand, and booted to betoken that he "was not a loose or low creeping prophet."

In his book on Elizabeth, Professor Neale reproduces a contemporary engraving of the artificial pond, with its ship, fort, and the rather odd "Snail-mount," the flag of St. George flying over each of them; and Professor Neale gives detailed description of the very elaborate goings on throughout the whole of the three-day visit. Mr. Ian Dunlop, writing about the *Palaces and Progresses of Elizabeth I*,[3] points out that Elizabeth was to be pleased not only by temporary entertainments but by permanent improvements at the houses at which she stayed. Aubrey notes that where Elizabeth went tended to create "a most parkly ground and romancy pleasant place" out of what was "heretofore all horrid and woody." Defoe suggests that to please Elizabeth country houses had to "shine among the trees as jewels shine in a rich coronet." At a distance they had to be "all nature, near hand all art; but both in the extremest beauty." Indoors, Elizabeth's insistence on improvement was even more noteworthy. "The times could still be remembered," wrote William Harrison, "when the goodman of the house made his fire against the reredos of his hall," and lay upon straw with a log for a bolster, covered only in "dog-swain and hopharlots." As for servants, there was not much nightwear over or under "to keep them from the pricking of the straws that ran oft through the canvas and razed their hardened hides." Mr. Dunlop, as I think rightly, comments:

It is here, and not in any consideration of styles or of architect, that the true significance of the Tudor House is to be found. The outstanding feature of the period is not the advent of the cornice and pilaster, but the extraordinary improvement in domestic comfort. The period begins with the laying of water to all the principal rooms at Richmond; it ends with the invention of the water closet.

Sir John Harington deserves to be remembered for constructing the first water closet in 1596, in his house near Bath. It was an installation commended to Her Majesty for her Palace at Greenwich and "other stately houses, that are oft annoyed with such savours as where many mouths are fed, can hardly be avoided."

The queen, wherever she went visiting, spared no comment on the household arrangements. Of a visit to Sir Thomas Gresham at Osterley, Mr. Dunlop quotes Fuller: "Her Majesty found fault with the court of this house, as too great, affirming that it would appear more handsome if divided by a wall in the middle." She awoke next morning to find the court partitioned as she had suggested. Gresham had at once sent in to London for workmen to erect the wall overnight. Mr. Dunlop adds a comment from the Ambassador Michael Soriano, who put into his dispatches that the English "attempt to do everything that comes into their heads, just as if all that the imagination suggests could be easily executed." Elizabeth might be exacting; she might indeed be kleptomaniac. There are diaries with remarks such as: "To grace his Lordship more, she, of herself, took from him a salt, and a spoon and fork of fair agate." But the net effect of Elizabeth's progresses was a vast improvement of country-house manners.

It is noticeable that Elizabeth's royal tours were confined to the South of England. She made progresses to Dover, Southampton, Bristol, Worcester, Stafford, Norwich; she visited Oxford and Cambridge, Kenilworth near Oxford and Hinchingbrook near Cambridge; she visited many another country estate. She never made a royal progress up the Great North Road to Lincoln, York, or the farther North. Perhaps her cruising radius was limited by the cumbersome nature of her tours. It is said that she expressed a wish to visit York, but was dissuaded by the awkwardness of such a visit at the time when Mary Queen of Scots was imprisoned there. My impression is that at no time would an ostentatious display of pomp and pageantry have been well received along the Great North Road. In the South of England, if some people shook their heads at exhibitions of wanton extravagance, it could be condoned by the suddenness of the wealth and the confidence of sudden power. But, broadly speaking, the people of the "inly-working North" were not sharing the prosperity or the sentiments of people of the South and West. In Elizabeth's time, why should the Danelaw rejoice? Evictions were going on, and if in the South there was the great upsurge of national pride and a quickening of spirit to be exploited by the poets and dramatists across London Bridge, was that a surge and spirit to travel up the Great North

Road? The Lollards had done their work too well for people with sectarian discontent to be appeased by the Elizabethan compromise which required conformity not, it is true, with the Old Church of which the pope in Rome was governor, but within the new Church of which Elizabeth was governor. There were many loose and low-creeping prophets who preached that such a change was no change, who reviled the conduct of the Elizabethan Court as much as they had reviled the conduct of the Vatican. On the same evenings on which poets and dramatists were returning across London Bridge to discuss their matters at the Mermaid Tavern in Cheapside, thence to disperse to their rooms near Little Britain, the presses of Little Britain were continuing to clack away with "news," for the Great North Road, of the excesses and extravagancies of the Court; "news," true or false, of plots and counterplots and machinations. There were too many hotheads and too many idle up and down the Great North Road for it to be regarded, in Elizabeth's time, as a Ceremonial Highway.

As Elizabeth's reign drew toward its end, it was not only the poorer people of the Danelaw who were discontented. There is the memory of the Earl of Huntingdon on his deathbed in 1595:

. . . the Bishop of York, being with hym, desired two Things of his hands; to prepare hymself to dye, which he did; not using many Words but such as did give good Assurance he died a good Christian; and to dispose of his Estate, which by no meanes he would harken unto; and said little to yt, only that yt was a wild world which he wold not thinck upon.[4]

Perhaps the evidence of a tired old man should not be brought in to indicate a general despondency. Nor, perhaps, are the actions of adventurers of much significance. John Smith came from Willoughby in Lincolnshire. John Smith is no evidence of a general discontent with home conditions, for he was of the type that, had home been happy, he would have gone away anyway. But if the area of the Danelaw had been a happy land in Elizabeth's time, I doubt if John Smith would have so readily enlisted companions such as Henry Spelman and John Rolfe, both of Norfolk. Rolfe was the gentle boy from Heacham who married Pocahontas, after that "unbelieving creature" had been converted, and claimed baptism; she was renamed Rebecca and was brought to England to die of the change of climate. Into a change of climate in the reverse direction, from England to Virginia, the Great North Road was sending off more of its unemployed to the Virginian "colonies." None knew quite where these colonies might be established. There were many willing to find out. There was Raleigh's impetus, and there was the brave boast of Master Thorne: "There is no sea innavigable, nor land unhabitable." In fact there was much wastage. It took time to learn that the triangle of the Western Ocean from Bermuda to the east, Cape Hatteras to the west, and Nantucket to the north is an area for unexpected and fierce gales. Some of the colonies which set forth for Virginia never got there. Some of the colonies which got there were never heard of after. One thinks of the lost colony of Roanoke. One thinks of the colony which set out for Darien in Panama, and more fortunately ended up at what is now called Darien, Connecticut. One thinks that some of the men who attempted these things attempted them because they were not happy at home.

I would not accept the enterprise of the earliest adventurers to Virginia as a complete indictment of home conditions. To the earliest adventurers there was the appeal of the coasts of illusion. Raleigh intended, like Drake, to strike it rich. John Smith persists in referring to Powhatan, father of Pocahontas, as "King" or "Emperor." On the coasts of illusion untold gold and jewels are always just a little farther on, even if the farther on is always on the other side of what John Smith has the honesty to call "the irksome woods." But by the end of the sixteenth century it was well attested that so far as instant wealth was concerned, what the Atlantic seaboard of North America had to offer was a most inhospitable climate, rocks and reefs, sand, scrub, insects, swamps, mosquitoes, thirst, and despair. There were two imports which might be of value: potatoes and tobacco. Potatoes might be acclimatized in England; tobacco could be grown only in Virginia. Colonies of sufficiently desperate men might go to Virginia and support themselves by trade in tobacco. The discontent was not confined to weary old men such as the Earl of Huntingdon, or to unemployed rogues and vagabonds. Discontent with the Elizabethan age is more effectively illustrated by the feelings of solid men; middle-aged farmers and worthies along the Great North Road between Scrooby, Bawtry, Doncaster, York—Robin Hood's land. That respectable solid people of these parts should be prepared to risk the known perils of "Virginia," with material possessions to depart from and with no expectation of gain—except freedom—is evidence that they were not much enamored of their governor who in the south was called "Good Queen Bess."

The group of "separatists" of whom I am particularly thinking was numerically small, and though their thoughts were desperate some felt it might be possible to stay in England after a change of reign. Some of them had tried to set up a "free" colony in Holland, but there was no more freedom to live and worship on their own terms in Holland than there had been in England, and they returned. Since 1564 in England they had been "branded with the odious name of *Puritanes*." These Puritans, the queen had complained, were "overbold with God Almighty, making too many subtle scannings of His blessed will, as lawyers do with human testaments." It was "dangerous to a kingly rule" to have private men citing Scripture against the Government. Separatists were left-wing Puritans; moderate Puritans felt the *"Liturgie, Ceremonies* and *Discipline* of the *Church"* might yet be further reformed. Separatists feared that there was nothing to hope for in any Established Church. Toward the end of Elizabeth's reign she was inclined to let matters slip. James, son of Mary Queen of Scots, was urged upon her by Burghley's son, Robert Cecil, as the least-worst nominee to become her successor. The troubles that were brewing could be left to James. In her seventy-first year, her death approaching, Elizabeth maintained a personal bravado. "We are frolic here at court," wrote Lord Worcester. Camden said "as the report now grew daily stronger and stronger that her sickness increased upon her" it was incredible to see "with what great speed the Puritans, Papists, Ambitious Persons and Flatterers of all kinds . . . posted night and day by sea and land to Scotland." Elizabeth herself had never traveled up the Great North Road, but these pressurers did, and when Elizabeth died in 1603 the Great North Road brought James, a Scotsman, to the throne of England.

Papists had hopes of James because he was the son of Mary, Queen of Scots; Puritans because he came from the Puritan part of Scotland. James traveled south with his queen, the stage-struck Anne of Denmark. Actor-managers had something to hope from Anne. As he approached London, James rested at Hinchingbrook, where in the Cromwell home he had, in his own words, the best reception since he had left Edinburgh. A little farther on toward London there was Lord Burghley's house, Theobalds, considered in Elizabeth's time to be the finest country house in England. Here James was entertained by Robert Cecil, Earl of Salisbury, son of Elizabeth's Lord Burghley and, in 1603, the most powerful man at Court: the same Cecil who had arranged for James's peaceful accession. James was delighted with Theobalds because its situation was favorable for hunting. On the spot Cecil made a deal with him, whereby James should take over Theobalds as his country palace. The upkeep of Theobalds was a considerable encumbrance, and it is likely that Cecil was not unhappy to part with "Tibbals" to the king, and to build for himself a smaller, elegant and compact home at Hatfield, replacing there the older palace in which the young Elizabeth had been staying at the time she heard the news that she was to be proclaimed queen. James came on from Theobalds to the Charterhouse beside Smithfield. It was beside the field where Wallace had been beheaded that James was proclaimed king. There had been no special pomp about James's progress along the Great North Road, and there was no spectacular pomp about his proclamation.

James's first pronouncements gave no satisfaction to anybody. As to the religious contest, here is a passage from his speech at the opening of Parliament in 1604:

At my first coming, although I found but one religion, and that which by myself is professed, publicly allowed and by the law maintained, yet found I another sort of religion, besides a private sect, lurking within the bowels of this nation. The first is the true religion, which by me is professed and by the law is established: the second is the falsely called Catholics, but truly Papists: the third, which I call a sect rather than a religion, is the Puritans and Novelists, who do not so far differ from us in points of religion as in their confused form of policy and parity; being ever discontented with the present government and impatient to suffer any superiority, which maketh their sect unable to be suffered in any well-governed commonwealth.

This statement is moderate, compared with James's outburst at the Hampton Court conference of clergy in 1604: "I will make them conform or will harry them out of the land." This again is moderate by comparison with his statement to Parliament of his doctrine of the divine right of kings: "Kings are not only God's lieutenants upon earth and sit upon God's throne, but even by God himself they are called gods. . . . I will not be content that my power be disputed on." The king was ordering Parliament to supply him with money; an order very soon "disputed on."

It was against papists that James promptly exercised laws which had been passed in Elizabeth's time but by her not always enforced. After several Roman Catholic priests had been hanged, an equally prompt retaliation was devised, the Gunpowder Plot of 1605. This plan was hatched in the restless Midlands: some of the plotters came from Warwickshire, the leader Rookwood lived at Holbeche in Staffordshire, and Guy Fawkes was a native of York. It was a plot against both Parliament and king, and their joint reaction resulted in common persecution of Jesuits: throughout the seventeenth century it was death for a Roman Catholic priest to wear his robes or to say mass openly in England.

But a common front against papists did not keep left-wing Puritans on the king's side. The anarchists of Scrooby continued as long as they could to lie low. They were as I said solid folk and well mannered. Nobody could find fault with the personal conduct of John Robinson, their clergyman, or with that of William Brewster, the Scrooby postmaster. To be postmaster on the Great North Road was a not unrespectable office. William Brewster the father, bailiff and postmaster under Elizabeth, was a man of sufficient substance to send his son to Cambridge; and the younger William Brewster was holding that position, with jurisdiction over the twenty-four miles of road between Tuxford and Doncaster, from 1594 for as long as he liked. Into the era of James, William Brewster continued to do as he had done; he refused to attend services at the parish church, but assembled at his manor house others of the separatist way of thought—Mr. Clifton of Babworth, near Retford; Mr. Bradford of Austerfield; Mr. John Smyth; and others who "met ordinarily at William Brewster's house of the Lord's Day; and with great love he entertained them when they came, making provision for them, to his great charge." This conduct was not without danger. We hear from Bradford of persecutions and imprisonments until the most of Brewster's group were "fain to fly and leave their houses and habitations and the means of their livelihood." But the flight of this particular group cannot be described as precipitate, and when it took place after seventeen years of James's reign the spur was less the spur of physical intimidation than of general disgust.

In every class of society, except among some of the opportunists and some of the Scottish hangers-on and except—it is a big exception—for the devotees of the theater, there was disgust with James. As soon as Cecil had sold James "Tibbals," and the king had taken over the great house as his permanent country palace, visitors made comments about the change of régime. Mr. Dunlop quotes from the diary of Lady Anne Clifford. Lady Anne and her mother and aunt had been most graciously received, "but we all saw a great change between the fashion of the Court as it is now and that in the Queen's, for we were all lousy by sitting in Sir Thomas Erskine's chamber." I can quote worse than that from Mr. Dunlop. Elizabeth, however imperious and unpredictable she might be, was personally abstemious and saw to it that her courtiers behaved.

When Theobalds had become a Royal Palace [says Mr. Dunlop] it was the scene of entertainments which were far from edifying. During the reception of Christian IV of Denmark the revels were brought to a standstill by general drunkenness. First a lady who represented the Queen of Sheba "overset her casket into his Danish Majesty's lap"; the King rose to dance with her, but fell, and had to be carried into an inner chamber. "Now did appear Faith, Hope and Charity in rich dresses"—but even the Theological Virtues had succumbed to intemperance; "Hope did essay to speak, but wine did render her efforts so feeble that she withdrew." Nor was Victory to fare much better "for after much lamentable utterance she was led away like a silly captive." John Harrington is stern in his censure of such debauchery, which was the more unfortunate because Puritanism was already beginning to make its uncomfortable presence felt in England.

The date of that particular debauch must have been round about 1607. John Harrington was right: news of such conduct, traveling up the Road, increased the discontent of sober people. Brewster resigned his postmaster's office in 1607. He would no longer serve such a king.

The one good result of the Hampton Court conference of 1604 had been the appointment of a committee—indeed six committees of fifty-four scholars working at Oxford, Cambridge, and London— to make a new English translation of the Bible from the original Hebrew and Greek. Of all the many scholars concerned in this translation, Lancelot Andrewes was the most notable. In beauty of language it surpassed the Geneva Version of 1560 which had previously been the most scholarly, convenient, and widely accepted translation of the Scriptures. The "King James Version" was published in 1611, at a price of ten shillings. It says much for the piercing beauty of the words themselves that in time they could overcome the double handicap of being issued as "Authorized Version" and of carrying the fulsome dedication to James. In 1611 the "A.V." did not instantly supersede among all private readers the previous Geneva Version which (as the American Bible Society points out with approximate truth) "was the Bible of William Shakespeare, John Milton, John Bunyan, and Oliver Cromwell." The Bible which went to America in the *Mayflower* (I am particularly referring to the copy which contains the charming scribbles and "portrait" of the first pilgrim child born in Massachusetts, Peregrine White) was the Geneva Version and not the Bible dedicated to King James.[5]

I suppose it must be said for James that he would have had to be superhuman to cope with the situation into which he had been pitchforked. A large part of the trouble he inherited was what Keynes calls the indirect products of Drake's expeditions. One of the products was "the revolutionary price changes" in England. To the bewilderment of common people an upward trend of costs went on and on, followed only at a great remove by rents and wages. Landlords and laborers alike found themselves deprived of income, although the capitalist was having undreamed-of opportunities. "Never in the annals of the modern world," wrote Keynes, "has there existed so prolonged and so rich an opportunity for the business man, the speculator, and the profiteer." Keynes emphasized how prolonged and how disastrous to many people the

"indirect products" were. The first quarter of the seventeenth century was the period of the "greatest economic confusion in our
history." The economy of England was upset in part because
treasure from the Americas had upset the whole of Europe:
throughout the whole it was a period of currency disorder, trade
crises; and "monetary confusion prevailed everywhere."

In such an economic situation James could find nothing in the
way of easy plunder with which to replenish his Treasury. Henry
VIII had found the Church to plunder, Elizabeth had in her time
been lucky with Drake, but James could find nobody to attack
but Parliament and the City. His approach to both was as inept as
possible. By attempting to hector Parliament with the "divine right
of kings" he very notably succeeded in encouraging that institution
to find itself an instrument of resistance to king's rule. In 1614
James was three-quarters of a million pounds in debt, and all that
Parliament would grant him was one contemptuous subsidy of
£70,000. Petulance on one side bred petulance on the other. To a
group of merchants in the City James granted a charter, in 1607,
for the formation of the Virginia Company to have monopoly of the
tobacco trade. The colonies which had been sent out by Raleigh
twenty years before had managed, those which survived, to make it
worth while to establish a new town, Jamestown, in Virginia, to be
dependent largely upon tobacco. Were it not true it would be incredible that James's contribution to the enterprise, and to the town
which bore his name, was that expressed in his own writing and
never withdrawn: his *Counterblaste to Tobacco:*

A custom lothsome to the eye, hatefull to the nose, harmfull to the
braine, dangerous to the lungs, and in the black stinking fume thereof,
neerest resembling the horrible Stigian smoke of the pit that is bottome-
less.

Tobacco, in the mind of the populace with whom the habit of
smoking had caught on, was identified with the brilliant, gallant,
violent character of Raleigh, and it may be that James in his
Counterblaste was primarily girding at Raleigh—who, on trumped-
up charges of treason had been confined to the Tower under
sentence of death since James's accession. When James was desperate for money, he bethought himself of releasing Raleigh for one

last fling to the Spanish Main. Raleigh had been thirteen years in the Tower when James presented this proposition, and the aging adventurer must have been in two minds about accepting; but he did accept the last fling, and for a king that he despised Raleigh and his son and a crew of desperadoes set forth in 1616 to find an Eldorado in Guiana. The expedition was doomed from the start. The Spaniards were forewarned, resisted, drove off the attack, in which Raleigh's son was killed. Raleigh got back to London to report his unsuccess and to face his execution. The execution was not in the Tower, but at Palace Yard, Westminster, on 29 October, 1618. Before he went to the block Raleigh called for a pipe of tobacco, and wrote some philosophic verses; then as his last words, the axman seeming to him to be reluctant to do his business, he cried out, "Strike, man, strike!"

In 1620 the small group of "separatists" at long last left their homes and possessions in that region of the Road in which they could no longer see anything, material or spiritual, to hope for. I mentioned that the *Mayflower* in which they sailed was a ripe old ship which had been discarded by the Turkey Merchants. I mentioned that the printing press which they took with them had an interesting future. It was put to work before the Pilgrims reached America. As the old *Mayflower* was taking punishment in heavy seas of the Western Ocean, one of her principal beams cracked. It was shored up with the printing press. Eventually by happenstance the voyage fetched up at what became known as Plymouth, Massachusetts, and thankfully the "separates" set to the immediate task of securing food and cover. The hand press which had saved the ship was presently offloaded, but not as yet put to any printing work. When the men and women rose from their knees, there were other things to do.

I had decided not to attempt to have any illustrations in this book on the Great North Road, but I think I must break my rule (see page 184) to include the scribbles in the copy of the "Mayflower Bible," with the very kind permission of the University of Texas, where the copy now resides.

This chapter I have called The York Road. It is with that stretch of two hundred miles that I am here concerned. Remembering that the kaleidoscope is always changing, I tried to picture

London at the base of the road, gradually outspreading until it was going to contain, as it does today, a fifth of the population of the whole island. (Imperial Rome, in its heyday, had contained about a fifth of the population of all Italy.) I pictured some of the Tudor country houses, some of the extravagancies and comforts of the wealthy and great. I pictured the Road as a spillway whereby some of the poor or desperate or separate-minded effected, or attempted to effect, escape. As in the time of James restlessness

Peregrine

became endemic (except for those whom Keynes lumps together as "the business man, the speculator, and the profiteer"), the island of Britain began to look like breaking up for good and all. We, with our hindsight, know it did not break up. But what, then, pulled it together? What effected one of the most extraordinary transformations of all history, the emergence of this disaffected little island as pulse and dynamo for—what shall I say?—for whatever it later on proved itself to be a pulse and dynamo. As the storm gathered, as the Great Rebellion became for most people a foreseeable ordeal which could not be evaded, England must indeed have seemed a land of darkness, where the inhabitants sat in the shadow of death. It must have been dark indeed upon the York Road, with the darkness which shows no light anywhere.

What part am I to say the York Road played in those bad times? For a very long while it had been a road of "news," spoken news or printed news, and most of it bad. Elizabeth had never traversed that road; it shared none of her glory. James had traveled the road southward; there was no pride to be found in that. Except for such adventurers as might escape, there was increase of idleness, and life without work or purpose can seem very long. On the road, as you leave Scrooby northwards, you cross the boundary between Nottinghamshire and Yorkshire. The boundary is a small river, crossed by a small bridge. That bridge used to be in William Brewster's beat as postmaster. The river is the river Idle. Disgust with idleness was partly what the Pilgrim Fathers were leaving behind. Disgust with idleness was felt by other farmers and gentry of the Danelaw whose religious views were more moderate than those of the Pilgrims, and who were even slower to forsake their homes and livelihood. But some of them could not continue to go on nursing a perpetual disgust. The pilgrims from the York Road who had settled at Plymouth, Massachusetts, in 1620 and who had managed to survive were, as I stressed, "separates." They had gone to America as refugees who had forfeited and forsaken any legal standing in England; as to the world they left behind them, they had given up political expectations; their deep wish was to escape and to be left alone. Their survival was, however, a matter which was reported back to England, and this was also part of the "news" on the York Road. The survival of the Pilgrims resulted in the further and larger emigration to Massachusetts Bay in 1630. The Massachusetts Bay Colony was led by Englishmen who had not forfeited their legal standing in England, men whose intention was "militant and expansive." I borrow that phrase from Professor Ralph Barton Perry's *Puritanism and Democracy*. I don't know precisely what the phrase implies: something, I suppose, which was regarded by authority as politically subversive, else why should a ship have been prevented, in 1636, from sailing to the Massachusetts Bay Colony? We attend to the detention of that particular ship because it was the one in which Oliver Cromwell, at the age of thirty-seven, had "sought passage for himself and family" to Massachusetts. Cromwell had represented Huntingdon in Charles's third Parliament, which had been dissolved in 1629; there was apparently no prospect of Charles calling another Parliament; and the reason given for Cromwell's proposed emigration was that he was "disgusted with the government." He "only remained in England because the ship by which he was to have sailed was detained by proclamation."

I had not appreciated what a near thing it was that Cromwell did not become an American colonist,[6] until I ran across the above remarks in the third revised edition of Messrs. Dent's *Everyman's Encyclopaedia.* I should go back here, I think, to watch how Cromwell's disgust arose. The two families, Stuarts and Cromwells, were in a personal way known to each other. I would indeed draw a comparison, rather than a contrast, between the situations in which the two men, Charles and Oliver, grew up. There is nothing to contradict the story that as boys Charles and Oliver played together, on occasion, in the grounds of Hinchingbrook House. There is nothing to contradict that other story, that after the execution of Charles in 1649 Oliver visited the room at Whitehall where the king's body lay and, looking at the face, muttered the two words, "Cruel necessity." The skeptical may say there is no real proof of either story, and that they fit almost too neatly. But I would not disregard historical epitaphy. What the stories convey is an essential truth that the Civil Wars in seventeenth century England involved close personal feelings and relationships to a degree unknown in the anonymous wars of our day. I said the situations of the Stuart family and of the Cromwell family were not wholly dissimilar. In the first quarter of the seventeenth century the Stuarts at Theobalds were not having a good time. The Cromwells at Hinchingbrook were not having a good time either.

It was in March, 1625, that James died, leaving to his son, Charles, "a load of debts and a legacy of mistakes." It was in 1627 that Sir Oliver Cromwell, unable to cope with his own debts, was forced to sell Hinchingbrook House to the highest bidder. The nephew, Oliver, was then a man of twenty-eight, married (he was married at St. Giles's Cripplegate) and with a son a year old. I skip a myriad of anecdotes of Oliver's boyhood, that he was a notorious "apple-dragon," that he indulged in "pigeon-stealing," that at Dr. Beard's Grammar School at Huntingdon he frequently came under the rod of that fierce Puritan. Such stories are a common form of seventeenth century biography; as also the stories of delicate health, and of his being required at times to wear "a piece of red flannel round his neck." I dwell a moment on the phrase that in youth at Huntingdon he was regarded as a "splenetic dreamer." Oliver, at Dr. Beard's Grammar School, does seem to me to have been in a rather odd situation. I don't know how to express it accurately. The nearest I can come to it is to say that in the flat East Anglian countryside there was something "alien" about the Cromwells; something "different"; they were not "natives." I doubt if that mattered to the Cromwells of Hinchingbrook House. I picture Sir Oliver as maintaining a pride in the Welsh blood, in the heritage of a Hinchingbrook acquired by royal favor, of a House which royalty continued to visit. I picture the nephew Oliver as, and consciously, of the younger and poorer branch, the Huntingdon branch of the family. There he was in Thomas Beard's Puritan grammar school in Huntingdon, and amongst all the plain Biblical names of the other schoolboys, the Matthews and Marks, the Abrahams, Isaacs, and Jacobs, amongst the Samuels, amongst the Gideons, he had to stand up and answer to the Norman name of Oliver. I don't know how to state the thought without overstating it; but the thought is that Oliver Cromwell as a boy was somewhat living in two worlds. As a schoolboy at Huntingdon he must have been put to it to reconcile the tensions.

As we look back, both of the worlds in which Oliver Cromwell was growing were worlds which were falling and falling apart. By the time that Oliver was a young married man the Hinchingbrook world had certainly fallen. Yet—it is a small thing, but worth noting—he gave his son the Norman name of Richard. But Hinchingbrook House, and the world that represented, was sold up. The Huntingdon branch of the family was affected by the rot; some of the Huntingdon properties had to be sold, and by 1631 the salvage for Oliver and his increasing young family was a grazing farm at St. Ives, five miles from Huntingdon, down the river Ouse.

Cromwell, we said, had represented Huntingdon in Charles's

third Parliament, dissolved in 1629. Relegated to the grazing farm
at St. Ives, though he might have been, in the phrase quoted, "disgusted with the government," he remained a locally respected
farmer, a regular attender of the parish church, and a parish overseer. Why should Cromwell not have been contented with his lot?
Others in that time could manage to put aside political worries
and do useful daily work and seek the consolation of a quietist
philosophy. A doctor of Norwich, six years younger than Oliver
Cromwell, like Cromwell also by birth a gentleman, living neither
in any considerable height nor yet in obscurity, could solace himself
by writing *Religio Medici*. Sir Thomas Browne was to live through
the whole period of the Civil Wars in England with only one reference in his writings, so far as I recall, which is remotely topical;
and that is the astronomical phrase, "the huntsmen are up in
America." After the Parliament of 1629 there was to be, in fact, no
Parliament for eleven years. Was that period politically insupport-
able? Clarendon, who as an old man in exile was writing of those
years, says it was a period of "the greatest calm, and the fullest
measure of felicity." One would think that if Cromwell had been a
gentleman of adequate resignation or of decent despair, he might at
St. Ives have gone on watching the river Ouse ooze slowly to the
sea. But after five years of St. Ives, Cromwell sought passage for
America. It indicates his temperament was not that of a Thomas
Browne, nor his opinion of the state of England one of agreement
with Clarendon.

I don't believe that if Cromwell had persistently intended to
emigrate to the militant, expansive colony of Massachusetts Bay,
the stoppage of one ship would have halted him. A piece of
family business came up in the same year, 1636, the inheritance of
another property at Ely, and it is possibly that which stopped him.
He and his family moved to the Isle of Ely; but as years passed,
'36, '37, '38, '39, the contemplation of the river Ouse at Ely gave
Cromwell no more comfort than the river Ouse at St. Ives or the
river Ouse at Huntingdon. One thinks of him riding to London on
occasion to see what he could learn from Pym, Hampden, or the
rest about the state of the nation.

I picture some of Cromwell's rides as taking him from Ely to
look up affairs remaining at St. Ives and Huntingdon, and then on

past Hinchingbrook House to join the London Road at Buckden, or, if you prefer to pronounce it in the local way, Bugden. Hinchingbrook House had been bought by a Montagu, and a wall was being built round the place. To interpolate and to anticipate, if Sir Oliver Cromwell had to make a forced sale, he might have found a customer less congenial to the younger Oliver than that branch of the Montagus, for Edward Montagu, a child of two at the time of the purchase of Hinchingbrook, was at the age of eighteen to join the parliamentary army, to attract Cromwell's attention for his valor, and to hold high office on land and sea under the Commonwealth. This was the same Montagu who after the Restoration was created first Earl of Sandwich, was appointed admiral, and proved himself most notably in naval action, defeating the Dutch fleet off Lowestoft in 1665, and again in the Battle of Solebay, in which he was killed in the moment of victory. The article of food called a "sandwich" was named after the dissolute fourth Earl of Sandwich (the "Jemmy Twitcher" of *The Beggar's Opera*) and not after the first earl. It is ironical that Edward Montagu is I suppose now most widely remembered as the patron of Samuel Pepys, and also ironical that Hinchingbrook House is most widely known for the references to it in Pepys's *Diary.* Those references are amusing, especially the references to the dependent cottage at Brampton—the cottage in which lived Pepys's sister who "grows old and ugly," and the cottage garden in which Pepys's father so "sillily" buried the gold. Pepys's references to the great house at Hinchingbrook are mainly about the many "chargeable works that my Lord hath done there," mentioning among them "his water-works and the Ora, which is very fine." From Pepys's *Diary* you would obtain no intimation that Hinchingbrook House had memories antedating his "my Lord Sandwich," nor indeed from Pepys's editors do you gather that the "water-works and the Ora" are but repairs and renovations of plumbing which the Cromwells had put in for Queen Elizabeth. I must not let these trivia distract me from the sweep of the great storm which in Oliver Cromwell's time was gathering on the Great North Road. But trivia do have their trivial place in history. I don't apologize for our having a stereoscopic view of Hinchingbrook House. The Great North Road does that sort of thing to me when I turn off at Buckden. But the sweep of my story must blow away interpolations and anticipations; for there was storm in the feelings of the middle-aged moody Cromwell as he rode past Hinchingbrook House on his way to London. The future of Hinchingbrook he couldn't know about; it was in new hands, they were building a wall around it. The past of the house, I fancy, he could remember. I fancy—I only say I fancy—that at such a time as Cromwell rode past Hinching-brook House to London—each time it possibly did, I don't know what, something to his metabolism.

There was a Parliament again in 1640. Short Parliament, Long Parliament, the sharpening of all the quarrels to the single issue, King versus Parliament—in what way does all that involve the York Road? At first it would seem as if the road was only accidentally involved. After Charles's personal intervention in Parliament in January, 1642, after that inconclusive and unseemly squabble, Charles moved his court from Whitehall to York. Was it the first time an English sovereign had traveled so far up the perilous path of the Great North Road? It was the first time for a long time and, as it happened, a journey of ill omen: Charles never again returned to Whitehall except as a captive. But I am not stressing the remove of Charles's court to York as a matter of significance to my story. What I regard as a real significance of the York Road is yet to come. It is of importance to consider that it was at York that Charles was joined by his impetuous foreign nephew, Prince Rupert, who had hastened to come over from Holland. It was a time when English-men, no matter how clear-cut the issue, were deeply reluctant actually to draw sword on fellow Englishmen, a time when on one side there was a man such as Falkland, on the other a man such as Hampden. No biography of Rupert indicates that he had any modicum of such conscience.

If it had to come to a long-term civil war, the sinews of warfare might reside in London, in Parliament, City, and control of ship-ping; but all immediate offensive striking power was with the king. Around Charles at York there gathered men eager for physical com-bat: Rupert the most notable. Rupert was scarcely more than twenty years old, but had been a soldier from the age of fourteen. He had experienced a hundred fights in the Danish and German wars; he had made his name as an irresistible cavalry leader; had proved himself, General Fuller stresses, "a man of reckless courage, headstrong, flamboyant and versatile." Rupert was the Cavalier superbly able to give *esprit de panache* to the gathering Royalists. "Dressed in a scarlet coat richly laced with silver, and mounted on a black Barbary horse, he rode about accompanied by a pet monkey," accompanied also by a white poodle. The poodle was named Boy, and Rupert had taught him the trick:

> Who name but Charles he comes aloft for him,
> But holds up his Malignant leg at Pym.

Royalist supporters came to York from the North and West. Rupert taught his cavalry to charge with the sword after the fashion of the Swedish cavalry he had seen in Germany, and for such type of whirlwind action he inspired immense confidence. By the summer of 1642 Charles was prepared to move south. In August he raised his Royal Standard on Castle Hill, Nottingham—"an appeal to his people and a challenge to Pym's Perpetual Parliament." It was the formal declaration of war. Charles's objective was London, but it was by a circling movement to the west, hoping so to gain larger forces, that the Royalists progressed, and the first major engagement with the troops which Parliament sent out was at Edgehill (October 23, 1642) in the Cotswolds.

The Battle of Edgehill was confused and indecisive. Two things stand out. One is that Rupert conclusively proved that wherever he chose to charge he could carry the day. He chased the Roundheads in front of him three miles to Kineton, and after that the mention of his name spread terror to Parliamentarians. The other fact that stands out is that Oliver Cromwell was at the Battle of Edgehill. At the age of forty-three it was his first experience of actual warfare. Cromwell was in charge of the 67th Troop of Horse, consisting of sixty men and three officers. Later, Cromwell records the talk he had with Hampden after the battle:

At my first going out into this engagement, I saw our men were beaten at every hand. . . . "Your troopers," said I, "are most of them old decayed serving-men, and tapsters, and such kind of fellows; and," said I, "their troopers are gentlemen's sons, younger sons and persons of quality: do you think that the spirits of such base mean fellows will ever be able to encounter gentlemen, that have honour and courage and resolution in them? . . . You must get men of spirit: and take it not ill what I say—I know you will not—of a spirit that is likely to go on as far as gentlemen will go—or else I am sure you will be beaten still."

After Edgehill the king was able to move slowly on London. Rupert carried Brentford bridge by storm, but the direct thrust was stopped by the "Trained Bands" assembled at Turnham Green. The Royalist army was not yet large enough to invest so large a town as London, and for the time being Charles and Rupert withdrew to Oxford, to raise more troops for the final and triple attack. The Royalist plan was simple. The king had three armies which could be counted on: that of the Duke of Newcastle to come down the Great North Road from the North, that of Sir Ralph Hopton to come from the Southwest, that led by Rupert to work from the Midlands along the line of the old Watling Street. The roads laid out by Aulus Plautius still governed the anatomy of Britain. Those were the three routes for the triple threat to London. The plan was hampered because behind each of the king's armies there were on each of these three routes towns which were firmly and obstinately Roundhead and which remained so throughout the war: Hull, Plymouth, Gloucester. Those were the towns which saved the Parliamentary cause by giving Cromwell time to raise his "men of spirit."

The sting administered by Rupert at Edgehill had roused the temper of a hitherto inexperienced captain of horse, and it is as if in personal opposition to the hero of the Cavaliers that Cromwell fervently set to work. In January, 1643, Cromwell returned with his troop to Cambridge. By March he had raised four more troops. These five original troops, each of sixty men, were proud to bear the name of "Gideon's Three Hundred." In this swift exertion of raising and training the nucleus of an army, Cromwell for the first time gives the impression of being supremely happy. The moody parish overseer is replaced by a man who has found his dedication: the dedication of a soldier. His happiness bursts from his letters. "I have a lovely company," he wrote, "you would respect them, did you know them. They are no Anabaptists, they are honest, sober Christians: they expect to be used as men!"

"Some time they must have for exercise," said Cromwell; and if his recruitment was from Cambridge, Ely, Huntingdon—attracting such young men as Edward Montagu—his ground for exercise was the Great North Road. The road from Cambridge and Huntingdon joins Route A1 at Alconbury Hill; northward from that road junction were Cromwell's first exercises. This is the significance which I find in the York Road: it was Cromwell's testing ground. Newcastle's army was probing from the North, Rupert's troopers were also "exercising" from Oxford. Rupert's fame was at its zenith. Wherever his Cavaliers charged, neither infantry nor cavalry withstood them. Rupert on reconnaissance from Oxford met John Hampden's regiment in the Chiltern Hills, charged and dispersed them, and Hampden was mortally wounded. In March, 1643, the Royalists took the town of Grantham on the Great North Road. It was a necessary exercise for "Gideon's Three Hundred" to chase them out. After that, Cromwell himself in May, 1643, scouting with twelve troopers at Gonerby Hill (pronounced Gunnerby) a mile or two north of Grantham, laid into and put to flight a troop of twenty-four Royalists. It was Cromwell's troopers who began to feel they had a leader who was irresistible. It was about this time that Cromwell clothed his troops with an issue of "russet" coats. More men joined his color: by September, 1643, he had ten troops of horse, early in 1644 he had fourteen, additional to the original "Three Hundred." By himself the one-time parish overseer had raised eleven hundred men in what came to be "red" coats, proud to be used as men; and more than that, by his exertion and example Cromwell had organized the counties of Norfolk, Suffolk, Essex, Cambridge, and Hertford into the "Eastern Association," a unit small in comparison with the whole of Britain, but one by now prepared to test its strength. Hull, Gloucester, Plymouth had done their work by delaying the Royalists' triple thrust to London, and Cromwell felt it was time for him to dictate a direct battle with Rupert.

"About this time," says Defoe, "it was that we began to hear of the name of Oliver Cromwell, who, like a little cloud, rose out of the East, and spread first into the North, until it shed down a flood that overwhelmed the three kingdoms." After Edgehill it had taken about eighteen months of immensely energetic work for Cromwell to feel ready to try it out with Rupert, eighteen months of finding "men." Cromwell never forsook his axiom that "an army is 'men.'" In 1644 he was telling the London Committee of Parliament that he would not be voted riffraff who were "only fit for the gallows here and a hell hereafter." He was also telling Parliament that he was going to face Rupert. He had exercised along the York Road. It was time to take York. This threat was bound to draw Rupert. It did. Battle was joined at Marston Moor near York at 5:00 P.M. on July 2, 1644. Rupert had the handling of the cavalry on the king's side, Cromwell on the side of Parliament. It was in the main a cavalry battle, and looked upon as an out-and-out contest of the two leaders and of what they represented. The battle ended in an overwhelming Royalist defeat. "It was the greatest battle of the war," says General Fuller, "and for Charles a disaster of the first magnitude. Rupert, having started with seven thousand cavalry, and having lost a thousand of them, withdrew in haste to Richmond." The dog, Boy, had been killed by a Roundhead trooper. With Rupert in flight, Cromwell swept round the rear of the Royalist army, and dispersed the cavalry on the other wing. He then attacked Newcastle's foot, who died bravely almost to a man. A fortnight after the battle York surrendered to the Parliamentarians.

"Old Ironside" was the nickname which Rupert, with rueful wit, bestowed upon Cromwell after Marston Moor, and "Ironsides" became the proud name of Cromwell's troopers. The Duke of Newcastle abandoned the king's cause, and the whole territory of the Great North Road was under Parliamentary control. Charles still held the South and West, the Royalists continued to win battles there, and Montrose was raising Highland clans for the king and making his name feared by Scottish Covenanters: so the Royalists had hopes for the campaign of 1645. But in the meantime Cromwell had persuaded Parliament to let him and Fairfax organize a New Model Army, the first regular standing army in English history. Royalist wits laughed at the "New Noddle Army," but it was a thoroughly professional body of 21,000 men with regular pay and with standard issue of new red coats. This army was well drilled throughout the spring in Windsor Great Park, and in the summer it caught up with the king's army at Naseby in Northamptonshire. Once again Rupert on his black horse led the cavalry for Charles, and Cromwell for the Roundheads, and once again it was Rupert who was outmaneuvered and defeated. Wherever it was directed the New Model Army was successful, and in May, 1646, Charles left Oxford in disguise and surrendered to the Scots garrison at Newark.

The Interregnum, the Second Civil War, the trial and execution of Charles, the Commonwealth, the Dutch Wars, the period of the Protectorate; Cromwell's relations with Parliament, his refusal of the crown—all these thoughts crowd in. Cromwell's ruthlessness in Ireland, his foreign policy, his conception of a British Empire; the careers of Blake and Montagu as "Generals-at-sea," of General Monk in Scotland; how the Restoration came about after Cromwell's death in 1658; the conduct of Charles II, reminiscent of "that chameleon" Augustus who had followed the first Caesar; recollections of how that famous army of Ironsides was reviewed for the last time at Blackheath and paid off and discharged from service—these thoughts, I say, crowd in. But what I must not let them do, is crowd me off my strip of Roadway. I can't follow all that came out of it, but I can see where the causation began. Much indeed began to stir, when Cromwell first began to use the York Road for his "exercise."

1558—the Accession of Elizabeth. 1658—the death of Cromwell. Elizabeth never used the York Road. Cromwell used every inch of it. Elizabeth's chief glory, I suppose, the poetry at London Bridge; and Cromwell's I suppose, the greatest all-round effort of an English commoner who, when the ship of state was most demonstrably in a bad way, stayed and righted it. It is with the York Road that I identify the beginnings of his effort, and it is with the York Road that after his death I identify Cromwell's bones. Myths are a part of the story of the Road. It is interesting in what ways myths repeat themselves, and in what ways they differ. I mentioned that as Malory tells the story, Launcelot's body was sent up the Great North Road. It went in stately progress, in the bier which had been used for Guenever, and with the hundred burning torches. I did not picture that progress as calling forth much devotion within the Danelaw. The myth about Cromwell is that after his death his body also, though without torches, was taken up the York Road. After the Restoration there was the recorded intention of having the coffin of Cromwell removed from Westminster Abbey and of having his body hanged in its shroud at Tyburn. But the myth to which I refer denies that it ever so happened. The myth about Cromwell's body seems to exist as a spiritual necessity. I don't know how many of Cromwell's original "Three Hundred" survived him, but the souls of those who didn't were in attendance at the last journey of the man with the Norman name, up the York Road to York, and a little farther.

Beyond York there is the village of Coxwold; beside Coxwold is Newburgh Priory; and it is in a wall of Newburgh Priory (with no external sign to prove it) that Cromwell's bones are sealed in their final resting place. Tourists know Coxwold because Laurence Sterne lived there, and wrote *Tristram Shandy*. My Uncle Toby lays down his pipe as gently as if it were thistledown, and is silent upon the matter. I believe in his silence. I also believe in the Yorkshireman who told me of the myth.

X »» *Postmen's Garden*

Immediately to the north of G.P.O. Headquarters Building, in the heart of Little Britain, a gateway leads from King Edward Street into Postmen's Garden. A recent signboard by the gate now labels it Postman's Park, but I prefer the older name.

There are three or four things to see and think about in Postmen's Garden. In a moment I hope to enter, find a bench to sit on, and relax and think about them.

But before that there seems to me a duty to be done. I was attempting to draw a contrast between the condition of England in the time of Elizabeth and the condition in the time of Cromwell, but I don't feel I managed it properly, and with permission would like to try it another way.

Hock-day.

Hock-day—few words have ever received so much etymological and historical investigation, but the origin has never been agreed—was the second Tuesday after Easter Sunday. Hock Tuesday, in former times, says the big *Oxford English Dictionary* (I don't see how you can travel the Road without carrying those thirteen volumes in your knapsack) was "an important term-day, on which rents were paid, and the like, Hock-day and Michaelmas dividing the rural year into its summer and winter halves."

So far, so good. What does the *O.E.D.* mean by "former times"? From early times, I gather. From the fourteenth century "and probably earlier" the *O.E.D.* reports that Hock-tide was a popular festival "signalized by the collection of money for parish purposes by roughly humorous methods." The "roughly humorous methods" invite attention. Hock-day was the second Tuesday after Easter, but we learn that Hock-tide was a two-day period of license. The term Hock-tide applied to both Monday and Tuesday, and the chief feature was the seizing and binding (by women on Monday and by men on Tuesday) of persons of the opposite sex, who released themselves by paying a forfeit.

Saxon fun, I feel. I feel it as a sort of downspreading of Æthelred's housewarmings, though by the later days of the fifteenth and sixteenth centuries it is clear from the references that regularization of payments for the sexual excitement had been taken over from manor house to Church. Such Hock-tide forfeits as were paid in cash were put into parish funds. The ever-useful *O.E.D.* provides a number of references: "1499 in C. Coates *Antiq. Reading* 214. It. rec. of hok money gaderyd of women xxs. It. rec. of hok money gaderyd of men iiijs. 1515–6 in *Archaeol.* VII 251. Received of the men for oke money *vs.* viiid. Item if the wyffs of oke money xvs. *id.*" And so on: it would be no trouble to multiply the references. It is interesting to note that women paid into parish funds more shillings and pence from their gatherings from men than men paid in from their gatherings from women. As a Church-licensed saturnalia, Hock-tide was frowned on after the Reformation, though it continued to have defendants. Wither wrote in 1613: "Because that, for the Churches good, They in defence of Hocktide custome stood." Two centuries after that, Hone in his *Every Day Book* (in 1826) mentions Hock-tide as a term that his readers will remember. "Kissing Day" in Cheshire provides the *O.E.D.* with a quotation from the *Liverpool Echo* as late as 1898, the celebration then still occurring on the second Tuesday after Easter.

I draw attention to the recorded power of survival of the "Hock-tide custome." The *O.E.D.* remarks that after the "custome" was officially renounced by the Church, "recourse was had to the plan of stretching ropes or chains across the streets and ways, to stop passers by for the same purpose." Brand writes in 1777: "On both days the men and women, alternately, with great merriment inter-cepted the public roads with ropes, and pulled passengers to them." Another thought reminds me of our discussion of Saxon manor houses, how sexual entertainment in the manor houses eased off into floor shows and music-hall turns, or was at any rate accompanied, in my surmise, with theatrical entertainment; for you find that "Hocktide custome" was regularly accompanied with open-air theatrical play performances. But it is a further thought which is the surprising one, that traditional Hock-tide plays had to do with Danes. If you are casually interested in the Great North Road it is probable that you will glance at Speed's *History of Great Britain*. The date of Speed's *History* was 1611. Speed was in no particular hurry: the reference I am making is to Volume 8, Chapter 5, Sec-tion 11, Folio 392. When you have gone buzzing along to that point, Speed suddenly bites your ear with the remark: "The day of his [Hardicnut's] death is annually celebrated with open pastimes . . . which time is now called Hoctide or Hucktide, signi-fying a time of scorning and contempt, which fell upon the Danes by his death."

Hypotheses non fingo, but I fingo the *O.E.D.* It comments: "State-ments going back to the 15th or 16th c. assert that *Hock-day* com-memorated either the massacre of the Danes on 13 Nov. 1002, or the death of Hardicnut on 8 June 1042. From the dates of those events it is difficult to understand how either was associated with Hock-tide."

I trust I am as candid as the great *Oxford Dictionary* about admitting a difficulty, but road works tell you that when you meet a difficulty you have to cope or run around it somehow.[1] So that was why, a long while since, when we were stopping at Lindisfarne and Jarrow and Whitby, I was laboriously dragging together indi-cations about the season of the year when Saxons would most par-ticularly wish to scorn or score off Danes. That was why I was struggling to ponder the season for Danes and dragons, for the special resentment of Saxon churchmen, for the irritability of Saxon warriors, even for the selection of St. George's Day for Saxon celebration, and the selection of St. George himself as patron saint of England—St. George and the Dragon. I doubt if anything gets into myth unless many meanings intertwine, and it is murder to dissect the meanings; but if you are presented with a great tapestry is it respectful not to pay what attention you can to the threads and the weave? When we were back at Lindisfarne I had the feeling that if ever the Saxons were going to get on top of the Danes and wish to crow about it, Hock-tide would be the crowing season. And so apparently it was, in Elizabeth's predominantly Saxon England. Consider the cockcrowing opportunity for play actors at Hocktide. Consider Laneham's remark in 1575: "Hok Tuesday by the Couentree men," and more particularly consider the remark from Dugdale's *Warwickshire,* also dated 1575: "Hither came the Coventre men, and acted the ancient Play, long since used in that City, called Hocks tuesday, setting forth the destruction of the Danes in King Ethelred's time."

It would be interesting to know the geographical distribution of the "various parishes" in which, in Elizabethan England, it was customary to applaud the ham actor's performance as "hockermocker," coincidental at Hock-tide with other "hugger-mugger" goings on. It is a question of a type not easy to answer: Could you, for instance, associate May games and Morris (Moorish?) dancing with one region of England more than another? Boisterous springtime merrymaking, sport, frolic, foolery, and entertainment are not confined to the Saxon part of the island, although in the far North springtime is naturally later in the calendar—at present the spring term day in Scotland is Whitsuntide instead of Lady Day as in the South. In Elizabethan times the Southerners remained scornful of "the inly-working North," yet so far as concerns physical exuberance I am sure the Maypole was as well understood in Yorkshire, say, as in Kent. In Yorkshire in 1583 "A May game was of Robyn-hood, and of his traine that time." Professor Child remarked in his *English and Scottish Ballads* that "Maid Marian is a personage in the Maygame and morris." Yet there is a point to the question, in that it makes one recall that even the most universal of springtime impulses were, in the Elizabethan age, interpreted locally and paro-

chially. The fundamental impulses might be the same all over the
island, and in hindsight the rejoicings may seem more or less
cognate, but all the same the individual expressions of the common
impulse reveal deep native cleavages, and indeed persistent hostilities. That is why I was so much interested to observe that Hock-
tide was associated, by Saxons, with scorning of Danes, with
taunting Danes for ineffectiveness: the Saxon Church abetting in
this raillery. If I had to guess which parishes relished the Hock-tide
celebrations, I would associate them more with the line of Watling
Street, the famous old dividing rampart between Saxons and Danelaw, than with any other region.

There is an "if"—and what an "if" it is—arising from the above
quotation from Dugdale. "If" in 1575 the Coventry players on their
stroll played their Hock-tide play at Stratford, then a Stratford
schoolboy of eleven might have watched them playing a play about
Danes. Or a year before or a year after, or young Shakespeare
might have watched the Coventry players year by year. There is
no shadow of proof that he did. There is no impossibility.

It is a monstrous skip from a schoolboy in Stratford who *might*
have seen Coventry players playing a play about Danes, to the
mature dramatist who made

> Those flights upon the banks of Thames
> That did so take Eliza and our James.

I would not make the skip to any purpose except to say that there
are more complexities in the background of Shakespeare's *Hamlet*
than are instantly evident if you are reading the text in the abstract,
as if it had sprung out of nothing, as if Shakespeare had been given
a free hand to invent an as it were "personal" character. Those
flights upon the banks of Thames were professional theatrical
ventures, and the ventures had several tastes to please—including,
I would agree, the author's own taste—but not offending tastes of
others. What was the "general gender" of the entertainment world
at London Bridge when Shakespeare was commissioned, or commanded or decided for himself, to redesign an older play about
Danes? "Our James" (when Ben Jonson used that phrase he was in
part alluding to the fact that he and James were both Scotsmen)
was a somewhat unknown quantity advancing down the Great

North Road to become King of England, with a stage-struck Danish queen, whose Danish friends at court were likely to prove themselves (as in that orgy at Tibbals) rather a raffish lot. How then was a King's Company of players to put on a production of *Hamlet* which could wholly go along with Saxon Hock-tide traditions? Yet also how could a play about Danes go wholly against the traditions? I am adding nothing to the study of *Hamlet*, the play, except perhaps an extra reason why Shakespeare worked harder on it, as is demonstrated by the internal evidence, than on any other play. Among whatever larger reasons, Hock-tide contributes a moiety to the puzzle Shakespeare sets about Hamlet, the character. The Prince of Denmark is presented by Shakespeare (as many critics have observed) as scarcely being a "person" at all; and perhaps it is because he is such an "impersonal" Hamlet that the play has proved to be such good theater. There are two ghosts in Shakespeare's *Hamlet*: the ghost of Hamlet's father, and Hamlet himself who is ghost of us all, about whom each of us can feel that we know him somewhat more intimately than can anybody else.

In my vision of the Great North Road I saw, at the southern end, London Bridge originating as a formidable Norman military instrument, intended as a catapult toward Europe. As such it failed, and I saw it being taken over, as Norman abbeys had been taken over, in a spirit that was domestic and parochial. It was not the business of the play boys to do anything else with London Bridge than to throw whatever ropes and chains they could across the southern end of it, to devise a good jigamaree, and to cozen whom they might into the playground, beer garden, bear garden or theater. The sport brought into being a wonderful galaxy of talent, a new variety of tradesmen. There is no disrespect in regarding Shakespeare, in that new trade, as the tradesman nonesuch. Ask any kind of play you fancied, cloth of gold or cloth of fustian, and there it was, laid out and cut to length and with such ease that you would scarcely think the making of the cloth or the cutting of it was a virtue. What was young Heminge's epithet?—*ingenious* Shakespeare. The only play in which you see Shakespeare in trouble is *Hamlet*. Well, that old rent in the garment of England between Saxons and Danes remained as something very difficult to stitch together. That is the big thing we are examining, how England got stitched together. The play boys at London Bridge couldn't do it: consider the physical limitations of their broadcasting. In a twentieth century world it requires an effort to appreciate how silent was the seventeenth century world, as to intercommunication; how separated were the parts. In Britain's recent times of woe the entertainment business was able to exert immense cohesive power: one needs only to mention the universal comradeship supplied by Tommy Handley and the radio program "It's That Man Again." In the bad times of James, with the fabric of Britain more and more obviously tearing asunder, there was nothing much that Jacobean dramatists could do, except to sink into the slough of despond, and to compare notes about malaise, acedia, and agenbite of inwit. Box-office business and other forms of patronage dropped off. Ben Jonson, we may recall, died penniless. Shakespeare had retired from the arena very early. Seven years after the advent of King James, roundabout the year 1610, Shakespeare at the age of forty-six slipped away from London Bridge. He slipped away to Stratford. For three more years or so he wrote, then wrote no more.

It is extraordinary that there has never been found any shred of a personal letter from Shakespeare after his retirement to any of his old friends in London, to "old Heminge" or to anybody else. I repeat, it is extraordinary. We scan the best biographies, and what they report is that after Shakespeare's return to Stratford there were six years of midnights without a letter to anyone. It is a shocking cipher in the great accompt.[2] The letters of Keats are of as much interest as his poems. Of Shakespeare's private thoughts no letter, not a scrap, nothing remains. There are the few legal documents and the will he made in 1616 a month before his death. Explain it how you may, after Shakespeare's retirement there is no comment to be made: the rest is silence.

I was drawn into simultaneous consideration of Shakespeare and Cromwell because they are so very close upon the time scale. Had Shakespeare, pulling away from London Bridge with whatever cargo he took with him made use of the Great North Road (I am not suggesting he did) Oliver Cromwell, at that date a schoolboy of eleven, might have seen him passing by. This is only another way of saying that Cromwell is to be thought of as a delayed Elizabethan; that is to say, a young man growing up in an England which was much divided, fragmented, and, in the country, much given to parochial customs embodying, in however merry a way, ancient antipathies. That was the reason, apart from the amusement of the custom, for thinking about Hock-tide. I was thinking about Shakespeare; born as it were on "the right side of the tracks" (the "tracks" in this metaphor means Watling Street) devising a London transmutation of a traditional knockabout Dane into a prince, who had he been put on would have proved most royally. It is not absurd to consider Shakespeare's Hamlet and Cromwell in the same breath, insofar as both were shaped to contemporary circumstance, Cromwell a real person (no doubt about that) and Hamlet a wraith. Cromwell, with his curious heritage, grew up with school fellows from "the wrong side of the tracks," that is to say, with fellows from within the Danelaw. The comparison between the characters, if we don't press it too hard, is permissible.

Everything on the time scale seems close in those days, though the motion of time itself, throughout the reign of James, seems to drag. I mentioned the long hesitancy before the Pilgrim Fathers actually chartered the old, decrepit *Mayflower*. Cromwell, as father of a family, as a farmer with local responsibilities, as an inconspicuous member of Parliament, was slow to push forward. As a moody young man we imagined him quick enough to agree with Hamlet that "the time is out of joint" but not at all hasty to assume

> O cursed spite
> That ever I was born to set it right.

It is not with that jingle that we associate Cromwell. But I do associate him with the words

> Sir, in my heart there was a kind of fighting
> That would not let me sleep.

I said that when he found himself in military action, and especially against Rupert, he was happy; yet when the Wars were over and he was military dictator of the whole of Britain—what then? He had destroyed the Throne of England; with impartial violence he had destroyed Parliament; there was no government except that of his own mailed fist—what then? His position was similar to Caesar's, and Caesar, we said, failed to find a way out. What was to be Cromwell's way out, when he was dictator of Britain?

My business is to trace what part was played by the Great North Road in Cromwell's conception of the future for Britain; and looking solely from this point of view, I see this Road as of immense importance to Cromwell, with a power of exercise above all others. We saw his use of the road for his troopers; he extended that use beyond York, beyond the border of Scotland, to win the decisive battle over the Scots at Dunbar—one of the decisive battles of the world. But it was not the military use of the Great North Road which was so important as the use of the Road as means of joining, as means of suture for an island apparently hopelessly disjointed and disordered. I don't see what else could have pulled Britain together, after the Great Rebellion, except the Great North Road; and this, so far as I am capable of gathering it, was Cromwell's view. The Bible, disseminated in its various translations, was providing something in common—at least something in common to bicker about—but the bickering of sectaries was so violent as to destroy, rather than to exhibit, any common religious faith. What Cromwell had first achieved was the implanting of a military faith upon the Great North Road: a military pride within the Danelaw. When that pride was so unmistakably followed by performance, the Saxon part of England had perforce to cease to jeer. That was the sewing of the old, old rent in England's garment. It was a suture which nowadays is mostly forgotten (though the soul of Alfred would remember)—which is best proof of good sewing. And, after Dunbar, the Great North Road might be a way of drawing Scots toward union. I would instance Cromwell's treatment of Scotland as in notable contrast with his treatment of Ireland. The Irish, apart from being papists, were of no use to Cromwell's immediate design: they received atrocious treatment, as having nothing but nuisance value. But Scotland—look at it as Cromwell looked on his map—was now on the Great North Road. That muscle of Road was bound to exert itself, and the instructions with which General Monk was sent back to Scotland were, I would guess, that proud Scots were to be taught not merely the strength but the use of that muscle. For, as it seems to me, that was part of Cromwell's conscious design. The Great

North Road should play its part in his way out. I see it as in his plan, to use the Great North Road as muscle; to use it as men; to send it oversea and round the world at a good round trot.

This second effort to send the Great North Road to sea differed from the former Norman conception, in that in Cromwell's time it looks like a forced diversion from the trouble at home. It would seem to be a universal axiom that when a dictator is in an uneasy situation it is best to find, or if necessary to invent, an outside enemy, or at the least some common interest away from home, and perhaps the farther away the better. When in 1646 Sir Jacob Astley had surrendered the last of the Royalist armies at Stow-in-the-Wold, he said to his captors, "You may now go play, unless you fall out among yourselves." Within Britain what Cromwell had to face was everybody falling out among themselves: ancient racial hostilities had been appeased, Saxons versus Danes, and it might be possible to appease Scots versus Southerons; but the storm of the Great Rebellion was unlikely to subside all in a moment. Paradoxically, the fighting had done something toward pulling Britain together, in that the conflict was so much larger than parochial, and tiny fragments had become larger pieces; but what common faith would cement them? A common secular faith might grow from victorious foreign wars and increase of foreign trade. I am sure Cromwell had plenty of midnight worries, but one possible way of composing them was to send the Great North Road to sea for the sake of peace at home. So

> Up from my cabin
> My sea-gown scarved about me, in the dark

he set about that task.

I must reflect that at the beginning of my journey I could run along the Road at the rate of four hundred years a chapter; but here, at the start of the British Empire, unless I am extra cautious the engine seizes. All things considered, we were traveling at a pretty fast clip until we ran into that contiguity in time between Shakespeare and Cromwell, and into the storm of the Great Rebellion. I said that in his lifetime Cromwell exercised the Great North Road, and made at the northern end a much more firm attachment to Scotland, and then from the southern end he set it to work at sea. If one is talking matter-of-fact, it is of course preposterous to say the Road was sent to sea; but talking matter-of-spirit (we faced this problem before with the Normans, and with the Pilgrim Fathers) it seems to me legitimate to remark that it was the spirit of the Road sent to work across the waters. It was the spirit Cromwell had exercised upon the Road which had encouraged Robert Blake, a West Country merchant, an Oxford man, to become soldier at the age of forty-five, and in the period of the Rump Parliament to accept appointment as "general-at-sea" (Edward Montagu was another). Cromwell with a file of soldiers marched into the House of Commons and in the famous scene of flinging the Speaker's mace on the floor ("What have we to do with this bauble? Take it away") completed the breakup of any free self-government in England. There was no government now, except that of the Lord Protector. The Lord Protector would not live for ever: all self-continuing institutions had to be rebuilt. The indirect way that could happen (at least the way it did happen) was by Cromwell routing up, his sea-gown scarved around him.

But though I feel the spirit of the Great North Road is legitimately to be thought of in thinking of the formation of the British Empire, to trace that theme in any detail will be agreed to be beyond my scope of power. It starts off comically enough. After the Civil Wars in England, Prince Rupert, shorn of his feathers but not of his energy, attempted to use the Channel Islands, to which he had escaped, as a base for privateering in the Narrow Sea. Blake's first commission, after he had reorganized the navy, was to chase him away. Blake chased Rupert to Lisbon, thence into the Mediterranean and out again, till Rupert fled to the West Indies. There, for a while, he had a lively time of buccaneering. Blake, returned to home base, was cruising with ten ships off Dover when he fell in with Tromp, with a Dutch fleet of fifty ships. According to old English naval custom, Blake ordered the English flag to be saluted (a demand to foreigners not abandoned until 1872) and Tromp at once resented the impertinent demand. Tromp opened fire, and Blake escaped only under cover of night. This episode triggered off the first of the naval wars with the Dutch. There were hard feelings on both sides. The Dutch had borne the real fury and sufferings of the wars with Spain, for which the English, who contributed relatively little, claimed too much credit. After six vicious battles in the home seas Blake was at last victorious over Tromp, but there was further sea warfare to come with the Dutch, and skirmishes all over the world. For example, the East India Company had attempted to found a factory at Amboyna in the Spice Islands; in 1623 the British merchants there had been set upon by the Dutch, some of the merchants killed and the settlement destroyed; this was not forgotten when later on the English had the chance of picking up a Dutch settlement in North America called Nieu Amsterdam and renaming it New York.[3]

The caprice and unexpectedness of what happened when the Great North Road went to sea in the seventeenth century is fascinating, and in a wealth of episodes it would be easy to concentrate upon those which exemplify a spirit of conquest, or a spirit of foreign trade, without recognizing that it was the blend of these two spirits which was to provide the secular faith which would establish stable government within the homeland. Trade and conquest, conquest and overseas trade: that was the combination which would redeem idleness in England and cause men to think together. Oversea commerce was no new conception, but was to be pursued with renewed energy. Spanish possessions anywhere in the world were obvious targets to Cromwell. He sent an expedition to the West Indies with instructions to capture Hispaniola; the captains concerned in that expedition mismanaged it, squabbled among themselves, were beaten away from Hispaniola, but not daring to return without something, picked up Jamaica instead. Cotton from the West Indies at once began to come into Lancashire to be fingered by the weavers of "Manchester cottons." The West Indian cotton did not compare favorably for all purposes (such as wicks for tallow candles) with the Sea Island cotton as shipped to England by the Turkey Merchants from the Mediterranean, but the extra quantity was useful, for the Turkey Merchants were clamoring for more and more manufactured cotton cloth. The color of the English cloth which was most admired was red; it was a standing order of the Levant Company to its export shippers, "When in doubt, send red"; and the phrase "Turkey red" is likely to be one of the phrases (such as "American cloth," "Russian stout") whereby a product is described not from its point of origin but from its destination. The all-over tonnages of those hand-loom days may seem to us small; I have no figures for the seventeenth century, but even by 1790 (just before the power-driven looms got to work) it is improbable that the import of raw cotton into England was much more than 30 million pounds, contrasting with something like 460 million pounds in 1840 when (thanks to the Industrial Revolution) the map of what had been the Danelaw was really turning black. I am not forgetting the wool textile industry, which we were looking at in its earliest days; this was and remains a main staple of Britain; in the 1950's the United Kingdom wool textile industry exports exceeded exports of aircraft and aircraft engines by more than £800,000. Cotton, in Britain, was younger sister to wool, and in Cromwell's time was very young, and needed protection. Cotton from Egypt was the best; there had to be safe passage in the Mediterranean; Cromwell sent Blake to show the English flag, to beat up the Barbary Corsairs (a task eventually completed by American Marines), to threaten the pope himself; and he dropped a letter "to Generals Blake and Montague, at Sea," suggesting they might take Gibraltar. This project did not appear to be convenient at the moment (Gibraltar was not captured until 1704). What Blake was doing was to fall upon the Spanish fleet in the harbor of Santa Cruz in Teneriffe; he sank the Spanish fleet and sent home thirty-eight wagonloads of treasure. But the treasure was aside from the main purpose, which was conquest for the sake of commerce.

At home in England, too much I think has been made of the sourpuss aspect of Cromwell's régime. City merchants found there was less austerity than under James or Charles. There was a wide variety in the new commerce: more raw silk was coming in from Persia, mohair was coming in to be used for buttons and buttonholes, tea was coming in, tea drinking began. Covent Garden (Convent Garden) was now a pleasure resort, ripe for its development, shortly to come, as a new theater center. As I see it, in many ways Cromwell had managed to prepare for the Restoration in England before the Restoration.

Cromwell died, some say of malaria, on September 3, 1658. There was, and naturally, a great deal of instant confusion. One of Macaulay's picturesque sentences describes:

Major-generals fleecing their districts, soldiers revelling on the spoils of a ruined peasantry; upstarts, enriched by the public plunder, taking possession of the hospitable firesides and hereditary trees of the old gentry; boys smashing the beautiful windows of the cathedrals; Fifth Monarchy men shouting for King Jesus; Quakers riding naked through the market-place; Agitators lecturing from tubs on the fate of King Agag.

There is no reason to doubt that there was momentary anarchy; but the remarkable thing is that the anarchy was so brief. After Caesar's dictatorship we noted that there were seventeen years of anarchy in Rome; it was within less than two years of Cromwell's death that a lasting constitutional government was redevised for Britain. Carrington and Jackson (whose *History of England* has been my map for this part of the journey) put the story succinctly:

In 1659 there was danger of civil war between General Lambert who commanded the army in London and General Monk who commanded in Scotland. At last Monk, who was an honest patriot and a plain blunt soldier, proclaimed that he was in favour of a newly elected Parliament, no sham packed Parliament like those of the last few years, but a real assembly of the Lords and Commons of England. At the end of the year his troops were swiftly concentrated at Coldstream on the Tweed and marched through bitter frosty weather to London, where the surviving members of the Long Parliament assembled to meet him. They voted Monk the supreme command; Monk issued writs for a new general election; the Parliament thus elected (known as the Convention of 1660) sent to Breda in Holland inviting King Charles II to return and ascend his father's throne. So Monk, the Roundhead soldier, restored King, Lords and Commons, with the help of many survivors of the old party of Pym and Hampden.

A first reflection on this Restoration of king and Parliament is that it would scarcely have come about unless on both sides (excluding extremists) there had been genuine wish for peace at home, in order to get on with the joint effort of expanding an empire over the world. Charles II accepted the throne on terms that his father had refused, and Parliament assembled in a spirit (again I exclude extremists) equally conciliatory. My subject, though, is not the subsequent constitutional history of Britain. It is a second reflection about the Restoration of a much-revised monarchy which occurs to me, and that is, how, and as if of natural right, the Great North Road—the internal segment of it between Scotland and London—continues to show up as an effective instrument. In the anarchy after Cromwell's death anybody other than Monk might have attempted an approach to London by any other road: but it was in fact Monk, whom Cromwell had sent to Scotland; and it was in fact the Great North Road which was there to be used for the frosty winter march at a moment of crucial importance. The men who made that march with Monk from Coldstream down the Great North Road won the name of the Coldstream Guards. The importance of the march was not forgotten: when it was agreed by king and Parliament that the rest of the Ironsides were to be disbanded, it was also agreed the regiment of "Coldstreamers" should be retained in the king's service. On the way down from Scotland, as he passed by York and Marston Moor, it is possible Monk thought of Cromwell. If so, I doubt if he felt it was defection of loyalty, to be setting up a reformed monarchy. Monk was not changing sides, nor was Edward Montagu who, having served Cromwell, then served the king and died in service. I don't think these men had to make a choice; they were no longer partisan; somehow there was by that time, after the Great Rebellion, a larger loyalty.

Cromwell's friend Blake never had to think about what he would do after the Restoration. Before that, one of the greatest of English admirals, he had died at sea, on his way home and within sight of Plymouth. I don't know the cause of his death, at the age of fifty-eight: the phenomenal overexertion, I suppose, of his five years of sea fights. In the name of the grateful nation, as recognition of his superb conduct and courage, the remnant of the Parliament which existed under Cromwell voted to give Blake a diamond ring. After his death he was accorded a most ceremonial burial in Westminster Abbey; whence, at the Restoration, his body was removed by the same fanatical Royalists who removed the body of Cromwell. The struggle for possession of corpses was one of the macabre features of the Restoration. No such fulsome ignominy was accorded to the body of Blake as was intended for the bodies of the regicides, Cromwell, Ireton, and Bradshaw. Blake's body was simply removed from the Abbey and

reinterred in the churchyard of St. Margaret's. But the House of
Commons which was to serve under Charles II publicly voted that
the dead regicides were to be hanged publicly: the sentence to be
carried out on January 30, 1661 (the anniversary of the death of
Charles I), in the presence of all London. John Morley quotes
(I know not whom): "This morning the carcases of Cromwell,
Ireton and Bradshaw (which the day before had been brought
from the Red Lion Inn, Holborn) were drawn upon a sledge to
Tyburn and then taken out of their coffins, and in their shrouds
hanged by the neck until the going down of the sun." Pepys wrote
of the affair: "which methinks do trouble me that a man of so great
courage as he was should have that dishonour." Pepys records later
in his diary (October 13, 1664) a rumor that instead of Cromwell's
body another body had been substituted. If my story in the previous chapter is to be regarded as true (as others have thought),
then I have to suspect some hanky-panky at the Red Lion in Holborn, where the coffins had been resting overnight.

At the moment of the Restoration it is not the antics of extremists
on either side but the moderation of the new temper of the middle-
man, the rising merchant class, which is most noticeable. The City
of London (speaking by and large) had heartily approved of
Cromwell, and moderate Royalists did their best to appeal to the
City. I know of no better example of the attitude of the moderate
Royalist than Thomas Sprat's *History of the Instauration, designe
and Progresse of the Royal Society of London,* published in 1667.
It is only another instance of how close together were the individuals of those days, no matter how they fought, to remark
that Robert Blake as a young man had come from Somerset to
study at Wadham College, Oxford. Thomas Sprat came from
Dorset to the same college. The warden of Wadham College was
John Wilkins. Within his cloisters Wilkins had formed a club—he
spoke of it as an "Invisible College"—to discuss the "advancement
of experimental philosophy." This club attracted the attention and
attendance of such men as Ward, Petty, Wren, Boyle, Wallis: it was
an "Invisible College" because all of these men were thoroughly
tired of conspicuous and acrimonious dissensions, and Sprat (who
was later to become chaplain to the Duke of Buckingham, and
later still Bishop of Rochester) was attracted to the club at Oxford

because of its purpose to discuss "calm, and indifferent things." At the Restoration the club felt it could throw off the cloak of invisibility; it moved its meeting place to the City of London—to Gresham College, just to the east of Postmen's Garden. It applied to Charles II for the permission, which it received, of being "incorporated by the name of the Royal Society." Sprat was deputed to write the history of the first five years of its endeavor. It is the temper in which that history is written, the temper of that influential Royalist group, which is worth a glance.

One of the "mischievs" by which "the greatness of the *English* is suppress'd," Sprat exclaims, "is a want of union of *Interest*, and *Affections*":

> This is originally caus'd by a Natural reservedness, to which our Temper is inclin'd: but it has bin heightened by our *Civil differences*, and *Religious distractions*. For the sweetning of such dissensions, it is not best at first to meet, and convers about affairs of state, or spiritual controversies. For those did first occasion our *animosities*, and the more they are rubb'd, the rawer they will prove. But the most effectual remedy to be us'd is, first to assemble about some *calm*, and *indifferent* things, especially *Experiments*. In them there can be no cause of mutual *Exasperations*; In them they may agree, or dissent without faction, or fierceness: and so from induring each others *company*, they may rise to a bearing of each others *opinions*; from thence to an exchange of good *Offices*; from thence to real *Friendship*; Till at last by such a Gentle, and easy *Method*, our several *Interests* and *Sects* may come to suffer one another, with the same peaceableness as men of different *Trades* live one by another in the same *Street*.

The last sentence is significant—the mention of trade. Sprat had to defend the pursuit of experimental science against those who feared that it might damage religious belief or moral theology: for if in the mid-seventeenth century there was no general fear that experimental science might release ungovernable forces and become a Frankenstein's monster, there was plenty of general fear that scientific experimentation, in so far as it was not mere folly, might easily be an impiety inviting God's punishment. In London two sudden and disastrous catastrophes had to be accounted for—the Plague Year of 1665 and the Great Fire of London of 1666. There were many who felt and others who openly said that these were "ominous" events, God's retaliation against Charles II, and the excesses of his Restoration, and all his works. The senior Fellows of the Royal Society did all they could to disinfect this superstition: John Dryden weighed in for the Royalists in 1667 with *Annus Mirabilis;* and it was as if to demonstrate the holiness of the intentions of the new science that another of the senior Fellows, Christopher Wren, set about the design and building of new City churches with incomparable inventiveness, skill, and speed. In Sprat's apologia for the Royal Society, his main argument is an adaptation of Cromwell's effort to inspire a secular faith: Sprat's argument is that "experimental science" is the "one common expedition" in which all Englishmen, from prince to artisan, regardless of private religious views, may join in a spirit of national unity. Sprat is at pains to present the spirit of the Royal Society as utilitarian. The Royal Society is first and foremost a mechanics' institute: the experiments which Sprat has most satisfaction in recording are those concerned with technology and commerce.

By the time of Sprat's *History* Newton had come down the Great North Road from Grantham to Cambridge, but had not yet made the further step from Cambridge to Gresham College, to deliver the *Principia* which was to prove that the Royal Society could stand for theory as well as for practical procedures. The flag of England was to fly in the heavens as well as on the seas. Leibnitz of Germany, the Bernoullis of Switzerland, the savants of the French Academy, the cognoscenti of the Italian *Lincei*, were later to pay intellectual respect. But there is no doubt that Sprat, of his moment, was artful in promoting the Royalist cause by asserting that the Royal Society was a group of researchers with the practical know-how to produce an expansion of English commerce. Within the Royal Society the "one common expedition" did not always proceed with the sweetness which Sprat so much commends—the Society divided with some acrimony on the question of investigating witchcraft (a very touchy subject). There was acrimony on behalf of the Royal College of Surgeons when Fellows of the Royal Society invaded their prerogative with experiments in blood transfusion. But as for experiments useful to navigation, as to barometers, telescopes, and ship design, Puritan merchants were quick to be interested in the work of the Royal

Society. Much of that work was just generally adopted without anybody knowing quite how it came about. The word "Royal" somehow coalesced with Cromwell's conception of empire. The sending of the Great North Road to sea appeased and altered a good many of the old rancors: we see Prince Rupert returning to England, becoming a prominent Fellow of the Royal Society, and combining with City merchants to form the Hudson's Bay Company. The speed with which English colonies and trading posts were established in the seventeenth century is impressive. Virginia, Bermuda, Surat, New England, Barbados, Madras had been established before the Civil Wars; Cromwell had added Jamaica and the suggestion of capturing Gibraltar; after the Restoration, Bombay, the Hudson's Bay Company, Pennsylvania, New York, are new entries in the ledgers, suggestive of more to come. The English were well launched upon a policy which reminds us of a phrase Gibbon applied to the Venetians: a policy "marked by the avarice of a trading, and the insolence of a maritime power."

It has often been asserted that the rapid growth of the British Empire was due, by and large, to Puritan impulse; it is equally interesting to observe how Royalists fell in with that impulse and how merchants fell in with the word "Royal." It was from the "Royal" Observatory at Greenwich that English ships, wherever they might be, were to reckon their positions: longitude measured from Greenwich as zero meridian, time everywhere adjusted to Greenwich Mean Time. This was a remarkable extension of the old idea that the Narrow Seas were an English lake, in which the English flag should be saluted; for the idea as it was here put over was that other ships of other nations might take their longitude and time, as if by Royal bounty, from the Royal Observatory. The general acceptance of Greenwich as the zero meridian I regard as a strange phenomenon. In the French Revolution one of the first impulses (change for the sake of change) was to reverse the rule of the road; and to drive upon the right, instead of the old Roman custom of driving on the left, became compulsory in most territories conquered by Napoleon or affected, as America, by French influence. But in the American Revolution, although the French rule of the road is adopted, there is no evidence whatever of an impulse to alter the English rule, the "Royal Observatory" rule, of the sea road. Nathaniel Bowditch of Salem in New England I regard with respect, and also as a case in point. Nobody could accuse him of not being anti-Royalist. He had learned Latin as a boy in order to read the *Principia* and, partly because it was a publication of the Royal Society, was delighted to point out an error. Bowditch scrutinized the best English tables of navigation and found no less than eight thousand errors. These he corrected in his *Practical Navigator,* and Bowditch's calculations were always so exact that (all seamen know the famous story) on a Christmas night, in the midst of a blinding snowstorm, no landmark to be seen, he sailed his own ship as straight to his Salem wharf as if it had been a sunny day in June. There might have been a bit of luck, but I don't doubt the story. Bowditch was a superb navigator and a supreme computer. Why, I wonder, did he not adopt Salem, Massachusetts, as being on the line of his zero meridian? He had opportunity to do so, but he didn't. Growing up as a boy in the full zeal of American Independence, aware of French influence (he translated Laplace) he nevertheless accepted, as if there could be no idea of thinking otherwise, that the "Royal Observatory" at Greenwich was the natural point of origin (with whatever corrections) for navigational reckoning.

I am saying that after the Restoration it was in common enterprise oversea that Royalists and Roundheads might the more readily combine. It continues to astonish me that the combination proved to be so effective, that the English, not having been hitherto especially prominent (except in their own estimation) in the art of navigation, established Greenwich and the initials G.M.T. as of international importance. It must have come about, preeminently, by the multiplication of English trading ships. A corresponding pride of merchant citizens at home is what marks the transition from the seventeenth to eighteenth century, expressed in 1722 by Steele in *The Conscious Lovers:*

I know the Town and the World—and give me leave to say, that we Merchants are a Species of Gentry, that have grown into the World this last Century, and are as honourable, and almost as useful, as you landed Folks, that have always thought yourselves so much above us.

Professor Bonamy Dobrée (*English Literature in the Early Eighteenth Century*) reminds me how the name of "Merchant" comes to be extolled, by Defoe in *Roxana* (1724) and later by Gay, not only in *Polly* but in *The Distress'd Wife* (1734):

> Is the name then [of merchant] a term of Reproach?—Where is the Profession that is so honourable?—What is it that supports every individual of our Country? 'Tis Commerce—On what depends the Glory, the Credit, the Power of the Nation?—On Commerce.—To what does the Crown itself owe its Splendor and Dignity?—To Commerce.

There is satire in these remarks, a laughter at "Commerce" being regarded as be-all and end-all, but it is because during "this last Century" (the Civil Wars forgotten) middle-class merchants, largely dissenters, had become fat enough to laugh. Gay would not have had a success with *The Beggar's Opera* unless there had been a transition from a period of general distress to a period when there was a new generality of theatergoers who were comfortable enough to smile at beggary.

The great transition from the seventeenth to the eighteenth century was the transition from religious rancor to economic rancor. There has always been a quantity of rancor in Britain, and perhaps it is a constant quantity; but this was a period of rearrangement. We must not accept the meliorative Sprat without remembering that there were furious quarrels, on theological grounds, within and among the Royalist churchmen: there is the case of William Chillingworth and Francis Cheynell. Cheynell was so venomous toward Chillingworth and the book that he had written that when it was his church duty to bury the body of dead Chillingworth he refused to do so without also burying a copy of the book, with language which I forbear to quote: "Get thee gone, thou corrupt, rotten booke . . . get thee gone into the place of rottennesse, that thou maiest rot with thy Author, and see corruption"—that, as an expression at a church burial, is all that I choose to excerpt. Among Puritan sectaries there were feelings as bad or worse: it was indeed a wise decision of the Royal Society, not to investigate the goings on of witchcraft in the swamplands of Essex at Maiston, under the sinister female Maeve, who gathered a brood of Ishtar of sufficient strength to stand off Cromwell's efforts to suppress them. The sexual orgies of the Brood of Ishtar and of similar "witches covens" elsewhere in East Anglia are hinted at rather than recorded; such records as there are remind one of the Voodoo cults in the West Indies: snake worship, goat sacrifice, black magic, elements of ritual impartially borrowed and distorted from Christian practice, Mithraism and the Cabala. It is possible that the notorious Maeve of Essex was in fact no more sinister than Tantie Sylla, proprietor of a present-day "shango" in Trinidad; but the belief that at the underside of Puritanism there were dark practices at work was sufficiently widespread to permit the torture or extinction of a good many probably harmless, and certainly unfortunate, old women. In Yarmouth, in 1644, Matthew Hopkins, "Witch-finder General," caused sixteen persons to be hanged for witchcraft; and the custom of witch hunting was one of the earliest and least admirable exports to New England. But I was saying that in eighteenth century England the quantity of rancor was beginning to be redistributed. With belief in commerce and trade as a universal secular religion, rancor shifted into the realm of economics.

And that, at last, brings me to Postmen's Garden.

I went to have another look at Postmen's Garden on Hock-Tuesday, 1960. The tulips there are good to see at this time of year. By coincidence or by tradition a nurse in uniform was at the gateway, collecting for the British Red Cross, selling the miniature flags which are, if you think of it, reminders of St. George. I was tempted to mention that this was Tuesday, not Monday; that it was really my turn to collect from her; but, cowardly, I did not dare. As you enter the garden from King Edward Street the first thing you see, rising above the beds of bright variegated Hocktide tulips, is the statue with one word incised on the pediment, PEEL. The statue represents Sir Robert Peel, after whom the London policeman came to be nicknamed a "bobby." This statue as I first remember it was at the western end of Cheapside at the junction with St. Martin's-le-Grand, and Peel looked toward Newgate Street, and reminded one of Newgate Prison and the eighteenth century expression, "as black as Newgate's knocker." At that site the statue came to be regarded as an obstacle. It was moved to this placid garden to be out of the way, and a traffic policeman, a living "bobby," was posted where the statue used to stand. I was intending to use the statue of Peel to lead into a discussion of cops and robbers, a theme in which the Great North Road plays a distinguished part; but a distracting thought is suggested by the eighteenth century church to the left of Peel, in the down-east corner of Postmen's Garden. It is a church of St. Botolph, and the distracting thought is concerned with the Boston Tea Party at the other side of the Atlantic pond. This is another theme to which the timetable now brings us. There is, by the way, a miniature pond in Postmen's Garden at the side of St. Botolph's church, with a small fountain from which water trickles down into a weedy basin. In the dark liquor of this basin (the liquor is too dark to be called water) there is (when you are lucky enough to see him) a very large carp, a Moby Dick of a carp (except that he is black) attended by two small bright goldfish. The goldfish often nip about at reasonable speed. The big dark carp scarcely bothers to move.

Reluctant as I am to grapple with any more big themes, Postmen's Garden, at the base of the Great North Road, compels me to think about the emergence of a "police era," and what kind of a police era, in England; and, in America, a war for "independence," and what kind of independence. These are big themes, and I would not wish to hurry either of them. They may wait for a next chapter. I propose here, in Postmen's Garden, to picnic for a few minutes. The garden, when you sit down on a bench and begin to study it, tells you it has been a garden for a long time. I am not going to retrace too far on the time scale, but I must surmise that in the fifteenth century it was a walled-in "garthyn with a hovell on it." Obviously—here I feel a tremor, for whenever anybody else uses the word "obviously" I instinctively dispute his opinion—as, whenever anybody uses the word "honestly" I at once suspect his intentions—but nevertheless, obviously it was at one time the garden of Northumberland House, a garden obviously with high walls, Little Britain walled off on the north side, Blow-Bladder Lane walled off on the west. The dog's-leg of the street now labeled Little Britain to my mind proves there was a wall on the north side of the garden: the church of "St. Botolph without Aldersgate" was possibly not included within the wall. The story of this St. Botolph's church would be interesting, if one had time to investigate. It was possibly from the beginning very "low." There is a suggestion, from the beginning, of "Salvation Army." The earlier church was destroyed by the Fire of London, but there was no question of its being rebuilt by the Royalist Wren. Northumberland House, facing St. Martin's-le-Grand (we are sitting, I say, in its garden) was indeed surrounded by radicals and reformers. On its right hand was the "pub" called Bull and Mouth, the stance from which Fifth Monarchy men preached from their tubs, and where George Fox preached before so fiercely going up the road to cry, "Woe to the bloody city of Lichfield"; and when upon its left hand the present eighteenth century edition of St. Botolph's Church was built, its associations are altogether with the evangelicals, especially with Charles and John Wesley.[4] Northumberland House gave up the unequal contest and moved westward; the garden was invaded by radical reformers; and we are sitting in it.

I am, as I said, for the moment picnicking. Many little questions flicker across the mind: mannerisms one has always assumed without question, but when you question, you don't know the answers. When I was talking about Cromwell, I should have mentioned that any date mentioned was a date "Old Style," before England adopted the Gregorian Calendar, a change which had been slow to come because it had been promulgated by the Church of Rome. Nations predominantly Catholic had adopted the change in the sixteenth century. Scotland had adopted the change in 1600. It involved making January 1st, instead of March 25th, the first day of the year, and the change from Old Style to New Style involved the illusion of the loss of eleven days. England was slow to conform to a calendar promoted by papists; but by 1750 the commercial impulse overcame the inconvenient religious scruple; the Calendar (New Style) Act was passed by Parliament and the change was effected by nominating September 2, 1752, as September 14th. The change was illusory, but not so for lawyers, countinghouses, or wage earners; and we mark and note the growth of an element in the life of England—the outcry from the mob, who went about shouting for the restoration of their eleven days. The mob—that is a theme to which we must return. Thought of the eighteenth century evangelicals started up another question about the calendar, which has puzzled me for a long time. We date a year after the birth of Christ with the abbreviation A.D., an abbreviation of the Latin *Anno Domini*. Skipping any incidental dispute as to the right number on the time scale to be given to the year of Christ's birth, we admit, without batting an eyelash, another abbreviation, B.C., as nomenclature—for years "Before Christ." But this is a hybrid nomenclature—A.D. Latin and B.C. English. How and when was the English abbreviation B.C. brought into the language, and who made it stick? I have no answer, except to say my guess is it came into the language through usage of evangelical preachers and teachers, conning their message in this part of Little Britain—a teaching transcending, if I may use the word, any hybridity of nomenclature. Such a mix-up could not have emerged from monastery or from university; an eighteenth century classicist, such as Gibbon, scrupulously avoids the letters B.C. But somehow, in later history books, there the abbreviation is: Caesar's second invasion of Britain is dated 54 B.C. Who brought into usage those initials, B.C.?

I advanced a thesis that Postmen's Garden was an old-time garden. In defense of the thesis I could quote that Tusser used to say it was proper for old-time gardens to have shelters in them: "Make drie ouer hed, both houell and shed." Postmen's Garden maintains both hovel and shed. The inconspicuous shed houses the garden tools with which in due course the Hock-tide tulips will be dug up and replaced with—with what? I wouldn't be sure till I see them. The "hovel," which in the beginning was a respectable word (as "penthouse" was a farm word in the beginning) implies a lean-to, a roofed porch—and there is one such here, which as we came into the garden from King Edward Street we passed on the left, before reaching Peel, before reaching St. Botolph's Church. This modern covered porch must not object to my calling it a hovel, for I am regarding it not merely with respect, but reverence, as an unusual variation on a very old garden theme. In fact, I haven't seen the like of this open-air porch elsewhere. If you rise from your garden bench, where we were thinking about whatever we were thinking about, to look into this porch, you find that under the lean-to roof the back wall of the porch is covered with Doulton tiles. It is a shock to find, react as you may, that each rectangle of tiling records some inconspicuous but actual sacrifice of life in an unexpected civil emergency. The Doulton tiles record (with an impression that they are as out of date as yesterday's newspaper) nothing much in common, except that somebody, generally speaking from the "lower" classes, was ready to volunteer his or her life in effort to save somebody else. The Doulton tiles are as out of date as Charlotte M. Yonge's *Book of Golden Deeds*. What they record transcends the mode of the recording: inconspicuous heroisms evoked by casual emergencies in the ordinary peacetime life of an industrialized society: fires, explosions, drownings—emergencies of that kind. There is no general inscription above the tiles. There are no flowers underneath. It is just a back wall, as if taken for granted. It reminds you of a department of the Sorting Office of the G.P.O. across King Edward Street, the department of Dead Letters. None of the names here recorded are names of Top People, with recognizable addresses. The memorials could not be delivered otherwise than here: letters uncalled for, remaining in Postmen's Garden.

It makes you think about "the mob," this open-air portico at the base of the Great North Road, for it is representative in its general way of the Fourth Estate, the unfranchised. I said the immediate result of the Norman effort to send the Great North Road to sea was, the effort being unsuccessful, the Wars of the Roses at home. The unexpected result of Cromwell's impulse to send the Great North Road to sea again, this time successfully, was the creation, at home, of the mob. I am sure this was an unintended result. I was so bold as to think that Cromwell envisaged a Restoration (he knew as well as anybody that his son, Tumble-down Dick—for whom one feels affection—could scarcely carry on) and the return to power of the first Three Estates was predictable. In seventeenth century England the Three Estates were in every thinker's mind—the problem of balancing the Lords Spiritual, the Lords Temporal, and the appointed Commons—and, broadly speaking, there was a mathematical solution to this problem of three bodies in the "bloodless Revolution" of 1688 which produced, in the next year, the famous Bill of Rights which ranks with Magna Carta as a statute of English liberty. According to right thinking, all should have been at ease. England was now well governed; the more farseeing of the Scots were contemplating Union; overseas trade was notably expanding; there was more money filtering into more hands, and less excuse for idleness. Through the reign of William and Mary, through the reign of Anne, through Marlborough's victories on the Continent (Blenheim, Oudenarde), through Rooke's picking up the Rock of Gibraltar, morale within England should have been never better; and it wasn't. What came into being in the first half of the eighteenth century was the Fourth Estate, the mob.

Perhaps not enough money was filtering through to servants; perhaps there was too evident disparity between the wretched poor and the wealthy and great; perhaps such an episode as the South Sea Bubble came into it; perhaps the freedom of the press —for after 1694 censorship was abolished, and a printer could print anything, even criticism of the government, so long as it did not break the laws against treason, libel, blasphemy, or indecency. Perhaps the main cause for the existence of the mob was the filtering downwards of the Bill of Rights; for when you start such a statement of liberty where do you stop it? There is a passage in Plato's *Republic* (VIII, 565 c.) in which, with humor, Plato illustrates that freedom, in the end, means anarchy, by describing the effect of freedom on animals. I disdain to quote Jowett's translation of the passage, for I don't think he expresses the fun of it, and I don't think Jowett (or his adjutant, Swinburne) knew much about animals. I prefer the translation by a sometime scholar of Lady Margaret Hall, Oxford:

As for the domestic animals, no-one who hadn't seen it would believe how much freer they are in the democratic state than elsewhere. Honestly, the bitches are equal to their missises, as the saying goes, and even the horses and mules are accustomed to journey along in a grand and carefree manner, bumping into anyone they meet on the road, if he doesn't stand aside. And everything else is the same, ready to burst with freedom.

That is the spirit which led to the eighteenth century clamor for "Wilkes and Liberty," and which led Tom Paine from Thetford, Norfolk, to the pub called the Red Cow in Smithfield, where he

sat down to write the first draft of the *Rights of Man,* a work
which he completed in Bleecker Street, New York. Paine went
to America with a letter of introduction from Benjamin Franklin,
who was from his youth well acquainted with Little Britain, for
he had come from Boston to this acre of the City of London in
1725 to learn more about printing and about newspaper work.
Franklin was then a bright boy of nineteen; he lodged in Little
Britain at the Golden Fan; and he certainly came to the right
place to learn about newspapers, for the first daily paper in the
world had been initiated by Samuel Buckley in Little Britain in
1702, the *Daily Courant.* The "weeklies" of Little Britain (for example, *The Spectator*) were before Franklin's time going strong
"in a grand and carefree manner," and in Franklin's eighteen
months in Little Britain he became attentive to the mode of distribution along the Great North Road. So one practice leads to
another: with reasonable certainty you may say that the idea of
Poor Richard's Almanac, and the *Saturday Evening Post,* and Franklin's work as postmaster of Philadelphia, derived much from the
scene at which we are looking when we sit in Postmen's Garden.

In my overture I spoke of the garden of St. Mary Aldermanbury
as the Publishers' Shrine. I was at that moment thinking of book
publishers. The shrine for newspaper publishers, the *fons et origo,*
would be this part of Little Britain, this piece of Postmen's Garden.
This was where things began. Any working journalist knows, or
should know, that Fleet Street is parvenu. I must repeat, the most
noteworthy and the most disgusting seedbed of English writing—
of every kind of English writing—was Little Britain. It was not
unnatural, in the eighteenth century, to wish to transplant from
Little Britain as soon as you could. The living and working conditions couldn't be tolerated any longer: Little Britain had to break
up, and away went its inhabitants, bumping into anyone they met
on the road. Writers, booksellers, printers, newspapermen, pulled
away from Little Britain; and the reason is simple—coaching days
had begun—you could get your stuff on the Great North Road from
any of a dozen coaching inns—you did not have to go on living
at the omphalos. The Royal Society pulled away from the disreputable neighborhood: it hovered a while in Fleet Street before it
settled in Burlington House. Among the landlords of Little Britain

there was consternation at the exodus of valued tenants. The name
of Blow-Bladder Lane was improved: it was renamed Stinking
Lane; it was then renamed Cow Lane; prodigious efforts to make it
savory. But unrest was in the air. The book trade, the newsmen,
discovered it was possible to remove; and once a general shift
begins, once people have decided to move, distance means little.
As Madame du Deffand remarked, it is the first step which counts.
Printers and writers moved westward, and how far westward
scarcely mattered. Some of the printers (I am thinking of Benjamin
Franklin) moved westward as far as Philadelphia; some of the
trade, along with the Royal Society, moved westward as far as
the West End.

But I sit in Postmen's Garden and think of it as the shrine for
the newspaperman, and think of what strange cargo the newspapers invented; for when and as they ran out of facts, there was
nothing for it but to invent fiction; and as I have said long ago, I
am often puzzled to know which of those two "f's" is more real.
I have moved out of the sunshine of Postmen's Garden, into the
shaded open-air portico with its back wall of Doulton tiles, and
I sit with my back to the tiles, looking straightway out upon
Aldersgate. There I see living passers-by upon the Great North
Road. If my imaginary forces are in good working order, I see
other pilgrims stumping northward past that gateway of Postmen's Garden: George Fox, John Bunyan, John Wesley. But of
people moving the other way, southward into the City, I see other
figures too: I see in particular two rather undersized and delicate
small boys. A moment ago I mentioned, with insufficient respect,
Benjamin Jowett, translator of Plato, the great Master of Balliol,
and, which means more than those facts might mean by themselves, guide and mentor to the governors of the British Empire
at the height of its Victorian pride. Jowett, when he was a puny
lad, won a scholarship to St. Paul's, and Geoffrey Faber's fine
book on Jowett tells me the boy was farmed out from the dreary
household in South London to a boardinghouse off the City Road
(which, a little to the north of us, cuts across the Great North
Road at the Angel) so from the boardinghouse he might, each
morning, walk past this gateway in front of us, to go to school.
Sir Geoffrey Faber wished to locate the boardinghouse of the school-

boy Jowett, in which particular crescent off the City Road. I believe I could have told him which crescent (but I was at that time working in Washington) for it is fairly well particularized by a newspaperman, Charles Dickens. Jowett's boardinghouse in the crescent off the City Road was next door to another boardinghouse, kept by a certain Mr. and Mrs. Micawber; in which there was lodging another little boy who was, within a matter of a month or two, the same age as Benjamin Jowett. This boy each morning had to leave his boardinghouse to attend, across the City, the blacking factory in which his stepfather, Mr. Murdstone, was interested. Now (in my imagination) those two boys of the same age walked day by day, in identical costume of round hat, short jacket, white pantaloons, and small black pumps—they walked side by side, past Aldersgate, past the gateway of Postmen's Garden, on which I am keeping a present wary eye. The two boys are in practically every way identical, in age, in costume and in circumstance—and tell me, if you please, which of the boys is to you the more real—Benjamin Jowett or David Copperfield?

One thing, in this overlong picnicking in Postmen's Garden, I am inclined to add, for it is all part of the meditation that newspapers and periodicals have been as important, perhaps more important, for the dissemination of fiction as for the dissemination of fact. The fact about the Great North Road which continues to intrigue me is not only the part it played in forcing the machinery of distribution for English prose—without hyperbole you could call the Great North Road the Path of Prose—but what is ancillary, the frequency with which the road itself crops up in English fiction. It would be a formidable task to compile an anthology of the references to the Great North Road in English fiction, from Defoe to Priestley's *The Good Companions*. I shall here content myself with a particular discovery, which happened this Hock-tide, about Sherlock Holmes. Everybody knows, of course, that Sherlock Holmes and Dr. Watson first met in Little Britain, at the laboratory in Bart's Hospital. Everybody knows, or should know, that the name "Sherlock" pops out at you in this part of the world. If, as Conan Doyle did, you stroll northward from Bart's to the Angel, and scout around a little (with or without Jowett and David Copperfield in your mind) you can scarcely miss *Sherlock Brothers Brush*

Factors, 357 City Road. You could scarcely miss (or, I wonder, could you?) Saxe-Coburg Square, which so pleasingly is the venue of the adventure of *The Red-Headed League.* Well now, you know all about Conan Doyle's methods, about the evident inconsistencies in that delightful story: errors of dates and everything else. Go, I ask you, to Saxe-Coburg Square, and thump on the pavement, and ask a man with royal blood in his veins, looking the while at his knees, the way (if you please) to the Strand—and see what you get for an answer. But what I am trying to express is the wonderful transmutation of dull fact into immortal fiction. Nothing in that particularly pleasurable story of Conan Doyle is more dramatic than the announcement to the unfortunate pawnbroker, Jabez Wilson, posted on white cardboard:

The Red-Headed League
is
Dissolved
October 9, 1890

Poor Jabez Wilson! Poor pawnbroker! He at once set off to find his employer at his alleged new address "17 King Edward Street, near St. Paul's." When the redheaded pawnbroker got to that address it was not what it ought to have been: "It was a manufactory of artificial knee-caps"—which in a way was reasonable enough (I am endeavoring to put myself in Conan Doyle's footprints) for if there had been a "17 King Edward Street" it would have been opposite Bart's Hospital. But if you try to put yourself in the footprints of the master, you find (not unexpectedly) that there is no such number as "17." King Edward Street (forget its previous names) is a short street: the numbers go to "16," and then stop. After "16," King Edward Street runs into Little Britain—Little Britain becomes the continuation, and number "17" is the first number of the coalescence of King Edward Street and Little Britain. But—this is what makes you feel you are stepping in the footprints of the master—Number 17 houses the offices of the British Pawnbrokers' Association, and the Pawnbrokers' Benevolent Society. It is one of those coincidences. Tell me where is fancy bred, in the heart or in the head, or in Little Britain?

XI »» The Post Road

It is time we began to look at the Great North Road from the other end, and a character naturally to be recalled is James Boswell. It was on Monday, November 15, 1762, in Edinburgh, at the age of twenty-two, that Boswell records: "Elated with the thoughts of my journey to London, I got up. . . . At ten I got into my chaise, and away I went. As I passed the Cross, the cadies and the chairmen bowed and seemed to say, 'God prosper long our noble Boswell.' I rattled down the High Street in high elevation of spirits, bowed and smiled to acquaintances. . . . I made the chaise stop at the foot of the Canongate . . . walked to the Abbey of Holyroodhouse, went round the piazzas, bowed thrice: once to the Palace itself, once to the Crown of Scotland above the gate in front, and once to the venerable old Chapel. I next stood in the court before the Palace, and bowed thrice to Arthur Seat, that lofty romantic mountain on which I have so often strayed in my days of youth. . . ."

Mr. Pottle, in his introduction to Boswell's *London Journal,* reminds us:

To reach London from Edinburgh in 1762, if one did not wish to make the trip by sea or on horseback, one had the choice of stage-coach or post-chaise. In either case, one went all the way in the same vehicle, but changed horses every few miles. There was perhaps not much difference in the time required, but the post-chaise was more gentlemanly. The stage-coach, a heavy, jolting vehicle, carried six inside passengers of every social status who got on and off at different places along the road; like a modern bus, it arrived at inns at inconvenient hours and allowed insufficient time out for eating and sleeping. In a chaise you travelled all the way with only one other person, picked your own inns, and were sure of spending the nights in bed. On this trip Boswell came up in a chaise. His time by the east road (with nights spent at Berwick, Durham, Doncaster, and Biggleswade) was four days; his mileage roughly one hundred miles a day. The trip cost him £11.

As I compute it, Boswell's journey occupied five days, which somewhat reduces the daily mileage, but no matter: it is the episodes on the road which are of interest. Two small accidents are treated as matter of course. Near Berwick "one of the wheels of our chaise was so much broke that it was of no use." Between Stamford and Stilton "there was a young unruly horse in the chaise which run away with the driver, and jumping to one side of the road, we were overturned. We got a pretty severe rap." There is another episode worth mentioning: near Biggleswade "During our two last stages this night, which we travelled in the dark, I was a good deal afraid of robbers. A great many horrid ideas filled my mind. . . . However, I affected resolution, and as each of us carried a loaded pistol in his hand, we were pretty secure. We got at night to Biggleswade." On Friday the 19th: "When we came upon Highgate hill and had a view of London, I was all life and joy. . . . I gave three huzzas, and we went briskly in."

Boswell's *London Journal,* with its moments of elation and its moments of repulsiveness, provides what must be accepted as an accurate picture, though scarcely a happy picture, of eighteenth century London. What Dr. Johnson called the "bursting with sin and misery" is hardly to be disregarded, though never can we disregard how many talents, and great men, emerged in the mire. The wonderful moments, which Boswell so diligently practised to record—the meeting with "the great Mr. Samuel Johnson"—

"Mr. Johnson," said I, "indeed I come from Scotland, but I cannot help it." "Sir," replied he, "that, I find, is what a very great many of your countrymen cannot help." Rather too easy for Johnson perhaps, as was the opening made for him by that other young Scotsman, Mr. Ogilvie, at the Mitre—the "noblest prospect which a Scotchman ever sees is the high road that leads him to England." I have sometimes surmised that Samuel Johnson had himself some Scottish blood, which if so would explain a good deal.[1] Boswell's picture of eighteenth century London is not a pretty one; but the picture of some other parts of Britain, in the latter half of the eighteenth century, is even worse.

Cromwell's use of the Great North Road had, I think, paved the way for the Union of the Kingdoms. The flag of Britain was now the Union Jack.[2] I am not suggesting that everything within the Union was politically happy; I am not one to disregard Jacobite loyalties; nor to think that even within remote country parts of England all was well. Perhaps "the fellows who cut the hay," in eighteenth century agricultural parts of England, had opportunity to grow up in conditions which were not physically intolerable; and though there were such glaring contrasts of riches and rags as we noticed at Castle Howard and Hinderskelfe, and evictions (such as we noticed in *The Deserted Village*) we may meditate that great country houses provided (as the monasteries had done long before them) employment and life for a good many people. The farm life that was in being and coming into being, as represented by Coke of Norfolk, or as later described in Cobbett's *Rural Rides*—as represented in painting by Gainsborough, Constable, Cotman, or in poetry by Bloomfield, Clare, Crabbe— as in Scotland represented by Burns and described by Scott—all of the rural life of Britain may exhibit sour moments but, on the whole, health. The arable land and the life upon it seem from the evidence to have been in good heart. But what could hardly have been envisaged by Cromwell who was concerned to get the island united, or by the Fellows of the Royal Society who were eager to bring together science and commerce, was the appalling disunion which this was going to create, and within England a cleavage far more serious than the old cleavages between Danes and Saxons, or between king and Parliament. I mean the cleavage between Capital and Labor, or if you prefer to put it in social terms, between a "them" and an "us."

The Union Jack, regarding it purely pictorially, has never seemed to me a flag of particular beauty; but symbolically I have never seen any harm in it. What is the harm in the intention of an agreed Union? The Union Jack represents the earliest of English-speaking "united" states. The White Ensign of the Royal Navy is to me, pictorially, a flag of beauty, and I cannot avoid a stir of affection and respect whenever I see the Red Duster of the Merchant Marine, old "blood and guts." But it is not a pleasing meditation to think how the flag of the British trading ship unintentionally effected such disunity within the homeland. If, a few minutes ago, I was quoting Plato's example of anarchy among animals when he supposes them to have the virus of unrestricted liberty, we have to remember the parable applies to all humans, top as well as bottom, to the drivers as well as the driven. Looking yet again into Mumford's *Technics and Civilization* I don't know whether the more to admire the skill with which he marshals his examples, or to be the more horrified at the material he has assembled. The sending of the Red Duster round the world, the expansion of commerce, the importation of raw materials for manufacture, the speeding up of every process, the degradation of the worker, these are all themes familiar enough to anyone who has considered the Industrial Revolution, yet never so familiar that they fail to suggest new meanings.

About the same time that Boswell and his companion were approaching Biggleswade on the Great North Road, "each with a loaded pistol in his hand," other chaises were being used to put the finishing touches on the factory system. Richard Arkwright, Mr. Mumford reminds me, was rattling around:

Arkwright, indeed, was a sort of archetypal figure of the new order: while he is often credited, like so many other successful capitalists, with being a great inventor, the fact is he was never guilty of a single original invention: he appropriated the work of less astute men. His factories were located in different parts of England, and in order to supervise them he had to travel with Napoleonic diligence, in a post-chaise, driven at top speed: he worked far into the night, on wheels as well as at his desk. Arkwright's great contribution to his personal success and to the factory system at large was the elaboration of a code of factory discipline:

three hundred years after Prince Maurice had transformed the military arts, Arkwright perfected the industrial army. He put an end to the easy, happy-go-lucky habits that had held over from the past: he forced the one-time independent handicraftsman to "renounce his old prerogative of stopping when he pleases, because," as Ure remarks, "he would thereby throw the whole establishment into disorder."

What then had been released, and especially within what had once been the Danelaw (Arkwright was a Lancashire man) was a contempt for any other mode of life except that associated with the machine: a demoniac possession which caused many of the masters to drive themselves almost as hard as they drove their men. In the era of the monasteries, we (in a detached way) could foresee with apprehension what was going to happen when there was to be no gospel save "work for work's sake"; but the reality when it emerged was more severe than any premonition. There is no squeamishness about some of the eighteenth century expressions of the desirability of the cleavage between capitalist and factory hand. The distinction was not primarily social. Anybody could become a capitalist who was a self-starter. Arkwright, if I remember, was a barber's apprentice at Preston who made his start by concocting a lotion for dyeing hair. But such poor boys (and women and children) who failed to be so ingenious were to be forced to become factory hands through pauperism; so the economic distinction quickly became a social one. There was nothing mealy-mouthed about it. Mumford quotes a writer of 1770 who had the right scheme for providing for paupers. "He called it a House of Terror: it was to be a place where paupers would be confined at work for fourteen hours a day and kept in hand by a starvation diet."

So what had been the Danelaw became black with factories, and I can't altogether fail to blame the roads, and the post chaise, which if it enabled a Boswell to get to London and meet Mr. Johnson, enabled an Arkwright to get around to the houses of terror. I am not suggesting things were everywhere the same. Some parts of England were still green and pleasant. Nobody can say that mechanical inventiveness is, of itself, bad. To anticipate a little (for I must cover the ground toward the Great Exhibition) there was another barber's apprentice at Bury St. Edmund's who invented that most amazing miracle, the glass marble in the neck of the fizzy-lemonade bottle. We noticed that the water closet was invented near the civilized city of Bath, and in the civilized town of Stroud, and without any particular damage to anybody (except for its noise) there was invented the lawnmower. That quiet, silent poor-man's chaise, the bicycle, was perfected on a flat stretch of the Great North Road, at Biggleswade. And the era of the Industrial Revolution did not destroy the handicraftsman. Mumford, who is severe on Arkwright, pays superb tribute to Maudslay—Henry Maudslay,[3] a bright young mechanic who had begun work in the Woolwich Arsenal:

Maudslay became not merely one of the most skilled mechanics of all time: his passion for exact work led him to bring order into the making of the essential parts of machines, above all, machine-screws. Up to this time screws had been usually cut by hand: they were difficult to make and expensive and were used as little as possible: no system was observed as to pitch or form of the threads. Every bolt and nut, as Smiles remarks, was a sort of speciality in itself. Maudslay's screw-cutting lathe was one of the decisive pieces of standardization that made the modern machine possible. . . .

These men [Mumford has gone on to mention Brunel, Nasmyth, Whitworth, Roberts, Muir, Lewis and Clement] spared no effort in their machine-works: they worked towards perfection, without attempting to meet the cheaper competition of inferior craftsmen. There were, of course, men of similar stamp in America, France, and Germany: but for the finest work the English toolmakers commanded an international market. Their productions, ultimately, made the steamship and the iron bridge possible. The remark of an old workman of Maudslay's can well bear repetition: "It was a pleasure to see him handle a tool of any kind, but he was *quite splendid* with an eighteen inch file."

Yet, and all the same, along with the good things, what the factory system in England at the beginning of the Industrial Revolution produced first of all was "the mob."

Regarding American history, regarding the history of Australia, regarding indeed India of the past or Africa of today, I find I have to think about "the mob" in England of the mid-eighteenth century. If you travel the Road, you have to travel it, and this is where we have got to. I said that Cromwell sent the Great North

Road to sea for a second time, at a good round trot. But the trot became faster, faster, a gallop for conquest and commerce. This should have resulted in equanimity at home. It didn't. The first Three Estates of the Realm had been reestablished by the Bill of Rights. At once what reared up was a Fourth Estate. The phrase is interesting. Many newspapermen believe that the Fourth Estate is "the press." This belief derives, I think, from Carlyle's remark in *Hero-worship* (1841), where he is speaking of Edmund Burke: "Burke said that there were three Estates in Parliament, but in the Reporters' Gallery . . . there sat a fourth Estate more important far than they all." Carlyle's remark was dramatic and widely adopted, though nobody has been able to confirm Carlyle's attribution to Burke of the use of this phrase in the application which the press adopted. The phrase was used earlier by Henry Fielding in the *Covent-Garden Journal* in 1752: "None of our political writers . . . take notice of any more than three estates, namely, Kings, Lords, and Commons . . . passing by in silence that very large and powerful body which form the fourth estate in this community . . . The Mob." Again Fielding says: "Nor hath this estate . . . been unknown to the other three." In the mid-eighteenth century the "Fourth Estate" is thus to be regarded simply as the "unfranchised." The press came to be associated with the term insofar as it represented, or was held to represent, *vox populi*.

In the mid-eighteenth century "The Mob" was not at all unknown to the other three estates; one of the most difficult problems of government was how to cope with organized riots. Here my researches led me to a book called *The Blind Eye of History* by Charles Reith. This is one of several admirable books by Mr. Reith on the origins and developments of police forces in different countries. As to London of the mid-eighteenth century Mr. Reith points out how riot-conscious people had become:

As riots became increasingly frequent and formidable, authority became incapable of controlling them. Constables and night-watchmen and City marshals were useless against them, and the only other form of law-enforcement machinery which was available was military force. Troops could not risk loss of power by dispersal in small bodies. Military force could not prevent riots or their recurrence, but it could repress them temporarily, by volley-firing or sabre charges. It could do this only after destruction had occurred. Authority could not use violent action by troops before violent action had been indulged in by a mob, and the ensuing helplessness from which it suffered could not be concealed. It is a remarkable fact that clear recognition of authority's weakness, clear understanding of its causes and of the immense political possibilities of exploiting it, were the product of the genius of a single individual at this period . . . John Wilkes.

"Wilkes and Liberty"—at the time of Boswell's *London Journal* Wilkes is beginning to be notorious. The great figures of the eighteenth century are not always very good-looking. Boswell remarks: "Mr. Johnson is a man of a most dreadful appearance. He is a very big man, is troubled with sore eyes, the palsy, and the king's evil. He is very slovenly in his dress and speaks with a most uncouth voice." Mr. Pottle remarks of Wilkes: "A man of learning and wit [at the time of Boswell's *Journal* thirty-five years old], of easy fine manners and imperturbable urbanity, he is in his political capacity capable of a degree of abuse for which 'licentious' seems too mild a word. A profligate, a sceptic, a cynic, an opportunist, but never a hypocrite. Cross-eyed, very ugly." It must be added that one of Wilkes's admirers was Sam Adams of Boston. I leave it to the reader to consult Mr. Reith and others as to details of correspondence between Wilkes and Sam Adams, and the influence of Wilkes's example on the organization of the Boston Tea Party and other mob actions in New England. Here I quote Mr. Reith's general thesis:

Authority's only means of dealing with riots in England was the use of troops. It could conceive no other, and the frequency with which it had to be employed established, solidly, a peculiar and very unmilitary set of strategic and tactical principles. . . . Its chief object on every occasion of rioting was to secure dispersal of the mob. . . . Its first step on the occasion of a riot was attempts to overawe the participants. There was an issue of pompously worded warnings. There was a parade of troops. They were then moved into position for attack. They never attempted to surround or capture a mob; their aim was to induce the rioters to go away. A route of escape and dispersal for them was always left open and clearly indicated. . . .

Mr. Reith goes on to suggest that this was a procedure which had to be so frequently exercised in dealing with riots in England, and was so "solidly" believed in, that it had much to do with the conduct as to the "riots" in New England:

England's feeble handling of the American Revolution has been the subject of endless controversy and discussion, but most of its mysteries disappear when they are examined in the light of certain easily seen but almost wholly overlooked truths. From first to last, ministers and generals were unable to rid their minds for long of the obsession that what they were dealing with in the American colonies was a London street riot of an unusually formidable, prolonged and unyielding kind. They could sense no difference between Englishmen there and Englishmen at home. . . . Their only means of restoring order was military force. They tried to avoid violence and bloodshed. They paraded troops in the sight of their opponents in the hope of inspiring awe. They issued pompous proclamations with the same purpose. They tried to avoid inflicting punishment and taking prisoners. They refrained from surrounding their opponents, taking care always to leave a safe and inviting route by which these could retreat and disperse. . . .

This is not what I was taught in school, but I am bound to say it makes Howe's conduct at Bunker Hill less unintelligible to me. Not thus in the Scottish wars did Cromwell behave, as to the capture of impregnable Stirling Castle: let Monk surround the place, let thirst and impatience do their work until the garrison makes fatal sortie. At Bunker Hill, the leaving of the obvious escape route, and then the fatuous frontal march of the redcoats up the slope, is to some extent explained if the British believed that all that they had to quell was a street riot; whereas colonials, or some of them, believed they were fighting a war. I leave it to heads more knowledgeable than mine to decide to what extent the obsession of ministers in London, as the American War of Independence went on, continued to be the objective of "voluntary mob-dispersal." I do agree with Mr. Reith that the English professional soldier, when it was a declared war that he was fighting, fought otherwise than at the beginning of the American War of Independence. If England had fought Napoleon the way England fought the "haughty Republicans" of America (Lord North's phrase), then England today would be using the metric system, beer would be served in litres instead of in pint pots, and we should be driving on the right-hand side of the Great North Road.

Speaking of the "ifs" of history, and of how close things often were to having been different, there is one odd link between Boswell and Napoleon. What time there were ferments for independence working along the American Post Road from Boston to Philadelphia, there were ferments in the island of Corsica for independence, and Boswell made his serious efforts to interest the British Government "in favour of the brave Corsicans." It was a bee in Boswell's Scots bonnet, for which Samuel Johnson reproved him:

I wish there were some cure, like the lover's leap, for all heads of which some single idea has obtained an unreasonable and irregular possession. Mind your own affairs, and leave the Corsicans to theirs. I am, dear Sir, your most humble servant,

SAM. JOHNSON

The British Ministry was not disposed to act for Corsica; the island was too vulnerable to the French, who took it over; and the Corsican leader, General Paoli, fled with his adjutant and a few others. Paoli escaped to London, where Boswell and other libertarians persisted in such support as they could; in the American colonies there were feelings for Paoli; from Philadelphia toward Valley Forge you may still travel by the train known as the "Paoli Local." It was my birthright to travel, as a boy, upon that train. It made one aware of Paoli. I was not aware until the recent publication of Boswell's *Journals* of Paoli's adjutant. The adjutant and his wife escaped with Paoli from Corsica, first of all to Leghorn. Paoli made arrangements to sail for London, to raise help against the French. To sail on to London?—the adjutant's wife refused to go. She was pregnant, and very near her time. She was already too lonely in Leghorn; she would be far more too lonely in London. So Paoli parted company with his former adjutant and the adjutant's unreasonable wife, and despite the fact that Corsica was now in the hands of the hated French, the wife and the adjutant returned to Ajaccio. There, a few weeks later, their child was born. It is in a way a pity, in the sense that history might have been different, that the child was not born in London. These women!—she did not wish to have her child in London; she wished to have her child in Corsica. The name of the child, by the way, was Napoleon Bonaparte.[4]

If this story is true, it was the closest Napoleon ever got to invading Britain, though later on it was going to take a lot of trouble to keep the emperor out. But though I don't regard Napoleon as being out of the theme, as I conceive it, of the Great North Road—my trouble is, that as I conceive it there is nothing that went on in the Western world which is not in some way related to that theme—I must not lose sight of the immediate subject of this chapter, this stretch of the road when it became not only, and in a new sense, the Post Road of Britain, but the first Post Road of North America, Route U.S. 1, in its beginning the limited segment from Boston to Philadelphia. Sea travel, coastal travel, by the youth time of Benjamin Franklin was still a normal means of transportation along the Atlantic seaboard: that was the way Franklin had gone, in the first instance, from Boston to Philadelphia—that was the natural carriage for people, commodities, and news. I wonder if biographers have commented (it is a point that I have not had time to restudy) how intimately Franklin's activities as Postmaster are associated with what he had observed about transportation and communications within Britain. It is not in disregard of the work of other men, or in disregard of that unspecifiable factor which we can only call "general development," that I particularly associate Franklin with the change whereby, in North America, the road became more important than the sea, more important than the rivers. It would be an interesting byway to get into, the exploration of procedures on the main Post Road of America, as deriving (so I would be tempted to believe) from procedures on the main Post Road of Britain. But I say it would be a byway which I have no leisure to explore—the direct connection between the Post Road of Britain and the Post Road of America—because what one has to brood about is not so much what procedures as what ferments were working along both working roads.

Here the general question is: Did the Great North Road play a part in the formation of the American Constitution? I would think one specific traceable influence might be found in what we have just been discussing, the power of the organized riot. In the creation of the American Constitution, if the Founding Fathers were most carefully debating and devising safeguards against unrestricted Executive Authority, no less noticeable is the way they kept looking over their shoulders at "the Mob." The power of the "rabble rouser" was much in the consciousness of those who had observed how difficult it was for Authority in England to cope with him; and after hotheads such as Sam Adams and Tom Paine had done work which was useful for obtaining independence, it is my impression that they fell swiftly out of favor. Power such as they had exerted should be trimmed. The grand principle of a society in "subordination," as expressed in England by Samuel Johnson, was to be resisted; but, in whatever other terminology, some system of subordination had to be devised. Safeguard against impetuosity of political behavior is so strongly recognized in the American Constitution that, speaking strictly and pedantically, the United States has never been, and is not now, a "democracy." The electorate was not to be allowed to exert direct action. After the War of Independence, "independence" had to be defined in a written Constitution: no easy matter. Fortunately the American autocracy had plenty of time to produce a good definition. There was little pressure from the mob, for behind the Eastern seaboard there was a whole continent, a wide and evident dispersal route. Thomas Jefferson could advise cultivation of the garden, for the garden seemed illimitable.[5] There was enough empire for everybody, to ease away the pressure and take away the heat from problems on the seaboard. When I reread *The Federalist* what most impresses me (apart from admiration for James Madison) is the absence of feeling of desperate urgency. Subject to correction, what I feel about the drawing up of the American system of government is that the Founding Fathers were apprehensive about mob rule and carefully guarded against it. Their relative good fortune was that at a time when the old Post Road within Britain was bursting with traffic, the new Post Road of America, from Boston through New York to Philadelphia and then through Baltimore and the new-invented capital city of Washington on through Virginia to points south—it now runs all the way from

Fort Kent, Maine, to Key West, Florida—this new road, rapidly growing though it was, was not yet working very hard.

The Founding Fathers of the American Constitution seem to have been under relatively little pressure, at a moment when England was hissing like James Watt's steam kettle. The composition of government in the shape of an equilateral triangle, with three sides—legislative, executive, and judicial—could be gone about, in that period of the American story, almost as if it were a blackboard exercise in a brand-new classroom. We all recall, of course, that Madison's two terms as President were regarded as stormy ones; but those storms were not hurricanes. We all recall that in 1814 British troops captured the Capital of Washington and attempted to burn down the White House; but we recall it as if it were a picture in slow motion. Before the White House was afire, Dolley Madison had sufficient time to save Stuart's celebrated painting of George Washington, and to seek out and save the original draft of the Declaration of Independence. There is an air of time and space about the America which was waking up from the eighteenth into the nineteenth century. The size of the bed was beginning to be appreciated; the breadth had been measured by Lewis and Clark; and any alarm clock which at that moment rang from Washington was only a Baby Ben. They slept well, the Founding Fathers, and whatever their trials, they lived long. George Washington died at the relatively early age of sixty-seven. Jefferson lived to the age of eighty-three; Franklin to the age of eighty-four; Madison to the age of eighty-five; and at the age of ninety Charles Carroll of Carrollton was continuing to keep up his energetic correspondence. These great figures in America do not seem to have been pushed too hard.

I am saying that at the turn of the centuries, eighteenth to nineteenth, progression on the new Post Road of America was leisurely. On the old Post Road of Britain the traffic was unresting. The impression is that the most active people in England of that time burned out more quickly. Chatham had lived to the age of seventy, and Burke to the age of sixty-eight. The hard-driving Arkwright snuffed out at sixty; then the death rate is worse—Charles James Fox dead at fifty-seven, the younger Pitt at forty-seven. The suggestion is that the pressures were severe; as to which there is other and abundant evidence. The American Revolution was physi-

cally at a distance: the French Revolution was across the Channel
—and the rioting in England, wasn't that the same thing? It is possible to consider that the Napoleonic Wars, no matter how costly
and dangerous, to some extent took the heat off a most explosive
problem within Britain. Professor Aspinall's book on *The Early
English Trade Unions* leaves one in no doubt that the Ministry's first
idea in dealing with workmen was to encourage them to breed
(more and more were needed) but to prevent them from combining. In the latter part of the eighteenth century this potentially dangerous Fourth Estate invented a habit of forming trade unions. "The
fact that, at the end of the eighteenth century there were more than
forty Acts of Parliament to prevent workmen from combining,
is suggestive both of the widespread existence of trade unions
over a long period of years, and of the willingness of the legislature
to support the labour policy of the employers. That policy was, in
brief, to suppress combination and to keep down wages. . . .
Adam Smith's view that liberty of combination ought to be
recognized by law was not the view of the Legislature before
1824."

What part did the Post Road play in this matter of labor legisla-
tion? I am interested by a passage from Professor Aspinall:

Both the Government and the employers were all too conscious of
the fact that in seeking to suppress combination they were fighting a
losing battle: as they were, too, in seeking, by means of severe laws
and punitive taxation, to prevent political information from reaching the
masses through the medium of popular newspapers. Propaganda through
the Press, through public meetings and through the various Radical
Reformist Societies which re-emerged during the last years of the
Napoleonic War, was powerfully contributing to increase the political
consciousness of the working class. The great improvement of the postal
service after 1784, and the multiplication of accelerated stage-coaches,
enabled the trade unions in time to organize themselves on something
wider than a merely local basis; and in an effort to destroy this new advantage the Home Secretary sometimes instructed local postmasters to
stop all letters addressed to suspected members of these illegal organiza-
tions. . . .

"To the public-house, too," the unions owed something, and
clandestine meetings might here or there be held under cover of

Benefit Clubs, which were permitted under the Friendly Societies
Acts. But the formation of the earliest unions was an underground
business, for persons found guilty of unlawful combination, upon
indictment could be sentenced either to seven years' transportation or two years' imprisonment. The severity of Pitt's "Gagging
Acts" of 1799 and 1800 to some extent defeated the intention, for
as with other punishments on the statute books there was sometimes a tendency to acquit an alleged criminal rather than to hand
him over for execution for some minor fault. In 1800 there were
in England two hundred crimes punishable by death: the sentence
for those convicted (I am thinking of Margaret Catchpole of Ipswich, a servant girl who loved a smuggler and stole a horse so she
might join him) was often commuted to transportation for life to
Botany Bay; at this length of time it is a pleasure to note that an
Australian edition of *Chambers's Encyclopaedia* speaks of such
convicts as "compulsory pioneers." Within England, in 1800, I
would suppose that not all employers wished to be punitive
towards skilled workmen: that some employers were ready to
connive at well-behaved "conspiracy." But undoubtedly there were
rough characters on both sides, and what is noticeable is that
there was more violence between labor and management after
the repeal of the "combination laws," in 1824.

Trade and industry [says Professor Aspinall] were flourishing in 1824.
The workers naturally tried to enforce their claim to a share of their
employers' prosperity . . . they had convinced themselves that the
combination laws were chiefly responsible for low wages, and believed
that repeal would be followed suddenly by a great rise. Now that they
were no longer under the ban of the law, trade unions sprang up everywhere. . . . There was an epidemic of strikes which quickly alarmed not
only the masters but the Government. It disquieted, too, the best friends
of the workers. . . .

There can be no question as to the gravity of the crimes that were
now being committed, the victims being workers who refused to join
the unions, blacklegs whom employers brought in to break a strike. . . .

These murders, attempted murders, including vitriol throwing,
were all the more shocking because they extended into an era of
reform in which, ever since Henry Fielding, there had been effort

to devise means of crime prevention. The "Peterloo Massacre" in Manchester (1819) had been, many hoped, a final example of the folly of calling in the military to disperse a riot: but what else were magistrates to do? Relaxation of the laws had not eliminated mob violence in industrial relations, and reduction of the number of offenses punishable by death had not eliminated crimes of violence on the Great North Road.

No journey along the Great North Road would begin to be complete without recollection of Jeanie Deans in *The Heart of Midlothian*, and, during her famous walk from Edinburgh to London and back again, recollection of the superbly told adventure with the robbers of "Gunnerby Hill"—the same Gonerby Hill near Newark where we noticed that Cromwell performed an exercise. Jeanie Deans made her journey in 1737, and Walter Scott points out that at that time it was an unsafe thing to do, and certainly Jeanie Deans's experience at "Gunnerby" makes your hair curl. A quarter of a century later we observed Boswell and his companion with loaded pistols in their hands for fear of robbers north of Biggleswade. What was reputed to be an even more dangerous stretch of the road was closer to London, where it crosses Highgate Heath. Here you had to watch out for Dick Turpin, and the other "Galloping Dick" (whose name was Richard Ferguson), and a third "Dick," Dick King, the "Gentleman Highwayman." It might be very bad news for a lonely traveler or a post chaise to run into one or another of this scurvy trio, or any other of the "Stand and Deliver" gentry. But as Scott suggests (writing in 1830), what made the road a safe road was precisely what Professor Aspinall noticed as one of the factors which encouraged the formation of trade unions: the improvement of the postal service and the multiplication of accelerated stage-coaches.[6] According to Scott it was simply the increase in the amount of traffic which defeated the highwayman:

In the present day, a journey from Edinburgh to London is a matter at once safe, brief, and simple, however inexperienced or unprotected the traveller. Numerous coaches of different rates of charge, and as many packets, are perpetually passing and repassing betwixt the capital of Britain and her northern sister, so that the most timid or indolent may execute such a journey upon a few hours' notice.

Jeanie Deans might be held up by the lowest grade of footpads. The individual horseman might be stopped upon the road. The post chaise, although when driving rapidly in the afternoon near Blenheim Park, Johnson might say to Boswell: "Life has not many things better than this"—although except for rain, or sun, or dust there was nothing more elegant than to be bowling along in a post chaise with a pretty woman—on the Great North Road there were plenty of stages where a post chaise was vulnerable to attack. The safety, and the glory, of the road developed not from the post chaise, but from the mail coach. G.P.O. London is now in King Edward Street. Then (when?—say about 1829) it was the Lombard Street Post Office, of De Quincey's famous description:

On any night the spectacle was beautiful. The absolute perfection of all the appointments about the carriages and the harness, their strength, their brilliant cleanliness, their beautiful simplicity—but more than all, the royal magnificence of the horses. . . .

Every carriage, on every morning of the year, was taken down to an official inspector for examination—wheels, axles, linch-pins, poles, glasses, lamps, were all critically probed and tested. Every part of every carriage had been cleaned, every horse had been groomed, with as much rigour as if they belonged to a private gentleman. . . .

Every moment are shouted aloud by the post-office servants, and summoned to draw up, the great ancestral names of cities, known to history through a thousand years—Lincoln, Winchester, Portsmouth, Gloucester, Oxford, Bristol, Manchester, York, Newcastle, Edinburgh, Glasgow, Perth, Stirling, Aberdeen—expressing the grandeur of the empire by the antiquity of its towns, and the grandeur of the mail establishment by the diffusive radiation of its separate missions. . . .

Every moment you hear the thunder of lids locked down upon the mail-bags. That sound to each individual mail is the signal for drawing off, which process is the finest part of the entire spectacle. Then came the horses into play. Horses! Can these be horses which bound off with the action and gestures of leopards? What stir! What sea-like ferment! What a thundering of wheels! What a trampling of hoofs! What a sounding of trumpets!

It was the mail coach which was glory of the road. The other coaches vied with the mail coach and with each other for speed, convenience, and service—such famous coaches as you might

book for at the Bull and Mouth, the Spread Eagle, the Swan with
Two Necks, the Green Man and Still, or the George and Blue
Boar in Holborn, from which the "Stamford Regent" started. It
was the multiplicity of coaches, as Scott said, which scared away
the footpads and defeated the highwayman. It is amusing to note
how they introduced other dangers: not only the intended elope-
ments to Gretna Green, but the unexpected marriages bumped
into on the way. I don't think Hazlitt had an intention of a
second marriage when he took coach (if I remember, at the
Angel) for his trip up the Great North Road; but when you are
jostled with a female inside a coach all day, and bundled at nighttime into the same inn, you might find it—or at least Hazlitt found
it—dangerous.

Coaches helped to clear the roads of crimes and violence, but
crimes of violence were not eliminated, nor were riots. Consider,
as Henry Fielding when he was Chief Magistrate of London had
to consider, the impossible problem—yet so far as possible to be
attempted—of prevention of crime. The organization of road-
services was going to diminish sporadic crime upon the roads,
but was going to introduce something more difficult to handle
—crime, which as it became more centralized became more organized. The significant criminals born in eighteenth century
England were not those you could catch up with—Jack Sheppard,
Jerry Abershaw, Sixteen-Stringed Jack, Thurtell and Hunt, Burke
and Hare—a more significant figure was the competent organizer
of syndicated crimework, who sometimes used Cock Alley, Cripplegate, as an office for operations: Jonathan Wild. To cope with
organized crime and to cope with organized riots was Henry
Fielding's problem, and it was he who struggled to devise a police
force which could be trusted by the people of England. Henry
Fielding was not blessed with good health, and his half-brother,
Sir John, who succeeded him as magistrate, was handicapped by
blindness. Sir John Fielding pursued the idea of making into a paid
profession what had at first been envisaged as a volunteer force of
citizens. Patrick Colquhoun further shaped "the new science of
preventive police, yet in its infancy, and only beginning to be
understood." Robert Peel finally steered through Parliament the
bill which created, in 1829, the Metropolitan Police of London.

Peel passed to two men, relatively unknown—Charles Rowan and Richard Mayne—the detailed planning and the shaping of police principles and behavior. An initial hostility to Peel's "bloody gang," as some Radicals called them, was considerably placated because they were unarmed, and under the control of civil magistrates: an altogether new departure from the conception of military police of Continental countries. After 1829 the police system as inaugurated by the Metropolitan police spread rapidly throughout Britain.

Mr. Burton Turkus and Mr. Sid Feder, writing of law enforcement in America, mention in their book *Murder, Inc.*, that "the Law never had or ever will have insurmountable difficulty with unorganized crime . . . but when the gangster discovered organization, when he converted from unorganized crime to Syndicate operations on the national scale, he developed an edge that law and order has not entirely matched, even yet." A continuing headache is caused in the United States today by "Syndicate" operations in some parts of the field of industry-labor relations, and a continuing headache is the misuse of government postal services for various "rackets." I said the mail coach on the Great North Road to a large extent eliminated open crimes of violence on the Road, but from the time of Henry Fielding to the time of Robert Peel, it was not crime which was eliminated—it was only that the open road had been made reasonably safe. The "bobbies" were going to have plenty to do in towns, but the mail coach had got rid of the highwayman.

Although of course the beauty of the mail coach with which De Quincey so much moved us—those horses which bound off with the action and gestures of leopards—was already doomed some time before De Quincey was writing. The mail coach was vulnerable in 1813 to a small, grubby, dirty, and displeasing-looking highwayman, whose name was "Puffing Billy."

XII »» The Great Exhibition

One exceptional moment at which the Great North Road within Britain seemed to be prepared to pause and take stock was the moment of the Great Exhibition of 1851.

We were reflecting that at the end of the eighteenth century there was leisure for some but not for others: a remark which does not mean very much unless illustrated; so we looked at the feverish activity of the Industrial Revolution, at Arkwright, at the competition to introduce machinery into factories, at the effort to force the rabble into becoming factory hands. We saw that if the unfranchised attempted to escape, there was the press gang to capture them for work at sea; or if crime was committed, there was the rope or transportation. Of none of this do you obtain much feeling from the conversations of Johnson and Boswell: more, to be sure, from Johnson than from Boswell; but consider the leisurely nature of such a conversation as this—the date is Good Friday, 1783:

On 18 April (being Good-Friday), I found him at breakfast, in his usual manner upon that day, drinking tea without milk, and eating a cross bun to prevent faintness; we went to St. Clement's Church, as formerly. When we came home from Church, he placed himself on one of the stone-seats at his garden-door, and I took the other, and thus in the open air, and in a placid frame of mind, he talked away very easily . . .

BOSWELL. "I wish to have a good walled garden." JOHNSON. "I don't think it would be worth the expence to you. We compute, in England, a park-wall at a thousand pounds a mile; now a garden wall must cost at least as much. You intend your wall should grow higher than a deer will leap. Now let us see;—for a hundred pounds you could only have forty-four square yards, which is very little; for two hundred pounds, you may have eighty-four square yards, which is very well. But when will you get the value of two hundred pounds of walls, in fruit, in your climate? No, Sir, such contention with Nature is not worth while. I would plant an orchard, and have plenty of such fruit as ripen well in your country. My friend, Dr. Madden, of Ireland, said, that 'in an orchard there should be enough to eat, enough to lay up, enough to be stolen, and enough to rot upon the ground.' Cherries are an early fruit, you may have them; and you may have the early apples and pears." BOSWELL. "We cannot have nonpareils." JOHNSON. "Sir, you can no more have nonpareils, than you can have grapes." BOSWELL. "We have them, Sir; but they are very bad." JOHNSON. "Nay, Sir, never try to have a thing, merely to show you *cannot* have it. From ground that would let for forty shillings you may have a large orchard; and you see it only costs you forty shillings. Nay, you may graze the ground, when the trees are grown up; you cannot, while they are young." BOSWELL. "Is not a good garden a very common thing in England, Sir?" JOHNSON. "Not so common, Sir, as you imagine. In Lincolnshire there is hardly an orchard; in Staffordshire, very little fruit." . . . BOSWELL. "A hot-house is a certain thing; I may have that." JOHNSON. "A hot-house is pretty certain; but you must first build it, then you must keep fires in it, and you must have a gardener to take care of it." BOSWELL. "But if I have a gardener at any rate?" JOHNSON. "Why, yes." BOSWELL. "I'd have it near my house; there is no need to have it in the orchard." JOHNSON. "Yes, I'd have it near my house.—I would plant a great many currants; the fruit is good, and they make a pretty sweetmeat."

Good holiday talk that was, friends at ease in Bolt Court off Fleet Street. About the same time John Byng (the Honorable John Byng, later Fifth Viscount Torrington) was taking off every holiday he could from affairs in London to ride on horseback up the Great North Road to observe how the countryside was getting on. The *Torrington Diaries* [1] stay for the most part to the southern side of Alconbury Hill—you may pronounce it Akenbury, or you may think of it as Cromwell's Corner, for Alconbury Hill is where the northward road from Huntingdon comes in to join the Great North Road. John Byng, in the last two decades of the eighteenth century, has a sardonic feeling about Alconbury Hill. "Alconbury Hill would make any person feel miserable for the wind, here, allways bleaks and saddens." That is a remark made in 1794: five years earlier in the diaries there is also a bad memory: "dinner . . . was to be prepared for us, at 3 o'clock at Alconbury Hill; where we did not arrive till ½ past that time; and then dinner not ready! We were rather peevish at the delay—for the half hour before dinner is allways a snappish time. The dinner was better than I expected in this filthy inn (the Wheat Sheaf) which to the miseries of a cold alehouse, joins the charges of a London Tavern: for 2 small Tench stew'd in a black Sauce were charged 7 shillings."

John Byng discloses less apprehension about highwaymen than he does about the charges of innkeepers:

Friday May 9, 1794:—More rain coming on, hurried us to the George Inn, a small public house at Silsoe (often mentioned in my tours). Here in the back room towards the garden, we employ'd ourselves in blowing the fire—and in waiting for something to eat. The day was cold and rainy—and this house is only for a hot summer's lounge.

GEORGE, SILSOE	
Eating	2–0
Beer	0–3
Brandy	1–3
Fire	0–6
Horses Corn & Hay	1–6
	———
	5–6

The expense was not high for 3 people? Tho' they screw'd up Hay one penny pr. horse.

If Byng on occasion chose to criticize the hospitality of this Bedfordshire part of the Great North Road, he would not permit others to do so. He ran into two Scottish ladies "of excessive vanity" who attacked the Sun Inn at Biggleswade "as *wretched, filthy*, &c., &c." and the road between Buckden and Biggleswade as being "*horrid! Oh horrid!* to the extreme." This really did touch off John Byng:

> Now, let me make a statement, in plain truth, of this—(*horrid, shocking*) road—betwixt Biggleswade and Buckden. As a road of fine gravel it is unequalled. Leaving the Sun Inn of Biggleswade (one of the cheapest, quietest inns I know) you pass the old bridge over the River Ivell, with a pleasing view of the river and its frequent navigation. A mile of flat road, thro enclosures, with a distant view of Wardon and Northill Churches to the left, and of the Sandy Hills to the right, leads into Lower Caldecote hamlet; hence a twining road of another mile to above Beaston hamlet, where you have a charming look of Sandy Church and village, with the two houses of Sir Philip, and Dr. Monoux, and closer to the right, the pleasant Vill of Stratford, back'd by the entire Roman Camp of Julius Caesar.

I cannot forbear to dwell a little longer on Byng's pride in the road:

> Passing thro this neighbourhood, any observer would be astonish'd at the culture, and gardening of the fields, surpassing everything I ever saw, but just about London; for every field is cropp'd by peas, carrots, parsnips, French beans, cucumbers, &c., &c., even the very open fields; and you cannot prevent your horse from smashing the cucumbers. (I once told this to a friend of mine, who smiled contradiction, till I led him into this garden of a country; and then he owned his surprise and conviction.) . . .
>
> After having gone thro that I think a road of unusual populousness, fertility—and pleasing views. Ten villages, or hamlets, are pass'd thro in 16 miles! There are 9 gentlemens seats close upon the road besides many others in view: 3 bridges over navigable rivers are cross'd.
>
> One Roman camp is seen; and at every mile a good public house may be enter'd in case of storms, or hunger: at Eaton there is an excellent inn much frequented. The George at Buckden is also excellent; and there is a brisk navigation upon the rivers. Now what can be compared to this in Scotland?

The eighteenth century pride in "this garden of a country" comes to be laughed at as, in the nineteenth century, the coaches gather speed. The inn at Eaton Socon to which John Byng refers was the White Horse, the stopping place of Wackford Squeers and his schoolboys in *Nicholas Nickleby,* on their way to York-shire. Dickens tends to be facetious about "Eton Slocomb," and the nineteenth century coach traveler in the *Stamford Regent* might not have been commended by John Byng—the traveler who knew Stilton only for its cheese, or Stamford only for its York ham. The cheese was never a product of Stilton. It was (and still is) a Leicestershire cheese which got the name because it was served at Stilton, at the Bell and the Angel; as, I suspect, "York ham" was not ham cured in York, but ham set out at coaching inns for travelers to York. It was the road which made it profit-able for the Bedfordshire market gardeners to grow so many cucumbers, and the road has influenced our eating habits not only by popularizing ham sandwiches but by inducing so much cab-bage. The mind roves back. What had made this part of Bed-fordshire "a land of cabbages" was originally such correspon-dence as emanated from St. Basil and Antipater and Gregory of Nazianzus; but what developed the *First and Best,* the *Early Offenham,* the *Imperial* and *Flower of Spring,* or the winter varie-ties, *Christmas Drumhead* and *January King—*and what brought the lettuces such as the devil sat on when the nun surprised him—and the cucumbers, and the asparagus—was the perpetual traffic of the Road toward London. I am interested in the leisurely con-versation between Johnson and Boswell, and in the leisurely journeys of John Byng; but in their time there was also urgency for everything—including vegetables—to grow faster, faster.

Speed, partly for the sake of speed, is a conception not confined to Arkwright and the other promoters of the Industrial Revolu-tion: one watches the quickening in the whole general tempo. Partly, perhaps, it was alteration of emphasis from theologic to economic; whatever it was, in every form of endeavor you detect a contest for speed. James Hogg, "the Ettrick Shepherd" (1770–1835), might still be taking his time over such a remarkable work as *The Private Memoirs and Confessions of a Justified Sinner,* but about his neighbor Sir Walter Scott (1771–1832) there is ever the feeling of the new urgency: the length of Scott's novels is due to his hurry. Sterne's *Tristram Shandy* may exploit a teasing slowness, but the nineteenth century George Borrow goes in for chapter headings with the explosive rapidity of Alfred Jingle. It was in 1811 that George Borrow as a boy, traveling with his mother, reached Norman Cross on the Great North Road. "And a strange place it was, this Norman Cross," is the way Borrow opens the part of *Lavengro* which is to introduce us to the Snake Hunter and to the Gypsies: here is the speed of the chapter headings:

IV. Norman Cross—Wide Expanse—Vive l'Empereur—Unpruned Woods —Man with the Bag—Froth and Conceit—I beg your Pardon—Growing Timid—About Three o'Clock—Taking One's Ease—Cheek on the Ground —King of the Vipers—French King—Frenchmen and Water.

V. The Tent—Man and Woman—Dark and Swarthy—Manner of Speaking—Bad Money—Transfixed—Faltering Tone—Little Basket—High Opinion—Plenty of Good—Keeping Guard—Tilted Cart—Rubricals—Jasper—The Right Sort—The Horseman of the Lane—John Newton—The Alarm —Gentle Brothers.

So "northward, northward still," along the road to Edinburgh Castle, goes young Borrow, with all the surge of energy of those early years of the nineteenth century.

An even better example of the surge of energy along this part of the road is a garden boy called Joseph Paxton. His father was a farmer at Milton Bryant in Bedfordshire; there Paxton was born in 1803; as a lad "my attention was turned to Gardening"; and after various preliminary jobs he got into the gardens of the Royal Horticultural Society,[2] then recently established at Chiswick. Paxton was then getting on for twenty years of age, "and unmaried." When in 1826 the Duke of Devonshire needed a gardener for his seat at Chatsworth he offered the post to Paxton, and Paxton accepted with alacrity. Did I say alacrity? Here are Paxton's words:

I left London by the Comet coach for Chesterfield and arrived at Chatsworth at half-past 4 o'clock in the morning of the 9th of May, 1826. As no person was to be seen at that early hour I got over the greenhouse gates by the old covered way, explored the pleasure grounds, and looked round the outside of the house. I then went down to the kitchen garden, scaled the outside wall, and saw the whole of the place, set the men to work at 6 o'clock, then returned to Chatsworth and got Thomas Weldon to play me the waterworks and afterwards went to breakfast with poor dear Mrs. Gregory and her niece; the latter fell in love with me and I with her, and thus completed my first morning's work at Chatsworth before 9 o'clock.

Twenty-five years later Paxton became the successful designer of the greatest greenhouse of all time, the Crystal Palace, which housed the Great Exhibition of 1851. It happened that when Paxton, with a roll of plans for the Crystal Palace under his arm, went to Derby railway station to get to London with all speed, he had "the good fortune to accidentally meet Mr. Robert Stephenson" of railway fame. They shared a railway carriage; Paxton exposed his plans; Stephenson was at once enthusiastic about the idea of the gigantic greenhouse; helped Paxton "like a brother" to get the plan accepted by Prince Albert. The plan was accepted, the Duke of Devonshire was "enchanted": the message from Chatsworth—from the niece whom he had "maried"—was "We are all in a state of great excitement at your most triumphant success. . . . The village bells have rung most merrily all day."

The accidental meeting of Paxton and Robert Stephenson at Derby railway station is significant of what was going on in the mid-nineteenth century. Consider the change of atmosphere from the discussion of greenhouses by Johnson and Boswell. In no department of life in nineteenth century England is there any stage at which the traveler may call a halt; there is no way of integrating an expression which contained so many variables; and yet there is that moment of the Great Exhibition when England just for the moment might try on its coat of many colors to see what it looked like. Pitt, in his speech at the Guildhall on Lord Mayor's day, 1805, had said: "England has saved herself by her own energy; and I hope that having saved herself by her energy, she will save Europe by her example." After Waterloo, when the hope was regarded as realized, a medal was struck to commemorate Pitt's last speech in four words of Latin: *Seipsam virtute, Europam exemplo.* The Great Exhibition of 1851 was to show to everybody, not by medallion but by display within the glass house, what had been achieved. The significance for my special theme is that in the promotion of the Great Exhibition I regard the Great North Road as having been at work: Paxton, a garden boy from the southern end in Bedfordshire: the Stephensons, father and son, from Newcastle-upon-Tyne. England was in transition from an agricultural to an industrial country: the Exhibition represents the midpoint of the transition.

Matthew Boulton had remarked to King George III: "I sell, Sir, what all the world desires—power." He meant a new source of power—steam—additional to man power, horse power, wind power, water power.[3] When in 1769 James Watt was working on the practical substitution of steam power, detractors of him and of Boulton also reported to George III that the idea was "drivelling delirium." The period abounds in disagreements. Malone found Johnson in his room at Gough Square in melancholy mood, pensively roasting apples at the fire, and reading the *History of Birmingham.* At that time it was not the "history" of Birmingham with which Boulton was concerned. In 1775 he organized the partnership of "Boulton and Watt" on Snow Hill, Birmingham, and their first engine, which was in use for more than a hundred years, is still in running order at the Science Museum at South Kensington. The craftsmanship of the mechanical age, as exhibited by Maudslay, was beginning. William Murdoch, a Cornishman who worked with Boulton and Watt, is said to have made a locomotive engine for colliery work in 1786; in 1803 Trevethick invented another which was taken up by the owners of Killingworth colliery in Northumberland, where George Stephenson worked as a boy. "Puffing Billy," the oldest steam locomotive which remains in existence, was built at Wylam colliery in 1813 by William Hedley. But it was George Stephenson who recognized that steam locomotives could be run on railways across open country to pull carriages for general traffic, human passengers as well as freight.

At first the coaching trade upon the Great North Road could well afford to laugh at George Stephenson's idea of railways. The surfacing of the roadway had begun to be improved, before 1819, by a Scotsman, John Macadam, who by a new process now called "macadamizing" produced a road surface superior to that which John Byng had described as "a road of fine gravel." On the macadam" roadway—part of Macadam's name was lost when it became "tarmac"—coach passengers and mail had little to fear from competition by the steam locomotive, which was not expected to travel at more than ten miles an hour, and would never be anything but "unsafe, incompetent, and a public nuisance." As for the transport of heavy goods, there was the "brisk" navigation upon the rivers referred to by John Byng, and there was also, between 1750 and 1830, the prodigious development of navigable canals. Canal navigators were called "navvies," and so were the laborers employed in the construction, and the term passed on to laborers in general. But the navigation of many of the rivers was not so much "brisk" as difficult. George Stephenson's first public railway from Stockton to Darlington was opened on September 27, 1825, to avoid the awkwardness of transport on the river Tees: it was a colliery line, but it also carried the first passenger train in the world to be hauled by a locomotive, Stephenson's *Active*. The Stockton and Darlington Railway was financed largely by Quaker capital, and the Quaker woolen merchant, Edward Pease, spoke in good Quaker spirit to an associate who was afraid to use it: "Thou hast the heart of a chicken. I am determined to try it."

If river transport was slow, so was canal transport. There was a glut of traffic to be handled. Transportation of cotton from the Mersey to the Manchester mills amounted in 1824 to 409,670 bales from America alone: it often took as much time for a consignment to pass from the Mersey to Manchester as the twenty-one days it had taken to cross the Atlantic. The two canals between Manchester and the sea—the Old Quay Canal and the Bridgewater Canal—were immensely profitable to their shareholders, and there were screams in *The Creevey Papers* at the possible competition of "this infernal nuisance—the locomotive Monster, carrying *eighty tons* of goods, and navigated by a tail of smoke and sulphur, coming thro' every man's grounds between Manchester and Liverpool." But the boilers were boiling. Locomotive race trials, to be judged by speed and pulling power, were arranged at Rainhill on October 6, 1829, where five entries were to compete before flag-draped stands for a prize of £500. The two outstanding contestants were the black and yellow *Rocket*, constructed and operated by George Stephenson and his son Robert, and the *Novelty*, in Swedish blue and copper, designed by John Ericsson, who had come to London from Sweden in 1826.[4] The *Rocket* was the heavier and sturdier, the *Novelty* the lighter and more fleet-footed. As they did their trials on what was somewhat of an improvised track, the excitement was intense: the two Stephensons and Ericsson and his partner, all in top hats, bouncing turn by turn on the open platforms behind their boilers, trying to get the utmost out of them. It is recorded that *Novelty* as a loose engine ran the measured mile in fifty-three seconds; but that, in the conditions, I take the liberty of doubting—I would think a minute had dropped out of the newspaper report. Both engines could do about thirty miles an hour: *Novelty* slightly the faster, *Rocket* the more reliable and the stronger for pulling power. *Rocket* won the prize. The Stephensons got the contract for the Liverpool to Manchester Railway, which was opened in 1830 after great difficulties had been overcome in crossing a swamp called Chat Moss. The day the line was opened was marred by the first railway accident. William Huskisson, the statesman, attempted to cross the line to speak to the Duke of Wellington and was knocked down by the *Rocket:* he was carried off to hospital at thirty miles an hour, but died the same day.[5]

John Ericsson was naturally disgruntled at losing the contest with the *Rocket*. The winning of £500 would scarcely have solved his personal problems, for he was already getting considerably into debt. I have pondered over the detail that within a fairly short time of his arrival in London this lively Swedish inventor had run up a bill with Messrs. Storey & James, Bond Street tailors, to the sum of £5,092 15s. This seems to me to show that round-about 1830, although wealth might be unequally distributed, there was disposition to extend a good deal of credit to plausible people. This was soon to be demonstrated in the new "Railway Age" in which there was a frenzy for investment, even in bogus railways, reminiscent of the South Sea Bubble. But a second ponderable is why at this date should a man so much interested in transportation run up such a large tailor's bill? The Regency period, the age of the "dandies," was over; however sad to see the last of brightly colored men's clothes of silk and satin, forward-looking men of business were toning down their dress to sober business uniform. Perhaps the bill for £5,000-odd was not wholly for clothes; perhaps

Messrs. Storey & James had lent money to Ericsson; at any rate the bill was not paid, and after it had run for some years Ericsson joined Mr. Pickwick in the Fleet prison for debt. Ericsson was an eccentric boffin. It is possible that his English wife's family bailed him out of the Fleet prison but reproached his conduct; certainly something turned him against his wife; he left her behind him in London and sailed for New York in 1839. The ship was the *British Queen,* which had auxiliary paddlewheels. The clumsiness of paddlewheels in the Western Ocean confirmed Ericsson in his conviction that screw propulsion was the most sensible way of driving a ship. Other ways of Ericsson's thinking were unaltered by the voyage. The customary tip to the ship steward cost him $6.66— the peculiar sum suggests it was the division of a collection—which left Ericsson short of cash on his arrival, and he was considerably short of credit: but his way of dealing with this problem was to check into New York's most fashionable and expensive hotel, the Astor House. It would be off my route to follow his subsequent adventures, but it must be mentioned that twenty-some years later he turns up in the history of the American Civil War as the designer of the *Monitor,* which was to cheer up the North by its combat, indecisive but regarded as successful, with the southern ship *Merrimack.*

What was happening in the Railway Age to the Great North Road? I have made it clear, I hope, that it was the Great North Road which was largely responsible for the Railway Age. The frenzy for speed of transportation came from within what had been the Danelaw. The first rails spread west from Darlington and Newcastle, but they soon spread south to London and north past Lindisfarne and Joyeuse Gard to Edinburgh and Glasgow. Along the route of the Great North Road there was in one sense no change at all by the addition of a third parallel, the so-called "permanent way" of iron rails, to the twin roadways initiated by the Romans. There were change of vehicle, change of speed of transport for people and freight, change of postal service. There was no essential change of spirit: but there were so many local changes and changes of habit as to be impossible to enumerate. A local change, for instance, was the decline in importance of Stamford and the return to importance of Peterborough. In monastic times Peterborough had been the more important of the two; even in those times Peterborough Cathedral gave a prophetic impression of being like a train shed—long and low, with no tower to speak of (because of the difficulty, in those marshy days, of foundations), with no rood screen to break the nave, it was almost like a blowpipe to expel a pilgrim onward horizontally toward Crowland, Boston, Lincoln. In most cathedrals you look upward; in Peterborough you looked outward, aware of the wide, flat, fertile plain of country, "as *level*," says Cobbett in one of his famous descriptions, "as the table on which I am now writing." After the draining of the fens this had become ideal railway country. Stamford, on the Great North Road, at the decline of the monastic period had rejoiced in its superior position. Stamford at that time had pretensions of becoming a second Oxford; like Oxford, in the pride of coaching days it resented and resisted any approach by rail; but Peterborough welcomed the railway and became more important than Stamford as a center for transportation. The addition of the third parallel, the "permanent way," meant many such local inversions of fortunes.

But the alterations caused by the railways cannot, as I say, be enumerated. Some of them one regrets: the alteration and standardization of many hitherto parochial country customs. A town spelled *Wymondham,* locally pronounced "Windham," has to be pronounced to a booking clerk the way it is spelled; "Hunston" has to be pronounced *Hunstanton;* and so all over the land. There is no argument. In the Monastic Age you had to accept the language of the clerk to get to heaven: in the railway age you had to accept the language of the booking clerk to get anywhere. The one could be as haughty as the other, for a new god was in being: the Locomotive God. And if one regrets the passing away of the beauty (as De Quincey described it) of the mail coach, one has also to admit the glory and the beauty which came in with the steam engine and the express train. The effect on children was mighty and instantaneous, and, among train spotters, the religion is strong today. The ritual of train service appealed spontaneously. A boy called Charles Lutwidge Dodgson was born in Daresbury, Cheshire, in 1832, the year in which the Parliamentary Reform Bill was passed. His father was a clergyman to whom, when

Charles was eleven, Sir Robert Peel presented a crown living at Croft-on-Tees, on the Great North Road a few miles south of Darlington. Charles was the eldest of eleven children, seven of them girls. The vicarage at Croft had a large garden; next the house there was a greenhouse in which there was a night-blooming cereus, and when that bloomed there was a party for the neighbors; but I draw attention to the garden. That is where Lewis Carroll (for it is less awkward to call him by his pen name than to go on using the other one) played with the brood of brothers and sisters, and the favorite game was "trains." The garden was large enough for a number of "stations" constructed by the children, at which the train—a wheelbarrow, a truck, and a barrel—could stop for real or pretended refreshments. Charles (or Lewis Carroll) as the eldest was Chief Station Master, also Ticket Agent: the Rules were written out and remain in his handwriting. Rule 3 follows:

Station master must mind his station and supply refreshments: he can put anyone who behaves badly to prison, while a train goes round the garden: he must ring for the passengers to take their seats, then count 20 slowly, then ring again for the train to start. The L one shall be a surgeon, the wounded must be brought there gratis by the next train going that way and cured gratis. There shall be a place at the L station for lost luggage. If there is anyone to go, a flag is to be hoisted.[6]

By 1843 it was just natural, and pleasurable, for children on the Great North Road to accept the Railway Age: so natural as to make one wonder how children could have existed before puffer trains came into being. Changes for grownups were also effected by new conditions of rapid transport. In recent years there has been much study of the changes of fashion in costume, male and female; and though I make no attempt at a detailed correlation of modes of clothing and modes of transport, such correlation has been learnedly observed. Extravagant fashions for men rapidly altered to clothing which was practical and utilitarian; but with outdoor wear women at first conspired (or were forced to conspire) to make it almost impossible for themselves to get about. At the beginning of the nineteenth century it was prevalent, not only in the West End of London, at Ranelagh or other places of fashionable resort, but also in county towns, for women to indulge "the naked fashion," white muslin worn with a minimum of under-clothing, occasionally with none at all. Apart from the extremely low necks, the gowns were sometimes slit at the side to reveal the legs. In winter smart women undressed to go out: they wore thicker clothes in summer. In the winter of 1804: "The only sign of modesty in the present dress of the ladies is the pink dye in their stockings, which makes their legs appear to blush in the total absence of petticoats. . . . Drawers of light pink are now the *ton* among our dashing belles, which through their thin muslin dresses exhibit a most inviting flesh colour." This was before the Jane Austen period, when outdoor dress became more decorous and prim, though for a while it was still possible, at the excuse of a puddle of rainwater in the street, to gather up an armful of muslin and disclose a pink stocking to the knee. Came then the tighter, stiffened skirt with high neck, long sleeves; the stiffened hem held it away from the ankles, so it was possible to walk without raising it; but since the top and legs of the female form were less disclosed, something had to be done about the equator. An earlier fashion of padding in front (cushioning known in France as *ventres postiches*) was superseded by the "bustle."

The beginning of the Railway Age shows men as eager to take advantage of the facilities of travel, and fashionable women as agreeing to make it as difficult as possible to do so. Jeanie Deans, walking the Great North Road in 1737, was far less handicapped than any well-to-do woman of a hundred years later. By the Railway Age, transition from hard work to machinery in the textile trades had been accomplished; the development of the power loom, the jacquard, and the spinning mule had brought an enormous increase in output and in wealth; and in some odd inversion of chivalry, the well-to-do female form was forced to carry, and submitted to carrying, as heavy a burden of armor as that of a medieval knight. At the time of the accession of Queen Victoria in 1837, the average housewife (then as now) "washed an acre of dirty dishes, a mile of glass and three miles of clothes and scrubbed five miles of floor yearly" (*Daily Telegraph*, September 29, 1937). But to display that one was not an average housewife and that one was above the working class also required, in 1837, heavy, although different, exertion. Sleeves, "Psyche wings," and pelerines made an enormous width of sloping shoulder; to set off this width above and below there had to be a tiny waist and tight lacing. Although the extreme tight lacing was not reached until the 1840's, a death from the practice is recorded in 1832. Below the waist corsets had spreading basques to uphold "a wide skirt of 7 or 8 breadths, lined with stiff muslin," and the pads for the bustle, which reached its extreme proportions in the 1870's, began to be carted by ladies of fashion. How to stuff the pads caused trouble: horsehair sometimes stuck through, air-tight pneumatic bustles sometimes burst, and to have a bustle stuffed with bran introduced an unexpected danger:

Ladies' Bustles. Caution. On Tuesday last as a well-dressed lady was proceeding down Watergate Street, a huge Jack-ass was observed to Throw up his nose, and snuff the air as if he smelt his Jenny from afar. Presently he kicked up his heels and with a most amorous Yeehaw, set off at the top of his speed down the street . . . which the lady no sooner perceived than she gathered up her garments and scampered away with all her might, amid shouts of laughter from the spectators. The relentless jackass still gave chase, calling to the fair fugitive with an occasional Yeehaw, to halt and surrender at discretion. At length he "ran into her," and, seizing her by that prominent posterior deformity which ladies call "a bustle," tore the skirts of her garments and under-garments fairly away from the body. The embarrassment and confusion, indeed the absolute state of fright, into which the lady was thrown under such circumstances may be more easily conceived than described. She was held fast behind, and escaped half denuded into one of the shops, leaving a stream of brownish powder to mark her route, besides a considerable quantity that had been emancipated by the donkey. The lady's bustle was stuffed with bran! Our fair countrywomen would grieve exceedingly if Nature had made them with one of these dromedary appendages on their backs; but if they will thus disfigure themselves, they will at least do well not to stuff their bustles with bran or oat-meal. There is more than one keen-scented and hungry donkey in Chester!

That quotation from the *Chester Chronicle* is filched from the delightful book *Browns and Chester* by "Mass-Observation"; but the episode (or leg pull) might just as well have come from York or Edinburgh. It is easy enough to make fun of our ancestors, who

have no opportunity of answering back; but the point of the reference is that well-to-do women, either by impulse or by compulsion,
tended to do the most they could, by costume, to assert or to
accept, that theirs was only a small cruising radius. For travel
the bustle was awkward enough: the subsequent crinoline was even
worse. The Englishman's Victorian home was his castle, from which
he might sally forth. A most effective castle wall was the crinoline.
No womenfolk could get far away in crinolines, which simply would
not pass a turnstile or go into a railway carriage. But in the end
it was the Road—the mechanization of the Road—railway, bicycle,
motorcar, aircraft—which did what it could to emancipate women.
Costume could not forever restrict women from travel: travel could
and did affect women's costume. In the 1890's "Mass-Observation"
records what a woman who had lived through the crinoline period,
and thought it was one which we "would wish to see erased from
history," could say as to outdoor clothes:

> Muslin frocks are only seen at garden parties, except in the country;
> silk has given place to the more serviceable woollen materials; and light
> colours are eschewed for obvious reasons of fitness and economy; every-
> thing for daily use must be quiet and unnoticeable, able to stand wear
> and tear, rain and dust, tumbling and creasing. The omnibus and the
> tram-car have much to answer for in toning down our costume from
> gay to grave. In these democratic days everybody rides in public vehicles,
> and this custom not only tends to produce a sober uniformity in dress,
> but is a great bulwark against any huge extravagance in fashion.[7]

I said it was impossible to enumerate all the changes which
accompanied the Railway Age, and content myself with two
more examples. If playing at trains gave pleasure to Lewis Carroll
while he was a rather peculiar left-handed little boy (the pleasure
is reflected in *Alice Through the Looking-Glass*), and if it gave a
new religion to those who could not fail to be impressed by the
Locomotive God,[8] it also started up a new game—or new business—
stamp collecting. Penny Postage (1840) started that. Under the
old system postage was paid on delivery of the letter, if not pre-
paid by obtaining a "frank" from a not always get-attable postmaster. Wordsworth had the privilege of franking letters, but it
was not always easy to find him, if he was out of doors composing

a poem somewhere along Striding Edge. In London, the cost of franking a letter to Brighton was eightpence. Rowland Hill (a statue to him is outside the Sorting Office of G.P.O. London) introduced a universal rate of one penny per half-ounce, and introduced to England the method of placing adhesive stamps on letters before posting. If I remember rightly, the French had antedated him with the idea of an adhesive wafer which would at one and the same time seal the envelope and demonstrate that the postage had been paid; but Rowland Hill's idea of the stamp on the front of the envelope won out; and Rowland Hill had a remarkable young assistant, Anthony Trollope, who brought in another idea—the pillar box, or post box. I never fail to marvel at the strange ways in which one civilization, or one age, carries over into another. Stephenson's choice of the 4 ft. 8½ in. gauge for his railway because that was the old Roman yoke: Trollope's choice of bright red for the English pillar box is another example. Whether or no we made out a good argument for the popularity of red with Robin Hood, it is provable that Cromwell put the New Model army into red coats, and the prestige of that army gave Gibbon occasion to remark (*The Decline and Fall,* c. lvii, n. 18): "in England the red ever appears the favourite and as it were the national colour of our military ensigns and uniforms." So for the smart huntsman, the color of the coat was automatically red. I don't recall if the color of John Peel's "coat so gay" is specifically mentioned; but what did you assume it to have been? [9] I do recall that Anthony Trollope, on his post-office inspections, combined fox hunting in a red coat with his post-office work as often as he could. So the red coat of Cromwell's soldiers, through the catalysis of fox hunting, came to stand to attention in the red pillar boxes of the postal service: the red pillar boxes which, when you see them, at once remind you that you are in Britain and not elsewhere.

Only one further interruption do I permit myself in this last burst upon the Great North Road. It has been a short journey, yet a long pull, from Claudius and his elephants to the Great Exhibition of 1851; and a well-stocked mind might have found many other things to think of than the thoughts which have prompted me. We have seen the railways regularizing place names and clothing; we should glance at the alteration of something which, until you come to think about it, doesn't seem very important—the English "street ballad." Here is how it was along the Great North Road in Shakespeare's Merry England—Autolycus, in *The Winter's Tale* (Act IV, sc. iv), doing his stuff with a country clown and his wenches:

Clown.	What hast here? Ballads?
Mopsa.	Pray now, buy some: I love a ballad in print o' life, for then we are sure they are true.
Aut.	Here's one to a very doleful tune, how a usurer's wife was brought to bed of twenty money-bags at a burthen and how she longed to eat adders' heads and toads carbonadoed.
Mop.	Is it true, think you?
Aut.	Very true, and but a month old.
Dorcas.	Bless me from marrying a usurer!
Aut.	Here's the midwife's name to't, one Mistress Taleporter, and five or six honest wives that were present. Why should I carry lies abroad?
Mop.	Pray you now, buy it.
Clo.	Come on, lay it by: and let's first see moe ballads; we'll buy the other things anon.
Aut.	Here's another ballad of a fish, that appeared upon the coast on Wednesday the fourscore of April, forty thousand fathom above water, and sung this ballad against the hard hearts of maids: it was thought she was a woman and was turned into a cold fish for she would not exchange flesh with one that loved her; the ballad is very pitiful and as true.
Dor.	Is it true too, think you?
Aut.	Five justices' hands at it, and witnesses more than my pack will hold.
Clo.	Lay it by too; another.
Aut.	This is a merry ballad, but a very pretty one.
Mop.	Let's have some merry ones.
Aut.	Why, this is a passing merry one, and goes to the tune of "Two maids wooing a man"; there's scarce a maid westward but she sings it; 'tis in request, I can tell you.
Mop.	We can both sing it: if thou wilt bear a part, thou shalt hear; 'tis in three parts.
Dor.	We had the tune on't a month ago.
Aut.	I can bear my part; you must know it is my occupation. Have at it with you.

There is an unbroken line of descent from Autolycus to "Tragedy Bill" who, just before the Railway Age, was doing the "gag and patter" at a London street corner for the ballads from the presses of Seven Dials:

Now, my friends, here you have, just printed and published, a full, true, and pertickler account of the life, trial, character, confession, behaviour, condemnation, and hexecution of that unfortunate malefactor, Richard Wilbyforce, who was hexecuted on Monday last, for the small charge of one ha'penny, and for the most horrible, dreadful, and wicked murder of Samuel—I means Sarah Spriggens, a lady's maid, young, tender, and handsome. You have here every pertickler, of that which he did, and that which he didn't. It's the most foul and horrible murder that ever graced the annals of British history. Here, my customers, you may read his hexecution on the fatal scaffold. You may also read how he met his victim in a dark and lonesome wood, and what he did to her—for the small charge of a ha'penny; and, further, you read how he brought her to London—after that comes the murder, which is worth all the money. And you read how the ghost appeared to him and then to her parents. Then comes the capture of the *willain;* also the trial, sentence, and hexecution, showing how the ghost was in the act of pulling his leg on one side, and the "old gentleman" a pulling on the other, waiting for his victim (my good friends excuse my tears!). But as Shakespeare says, "Murder most foul and unnatural," but you'll find this more foul and unnatural than that or the t'other—for the small charge of a ha'penny! Yes, my customers, to which is added a copy of serene and beautiful werses, pious and immoral, as wot he wrote with his own blood and skewer the night after—I mean the night before his hexecution, addressed to men and women of all sexes—I beg pardon, but I mean classes (my friends it's nothing to laugh at), for I can tell you the werses is made three of the hard-heartedest things cry as never was—to wit, that is to say, namely—a overseer, a broker, and a policeman. Yes, my friends, I sold twenty thousand copies of them here this morning, and could of sold twenty thousand more than that if I could of but kept from crying—only a ha'penny!

There were the "Standing Patterers," such as "Tragedy Bill," and there were the "Running Patterers," usually a "mob" or "school" from whose combined clamor only a few leading words were audible, "Horrible," "Dreadful," Murder," "One Penny," "Seduction," "Pool of Blood," and the like. I take these details from *The*

Common Muse by V. de Sola Pinto and A. E. Rodway,[10] who go
on to quote that the broadsides offered by the Running Patterers
"usually deal in murders, seductions, crim-cons, explosions, alarm-
ing accidents, deaths of public characters, duels and love-letters.
But popular or notorious murders are the 'great goes.' " The sales of
such ballads, written with great speed (allegedly by the criminal on
the night before his execution) were (if we may trust contemporary
statistics) stupendous:

1828	Corder ("Maria Marten")—	
	Murder in the Red Barn	1,166,000
1840	Greenacre	1,650,000
1840	Courvoisier	1,166,000
1849	The Mannings	2,500,000
1849	Rush's murder	2,500,000

Sales figures of this order are the more stupendous when one
considers them in relation to population. In 1700 the population
of England had been about 6 million, four-fifths of Englishmen
then living in the country. In 1900 the population was about
36 million, four-fifths of Englishmen then living in towns. For
any moment of the transitional period one may make the best
guess one can; but the ratio to the total population of ballads
printed and sold seems remarkably high. In the early part of the
nineteenth century there was competition between balladmongers,
notably in the towns which had grown in what used to be the
Danelaw: there were presses producing ballads in Liverpool, Manchester, Birmingham, Leeds, Nottingham, Newcastle. We know
(as for instance from the life of John Clare) that the sale was not
promoted solely by the Standing Patterers or Running Patterers
in towns, but also, as in the days of Autolycus, promoted at country
fairs. John Clare's father was a penniless farm laborer at Help-
stone, beside the Great North Road in Northamptonshire, and John
Clare was put to farm labor at the age of seven, yet he records
that his father's one extravagant passion was to stuff the primitive
farm cottage with ever-the-latest ballads.

In town and country, it was the success of the ballads which
destroyed them. In towns the Standing Patterer and the Running
Patterer came to be nuisances, and after 1829 the balladmonger

could be more easily discouraged by prosecutions for mendicity and obstruction: the entertainment of the streets was pushed by the police into the music hall, and a George R. Sims became a lineal descendant of a street-corner "Tragedy Bill." As to the journalistic functions of the street ballad, as soon (1839) as the stamp duty on a newspaper was reduced from fourpence to onepence, and even more rapidly after the penny duty was wholly abolished in 1855, the ballad presses switched to a greater regularity of news work, and began to profit by the sweet uses of advertisements. In talking about ballads I must make a distinction between murder ballads and the more or less lyrical folk songs which for generations had emerged all over Britain, Scotland as well as South Country: ballad sellers of such folk songs moved in two directions, bringing songs from towns to be sold to country singers, and collecting songs in the country to be taken back to town to be printed on new ballad sheets, and to be sung in drawing rooms. The murder ballads, with their particular blend of horror and morality, seem to me to contain trace elements of the old-time "news from Smithfield," and if it was possible in 1849—that is to say, if the above figures are reliable—to sell copies to the tune of two and a half million, the mechanical expertise for production and distribution on that scale would automatically lead to the development of newspapers: the development of the provincial press. The most notable of the English "provincial" newspapers are to this day associated with centers where presses had formerly been busy with murder ballads. The suggestion is that the success of ballads and of the "Patterers" spread in two ways: into music halls and into provincial newspapers. The ballads themselves were superseded.

I talk about trace elements in a civilization as if they were elements easily to be identified. None of the simple things are easy: I have yet to meet an organic chemist who has language to differentiate between a bee sting and a wasp sting. I have a deplorable temptation to oversimplify: to go on talking as if the Danelaw of the nineteenth century were of direct, unmixed, descent from the original hard yellow chunk of Danelaw on the map of Britain circa 900; to go on talking as if the sting of Danes and sting of Saxons in our heritage could be differentiated. I think that within Britain at the time of the Great Exhibition some traces of the old

Saxons versus Danes contest do remain; but at the center of things in London there is such an admixture of heritages from other racial elements and other contests, each in the passage of time partially but not wholly resolved and not wholly obliterated, that it is difficult indeed to tease one thread from the whole skein. Consider the contests which the journey on the road has made us think about: Britons versus Romans, Saxons versus Britons, Danes versus Saxons, Normans versus Danes, Gentles versus Simples, Roman Catholics versus Protestants, Cavaliers versus Roundheads—each contest leaves its traces, and by the first half of the nineteenth century there are fresh ones: country versus towns, conservatives versus liberals, and a new situation in the realm of labor, where it has to be fought out whether "work" is a matter of "status" or "contract." It is possible that one might be able to perceive some of the remote trace elements in our civilization less obscurely upon the fringes and frontiers than where they have become confused and blended at the center. That is why it occurred to me to touch upon so remote a subject as whale hunting.[11]

I mentioned the early whaling exploits by the Basques in the Bay of Biscay. The first excitement, I would think, might have been ritualistic rather than economic. We touched on the Mithraic bull-slaying ritual. Whaling was the bullfight performed at sea. It was essentially an all-male mystique, and in a low-class way it ties in, as bullfighting did on land, with the upper-class mystique (with its Mithraic elements) of chivalry. Traffic in whale oil at Biarritz I regard as having been at first subsidiary. I would suppose the flesh of bulls killed in bullfights has to be disposed of somehow, and fairly soon it would occur to somebody that the blubber of a whale that had been towed ashore had better be rendered down. Came then, as I described, the interest of Richard Coeur de Lion and King John, and the northern demand for whale oil for ships' lanterns and for lamps on land. Came then the secondary, practical development of whaling, less for the sport or ritual than for the product. Came then the importance of whale hunting for British seamen, spilling off the spillway of the Great North Road. Came then the exodus of some of those seamen from the Danelaw to New England, and the continuation of whale hunting from Connecticut and Massachusetts. Before the end of the seventeenth century a small but regular trade had started in New England. In 1688 Secretary Randolph wrote home to England: "New Plimouth Colony have great profit by whale killing. I believe it will be one of our best returns, now bever and peltry fayle us."

My concern at the moment is not with the history of whaling for its own sake, but with the reflection which the whaling industry of New England throws back upon the spirit and character of the Danelaw, from which the industry had been exported. As you derive a feeling about the extent of witch hunting in East Anglia from the immediate outbreak of witch hunting in New England when it was peopled by East Anglians who could behave without restriction—so I think I learn something about the Danelaw from the spirit of the New England whaling. If so, I learn a queer thing: namely, that after the hard hammering by the Normans some of the people of the Danelaw adopted and adapted some of the features of "the Heresy" which the Normans had brought with them from France; and in due course a transmutation of these Cathar elements went over to New England and there flourished. There was a surcharge of fascination about open-boat whaling which I can explain in no other way than by saying that over and above the commercial reward it represented (as it had done in the early days of the Basques) a pseudoreligious ritual. The ritual was, so to say, "canonized," because there was commercial profit in the industry; but the strange thing is that open-boat whaling did not cease as soon as there were better profits elsewhere. The trade did begin to decline in England. William Murdock had invented gas lighting and installed it in Boulton and Watt's foundry at Birmingham in 1803. Pall Mall in London, and Westminster Bridge, were shortly afterward illuminated by gaslight. The only apparent carryover from whaling tradition in London was the "fishtail" gas burner. For hand lamps, coal oil was quickly found to be superior in every way to whale oil. This was as true for the Atlantic seaboard of North America as for Britain. But New England, it seems perversely, attempted to keep on increasing its whaling fleet. Why? There is something ancient here, some ancient stubbornness. Profit apart, there was some kind of mystique about the whale kill; it is an odd coincidence that there is today a whaling museum located at Mystic, Connecticut; and the perversity of the mysticism and the peculiar form of whaling pride—the New Englander's bullfight—is dwelt upon by Herman Melville in *Moby Dick,* a work in which there are as many trace elements of Mithraism as there are in the *Morte d'Arthur.*

You would think that nobody in New England could have been unaware of the sadism in open-boat whaling, or of the disgusting working conditions in the whale ships. Melville was certainly not unaware. There is a note of his:

What became of the ship's company on the whale-ship *Acushnet,* according to Hubbard (who came back home in her after more than a four years' voyage and visited me in Pittsfield in 1850).

Captain Pease—returned and lives in asylum at the Vineyard.

Raymond, 1st Mate—had a fight with the captain and went ashore at Payta.

Boatswain, either ran away or killed at Ropo, one of the Marquesas.

Smith, went ashore at Santa, coast of Peru, afterwards committed suicide at Mobile.

Barney, boatswain, came home.

Carpenter, went ashore at Morvee half dead with disreputable disease. The Czar.

Tom Johnson, black, went ashore at Morvee, half dead (ditto) and died at the hospital.

Reed, mulatto—came home.

Blacksmith, ran away at San Francisco.

Blackus, little black, ditto.

Bill Green, after several attempts to run away, came home in the end.

The Irishman, ran away, coast of Colombia.

Wright, went ashore half dead at the Marquesas.

Jack Adams and Jo Portuguese came home.

The Old Cook, came home.

Haynes, ran away aboard of a Sydney ship.

Little Jack, came home.

Grant, young fellow, went ashore half dead, spitting blood, at Oahu.

Murray, went ashore, shunning fight at Rio Janeiro.

The Cooper, came home.

Of the twenty-three mentioned, approximately ten came home (I can't tell about The Czar). At the time of Melville's note there were still something like 329 whaling ships from New Bedford continuing their displeasing traffic round the world.

My thought was it might more readily indicate some of the elements present in that part of Britain which had been the Danelaw, by considering how the derived impulses worked out in New England, where they had, as it were, free play. Contemplation of New England, of the witch hunting and the whaling, suggests, for instance, that a curious amalgam had occurred between Norman elements and Danish elements within the Danelaw; and the word "amalgam" is scarcely right, for what I am trying to indicate is how explosive the combination could be. I see trace elements of Norman "purism" in "Puritanism," and I see trace elements of "the Heresy" in New England whaling. What else were New Englanders wholeheartedly emulating?—for that will tell us what was being valued in the homeland.

Boys in Boston, Van Wyck Brooks remarks, were confident, in the early years of the nineteenth century, that they could "lick creation." How did they propose to do so?

Factory towns were rising on every hand, in eastern Massachusetts and New Hampshire—Lawrence, Lowell, Fitchburg, Manchester, Lynn. Every village with a waterfall set up a textile-mill or a paper-mill, a shoe-factory or an iron-foundry; and as Boston remained the financial centre, as well for manufacturing as for shipping, the mercantile fortunes of the inland counties were joined with those of the magnates of the seaboard. . . .

The zeal with which the Industrial Revolution was emulated shows there was something to emulate; but it shows more than that; the "show-off" spirit of New England shows there was "show-off" spirit in the parent Danelaw. What did the boys in Boston propose to do with "creation" when they had licked it? Ralph Waldo Emerson in 1844 gave one of his lectures to the Mercantile Library Association of Boston:

Who has not been stimulated to reflection by the facilities now in progress of construction for travel and the transportation of goods in the United States? . . . Not only is distance annihilated, but when, as now, the locomotive and the steamboat, like enormous shuttles, shoot every day across the thousand various threads of national descent and employment, and bind them fast in one web, an hourly assimilation goes forward, and there is no danger that local peculiarities and hostilities should be preserved. . . .

The railroad is but one arrow in our quiver, though it has great value as a sort of yardstick, and surveyor's line. The beautiful continent is ours, state on state, and territory on territory, to the waves of the Pacific sea:

> Our garden is the immeasurable earth,
> The heaven's blue pillars are Medea's house.

The task of surveying, planting, and building upon this immense tract, requires an education and a sentiment commensurate thereto. A consciousness of this fact is beginning to take place of the purely trading spirit and education which sprang up whilst all the population lived on the fringe of sea-coast. . . .

Substitute British Empire for United States, and this passage seems to express very accurately the spirit of the parent Danelaw.

The Great North Road had been turned into a railroad; the railroad quickened the dissemination of news; newspapers throve on a subject more staple than the sporadic murders which had prompted the murder ballads. Murders were all very well in their way, but the real news staple was gold, and how to get it. There were the complicated methods, but for the ordinary simple fellow the attractive way to get gold was just to pick it up off the ground.[12] That this could be done was headline news. Drake, Raleigh, John Smith, and the others had been right after all: there was gold in America just for the picking. Fifty years after the War of Independence (England would have fought that war much harder had the discovery been made fifty years earlier) a North Carolina Negro known only as Charley, while trapesing southward on foot, picked up a nugget of gold on the bank of Dukes Creek, in northern Georgia. History does not record what happened to Charley. The first nineteenth century gold rush developed. The richest deposits were quickly traced to Indian lands belonging to the Cherokee. The Cherokee were dispossessed. Perhaps fortunately for themselves, New Englanders looked in vain for gold along the tributaries of the Connecticut; but at the far side of the wide continent a yellow glint in a California millrace caught the eye of a boss carpenter, Jim Marshall. Marshall was in the employ of his friend, Colonel Sutter, who as a good Emersonian was attempting to get away from the "purely trading spirit" of the eastern seacoast;

he was also a devotee, it seems, of Rousseau. At Coloma, on the American Fork of the Sacramento River, Sutter was attempting to establish an estate, hopefully named "New Helvetia." Marshall's quick eye brought himself and Colonel Sutter to ruin. Marshall waded into the millstream, picked out the nugget of gold, and that was news. The result was swift and inevitable. A mob of gold hunters simply took over New Helvetia; Colonel Sutter was powerless to evict the squatters; they slaughtered his cattle, felled his timber, and treated him no otherwise than a Cherokee.

It was in that era of immeasurable possibilities that the Great Exhibition was devised. No comparable show-off to the world had ever been thought of before. It was, I repeat, primarily the pride of the Danelaw. Paxton was a gardener, and gardening was not forgotten. The Crystal Palace in Hyde Park was the great exemplar for a rage for hothouses, for conservatories, for the imitative little greenhouses which are as much of a feature of life in English suburbs as are pillar boxes. A pattern was set for local flower shows; respect was obtained for botanical gardens—gardens not merely for private display but for public benefit, with emphasis on what was utilitarian. Queen Victoria had given Kew Gardens to the nation in 1840, but the value of the gift came to be appreciated when after repeated experiments at Kew it was found that the cinchona tree (long known as the source of "Jesuits' bark," or as we say "quinine") could be transplanted and introduced to India; and though the famous theft of rubber seeds from Brazil (by Sir Henry Wickham in 1876) did not take place for a quarter of a century after the Great Exhibition, it was the result, I would think, of ideas encouraged by the Exhibition.

The aim of the Great Exhibition was to demonstrate that peace and prosperity could be extended the world over through the benefits of science and inventions. It was in part a horticultural exhibition, in part an "ideal home" exhibition: foreigners were invited to contribute and to pool their notions, and many did, in realms of domestic heating, refrigeration, and gadgets. Unless I am mistaken, the Exhibition encouraged fish knives, a massive amount of electroplate, Liebig's meat extracts and baby food, purdoniars, and Isaac Merritt Singer's sewing machine. But as befitted an exhibition prompted by the Great North Road, there

was also an emphasis on transportation away from home. It came
at a moment when plant hunters and naturalists were much on
the move: Darwin's *Voyage of H.M.S. Beagle* was published—the
two parts of it—in 1839–1842. Bates and Wallace sailed together
for the Amazon in 1848. In 1848 there was the sufficiency of political
troubles in Europe to shift a great many people. Herbert Agar (in
The Price of Union) tells me that during the 1840's the United
States received 1,713,251 immigrants; during the fifties, 2,598,214.
I have no means of checking these figures or of knowing where the
immigrants came from: some I am sure were stirred by the California gold rush. Plant hunting, gold rushing, movement, were in
the air. Telegraphs (though the first Atlantic cable was not laid till
1858), newspapers, railways, steamships agitated everybody, those
who went or those who profited by transporting other people. It
was good for British shipping when gold mines were discovered
in 1851 in Australia; in 1868 in Gabriel's Gully in New Zealand;
and later on, the Rand, in South Africa.

The Great Exhibition of 1851 is possibly a fitting place for me
to end my journey. In one sense the Great Exhibition greatly
succeeded. It was the first of great "international" exhibitions for
the development of trade, for the speedy and profitable transportation of "goods." One could linger over any of a thousand
ingenuities which it encouraged, of "packaging" and salesmanship.
One which amuses me is "barley sugar." At the time of the
French Revolution some of the French émigrés brought to England
the elegant Parisian pastime of lowering a piece of string into a
glass which contained a supersaturated solution of sugar: the result
was the formation of "rock-candy." The name in French was *sucre
brulé*. The English came to call it "barley sugar." There is no
connection with the grain "barley." But like anything else, at
the time of the Great Exhibition it could be mass produced, com-
mercialized, and sold. It could be and was packaged and resold
to France under the label of *sucre d'orge*.[13] Such divertissements
of the period are good clean fun; also the fact that the Great Exhibition of 1851 made a considerable amount of money, which was
shrewdly invested. If you care, today, to look into the London
telephone directory, you will find a telephone number for the
"Royal Commission for the Exhibition of 1851"; an office which

continues wisely to administer funds which resulted from the original show in the Crystal Palace; including support for the "British School in Rome." That is a thought which cannot fail to make you think back to Claudius and his intended exhibition: the exhibition which, when it took place eighteen centuries after, preserved instinctive connection with the original root of the Road.

In another sense, the ironic element in the comparison of the two exhibitions, the one intended by Claudius and the other achieved in 1851, cannot be excluded. The Great Exhibition which succeeded was intended to usher in a new age of universal peace and prosperity. Within three years there was the war with Russia, the "Crimean War" of 1854–1856; there was swiftly afterward the Indian Mutiny (1857–1858); and the American Civil War of 1861–1865. Among the causes of the American Civil War I cannot exonerate the Great North Road. I must not exaggerate special factors; but it would be just as wrong to disregard all special factors. A special factor in the conflict between North and South in America was the transcontinental railroad: the race by railroad towards the western sea.

In the quotation above from Emerson, I felt his reference to Medea (the sorceress) was unfortunate; I felt his reference to the railroad as "one arrow in our quiver" displayed an insufficient apprehension of what a perilous arrow it might be. When Emerson was speaking there were nearly sixteen million people in the North and West of America; in the eleven states which were to form the Southern Confederacy there was a population of little more than seven million. The North had the greater numbers, and more wealth, and an increasing flow of immigrants from Europe: the South had the burning feeling, not to be subjected to the numerical majority resident above the Mason-Dixon Line. That "line," running inward from the eastern seaboard, was a mere surveyors' figment, although it is interesting that flora and fauna pay some attention to it—oysters from the north side of the Mason-Dixon Line differ from oysters to the south. But a line of acrimonious human contention was the line of the railroad. A transcontinental railroad required federal land grants; it was widely believed that only one such railroad would be built; and North and South both wanted it. Every kind of greed came in; not only were regional jealousies involved, but the competition of land speculators; and the deadlock in the Congress between the friends of Jefferson Davis's southern route to California and the friends of Douglas's Nebraska route was exacerbated by the slave question. Was slavery to be extended westward? Or was the plantation system, said the southerner, to be hemmed in?

It is horrible to think that the Great Exhibition of 1851, financially successful, exuding prosperity, exploiting the pride of industry and peace, was so swiftly followed by the Crimean War with Russia, the Indian Mutiny, and, worst of all, the American Civil War. I am not regarding Paxton's giant greenhouse as responsible: only as exhibiting, as other events exhibited, that the pulsations along the Great North Road had got horribly out of control. It was in the 1850's that winds were sown, of which we have reaped whirlwinds. The first wind may blow with righteous indignation: along the Great North Road it has often done so. There is, I believe, a defect of vision which is called "askopia." It is a physical counterpart to the disease of the spirit which St. Thomas Aquinas describes theologically as "acedia" or "sloth": the disease (which, he says, usually attacks monks about the third hour) of looking far away, and of being unable to see what is under one's nose. Herman Melville's morbid view of life, his preoccupation with death wish, was perhaps less dangerous than the view of Emerson and his colleagues who seemed not to ponder why more than half the seamen in the whaling-ship *Acushnet* were either unable to return, or preferred not to return, to New England. There was a similar askopia in the parent Danelaw of Old England. In the period of the Great Exhibition there was a revolution in the English book trade about slave labor. It was not about the slave labor, which manifestly then existed, in English printing plants; it was excitement over slavery in America. Within the twelve months following its publication in England in 1852, *Uncle Tom's Cabin* ran through forty editions and sold one and a half million copies. This was as good for the presses as murder or gold, and whips did not fail to crack in English factories to make such production possible. It was the beginning of mass production of books; it was followed in 1854 by the mass production of *Westward Ho!* West, was the operative word: "Go west, young man":

that was "manifest destiny" (the phrase was invented, I believe, in the summer of 1845). In the rivalry between North and South in America for the control of the route to the West, every advantage resided with the self-righteousness of the abolitionist New Englander (not all New Englanders were abolitionists), and with the superiority of the North as to wealth and numbers and machine tools. Calhoun in the South and Lincoln in the North had done their best to avoid the bitterness of the Secession; but it could not be evaded.

Slavery was not the main issue, but it was a most inflammatory issue. It could be played up as a main issue. In October, 1859, a young man called John Brown declared his private war on slavery. He had retired to Canada to think about it; he had decided it was his dedicated mission; he had collected an army of seventeen white men and five Negroes who agreed with him. His chosen entry to the South was at Harpers Ferry in what is now West Virginia, at the confluence of the Shenandoah and Potomac rivers; there had been a government armory and arsenal there since 1796; Lewis and Clark had started from Harpers Ferry on their expedition across the continent. John Brown surprised and seized the armory, but within a matter of hours a detachment of United States Marines arrived; the commander of the detachment happened to be Colonel Robert E. Lee. John Brown and six other survivors were captured, held for trial at a nearby county seat; they were convicted, and they were subsequently hanged. Herbert Agar suggests that John Brown's chief crime was that he killed the hope of conciliation between North and South. Some of the best-known of New England moralists can scarcely be cleared of complicity. Of John Brown's impetuous raid at Harpers Ferry, Emerson, that preacher of restraint, spoke up instantly: "a new saint awaiting his martyrdom, and who, if he shall suffer, will make the gallows glorious like the cross." Thoreau called John Brown an "angel of light." Wendell Phillips declared he carried "letters of marque from God." When Northerners, uncertain about other aspects of the Civil War, felt uneasy, they could unite upon a marching song: "John Brown's body lies a mouldering in the grave, His soul goes marching on."

A great man, one of the greatest ever, was elected to the Presidency of the United States in 1860. The map of how the states voted shows how Disunited, at that moment, the States were. In the eleven states which were to form the Southern Confederacy, not one electoral vote was cast for Lincoln. On the announcement of Lincoln's election by the northern states, South Carolina, and then the other southern states, promptly seceded. Lincoln's Inaugural Address contains the passage:

> Physically speaking, we cannot separate. We cannot remove our respective sections from each other, nor build an impassable wall between them. A husband and wife may be divorced, and go out of the presence and beyond the reach of each other; but the different parts of our country cannot do this. They cannot but remain face to face, and intercourse, either amicable or hostile, must continue between them. Is it possible, then, to make that intercourse more advantageous or more satisfactory after separation than before? Can aliens make treaties easier than friends can make laws?

Not much otherwise, a thousand years before, had Alfred endeavored to speak to the divided Saxons and Danes of Britain.

A thousand years after Alfred, eighteen hundred years after Claudius, it did not look as if the Great North Road had done much good to the Western world. By turning itself into a railroad, by transfer across America, it was an effective instrument of cruel destruction to the Old South. The transportation system which for a long time had tied the West to the South was the river traffic. In 1852 the United States had less than 11,000 miles of railroad; in 1860 it had more than 30,000, and most of the new lines were tying the Northwest and the Midwest to the East, contradicting the river system. "The parallels," writes Allan Nevins, "had conquered the meridian lines of commerce . . . by 1860 the Northwest and Northeast marched arm in arm." The South had not been pushed aside without a struggle in the railroad competition, but the North, with more voting power to manipulate land grants and federal aid, with more capital available and with increasing income of immigrant labor, was far ahead in the race of railroads before the Civil War began; and when it came to the fighting it was inevitably the railroads which played a most important part in the military problem of getting there "fustest with the mostest."

If it is permissible to take a long view of ancient heritages, it is

possible to think that after a thousand years, and in a new, immeasurable territory, the heritage of the Danelaw and the heritage of Saxon England fought the old fight all over again in a
war which cost more American lives than the last two world
wars put together (Gerald W. Johnson, *Our English Heritage:*
Lippincott, Philadelphia, 1949, page 241). Events which territorially
were far away, were, one feels, affected by the hubris [14] exhibited
in the Crystal Palace. But once the Great North Road had been
turned into a railroad the ramifications of my theme are beyond
me. Except for a few mild observations I have reached the end of
my version of a story which has no end.

The first of the mild observations is that even out of the mistakes
and miseries of the Crimea, if the price was ghastly, yet some good
emerged; as with the Indian Mutiny; as with the American Civil
War—the price of Union will not bear contemplation, but the
result was Union. A story is told about the English Civil War,
that before the battle of Edgehill a local squire hunted a pack of
hounds between the two opposing armies—indifferent to the fate
of king or Parliament. Despite the ferocity of the American Civil
War, there are examples, not of fox hunters but of gold hunters,
who seemed to care nothing about it. My guide is George Willison,
with his book *Here They Dug the Gold*. The Californian gold rush
of 1849, drawing the adventurers who overwhelmed Colonel Sutter,
denuding ships which touched at San Francisco, had reached its
peak by 1852.

From such booming camps [says Willison] as Downieville, Jersey
Flat, Nevada City, Grass Valley, Rough and Ready, Sailors' Slide, Placer-
ville, El Dorado, Fiddletown, Coloma, Angels' Camp, Jackass Hill, Bed-
bug, Freeze Out and Sonora came the tons of yellow metal. . . .

By 1859 those fields were petering out, but in that year there was
discovered the Comstock Lode on the Nevada-California boundary
and, a thousand miles to the east, the Colorado mines which started
the Pikes Peak gold rush. What was the Civil War to that sort of
excitement? The capital of the Comstock was Virginia City. There,
one day in 1862, a man of twenty-seven arrived after a trek across
the desert and got a reporter's job on the *Territorial Enterprise*,
under his own name, Sam Clemens. Soon he established a pen

name, Mark Twain. The book which put Mark Twain on the road
to fortune, *Roughing It,* was not written in Virginia City, but on
Jackass Hill, whither he had repaired to keep away from sundry
creditors. "Sundry creditors" have often been responsible for a
lot of penmanship. While Mark Twain was holed up at Jackass
Hill, another young man, Bret Harte, was momently roving the
gold fields. He was looking for a job as a schoolmaster: a job the
more difficult to find, in that the mining camps had no schools. Bret
Harte eased his disappointment by writing such stories as *The Luck
of Roaring Camp, Tennessee's Partner,* and *The Outcasts of Poker
Flat.* I wish I knew how these stories got to England: they did,
and were very popular. Bret Harte came to London, and never went
back to any other gold field.

It was the gold and silver from the fabulous Comstock Lode
which, far away from the war area, enabled the Central Pacific
to begin laying its tracks eastward from San Francisco in 1862.
"It took six years to get them over the Sierras to the vicinity of the
mines and in 1869, at Promontory Point on the north side of the
Great Salt Lake, they met the tracks of the Union Pacific building
westward from the Missouri and the two lines were joined with
the driving of a golden spike." [15] The gauge was the same old Roman
yoke, 4 ft. 8½ in. That, it might seem, could be for me another fitting
end; when the Great North Road had been turned into a railroad
and had been pushed across the North American Continent, and
there was readiness to push more railroads almost anywhere elsewhere. Yet that would be a mistake. I said this story has no end.
The Great North Road was certainly not ended by the Railway
Age. The fact which I had not appreciated until I came to make
this survey is that while the railways were still gathering steam an
altogether new thing had happened: the Great North Road had
taken to the air; and that, if you like, is a strange and curious
story.

The airlift begins in Yorkshire, with one of the most remarkable of the many eccentric Yorkshire squires; by name Sir George
Cayley, "*le véritable inventeur de l'aéroplane,*" as the leading French
authority puts it. I must be very careful in my statements; I do
not profess to be an aeronaut. First let me get the place right.
Eastward from the Hambleton Hills of Yorkshire, eastward of

Rievaulx Abbey, is the Vale of Pickering. If you follow it you will get to Scarborough; if you turn north at Scarborough you will get to Robin Hood's Bay; and you may if you wish spend a little time at the detective work required to identify, precisely, the location of the Shivering Sands which are of unforgettable importance to anyone who has read Wilkie Collins's story *The Moonstone*. But if you are less subject than I am to diverticulations, and are more serious about the serious problem which has suddenly cropped up, about seven miles before you get to Scarborough you will pass through Brompton; and Sir George Cayley lived at Brompton Hall. It was there that he brooded on the basic principles of the modern aeroplane, and of modern aerodynamics, as early as 1799, and aeronautics remained his chief passion until his death in 1857. Now as I say, I must be careful in my statements. Since Icarus, since Leonardo da Vinci, since innumerable others, there had been ideas about flying machines. Cayley's vision, as expressed in an article *On Aerial Navigation* in *Tilloch's Philosophical Magazine* (February, 1816), was this:

An uninterrupted navigable ocean, that comes to the threshold of every man's door, ought not to be neglected as a source of human gratification and advantage.

Which naturally could be regarded as "drivelling delirium." It was a vision beautifully expressed; yet unsupported by practice in aerial navigation, what did the statement amount to but science fiction? The vision, however, was perpetuated by Cayley's repeated and repeated experiments which resulted in full-size man-carrying gliders. Insofar as he had licked the main problems of the glider, Cayley should, it would seem, be accorded the tribute paid to him by the late J. E. Hodgson, that "the giant airliners of today are definitely descended from the efforts of Yorkshire's pioneer of aerial navigation." It is an opinion I would have no claim to support, were it not also authorized by Captain J. Laurence Pritchard, by Mr. Charles H. Gibbs-Smith, and by Mr. Oliver Stewart. For, if Mr. David Low is my mentor as to pronunciation of Latin, these are my mentors as to aeronautics.

Cayley's vision had been expressed as far back as 1809, when

in submitting to *Nicholson's Journal* what is now found to be an
epoch-making paper, he had written:

I am induced to request your publication of this essay, because I
conceive in stating the fundamental principles of this art . . . I may be
expediting the attainment of an object that will in time be found of great
importance to mankind; so much so, that a new era in society will commence from the moment that aerial navigation is familiarly realized.

The vision, and the theory of aerodynamics, were accompanied
by a persistence of experiments, at first with dead weights; then,
as his model gliders became larger, he entrusted to one of them
a young boy. This experiment was made, and I believe repeated,
in 1849: Cayley described the experiment for the French Aero-
static and Meteorological Society:

A boy of about ten years of age was floated off the ground for several
yards on descending a hill, and also for about the same space by some
persons pulling the apparatus against a very slight breeze.

Captain Pritchard has discovered a letter in June, 1849, from
Charles Clark to Cayley:

I have never been able to meet with such success as you appear to
have met with when experimenting with the boy. Poor fellow! I daresay
he feared the fate of some of our early aeronauts.

But despite the courage of the unnamed boy, this does not really
qualify as the first flight of a "manned aeroplane," because as Mr.
Gibbs-Smith says, the airborne distance was only a few yards,
and the glider was virtually a large model and not a full-size
machine. It was in 1852 or 1853 that the persistent old gentleman
achieved the first true full-size aeroplane in history to fly with a
man. The victim, this time, was Sir George's coachman. The best
account is that provided by Cayley's granddaughter, Mrs. Thompson, who at the time of the flight was about nine years old:

I remember [says Mrs. Thompson] seeing a large machine being
started on the high side of the valley behind Brompton Hall where he
lived, and the coachman being sent up in it, and it flew across the little

valley, about 500 yards at most, and came down with a smash. What the motive power was I don't know, but I think the coachman was the moving element, and the result was his capsize and the rush of watchers across to his rescue. He struggled up and said: "Please, Sir George, I wish to give notice. I was hired to drive and not to fly."

That was life in the dales of Yorkshire, at the time of the Great Exhibition. Sir George, at the age of seventy-nine, drew up his report:

It need scarcely be further remarked, that were we in possession of a sufficiently light first mover to propel such vehicles by waftage, either on the screw principle or otherwise, with such power as to supply that force horizontally, which gravitation here supplies in the descent, mechanical aerial navigation would be at our command without further delay.

Those were indeed prophetic words. The Locomotive God at that time was not prepared to listen. With as much stubbornness as New Englanders had pursued open-boat whaling, the steam engineers were pursuing not light power-units, but those which were ever larger and heavier. Size was the fashion: Brunel (who had wished a wider gauge for railways) built the *Great Eastern* in 1858. The first iron-clad warship, the *Warrior*, was built in 1860. A "light first mover" was what Sir George Cayley cried out for, to sail into that "uninterrupted navigable ocean, that comes to the threshold of every man's door." But everything suggested by the "permanent way" of the railway seemed to lend to more and more weight.

It was, as I like to think, the original Great North Road which fought back at the "permanent way" and enabled the world to be airborne. Whether that is for good or bad is not for me to say. I am inclined to trace the transition to that most harmless of inventions, the bicycle. It took some time to develop the safety bicycle (I don't doubt that on a springless penny-farthing you were bounced around as dangerously as ever the Stevensons or Ericsson had bounced behind the *Rocket* and the *Novelty*), but when the *Rover* safety bicycle came in, in the eighties, what seems of importance is that male and female created he them; and Dunlop created pneumatic tires; [16] and then at once was a variety of "light" vehicles—single cycles, tandems, tricycles, four-wheelers—the only catch being, that as with Sir George Cayley's man-carrying glider, there had to be some horizontal moving element. Easier for the legs if there could be some other prime mover. Here it was Gottlieb Daimler (who worked for a time at Whitworth's, Manchester) who conceived the idea of increasing the usefulness of oil and gas engines by making the working parts lighter and lighter, with greater velocity of rotation. Daimler's first motor bicycle in 1885, followed in 1887 by his gasoline-driven car—when this invention, developed away from the Great North Road, was admitted into Britain—and when the Wright brothers in America put the "sufficiently light first mover" of gasoline engine to successful and practical work in the air—there I may really leave my story. I hired myself to drive and not to fly.

XIII »» One for the Road

With the prosaic motor the Road fought back against the Railway, and you might have thought the motor might have removed any present-day excitement. Have a word with Mr. J. B. Priestley:

Then there came a great moment. He had been dozing a little but was roused by the lorry slowing down, sounding its horn, then swinging round into a road that was different from any they had been on so far. It was as smooth and straight as a chisel, and passing lights showed him huge double telegraph posts and a surface that seemed to slip away from them like dark water. Other cars shot past, came with a blare and a hoot and were suddenly gone, but the lorry itself was now travelling faster than he thought any lorry had a right to travel. But at one place they had to slow down a little, and then Mr. Oakroyd read the words painted in large black letters on a white-washed wall. *The Great North Road.* They were actually going down the Great North Road. He could have shouted. He didn't care what happened after this, He could hear himself telling somebody—Lily it ought to be—all about it. "Middle o' t'night," he was saying, "we got on t'Great North Road." Here was another town, and the road was cutting through it like a knife through cheese. Doncaster, it was. No trams now; everybody gone to bed, except the lucky ones going down South on the Great North Road.

"By gow!" he cried, "this is a bit o' life, this is."

The Good Companions was written after the First World War. I think the operative phrase in Mr. Oakroyd's enthusiasm about the lorry going through Doncaster is that it was in the middle of the night. I have not always gone through Doncaster like a knife through cheese. But whether or no I get stuck behind what Shakespeare called the "heavy-gaited toads," when I have been on the Road I have sometimes known the feeling so well expressed by Mr. Priestley.

Let us have another memory of Guy Gibson during the Second World War:

We stopped, the driver and I, at Grantham, on the way, and I saw the S.A.S.O. He said, "I'm sending you on a journey down south to meet a scientist who is working on your project. He's going to show you nearly everything, but remember only the A.O.C. and myself and four others know anything about these matters, and you'll be the seventh. I can't stress too much the need for secrecy. It's absolutely vital."

We went on, down the winding Great North Road, meeting very little traffic except vast army convoys going north.

That was a journey also in the middle of the night.

After the First World War, I was present at a Christmas Feast at Trinity College, Cambridge, seated next to (as he was then styled) Sir Ernest Rutherford; as his friends recall, an enormous man, red-faced, blue-eyed, with hands like hams, with which he had recently manipulated a trivial piece of apparatus, a glass tube no bigger than a baby-tonic-water bottle, and, bending over and peering at this thing, had recognized that he had split the nitrogen atom. Nobody, not even Rutherford, knew what the result might be; but clearly it marked the beginning of a different era; and—Rutherford being a man to whom it was possible to ask questions—it was possible to ask about the result. So, as I remember, the conversation (taking place, I repeat, at a Christmas Feast at Trinity, with Holbein's portrait of Henry VIII looking down) came quickly to the insoluble problem: What governs inventiveness, and who guards the guardians? We talked about Singer—about the fact that the same man who devised the sewing machine also devised interchangeable parts for the Union rifles in the American Civil War. We talked about Whitehead—the fact that the same man who had improved the Silo had also invented the Whitehead torpedo. In a pleasantly animated way we were getting on with our discussion when the awful thing happened. We were getting on so friendlily that I (although only a young squirt) ventured to ask Rutherford: "Tell me, what started you off?"

The awful thing was that at that moment there was one of those moments of silence at the High Table at Trinity which probably presaged that the Master was about to say grace, after which we would retire to the Combination Room. But into the general hush came that personal question, sounding out, in the hush, much louder than intended, from an unknown visitor to the great Rutherford: "Tell me, what started you off?"

Rutherford swiveled round at me, and his red Sc.D gown and his red face and the size of him made him seem as angry as a turkey cock, and in the general silence, and with everybody looking on, I could have died. Rutherford's voice, when he wished to speak, was not silenced by any academic silence; and as I was drooping with shame, and the Master was waiting for grace, Rutherford boomed out: "That's a damned intelligent question. It's the best question I've heard in a long time; and what's more, I can tell you the answer. When I was a schoolboy in New Zealand they put me, in vacation, to minding sheep; and I had a stick, and there was a pond, and the sheep were getting on all right, so I stuck the stick in the pond. When I stuck the stick in the pond, it was bent; when I pulled it out, it was straight. Stuck it in again, bent; pulled it out again, straight. Well," boomed Rutherford, "made you think, didn't it?" The Master said grace, and we went upstairs.

At any moment that the sheep are getting on all right, I like to get upon the Road. I don't know that I think very well, but it makes me ponder. There is too much for my comprehension. I like to get upon the Road at its beginning at Aldersgate, and I like to make my quiet progress (as I have done so many times) to

the very tipmost top of Scotland. A dull road, said Sir Walter Scott;
but I find plenty to think about, perhaps too much.

I like to get on the road at its beginning at Aldersgate, and I
have indicated a few things that it has meant to me. There is a
lot behind the Road, a lot to it. You can take it inch by inch and
brood about it, according to any inclination. You pretty well have
to take it inch by inch at its beginning because of the heavy-gaited
toads ahead of you, and you can't stop because of the hot breath
of the heavy-gaited toads behind. But from beginning to the end,
you may think of what you choose.

> Garlic and sapphires in the mud
> Clot the buried axle-tree.

You may think of Aldersgate in the unruly days when the man
came to George Fox and set a naked sword to his side, and Fox
said: *I looked up at him in his face and said to him "Alack for thee,
it's no more to me than a straw."* Perhaps that episode was not at
Aldersgate? Never mind, Fox preached outside the Bull and Mouth,
and you think of him. Or you think of that café in Aldersgate
Street where, on an afternoon in 1922, Frederick Bywaters and
Edith Thompson had their last unfettered conversation before
he killed her husband.

You think of all the things the Road has seen, and make your
own choice. I don't think about much in Goswell Road, as I
drive north from Aldersgate, except a passing thought for Mr.
Pickwick (but I prefer Dickens's later novels) and for the exact
location of Saxe-Coburg Square (about which Sir Arthur Conan
Doyle and Sherlock Holmes and Dr. Watson and I have several
times been puzzled). Goswell Road is not much to look at, but the
traffic is such that you don't look at it. When you have passed
the Angel, at Islington Green you may if you so wish think about
"The Bailiff's Daughter"; but I doubt if this was the Islington of that
polite ballad—it was probably an Islington in Yorkshire. When
you have entered Holloway Road you may be thinking of Edward Lear of the *Nonsense Rhymes,* one of England's greatest
examples of Danesmanship. Lear was born (May 12, 1812) at
Bowman's Lodge, at the corner of Bowman's Mews which (it is
difficult to find) is close to the corner of Seven Sisters Road and

Holloway Road. Edward Lear had more than seven sisters; he was the youngest of the twenty-one children which his mother (who came down the Road by coach from Durham) produced for the Danish stockbroker who speculated his way from Holloway to poverty and the King's Bench Prison.

Holloway Road brings me to the Archway. At the Archway Tavern the road forks. The left-hand is Highgate Hill, and a steep hill it is, winding between hospitals, past Whittington's Stone, to Highgate Cemetery: where, as you may think, strangely enough, among representatives of mercantilism, men in their time of means and power, is the grave of Karl Marx; above the sprawling city which, though it harbored him, was a city hostile to his way of thought. But unless you wish to see the tomb of Marx, the direct road north from the Archway Tavern is under the viaduct (which was one of the wonders of 1900) and along Archway Road, a milder slope than that of Highgate Hill. Shortly after the viaduct, there is on the right a Baptist chapel, and after that a turning to the right which takes you to Orchard Road, where, at Number 16, a certain Mrs. Heiss advertised by a card in the window (I am speaking of December, 1914) that she let lodgings. It was possibly the Baptist chapel which caused George Joseph Smith, with his latest bride, to turn off Archway Road at this point, for he had the worst of purposes in mind and therefore needed to impress his wife that he was "a thorough Christian man." She, poor woman, formerly Miss Lofty, an impecunious clergyman's daughter who had spent her life so far as companion to elderly ladies, was the last of "the brides in the bath." Smith was at the moment calling himself John Lloyd. Mr. Lloyd halted at Number 16 Orchard Road, interviewed Mrs. Heiss, and particularly asked to be shown the bath. He observed it was small, but remarked, "I daresay it is large enough for someone to lie in." There was something about his demeanor which was unattractive to Mrs. Heiss. He was ready to engage the lodgings, but she asked him to provide references, which he was unable to do, and she turned him away. He made the mistake of being so offensive that she remembered the occasion, and her testimony was of importance at Smith's trial. When turned away by Mrs. Heiss, Smith went on to find a lodging in Bismarck Road, where the landlady was less suspicious; where there was a bath upstairs, and, downstairs, a harmonium. The Bismarck Road lodging pleased "Mr. and Mrs. Lloyd"; she wrote to apprise her family of her sudden, happy marriage, while he strummed hymns on the harmonium. I quote from Browne and Tullett's *Life of Bernard Spilsbury:*

She had already insured her life for £700, and without more ado Smith's famous system, with its dreadful stereotyped sequence, was put in hand. . . . The visit to the doctor came first, on that same evening of the 17th. The call on the lawyer followed the next day, and "Mrs. Lloyd" made her will, bequeathing everything—£19 and expectations under the insurance policy—to her husband. Back at Bismarck Road, a bath was ordered for that night. Just after 7.30 the landlady, ironing in her kitchen, heard splashing in the bathroom upstairs, and a sound as of wet hands being drawn down the side of the bath, and then a sigh. A few minutes afterwards the harmonium in her sitting-room boomed out. "Mr. Lloyd" was playing *Nearer, my God, to Thee.*

Archway Road leads on through Finchley. In the High Road, Finchley, is Tally Ho Corner; just beyond, on the left, there is a pull-in at a gray and yellow pub with an odd name, the Swan and Pyramids. It is not a beautiful neighborhood; but often a busy one. There are garages to which overnight lorries come from the North; it is a point of transshipment, a place of snack bars for casual workers. Behind Tally Ho Corner in North Finchley there was living, in 1930, an inconspicuous man called Alfred Arthur Rouse. He was at that time thirty-six years old. He had served in the First World War, had been buried by explosion, and returned to civilian life with damage perhaps more psychic than physical. He was voluble, vain, and apparently a useful small-type salesman. He became a "traveler" for a firm of brace and garter manufacturers. He and his wife had no children; she was sorry for that and sorry for him, for it was his pride to have children. Nobody, in the "Blazing Car Mystery" of 1930, and in the subsequent trial for murder of Alfred Arthur Rouse, comes so well out of it as his wife, who had taken into her home one extramural child—and who had created, so far as neighbors could see, a happy home. Throughout the trial Mrs. Rouse remained steadfast to her husband; and indeed it seemed that after his fashion

he had intended to be steadfast to her: the insurance money for the
"Blazing Car," could it have been collected, was to have been
hers. The trouble was, the "harem-minded" salesman couldn't re-
strain his fondness for too many children and too many households
in too many directions. It was reported at the trial that at one time
or another Rouse had eighty maintenance orders against him. It was
not that his "wives" were not fond of him, or that he tried to do
them in: it was rather that on the pay he was getting he could not
support them all; and so decided the only way out was to die
temporarily.

The completely callous thing was that for Rouse to disappear,
a corpse to be identified as his had to be found in the "Blazing
Car." A suitable somebody else had to be the victim. Prowling
round the snack bars near Tally Ho Corner, in the High Road, or
in the public bar of the Swan and Pyramids, Rouse found his
victim. Rouse may have met him outside, but it was in the public
bar of the Swan and Pyramids that the stranger was talked into
his last ride. Nobody to this day knows who the victim was.
"He was the sort of man no one would miss," said Rouse, "and I
thought he would suit the plan I had in mind." So on the Guy
Fawkes Night of 1930 Rouse and "the sort of man" set off from
the Swan and Pyramids. Rouse bought a bottle of whisky to take
along—he himself did not drink spirits—so the man might con-
sole himself. Rouse dawdled on the road "because I wanted it to
be late." He stopped beyond St. Albans partly for a rest, partly
to fill in time, partly perhaps to make sure that his friend was
getting well and truly drunk. He turned off the Great North
Road for Northampton, and it was at the village of Hardingstone,
a mile or so south of Northampton, close to the "Eleanor Cross,"
about two o'clock in the morning of November 6, 1930, that the
"Blazing Car" murder took place. Rouse might conceivably have
got away from the charge of murder if he had lain doggo in the
ditch, but as two country fellows happened to pass by, he stood
up to call to them there was a fire; which so far as his plan went,
disproved his whole purpose. It indicated to two witnesses that
besides the corpse in the car there was somebody else—and somebody later to be identified as Rouse—in the vicinity.

Why do I dwell on these murders?—the "Brides in the Bath,"

the "Blazing Car." I don't dwell on them: I only say there they are. This that we have been talking about is not always a pretty Road, and you can't blink that. The Road has evoked, and gone on evoking into our times, things at which the delicate eye might prefer to be averted; but the dirty road accidents have to be coped with. As you go along the Road there are always, of course, distractions. I mentioned, at Hardingstone, the "Eleanor Cross." I don't know whether the fate of the Infanta of Castile, who came to marry Edward Longshanks:

> The King of Spain's daughter
> She came to marry me. . . .

was better or worse than the fate of the Miss Lofty who came to such a quick end alongside Archway Road. Miss Lofty had at least no time in which to reproach her husband. The Infanta (this admittedly is going back to the thirteenth century) had considerable cause to be tired of the little nut tree. Before she was forty-five she had provided Edward with nineteen children (count them up if you like, two in the Holy Land, two in Wales, one in Italy, two or three in Gascony, the rest in England) and in 1291, in the country which was disposed to make rhymes about her, she fell into what is translated as "a slow fever." Whatever it was, at the age of forty-five she was seriously ill. Edward, however, was impatient to visit Scotland, and urged her up the Great North Road. She died at Harby, between Lincoln and Scrooby, despite syrups and medicines which were brought to her from Lincoln. Edward's conduct, be it said, was impeccable: after the event he blamed himself for forcing the unwelcome journey on her; called off the rest of the trip; and followed the bier the whole way, two or three leagues behind, from Harby back to London. The showmanship, it strikes me, was almost excessive. The funeral procession left Harby on December 2nd; it went to Lincoln, thence to Grantham, Stamford, Geddington, Hardingstone, Stony Stratford, Woburn, Dunstable, St. Albans, Waltham and finally, at London, to Charing Cross. At each place, wherever the bier rested, Edward caused to be put up an elaborate stone "Eleanor Cross." Of the eleven crosses outside London, three remain—Geddington, Hardingstone, Waltham—and in London

itself, Charing Cross. The Charing Cross in London was shifted
and reconstructed in front of the railway station. The Cross at
Hardingstone has been broken. I have not viewed the others.

Take it how you like, there's a lot of this Road. Finchley, Barnet,
Hatfield, Welwyn, Stevenage, Baldock, Biggleswade; Sandy, Eaton
Socon, Alconbury, Stilton, Norman Cross, Stamford—you may ring
your own changes—but you should get to Stamford, and to Grantham, and to Newark—which if you go slap through is like nothing
whatever—but if you get into the town itself is rewarding. Retford,
Bawtry, Doncaster, Selby, York—well, there has been much on
either side to stop for—but now I am in a hurry. Northallerton (I
skip Scotch Corner because I wish to pass through Croft-on-Tees),
Darlington (pausing in the railway station), Durham—ah, noble
Durham, and such noble adventures you may have, driving up to
the cathedral—and such reward, if you get there! Then you may
take your choice, but on this run I go for Newcastle (beautiful dark
city) and the coast road through Alnwick (then past the Holy Isle)
to Berwick, where George Borrow burst into tears—tears at the
beauty of the river Tweed—and Dunbar, and the interminable
Leith, and EDINBURGH. Please do not misread my capitals; I am
not proposing to be sentimental about Auld Reekie; I am going
straight through so fast as I can for the Queensferry.

Scotsmen, please think me not perfunctory if at this urgency I
stop not in Edinburgh. Many a time and oft I have had that courtesy,
but I am eager to get across Queensferry before the new bridge is
built (and, as I cross) to think of Alan Breck, (and of Dr. Johnson
and the fishbones) and then, before the rain begins in earnest, I
must get at least as far as Perth. Inland then after Perth, over the
Grampian Hills ("my name is Norval") by that fast and lovely road
through Pitlochry, past Killiecrankie, Blair Atholl, over the pass of
Drumochter (I've known snowbanks there that were ten feet high—
but this is summer) through Dalwhinnie, Kingussie, Aviemore
(here is where you begin to feel you have passed an invisible line
and are really in the Highlands) and, leaving the Cairngorms behind you, on to Inverness. I am not sneering at the western road
and Rannoch Moor. (George Blake, do you remember when you
and I and Tom Eliot and Donald Brace were there, on Rannoch

Moor, long, long ago, a champagne day—but in November, so Don was wearing that enormous bearskin overcoat, which caused an unknown motorcyclist so fearsome a swerve. Do you remember it, George?—Tom made a poem out of it, and I, a memory.) But it is the eastern road, which I have now been following, which is the straight continuation to Inverness—or shall we say the straighter of the continuations—of our old friend the Great North Road, questing from Aldersgate (and, behind that, from Rome).

Tom Eliot is not the only Sassenach poet to have been in the Highlands; he was preceded, for example, by John Keats. I can't find my volume of Keat's *Letters,* but whoever can find the *Letters* will verify how, in those days, his spirit overtaxed his body, and he had to be shipped home from Inverness by sea. I don't know if Mr. Eliot ever got much farther north than Inverness; we were usually intercepted there by Neil Gunn. But there have been other times when I, of lesser breed, have pushed on through Dingwall, Invergordon, Tain—I have even stopped at Geanies. If you have the right day for it, there is no run in the world more beautiful than the coastal road along the Cromarty Firth and up the Dornach Firth to Bonar Bridge and back again toward Dornoch and to Brora. (Brora—Ralph Peck, do you remember?—where you killed a fish and spilled the inkpot?) But I go on, that lovely road, Brora to Helmsdale. I remember learning a lesson at Helmsdale. Once, when leaving Brora, I was cursing the fact that I was driving in teeming rain; the words I repeat; I was cursing, the rain teeming; and then came the brain-wave—I was probably sitting under one particular cloud, which was moving above me at precisely the same rate of knots. I, as a bonafide traveler, stopped at Helmsdale and had one for the road. The cloud, poor thing, went on. I could then follow in a lovely sunshine, in which everything glistened.

Since then, I have often stopped to let the showers pass, and that is worth doing on the coast road from Helmsdale to Lybster; and there, if you are going the way I am going—which is to Dunnet Head, you have to make a decision. You have now passed away from the Highlands, and are in Caithness, a different country. I have no Caithness blood in me, but my children have. So instead of cutting off from Lybster—or indeed before that, at Janetstown—for Thurso—some people might prefer to do so, for Thurso is a good town—I have reasons for going to Dunnet Head by way of Thrumster and Wick. I like to go to Dunnet Head because it is the tipmost top of Scotland (I like to sneer at John o' Groats). And what do I see at Dunnet Head? I can look across the Pentland Firth and see the Orkneys. I recollect times of seeing Dunnet Light from the sea (the Pentland Firth can be a very nasty customer). I recollect a moment (I wonder if you remember, Ian) when a boatload of us were as near as dammit to catastrophe in Dunnet Bay. And I recall the ever-memorable hospitality of Castlehill, the house (his shooting box, Mr. Crum-Ewing called it) above Castletown's tiny harbor: where the stone quarry was from which the Caithness slabs were shipped, in other days—and Boswell met one of the factors who shipped them—shipped, where do you think? Why of course these Caithness flags were shipped from Dunnet Bay to serve as paving stones for London pavements.

So in my little run, along the spine of England and the lovely coast of Scotland, in my end I come to my beginning. Here at the topmost tip of Scotland, I think of London pavements; of the City of London; of London *ab urbe condita;* of the Great North Road. I try to think of all that it has meant. All told, it could be quite a story.

At my start, I had to cast around for new beginnings. I have to cast around for a new end for my short pilgrimage.

I had never promised that the pilgrimage would be an easy one, but I had hoped that when in the end I got to Dunnet Head, and gazed upon the stone quarry from which Caithness slabs went to form London pavements, by that time things would have somehow sorted themselves out. I had the innocent idea that by linking the clean and lovely top of Britain with dingy Aldersgate and London Wall—that by the time I got to Dunnet Head and looked across to Orkney, whence came King Lot's wife—the many workings of this supreme working Road would have become clearer to me.

My story, like the story of a greater book, began in ruins. "It was among the ruins of the capitol that I first conceived the idea," says Gibbon in the last sentence of *The Decline and Fall*, "of a work which has amused and exercised near twenty years of my life, and which, however inadequate to my own wishes, I finally deliver to the curiosity and candour of the public."

The coda which Gibbon permitted himself is in his autobiography. "I have presumed to mark the moment of conception," he remarks; "I shall now commemorate the hour of my final deliverance."

It was on the day, or rather the night, of the 27th of June 1787, between the hours of eleven and twelve, that I wrote the last lines of the last page in a summer-house in my garden. After laying down my pen I took several turns in a *berceau* or covered walk of Acacias, which commands a prospect of the country, the lake and the mountains. The air was temperate, the sky was serene, the silver orb of the moon was reflected from the waters, and all Nature was silent. I will not dissemble the first emotions of joy on the recovery of my freedom, and perhaps the establishment of my fame. But my pride was soon humbled, and a sober melancholy was spread over my mind by the idea that I had taken my everlasting leave of an old and agreeable companion, and that, whatsoever might be the future date of my history, the life of the historian must be short and precarious.

Though Gibbon had no easy time, he did have his golden snuffbox embossed on the lid with cupids attending an altar, which is now in the British Museum; he did have his glass of madeira; and ridiculous as it is for me to contrast my pencil sketch of the rise of Britain with his great oil painting of the fall of Rome, he set himself the less difficult task. Vast as his subject was, and reluctant as he was to leave it, the revolutions which Gibbon studied comprised only those of a mere thirteen centuries, and the period of his study came to an ascertainable end. So having a mind to do so, Gibbon could produce—"Lo, a Truly Classic Work."

It would be inconceivable for anybody to attempt a classic work about the creativity, the revolutions of twenty centuries within Britain, the transportations and effects around the world, a story which has no end. But as I stumbled through postwar ruins in a part of the City of London, it came over me that I ought to wonder how some of the creativity had started. I was soon humbled by the consideration that there were so many things about which I simply did not know. This final bit of skittering up the road and into Scotland has not taught me so much as it should have done. I have gone too rapidly, missing too much. Up there at the top of Scotland, at Dunnet Head, I was thinking that I ought not to have skittered past Little Gidding or past Southwell Abbey (remembering of course the origin of the Bramley's Seedling),[1] past Melton Mowbray and Market Harborough where the Canadian pondweed got into the canal system; and most particularly I ought not to have skittered past Gumley. I do not so much mind having skipped Scotch Corner or even Barnard Castle (with the fascinating and sad memories of Sir Walter Scott), but I do mind having skipped Gumley.

Gumley, if you should have missed it in your travels, may be recalled by the statement that it is where Evelyn Cheesman, in *Things Worth While*,[2] records that she noticed badgers' spoor. Of course, even if your employment is that of a governess, if you notice badgers' spoor you at once decide to spend the night out badger watching, under the jurisdiction of Atkins, earth stopper to Fernie's Hunt. Atkins?—it is a known name—I have heard of it elsewhere. The nighttime in the badger wood adjoining the garden at Gumley, as described by Miss Cheesman, is a recollection which she admits dates from some years ago. In the middle of the wood, in the middle of the nighttime, Miss Cheesman says it was very dark. "Not having netted badgers before," she confesses, "I had no clear idea of the correct procedure."

"Atkins, what do you do when a badger is near the net?"
"Go for him and bouffle all you can," was the answer.

In the mood in which I began this book, it seemed to me the Great North Road might be my Atkins. And running back and forth along the few miles of it, and the many centuries, even if it was obviously impossible to attempt a classic work, whenever any badgering question (no matter how formidable) came near the net, and whether or no I had a clear idea of correct procedure, or whether the forms were forms of things as yet unknown, the Road spoke in the tone of Atkins:

Go for him and bouffle all you can.

Acknowledgments, Notes, and Queries

I do not think so informal a book calls for a formal bibliography. So far as I could do so without using footnotes, I have tried to acknowledge specific references in the text. A few special acknowledgments may be added here, together with a few notes and queries.

I Farewell

1. Later I was happy to find that Stationers' Hall had not been erased in the bombing of London, but only damaged.

2. My impression of the exceptionally low tide in the Thames during the particular blitz of December, 1940, was derived, I think, from *Buried London* by William Thompson Hill.

3. James Bone, Scotsman who knows London better than most Londoners, author, among other noble books, of *The London Perambulator,* was at the time I speak of, and for many years after, London Editor of the *Manchester Guardian.* Gerard Fay, present London Editor of the *Guardian,* reminds me in his recent book, *Passenger to London,* of one of the many stories by which James Bone used to promote the primacy of

London. A sailor in Vancouver was asked where he came from. "London." "London, Ontario, or London, England?" "Not London, Ontario, or London, England," he answered. "Just London All the Bloody World." I confirm that Jim used to tell that story, and I think I knew that sailor, who was also a Scotsman. Gerard Fay is, by the way, an Irishman, a Dubliner, a scion of the Abbey Theatre, and I owe him acknowledgment for his courtesy in reading the proofs of this book and for correcting me in many places.

4. I hesitated over the spellings of Caractacus and Boadicea. People nowadays tend to spell his name Caratacus and hers Boudicca. But nobody really knows how to spell their names, and possibly they did not know either. In my nursery days Tennyson introduced me to Boadicea, so Boadicea she to me remains; and Caratacus, although authorities now tell me that spelling is right, when I first met him was still wearing a "c" in the middle. The spelling of ancient names is a problem that defeats everybody. I have spelled "St. Alphage" that way, because that was the way the particular church I was visiting was spelling itself at that moment. Personally I prefer "Alphege" for the gallant old saint whom the Danes pelted with ox bones. At Greenwich the church dedicated to this same saint features a Saxon "f." Was it within St. Olfege's at Greenwich that Bella Wilfer and "John Rokemsith," in *Our Mutual Friend,* were married?

5. I was unable to quote, without distracting the narrative, the haunting passage from Defoe's *Journal of the Plague Year,* concerning St. Giles's Cripplegate.

6. The new view of St. Paul's had been opened by the partial destruction of Greyfriars, where, as is later mentioned, Sir Thomas Malory was buried.

7. The phrase about "the road to Athens" comes from Plato, *Symposium* 173B. I cannot now recall where, many years ago, I read the passage from Pico della Mirandola, but I recall how enchanting the whole of his paragraph was. All that I can quote from memory is the opening phrase, but the whole paragraph has often been referred to, I believe, as illustrating the spirit of the Renaissance.

8. *Homo Ludens: A Study of the Play Element in Culture,* by J. Huizinga (Late Professor of History in the University of Leyden), was published in England in 1949. It had been published in German in Switzerland in 1944, but parts of the thesis had been advanced in

Professor Huizinga's lectures and writings dating back to 1903. Perhaps Huizinga's *The Waning of the Middle Ages* is better known to a general public than *Homo Ludens*.

9. The reference here, if we wish to be precise about it, is to Holme, *Armoury* III, xix (Roxb. 154/2). The date is 1688. "The seuerall Beates or points of Warre are these. . . . (4) A Voluntary before the March."

Another "Beate" or "point of Warre" for a dashing army officer in the seventeenth century, before or perhaps especially after a "March," was to eat ice cream. The earliest reference to ice cream in my big *Oxford English Dictionary* is, in the main text of that work, dated 1769. In the supplementary volume of the *O.E.D.*, which always also needs to be consulted, there is an earlier reference, dated 1744. But if you go to Mr. Neville Williams of the Public Record Office, he can give you an entry in the accounts of the Lord Steward's Department for 1686 of a dozen dishes of ice cream, costing £1 each, as part of the fare provided for James II and his officers at camp on Hounslow Heath. Earlier than that, it has been conjectured that at five o'clock on the July day of 1644 it was because of the temptation of a dish of ice cream that Prince Rupert retired for the moment from his front line at Marston Moor, and Cromwell seized that moment for attack. Those dishes of ice cream for James II, costing £1 each, were presumably partitioned into "sundaes" served perhaps with strawberries, perhaps with hot sauce. I suspect that "ices" are older than the seventeenth century: I seem to remember Francis Bacon experimenting with refrigeration; and as for sundaes served with a hot sauce, in my childhood that is what I thought Shakespeare was talking about in *A Midsummer-Night's Dream* (V, i, 59) in the phrase "That is hot ice and wondrous." That phrase aroused me, as, in reading Xenophon, it made the *Anabasis* come very much alive when he talked about the Armenians using straws for drinks (*Anabasis* IV, v, 26, 27) just as I was accustomed to doing at the soda fountain at the drugstore, corner of Park and North Avenue, Baltimore. Re-reading the *Anabasis* has not deprived me of the feeling that the Armenians were the originators of some of our bar and soda-fountain customs.

II Fare Forward

1. I wish I knew what the Roman number was for our Route A1. The major Roman roads were enumerated. If the numbers were recorded in a Record Office in Rome, the main roads started by Aulus Plautius in Britain were possibly far down in the list.

I don't even know how the Romans managed to keep track of all their road accountancy. In this book I shall presently be brooding on the problem confronting Latin scribes, when asked to devise notation to record the Anglo-Saxon speech; it was not all an easy problem, nor is arithmetical notation. A trivial example occurs to me. When I handed in the manuscript of this book to my London publisher, I noticed that in his records it was given the serial number 33389. It would take me some time to write that in Roman numerals. Is 33389 a prime number? In our numerals it does not take me much time to find out. But how could I go about such a simple question, using nothing but Roman numerals?

It has often been said that the Roman Empire broke down through excessive taxation; I suspect the tedium of the paper work had something to do with it.

2. My references to "Collingwood and Myres" are to that great book *Roman Britain and the English Settlements* by R. G. Collingwood and J. N. L. Myres (Oxford University Press, 1936). This volume I found indispensable, as also is *The Roman Revolution* by Professor (now Sir) Ronald Syme (Oxford University Press, 1939). It is of course the Loeb Classics which have made it a pleasure for the likes of me to read and ponder what the ancients themselves had to say. I thank the Loeb Classics for making it attractive, for instance, to read Caesar's *Civil Wars* in addition to the *Gallic Wars* which was unduly (though understandably) emphasized in our perforce meager school curriculum.

I picked up the particular marching song of Caesar's legion from a footnote in *The Wandering Scholars* by Helen Waddell, chap. 1. Miss Waddell quotes a comment of Suetonius which explains that it is rather "low" Latin. I think there will be found in Dio suggestion of some legionary marching songs considerably lower in tone than the one here quoted.

3. The capricorn emblem of XIV Gemina (who, by the way, were the Twins?) reminds me of some old thoughts about sheep and goats. In primitive nomadic tribes the goat, as an animal, was naturally more esteemed than the sheep: as for example in the *Old Testament*, to separate the sheep from the goats was to separate the less valued from the more valued. By the time of the *New Testament*, and owing I think to the powerful image of the Good Shepherd, it came about that the values were reversed. Throughout the long warfare of Christianity against paganism the goat, as a pagan symbol, was persistently reviled by Churchmen. Until early Church Fathers discussed the animals, the

billy goat had no more stink than the ram. Milk goats are in every way much sweeter creatures than ewes. Having kept both breeds, I would myself sooner keep goats, any day, than sheep.

4. In preparing this book for publication it has been difficult to decide what to do about inserting maps of Britain. Here, for instance, it might be regarded as helpful to see at a glance precisely where the Battle of the Medway took place. But, supposing one could provide an agreed topographical map for the Battle of the Medway, it would only destroy the whole point of my subsequent remarks about Aulus Plautius; for Aulus Plautius had no means of knowing precisely where he was in Britain. I think it is best to leave it to a general impression that the river Medway is south of and roughly parallel to the lower reaches of the Thames, and that Aulus Plautius had to cross the Medway before he could reach the lowest crossable point of the Thames, at London. At this moment of the narrative it would be a mistake, I think, to know precisely where the battle was, for that, as I imagine it, was what Aulus Plautius could not feel sure about. He may have known that he was somewhere about forty miles southeast of London, and that there was a British center some twenty miles northward of London (now St. Albans) and another some fifty miles northeast of London (now Colchester) to either of which the Britons might retire. But as I picture it, the seriousness of the Battle of the Medway considerably startled Aulus Plautius and, because he could not know exactly where he was, led on to the idea that if he was not to be caught out again, the island had better be divided up into concentration camps.

5. I pray there will be educated readers who recognize that this reference to Sherlock Holmes relates to his conduct, when on the 11:15 train from Paddington, he and Dr. Watson had passed through Reading on their way to *The Boscombe Valley Mystery*.

III   The Road

1. The passages from Mr. David Jones have been taken with his permission from a broadcast talk by him, reprinted first in *The Listener* in 1955 and subsequently in his latest book, *Epoch and Artist*, 1959. No other artist of my age has exhibited such feeling for the Roman *viae* as Mr. David Jones.

2. The best known of Mr. Owen Barfield's works is, probably, his book *Poetic Diction*. The passage of thirty years since I first read it has

not diminished, but increased, my respect for that book; therefore when I was forced to contemplate the vast complex of literature that exists about the large questions of the decline of Latin as a living language in Britain and about the emergence of an English language, I felt that nowhere might I find so convenient and congenial a first guide as in *History in English Words* by Owen Barfield. I refer to the edition reprinted in 1954.

3. The quotations from Professor C. F. G. Hawkes are taken from his chapter on "The Jutes in Kent" in the symposium entitled *Dark-Age Britain* (edited by D. B. Harden, 1956).

IV   Merry England

1. The word *Marcescent* was introduced to me by H. C. Wyld's *Universal English Dictionary* as a word deriving from the same root as *Merry*. It seemed to me interesting that two words deriving from the same root could develop opposite meanings. Professor Wyld's dictionary has given me a lot of pleasure. Professor Henry Cecil Kennedy Wyld (b. 1870, d. 1945), B.Litt., M.A., Hon. Ph.D., Upsala, Honorary Member of the Linguistic Society, and of the Modern Language Association of America; Merton Professor of English Language and Literature in the University of Oxford, was one of a great generation of British scholars (I think of Saintsbury, Grierson) who were not above combining their extensive, accurate learning with individual humors. Witness in the above-mentioned dictionary Wyld's primary definition of the word "bun." The definition reads: *bun* n., M.E. *bunne:* "Small round sweet spongy cake with convex top and too few currants."

2. Quotations here and later are from the first volume of *English Historical Documents* (Oxford University Press, 1955). The general editor of this most helpful compendium of documents is Professor David C. Douglas of Bristol University: I shall presently have need to quote his own volume covering the Norman Conquest. Volume I, covering the period c. 500–1042, is edited by Dr. Dorothy Whitelock.

The paramount importance of the language problem in the beginnings of any society is illustrated in an article on Papua from a Special Correspondent to *The Times* (London) a few years ago:

"A common language is urgently needed. Papua and the Trust Territory of New Guinea between them have 460 languages—not merely dialects, but distinct languages. One village may speak a totally different tongue from the village on the mountain-top across the ravine. It is impossible even to begin planning for an integrated self-governing community until a common language is spoken by all."

I preserved the clipping, but stupidly failed to record the date. That does not much matter, except that I would wish to pay respect to that particular correspondent. He points up the situation of which Alfred the Great was well aware, toward which some space is devoted, and my distant humble homage paid, in the next chapter.

3. Professor Brandon's article on *Salvation: Mithraic and Christian*, from which I quote, may be found in the *Hibbert Journal*, Number 221, January, 1958, p. 123. The phrase *Hominibus vagis vitam* to which I refer on the next page (and later), may be observed among Mithraic remains in the Guildhall Museum (now housed in the Royal Exchange).

4. Augustine of Canterbury was of the Brethren who were sent by Gregory to Britain; not to be confused with Augustine of Carthage.

5. There have been many histories of English Literature since George Saintsbury, but none more to my liking. The snatch of Caedmon, and Dr. Dorothy Whitelock's translation of it, I found in her volume *The Beginnings of English Society* (Pelican History of England, Vol. 2, p. 206).

6. An anthology translated into English of some of the correspondence of the early Christian Fathers is provided by *A Treasury of Early Christianity* by Miss Anne Fremantle (1953).

V   The North Road

1. I took the quotation from Robert of Gloucester from Saintsbury's *History of English Literature.*

2. *Enemy Coast Ahead* (1946) by Guy Gibson, V.C., D.S.O., D.F.C.

3. Again I am grateful to Dr. Dorothy Whitelock for this quotation from Alfred the Great.

4. Gibbon speaks of *glis glis* as a "squirrel." He knew that the edible dormouse was not the same as the little red squirrel familiar to our forefathers of the eighteenth century, but deemed it as of his moment to be the best translation—as, had he been in America, he might have spoken of *glis glis* as being something like a chipmunk; or, had he been in Siberia, he might have said something like a *bundureek.* I am anxious

only that Gibbon's word should not be misinterpreted as meaning that more elongated, chattering animal, the "gray squirrel." The gray squirrel was not introduced to Britain until late in the nineteenth century. After the Great Exhibition there was among country gentlemen much competition to introduce novelties to their parklands, and the gray squirrel was regarded as one such novelty. There were repeated failures to get the breed to take to the English climate, but eventually it was a Duke of Bedford (so I have been told) who succeeded in cherishing the pest at Woburn. Not to be outdone in the transportation of pests, Cecil Rhodes in the 1880's introduced the gray squirrel to his home at Groote Schuur, whence the animal spread in South Africa.

Mr. Antony Wysard, Editor of *Wheeler's Review,* has drawn to my attention an account by Lord St. Oswald of a meal which involved mouse eating "on the Left Bank of the Mekong River, with three Chinese Generals" (Wheeler's Review, 3rd Qtr., 1958, p. 129). The date of the ceremony is not mentioned, but it could not have been very many years ago. Lord St. Oswald speaks of "two large earthenware bowls, set next to each other, contained, the one honey and the other newly born mice. The process was to dunk and thus drown one mouse at a time, before munching it. I was regrettably clumsy."

5. The custom of a "rule of the road," and the historical development of different rules (for instance "left" in Britain, "right" in France), have bothered a good many people. Plato, when discussing the matter in the *Laws,* is not concerned with whether to walk on the right or left, but rather with what fruit on either side of the road may be regarded as fair game *en passant.* It will be remembered that he lays it down that grapes, pears, apples, and pomegranates are fair game for the wayfarer, if the wayfarer can prove that he is more than thirty years of age.

A traffic rule, in the sense of upon which side of each other opposing horsemen or vehicles or columns of marching men were to pass, came in, it would seem to me, with the Romans after the initiation of paved roads in Italy. I am fairly well convinced of the suggestion in the text, that the Roman regimentation was to drive on the left. That "a" rule of the road was inherited in medieval Italy is suggested by a passage in Dante (*Inferno,* Canto XVIII, 28–33) in which it is indicated that because of the great throngs attempting to pass on the bridge of Castello Sant' Angelo in the year of the Jubilee, the bridge was longitudinally divided (some say by a fence) so that the party going to St. Peter's were on the one side, and the party coming away were on the other. I cannot make out from Dante's text which rule of the road obtained—left-hand or right-hand.

I must leave it to a better scholar to look up G. Villani, who was present at one of the Jubilees and who may have described the order that was preserved. If I were putting in for a professional degree of D.Hod. (Doctor of Hodology) I should pursue Villani, Lib. VIII, c. xxxvi, but here I am content to note the frontispiece to the first volume of the symposium Medieval England, edited by Austin Lane Poole (1958). This frontispiece, reproduced from a medieval manuscript (but I do not know which manuscript), depicts, as incidental background, riders using the left-hand rule.

There must be many other medieval illustrations, and what I would look for is whatever is portrayed as customary, normal background—whichever rule of the road is normally taken for granted. I think the probability is that the left-hand rule was normal on all the roads inherited from Rome, until you come to a dramatic change at the time of the French Revolution. The second part of the thesis for the degree of D.Hod. would have to deal in some detail with why and how the change to right-hand rule was promoted on the Continent and in North America.

The idea of automatic traffic lights is a recent one, and here again there has been a curious change of custom. To a present-day motorist red for "stop" and green for "go" has become habitual; so habitual to me that I notice that automatically I used red for "stop" and green for "go" on pages 316–317 of the text. But see the note about railway accidents, Chapter XII, Note 5.

6. There is, and rightly, an enormous number of scholarly works on the history of Lincoln. I have found Sir William Savage's book, *The Making of Our Towns* (1952), here, as previously at St. Albans, a most valuable first guide.

VI The Questing Beast

1. I am familiar only with those of St. Augustine's letters which have been translated in the Loeb Classics, and very wonderful letters they are. I have made use of suggestions provided in the notes to the Loeb edition by James Houston Baxter, B.D., D.Litt., Regius Professor of Ecclesiastical History in the University of St. Andrews.

2. I am referring to the second edition of *The Arrow and the Sword* by Hugh Ross Williamson, published in London by Faber and Faber (1955).

3. The relevant passages of Versions C, D, E of the *Anglo-Saxon Chronicle* are conveniently reproduced in parallel columns in Vol. II of *English Historical Documents*. This volume is edited by Professor David C. Douglas and George W. Greenaway.

I might have spared myself unnecessary effort if, before struggling with the problem of "dates" in the Middle Ages, I had consulted the useful series of handbooks called *Helps for Students of History*. No. 3 of that series is *Medieval Reckonings of Time* (1935) by Reginald L. Poole, M.A., LL.D., Litt.D., Keeper of the Archives of the University of Oxford. I find with relief that my speculations are not ruled out of court by Dr. Poole's more thorough study.

4. The reference to John Rhys is to his introduction to the *Everyman* edition of the *Morte d'Arthur*.

5. The phrase for Arthur's Seat, "an old volcanic vent," is strictly geological, as may be verified by anybody who looks at the geological maps of Britain, posted in the Library of the London Geological Society at Burlington House.

6. The quotation from Leyden is taken from the same introduction. the punctuation of Leyden's verse is slightly perplexing. I should favor omitting the comma after "falchion"; but I assume that Mr. Rhys was following Leyden's own punctuation.

7. The "broad arrow" the huntress shot into Launcelot's buttock—how did the "broad arrow" come to be in England, for a time, the distinguishing mark of a convict's uniform? Why any sort of arrowhead for that distinction?

VII The Road North and the Road South

1. The phrase "sullen, self-willed, local Yorkshire nature" occurs, if I remember rightly, in a volume of *Household Words*, dated somewhen in the 1850's.

2. *The Story of Cheese-making in Britain* by Valerie Cheke, Department of Dairying, Reading University (published by Routledge & Kegan Paul, 1959), is the authoritative work.

3. The statistics about Rievaulx Abbey are taken from the pamphlet by Sir Charles Peers in the invaluable series of pamphlets on English Monuments and Historic Buildings, available at Her Majesty's Stationery Office.

4. *Technics and Civilization* by Lewis Mumford, an epoch-making book, was first published by Harcourt, Brace & Co., New York (1934). With Mr. Mumford's permission I shall be quoting from it again. I would wish to acknowledge in the warmest possible terms the personal encouragement given to me by Mr. Mumford, what times (and they were many) that I was fainting on the road.

5. *The Ordnance Survey Map of Roman Britain* is something the Romano-Briton never saw. It is a beautiful piece of map making, produced by modern *pietas*. The edition in front of me is Printed and Published by the Director General of the Ordnance Survey—that is to say, the modern British Ordnance Survey—issued at Chessington, Surrey, 1956, and obtainable from H.M.S.O.

6. *The Lost Villages of England* by Maurice Beresford, Lecturer in Economic History in the University of Leeds, was published by Lutterworth Press, London (1954).

7. Many of the details about London Bridge I have taken from Jusserand's *English Wayfaring Life in the Middle Ages*. I should have acknowledged, when I mentioned this classic book as a boyhood companion, that I first read it, and still do, in the admirable translation by L. Toulmin Smith. I am happy to see that the book continues to be reissued, but alas without the full complement of the illustrations which added so greatly to the stimulus of the early editions.

8. The passage about Malory is quoted from Miss Bradbrook's contribution to the series of pamphlets published for the British Council.

9. From this point and for the rest of the book I found it very necessary to have beside me a reliable one-volume history of England. There is much choice. The book I chose for my road map is the *History of England* by C. E. Carrington and J. Hampden Jackson (Cambridge University Press, 1934). This is not to imply that I have not looked at other road maps, but the volume by Carrington and Jackson has been for me perpetually useful, congenial, and handy: I have pinched from it many more times than I have been able to acknowledge in the text. Messrs. Carrington and Jackson had prepared their book for use by boys and girls in English schools, and they had assessed very well the speed of journeying of which I was capable in my weather-beaten condition. Any reader who has recently "done" English History in school may be irritated with me for mentioning details which he or she knows much more about than I do; but I should ask such a reader to bear in

mind that many of the details are not familiar to those of us who were brought up, or who perhaps are being brought up, at a distance.

VIII   Little Britain

1. Mr. D. M. Low, M.A., F.R.S.L., formerly Senior Classics Tutor at King's College, London, who has rescued me from I don't know how many howlers, takes strong exception to my phrase "landowners who came down the road." "If they were going to London," says Mr. Low, "I humbly or not so humbly plead that they came *up* the road. I deplore the modern heresy which in deference to Wigan and the Scotch speaks of coming down from the North. Gibbon, Boswell, Dickens, Trollope, to mention no others, knew better, and so still do our own good British Railways. . . ."

It is one of the many points on which I have been racked with indecision. Unfortunately, on the map North is up and South is down. Sir Herbert Read has a different method of evading the collision of ideas. Somewhere in *The Innocent Eye*, that beautiful narrative of his boyhood in Yorkshire, he remarks: "We faced north; the south was behind." Elsewhere in an inscription he has recorded: "The Way North is the Way into the Unknown." To me that is a true feeling which I always feel when I am driving on the Great North Road and see the sign which bears the three words: "To The North."

2. The mention of the plowhorses Brok and Scot was suggested to me by *Ask the Fellows Who Cut the Hay* by George Ewart Evans (1956), a book full of the realities of East Anglia.

3. The reference is to *Language in History* by Harold Goad (Pelican Edition).

4. If I may claim a share of credit in drawing the attention of Mr. Robert Giroux to Heminge and Condell (at a time when Mr. Giroux and I were associates in business in New York) he has most amply repaid by acquainting me with his researches into the goings-on of "old Heminge" and of his son William. It was Mr. Giroux who supplied me with the text of William Heminge's *Eligie* from the Ashmolean collection.

I don't suppose that William Heminge has anything whatever to do with the mystery of "Mr. W. H.," but I do note that there is a distinguished Hemming family (there are various spellings) which is still to be associated with Stratford-on-Avon.

IX   The York Road

1. The quotation is from *Mary Tudor* by H. F. M. Prescott (revised edition, 1952).

2. Here and subsequently I am quoting from *Queen Elizabeth I* by J. E. Neale (18th impression, 1954).

3. Mr. Ian Dunlop has most courteously permitted me to quote from his manuscript on *The Palaces and Progresses of Elizabeth I*. I cannot give reference to it as a published book, for at the time this goes to press Mr. Dunlop's book has not yet been published. From my quotations it should be easy to discern what lively material Mr. Dunlop has assembled and how apt his comments are. May any publisher who is lethargic as to publishing Mr. Dunlop's manuscript suffer most horribly from dogswain and hopharlots.

4. I cannot recall where I obtained this memory of the Earl of Huntingdon on his deathbed in 1595.

5. The details about the Mayflower *Bible,* and the drawings within that copy which I have reproduced for their human interest, come from an article in the *Texas Quarterly* (Winter, 1959) by Evart Mordecai Clark, Professor Emeritus of English at the University of Texas. It makes me feel the Pilgrim Fathers were not always so severe as they are often presented, to find that there were some who were not afraid to scribble in the Book. I like the fact that one little figure (a latter-day Austalis?) seems to be escaping from the meetinghouse. Even by the time Peregrine White (the first Pilgrim child to be born in New England) had become so large and handsome as he appears (in his gay frock) in the Mayflower *Bible,* scribble paper must have been a rarity. Possibly much use was made of the smooth inner skin of the birch tree, which obligingly provides natural feint lines to help the scribe. But the inner skin of the white birch becomes fragile, and many a love letter, or verses, written on birch bark may have failed to survive. There is no reason to suppose that Pilgrim coevals of Marvell and Milton did not write verses —but on what could they write them?

I should like to be told who took the first copy of Shakespeare to North America. It would fit with my general thesis to suspect that the works of Shakespeare went in the first instance to Virginia.

6. Doubt is raised in my mind about putting too much emphasis on the story of Cromwell's proposed emigration to the Massachusetts Bay

Colony in 1636. There must be some authority for this story, for otherwise it would not have been included in the 3rd revised edition of *Everyman's Encyclopaedia;* yet I note that in the 4th edition the story is omitted. The omission does not necessarily mean that the story has been disproved. I should guess that the article on Cromwell in the 4th edition was rewritten by somebody else and that some of what had gone in earlier was squeezed out merely by the need to include, in limited space, additional material.

My Mentor on Cromwell is Captain Jepthah West, R.N. He is not to be blamed for any of my speculations, but I have had the great benefit of his comments. The Yorkshireman who told me about Newburgh Priory (at the end of this chapter) is Sir Herbert Read.

X   Postmen's Garden

1. In the light of my earlier comments on the problem of medieval reckonings of time, I am puzzled to know on what authority the *Oxford English Dictionary* says so precisely that the massacre of Danes occurred on 13th November, 1002, or the death of Hardicnut on 8th June, 1042.

My speculation in the text, that in course of time it was perhaps not unnatural for the scorning of Danes to be associated with Eastertide, cannot possibly be presented as proved. The whole matter is deep and mysterious. The word "hock" is very ancient. Many of the interpretations have to do with money raising. Although "hock-tide" is most usually associated with Easter, it will be remembered that Herrick speaks of the hock-wain at the end of the rural year, when reap payments were due after harvest.

I have never been taught precisely how words were pronounced in Shakespeare's time. I gather that the sounds of the words "hawk" and "hock" were sufficiently indistinguishable to admit a certain amount of word play. As I review this chapter, the way my feelings have been drifting, and the wind being uncertain, I could not possibly be sure of telling a hock from an answer.

2. I am tempering Shakespeare's phrase (*Henry V*, opening chorus, 1. 17) by using "cipher" in a later, cricketing sense. In that sense "to assign a cipher to the score" is to be put out without adding to the total of the innings.

3. Here, as well as later, I am pillaging from the *History of England* by Carrington and Jackson.

4. John Wesley and his brother Charles (four years younger) were Lincolnshire boys, born at Epworth Old Rectory, between Gainsborough and Goole. John (b. 1703) went to America as a young man, but returned to England, and it was after his conversion in Little Britain that he and Charles initiated the Methodist movement. The World Methodist Council at a recent meeting at Lake Janaluska, North Carolina, authorized the expenditure of $30,000 toward the restoration of Epworth Old Rectory.

XI   The Post Road

1. My remark about Dr. Johnson having some Scottish blood derives from nothing but his observably peculiar feeling for Scotsmen.

The most illustrious authority on Johnson's ancestry was Aleyn Lyell Reade, who died at Bootle in 1953 at the age of seventy-six. In 1906 Mr. Reade published his first volume about the genealogy of the Reades of Blackwood Hill and of their connections with Dr. Johnson's family. This was followed by a series of eleven volumes of *Johnsonian Gleanings*, published at irregular intervals during the period 1909–1952. The final volume contains a consolidated index of names, consisting of over 20,000 entries. There, I point out, is the corpus of knowledge; but I have not examined it.

2. Captain Jepthah West objects to my phrase "the flag of Britain was now the Union Jack." Captain West is correct. A jack is a jack only when it is a small flag flown from the jack staff of a vessel to indicate its nationality. The "Union Flag," bearing the crosses of St. George and St. Andrew, came into use two or three years after the accession of King James I. James ordered the Union Flag to be borne at the maintop of all British ships, except ships of war, which bore it upon a jack staff at the end of the bowsprit. Hence the confusion between "flag" and "jack."

The "Union Flag" was apparently not flown on English ships during the period of the Commonwealth. Was it resumed, I wonder, in the days of Blake, or only after the Restoration? The three British ensigns, white, blue, and red, each with the upper corner near the staff occupied with the union device, were at first distinctive of the white, blue, and red divisions of the fleet. In 1864 these divisions were done away with and new uses were allocated to the three ensigns. The white ensign is the exclusive flag of the Royal Navy and the Royal Yacht Squadron and may be flown by no other vessel. The blue ensign is flown by the Royal Naval

Reserve, by vessels in services of public offices, and by certain yacht clubs. With various distinctive badges in the fly, the blue ensign is worn by Dominion warships. After 1864 the red ensign was flown by British merchant vessels and ships not belonging to the navy.

After the union with Ireland in 1801 the cross of St. Patrick, a red saltire on a white ground, was merged with the crosses of St. George and St. Andrew to form the new "Union Flag," and this was used as identification at each man-of-war's jack staff and at the upper corner at the hoist of each ensign. "As a child," says Mr. Low, "I had a fascinating thing by which one built up the flag by folding over successive layers of crosses."

However improper it may be to nautical purists to speak of the "Union Flag," when not flown at a jack staff, as the "Union Jack," there is nothing to be done except to accept the confusion. I have in front of me a colored aquatint (by E. Duncan after W. J. Huggins, 1833) of *Sir David Scott,* an East Indiaman built in 1821. In this print she is shown in the Straits of Sunda, in 1830, flying the red ensign. She is a merchantman, but she has an impressive row of gun ports. She is flying no jack, but the ensign must be taken in lieu of a jack. Wherever the "Union Flag" went ashore from a ship, whatever it was flown from was in lieu of the jack staff which was metaphorically represented.

The export of the "Union Flag" to many parts of the world by a maritime nation led very naturally to the confusion that it was the "Union Jack" which had been exported; and with all deep respect to Captain West, I think a metaphorical defense might be made for the phrase about the flag of Britain having become the Union Jack. It was as a "jack" that the "flag" was going round the world. But not to labor that metaphorical justification, in a practical way if you use the phrase "Union Jack" people almost anywhere will identify it with Britain and know what you mean, whereas to say "Union Flag" will have a wholly different set of connotations in North America or South Africa or elsewhere.

3. An illustration to an article by Archibald Williams in the *Mechanical Boy* for November 6, 1924, provides a beautiful close-up of one of Maudslay's lathes. I am referring to Vol. 1, p. 226, of the *Mechanical Boy* (edited by H. T. Marshall).

4. The story about Napoleon's mother is to be found in the introduction to *Boswell in Search of a Wife,* edited by Frank Brady and Frederick A. Pottle (the Yale Editions of the Private Papers of James Boswell, Trade Edition, Vol. VI, p. xviii).

5. When Thomas Jefferson was Minister to France he paid a visit to England, in the spring of 1786, and was especially interested in English gardens. Writing to John Page of Virginia, he remarks about England: "the gardening in that country surpasses all the earth." The notes which Jefferson made on his tour were not without influence on his laying out of the gardens at Monticello.

6. The theme is here to instance, once again, the unexpected, unintended, and unforeseeable problems which have sometimes resulted from the existence of the Road and from the desire to make "improvements" on it.

In the eighteenth century nothing could have been regarded, on either side of the Atlantic, as more desirable or rational than the establishment of an efficient, cheap, and uncensored postal service.

In 1737 Benjamin Franklin, having studied the English system, and clearly being a man of enterprise, was appointed Postmaster of Philadelphia; by 1753 he had risen to the Deputy Postmaster General for the American Colonies. Franklin's original appointment, I assume, was from London—I don't know enough about Colonial history to say, but I am sure I can be corrected if I am wrong. In some ways he adopted English customs: for instance, he set up milestones on the main Post Road from Boston to Philadelphia, and followed the postal organization, and so far as there was any rule of the road (which I don't imagine there was until roads were decently surfaced) I imagine Franklin kept to the left. He was inventive as to speeding up communications from England; not much was known before his time about the Gulf Stream, but he deduced that there was something that was unduly impeding west-bound mail packets; and he initiated the experiment of altering the west-bound route.

In 1775, the War of Independence being imminent, Franklin, having proved himself a most able administrator, was made Postmaster General by the Continental Congress. He appointed William Goddard (who had begun his business life as a printer in Baltimore) to be "Surveyor of the Post Office." Noah Webster was (in 1793) a later Surveyor.

No better men could have been chosen to devise, for North America, an efficient postal service.

A present result in the United States is that since World War II pornography has become a $500,000,000 a year business, operating through the postal service.

My authority for this statement is *The Silent Investigators* by John N. Makris (E. P. Dutton, New York, 1959). Mr. Makris has been in a position to know what he is talking about. He gives a very interesting account of the problems of the Postal Inspection Service in dealing with Sam Roth, who was eventually convicted in 1956.

Any kind of government control of the efficient machinery of the postal service without destroying the good with the bad is very difficult to devise. Government caught up with Sam Roth, but there remain other big operators who use the postal service for immoral purpose with immunity. Why not? By way of first-class mail which cannot be opened for inspection any American home may be on the receiving end for illustrated circulars, booklets, catalogues touting not mere harmless nonsense but subsequently, according to the first responses, every kind of depravity and degeneracy.

Mr. Makris gives details of how the "sucker-lists" are compiled and pooled until "some of the big dealers mail anywhere from two to three hundred thousand pieces of 'come-on' literature at one crack." Mr. Makris regards the impact on children as the worst feature of misuse of the postal service, and quotes the concern of Dr. Benjamin Karpman of St. Elizabeth's Hospital, Washington, when testifying before a Senate Subcommittee, under the chairmanship of Estes Kefauver. Dr. Karpman said, "You can take a perfectly healthy boy or girl and by exposing them to abnormalities you can virtually crystallize and settle their habits for the rest of their lives."

This may be only expansion of a practice which has existed in every country from the beginnings of postal service. It is the more noticeable as a service becomes the more efficient and as the misuse becomes the more organized. The statistics given by Mr. Makris, if, as I assume, they are accurate, exhibit that a piece of social machinery, initially a road service, may go on working in unintended ways.

XII   The Great Exhibition

1. A one-volume redaction of the *Torrington Diaries* was published by Eyre & Spottiswoode, London, in 1954.

2. Here my handiest authority about Joseph Paxton has been *A Horticultural Who Was Who* by A. Simmonds, M.C., V.M.H., Deputy Secretary of the Royal Horticultural Society (R.H.S., London, 1948).

3. It is made clear in Mr. D. L. Howard's book on *The English Prisons* (1960) that into the first third of the nineteenth century the phrase "man-power" very often referred to the treadmill in prisons. There were few prisons in England in which by the time of Sydney

Smith the "everlasting staircase" had not been installed, and of its use as a source of power for turning a mill or other machine or engine, Sydney Smith wrote that it was "economical, certain, well-administered, little liable to abuse, capable of infinite division, a perpetual example before the eyes of those who want it, affecting the imagination only with horror and disgust, and affording great ease to the Government."

I am not certain how Sydney Smith intended that remark to be taken. Mr. Howard mentions examples of prison governors hiring out the labor of the prisoners to local millers "as they ground the treadmill round like so much water power or steam." "Some magistrates kept their prisoners treading from morning till night, till they half-killed them; others were content with requiring a modicum of wholesome exercise on the wheel for three or four hours a day."

In spite of many efforts to have the treadmill abolished, it was not legally prohibited in English prisons until 1898.

4. My details about John Ericsson are derived from *Yankee from Sweden* by Ruth White (1960).

5. The railway accident of 1830, causing the death of a man so widely known as William Huskissen, was, I suppose, the origin for those who wished to cross the line, of the warning: "Stop, Look, Listen." As for the "listen" part of this exhortation, I note that in 1835 the Leicester and Swannington train was hauled by *Samson,* that noble locomotive which was the first in the world to be fitted with a whistle, then known as a "steam trumpet." It is my impression that the original "steam trumpet" had three tones. In American railroad history the famous Casey Jones had on his engine a six-tone calliope whistle, and everyone on his route knew his signal:

> The switchmen knew by the whistle's moans
> That the man at the throttle was Casey Jones.

Casey Jones—his name was John Luther Jones, but he came from "Cayce, over in Kentucky," and so was known as Casey Jones for the rest of his life—met his death on the Cannonball, the No. 1 New Orleans Special of the Illinois Central line, on April 29, 1900. Long before that, the "Look" part of the exhortation "Stop, Look, Listen" had to be agreed upon, both by those who drove the locomotives and by those who wished to cross the line.

This leads to a curious speculation. I invite attention to the last paragraphs of Chapter IX, Book III of *Our Mutual Friend,* written by Charles Dickens in 1865. The Secretary and the lady who was beginning to fall in love with him, the "boofer lady," were to return by train from the borders of Oxfordshire to London. As they approached the station, understandably they were loitering, but "the railway, at this point, knowingly shutting a green eye and opening a red one, they had to run for it." Then, when the lovers were in the train, the railway continued to express its sympathy for them: "Something to this purpose surely mingled with the blast of the train as it cleared the stations, all knowingly shutting up their green eyes and opening their red ones when they prepared to let the boofer lady pass."

This is a curious passage. I attend to it because Dickens is presenting it as normal background stuff, and at a first reading it looks as if he were saying that for the engine driver a red lamp meant "go" and a green lamp meant "stop." That seems to us contrary to nature; yet the presumption is that at that moment a red lantern would be showing red all round. It would be "red for danger" for the other fellow, a warning not to cross your path. In early days of motoring a man with a red flag preceded you, and what the red meant was "Here I come" and, as driver, so long as the red showed ahead of you, you had given your warning and you went.

In the beginning of railway practice each company may have had its own rules for signaling. I believe red and white were sometimes used as contrasting colors, but snow could make them indistinguishable and cause accidents. The odd thing is the transition, for the driver, from red as being his signal for all clear ("I have given warning") to green for "clear." At sea, a wreck to be avoided is marked by a green signal. Practice at road crossings was affected when traffic lights began to have blinkers, so that red one direction showed green the other, but that does not alter the puzzlement of the question, how for the driver red for "go" became red for "stop."

6. This particular reference to the childhood of Lewis Carroll and the playing of "trains" in the garden at Croft-on-Tees is drawn from *Victoria Through the Looking-Glass* by Florence Becker Lennon (1945).

7. *Browns and Chester*, by "Mass Observation," was published by Lindsay Drummond, London (1947). He gave me my copy of the book; I wish he had lived to accept this gratitude.

8. I intended the reference to the Locomotive God to recall, to those who might recall it, the very remarkable work with that title by William Ellery Leonard, once upon a time Professor at the University of Wisconsin.

9. Another school of thought, about the color of John Peel's coat, is strongly represented to me from Cumberland, and from purists, and from those who have associated with hunting men in their cups. This school of thought asserts with truculence that John Peel's coat was "gray." I am bound to say that I like this contention, with the hint that John Peel was an honest farmer and all against the foppery of red coats. But here we are at a fork in the road, and you may take your choice.

10. *The Common Muse*, by V. de Sola Pinto and A. E. Rodway, was published by Chatto & Windus, London (1957).

11. Some of the details of the history of whaling are repeated from *Whaling North and South* by F. V. Morley and J. S. Hodgson (1927). In that book I don't think I sufficiently appreciated the importance of the British whale trade in the sixteenth century. Not much is recorded until the seventeenth century, but I have come to feel (for reasons expressed in the text) that in Elizabethan times whaling was regarded as one alternative for idleness in the wool trade. Notice that Shakespeare, in the quotation alluded to on page 132, speaks in the same breath of wool and whales, and regards the whale as something which will be familiar to a general audience.

As of this moment of writing, in 1960, whales have gone out of our consciousness, like Claudius's elephants. But I have met the whale, and do remember.

12. I am quoting, and on following pages, from *Here They Dug the Gold* by George F. Willison. (My edition is the one published by Eyre & Spottiswoode, London, 1950.)

13. I don't know where my barley-sugar story comes from: probably from Skeat, for I don't find it by looking again into the *Dictionary of Phrase and Fable* by the Reverend Dr. Brewer. I have been, I fear, perfunctory in my investigation into the innumerable ingenuities which can be attributed to the Great Exhibition. The article of furniture which I have spelled "purdonian" is one which Mr. T. S. Eliot prefers to spell "purdonium." On this important matter he chooses to correct me. "The *purdonium* (note the spelling) is an article I know well," he comments. "In case you do not know what is a Purdonium, I will try to sketch it for you: the main point was that a kind of metal coal scuttle fitted inside a decorated wooden box with a brass handle, in such a way that you did not see the coal except when it was opened to feed the fire."

I wish I might have reproduced Mr. Eliot's penciled sketch of the article, for his treatment of perspective is fully as good as that exhibited in the sketches in the Mayflower Bible. As to the spelling, it is my impression that this refined coal scuttle was invented by Mr. Purdon, who named it after himself as a "purdonian," and I think a chap who invents a thing should have some right to spell it as he chooses. Mr. Eliot is, I think, working away at some theory that "purdonium" is a neo-classic word, suggestive of a "gift of fire." I stand by Mr. Purdon, but Mr. Eliot may be correct in the speculation that the word got into the language because it was assumed to be Greek. The Victorian period was one of wonderful flowery pseudo-Greek coinages. The "pantechnicon" which shifted your furniture to a more expensive house flourished in very large letters the legend "ECOSIVEPHORON."

14. I found it difficult here to avoid using the Greek word *hubris*, in that I was unable to think of any single word in the English language which succinctly expresses the idea. The idea, central in Greek tragedy, relates to the "overweening presumption," especially against the gods, which creates the form of its fall. Dr. Arnold Toynbee spends some time examining the idea in *A Study of History* (Vol. IV, p. 258) under the general heading of "The Nemesis of Creativity." My first acquaintance with the word *hubris* came from Gilbert Murray. He discusses the crime of *hubris* in several of his books, notably in his introduction to *The Persians.*

Gilbert Murray could not find in the English language any one word exactly equivalent to *hubris*, and I can't either. This is the more strange in that the commodity has not been rare in the modern world: there has been plenty of *hubris* about.

"In the specialist field of national boasting," says Mr. Gerard Fay in *Passenger to London*, "I have never found a contrast so extraordinary as between the Great Exhibition of 1851 and the Festival of Britain of 1951. Two events have more to say about the social and economic life of their times than could be written in a hundred volumes by a dozen historians."

Some figures to support the contrast between the economies of those two Exhibitions may be found in the *Manchester Guardian* (London Letter, July 30, 1957).

15. Research is needed as to what happened to the golden spike which for a time united the rails of the Central Pacific with the Union Pacific.

16. The marks left by bicycle tires soon excited the keenest intelligences of the period. Raffles, most astute as well as most daring of Amateur Cracksmen, is reported by E. W. Hornung as having favored Dunlop tires:

"They seem the most popular brand . . . more Dunlop marks than any other kind. Bless you, yes, they all leave their special tracks, and we don't want ours to be extra special; the Dunlop's like a rattlesnake, and the Palmer leaves telegraph-wires, but surely the serpent is more in our line."

It has been noticed by scholars that in 1893 Hornung (originally a Yorkshireman) had returned from Australia, and had married Constance Doyle, sister of Arthur Conan Doyle. It was soon after that, 1894, that Sherlock Holmes returned to life and became very much interested in bicycle tires. It is true that tire marks play no part in *The Adventure of the Solitary Cyclist*, yet in the next story, *The Adventure of the Priory School*, Conan Doyle records how systematic and how thorough Holmes's study had been, after his return from Tibet. In *The Adventure of the Priory School* Holmes comments on the bicycle tracks left behind by the courageous but unfortunate German master Heidegger—and by somebody else:

"A bicycle, certainly, but not *the* bicycle," said he. "I am familiar with forty-two different impressions left by tyres. This, as you preceive, is a Dunlop, with a patch upon the outer cover. Heidegger's tyres were Palmer's, leaving longitudinal stripes."

Soon, in a miry path, Holmes found "an impression like a fine bundle of telegraph wires." It was the Palmer tyre. "Here is Herr Heidegger, sure enough!" cried Holmes, exultantly. After that it was not too difficult to identify the Dunlop tyre, with the patch on the outer cover, with Mr. James Wilder, unacknowledged elder son of the Duke of Holdernesse. The upshot was that Mr. James Wilder became a compulsory pioneer in the continent from which Hornung had recently returned, and Sherlock Holmes became less poor a man by a matter of six thousand pounds, and he never had to divulge any of his intimate familiarity with the other forty tire marks additional to the two to which Raffles had paid attention, Palmer's and Dunlop's.

XIII   One for the Road

1. In the garden of England a distinction is to be made about apples. The distinction is between eaters and cookers. If you are thinking about dessert apples, you probably think about Cox's Orange Pippin, and that would take me away from my route, to Slough in Buckinghamshire. But if you are thinking about cooking apples in commercial plantations in England and Wales, more than a third of them have been derived from Bramley's Seedling. Who was Bramley?

There is a nice piece of detective work here, which is discussed by Mr. Simmonds in the *Horticultural Who Was Who* from which I previously quoted. According to Mr. Simmonds, Bramley was not the shoemaker he is popularly supposed to have been, nor did he raise the apple; but inhabitants of Southwell, Nottinghamshire, may go on breathing easily—for whoever it was who planted that Seedling, it seems certain that it was first planted at Southwell.

2. *Things Worth While* by Evelyn Cheesman (1957) is in large part concerned with her eight remarkable solo collecting expeditions in New Guinea and the Southwest Pacific. I found the early part of her autobiography no less fascinating. The passage to which I refer is in the early part, pp. 33–39.

❂   ❂   ❂

And so Farewell to these brief Notes and Queries about the Great North Road, that mere 400 miles.

I shall refresh myself by reading *Gryll Grange* by Thomas Love Peacock:

THE REVEREND DOCTOR OPIMIAN
You are determined to connect the immaterial world with the material world, as far as you can.

MR. FALCONER
I like the immaterial world. I like to live among thoughts and images of the past and the possible, and even of the impossible, now and then.

What would Mr. Falconer have done without the corrections and help of The Reverend Doctor Opimian? It will I hope have been noticed that I have attempted to acknowledge the generous assistance given me by many, who might be irritated with me if I were to mention them here all over again. But there are some whom I have not been able to mention, whose help has exceeded all other: my wife, and Mrs. Ruby Millar, and Miss S. N. Brown; and far beyond any legitimate claim on their assistance, additional proofreadings have been given to me by Ronald Arthur Bargate of Beaconsfield, Buckinghamshire, and by my brother Felix Morley, of Gibson Island, Maryland.

Index

This index is selective. It is followed by a list of authorities quoted or mentioned.

Authorities Quoted or Mentioned

Alice, 89, 262; Aspinall, A., 241–243; Barfield, Owen, 46, 47, 302–303; Beresford, Maurice, 132; Bone, James, 4, 298; Borrow, George, 85, 252, 293; Bradbrook, M. C., 141, 308; Brandon, S. G. F., 60–61, 304; *Browns and Chester*, 259–261, 317; Carrington, C. E., and J. H. Jackson, *History of England*, used and referred to throughout, *see* 308–309; Carroll, Lewis (Charles Dodgson), 258–259, 262, 317; Cheesman, Evelyn, 297, 321; Cheke, Val, 126–128; Cicero, 19, 27; Collingwood, R. B., and J. N. L. Myres, 20–22, 28, 32, 33, 40, 44, 54, 301; Defoe, Daniel, 145, 173, 194; Dante, 305; De Quincey, Thomas, 244, 258; Dio, 17, 301; Dobrée, Bonamy, 217; Douglas, David C., 109, 303; Doyle, Arthur Conan, 35, 226–227, 288, 302, 320; Dunlop, Ian, 173, 174, 180, 310; Eliot, T. S., quoted here and there, mentioned, 300, 301,

6/15/61

DATE DUE

GAYLORD   PRINTED IN U.S.A.